AAV-7834

INTRODUCTION TO LIBRARIANSHIP

McGRAW-HILL SERIES IN LIBRARY EDUCATION
Jean Key Gates, Consulting Editor
University of South Florida

Gates: INTRODUCTION TO LIBRARIANSHIP

INTRODUCTION TO LIBRARIANSHIP

Jean Key Gates
University of South Florida

McGraw-Hill Book Company
New York   St. Louis   San Francisco   Toronto   London   Sydney

INTRODUCTION TO LIBRARIANSHIP

Library of Congress Catalog Card Number 67-12623

ISBN 07-022976-7

8 9 0 DODO 7 9 8 7 6 5 4 3

To Wylie, Helena, Corine, and Johnie
and
To the memory of our mother and father

PREFACE

The purpose of *Introduction to Librarianship* is to set forth some of the most fundamental elements of librarianship in sufficient detail to help the student acquire a foundation of historical background, an understanding of major library objectives, services, and needs, and an appreciation of librarianship as a profession and a career which will prepare him for—and support—the complex and specialized concepts and problems with which he will deal in later courses, studies, and investigations.

It is not possible to cover, in an introductory course, all aspects of the broad and rapidly expanding field of librarianship. The topics which have been included are the major ones which are, in general, recognized as making up the course called Introduction to Librarianship, Library in Society, or by some similar title. These areas are the history of libraries, books, and printing; the place of the library in and its contribution to its society; the kinds of libraries and library services; the library profession—its organizations, its educational requirements, and its specialized literature; some current trends, issues, and problems; and outstanding library leaders.[1]

It is recognized that the degree of emphasis on each of these aspects of librarianship varies from school to school depending upon the objectives of the institution of which it is a part; the purposes of the course; the available teaching materials, facilities, and resources; the academic level of the students; the methods of instruction; and other factors. Thus, one school will give particular atten-

---

[1] Wayne S. Yenawine and Martha Boaz, "The Conferences That Were," *Journal of Education for Librarianship*, IV (Spring, 1964), 194.

This choice of topics is based also on the results of a study made by this author in 1965 of library education programs in colleges and universities in the United States. An analysis of the catalog descriptions of more than one hundred courses in introduction to librarianship—in as many schools or departments of library science—revealed that the areas usually included are those listed above.

tion to the public library; another to the school library;[2] another to the historical development of libraries, books, and printing; still another to the library as an essential educational, social, cultural, or utilitarian agency; and so on. It is the aim of *Introduction to Librarianship* to present an overview of all these areas in order to give the student a broad view of the field and to provide, at the same time, adequate references to enable the student, teacher, or interested layman to pursue any given topic to greater lengths. A serious effort has been made to document dates, statistics, and other hard-to-find items of information.

The material is organized into three parts. Trends, issues, and problems are discussed with the topics to which they relate rather than as separate topics; library leaders are introduced throughout the text apropos of their particular contribution or interest, or in bibliographical references; and new Federal legislation is presented in the appropriate chapters. Numerous cross references throughout the text and a detailed index provide easy access to all discussions.

I am greatly indebted to the authors, publishers, and holders of copyrights for their kind permission to use their material.

I should like to express my appreciation to my professional colleagues, especially at the University of Maryland and the University of South Florida, for their encouragement and support; to Miss Sarah R. Reed for her favorable interest in the Library Education Series and to other members of the Library Services Branch of the U.S. Office of Education for their assistance and cooperation; to innumerable librarians who helped to locate materials and allowed special privileges in their use; and to my students whose reactions to portions of this volume have aided me in organizing and presenting it.

I am grateful to my family and friends for their continuing interest and patience, and my special thanks go to my husband for the constancy of his encouragement and the helpfulness of his criticism throughout the enterprise.

Jean Key Gates

[2] In a number of courses in introduction to librarianship the major emphasis is given to the school library. This fact accounts for the somewhat extensive coverage of this subject in this volume.

CONTENTS

INTRODUCTION

The student who enters the many-faceted career field of librarianship needs to acquire early a basic understanding and appreciation of the historical foundations and significance of libraries and librarianship; of their role in society—historically and presently; of the types of libraries, the kinds of services they offer, and the clienteles they serve; of the professional preparation and responsibilities of librarians; and of some of the problems, issues, and opportunities facing libraries and librarians in this age of accelerating change, explosive ideas, continuous experimentation, and technological innovation.

Introduction to Librarianship provides an overview of librarianship:

1. By presenting the historical development, current status, and future prospects of the library in the context of the educational, social, cultural, economic, or utilitarian needs which call it into being, pointing up the fact that the library shares the problems and opportunities of its society and that its importance rises or falls depending upon the "exaltation of the idea most prevalent in that society"

2. By tracing the development of each kind of library service, emphasizing the influence of conditions, movements, trends, and individuals, and by interpreting the functions, organization, and services of the various types of libraries

3. By introducing the student to the profession and to some of its basic attitudes and guiding principles, to the professional preparation for librarianship, to the organization of the profession, and to the professional responsibility of librarians

4. By discussing some of the current issues, trends, developments, and opportunities growing out of the continuous effort to improve and extend library service and librarianship

Introduction to Librarianship is designed to provide a body of basic material for an introductory course in librarianship, whatever the specific title of the course may be. In addition, it can be used to supplement other courses in library science in such specific areas as the history of books and libraries, administration and management, and the various types of libraries and library service. For the new student (the new recruit) *Introduction to Librarianship* provides material which will help him to develop some of the basic understandings and appreciations required in his newly chosen career and to lay the foundations for many of his future courses. It is hoped that for the student who has some background of study and experience in library science, it will serve as a review and a helpful and provocative summary of the field and introduce him to a sampling of recent developments, problems, trends, experiments, and new materials. For librarian, would-be librarian, or interested layman, *Introduction to Librarianship* seeks to offer a panoramic view of the broad reach of librarianship from its historical and traditional beginnings through centuries of indispensable service in behalf of some of the most vital needs of civilized peoples, to its present period of expanded activities, prestigious growth, and future promise.

INTRODUCTION TO LIBRARIANSHIP

PROLOGUE

Ask almost any group of individuals what a library is and usually you will receive as part of the answer, "a collection of books for use." Depending upon their experience and sophistication in using such a collection, they may add a few words about services and purposes.

As early as 1374, according to *The Oxford English Dictionary*, the word "library" was used in English in the sense of being a place where books were kept for "reading, study, or reference." By the nineteenth century, a library was also "a building, room, or set of rooms containing a collection of books for the use of the public or some portion of it, or the members of a society; . . . . a public institution or establishment charged with the care of a collection of books."[1] In time, the concepts of circulation and administration of the collection of books were added to the definition.[2] Thus the word "library" has long been established in our language.

It is a word which is in almost everybody's vocabulary and an institution which is a part of almost everybody's experience—its meaning for each person depending upon the nature and extent of that experience. For most people, the addition of a descriptive word, such as "public," "school," or "college," calls to mind some particular characteristics of the type of library described—such as size, location, purpose, and accessibility. Thus, although *a* library is a building or an institution for the custody, circulation, and administration of a collection of books (and other materials), there are definitely established *kinds* of libraries.

The library has inspired some of our most munificent philan-

[1] Sir James Augustus Henry Murray and Others (eds.), *The Oxford English Dictionary*, being a corrected reissue, with an introduction, supplement, and bibliography, of *A New English Dictionary on Historical Principles* (12 vols. and supplement; London: Oxford University Press, 1933). By permission of the Clarendon Press, Oxford.
[2] *Webster's New International Dictionary of the English Language* (2d ed.; Springfield, Mass.: G. & C. Merriam Company, Publishers, 1959).

thropy and some magnificent language: It is frequently referred to as "the heart of the institution"; it has been called "the mind of society . . . the only effective repository of . . . the racial memory";[3] "a live depository of the cultural past and sustainer of the intellectual activity that anticipates the future."[4] And so on.

What is seldom mentioned is that the library does not function alone, that "a library, above all, is a human enterprise and that it depends ultimately upon the skilled minds and talents of librarians if it is to perform its proper role in our changing society."[5] This fact leads to a consideration of librarians.

Neither the dictionary nor the phrasemakers (outside of the profession) have found a great deal to extol in librarians. To the lexicographer, the librarian was for many generations "one who has the care or charge of a library"[6]—a definition strongly suggesting a "keeper," one who watches and guards. And while these have often been characteristics of librarians, they have not been the only characteristics In *Webster's Third New International Dictionary* a librarian is defined as "a specialist in the care and management of a library," but this definition is somewhat diluted by the second meaning: "one whose vocation is working with library books (as by cataloguing)."[7] *The Random House Dictionary of the English Language* adds to the definitions the phrase "trained in library science"[8] (not educated).

One might reasonably expect that the persons who have the "care, or charge, or management" of "the heart of an institution" or the "mind of society" would merit a definition indicative of

[3] Frank G. Jennings, "Carpe Diem," *Library Journal*, XCII (February 1, 1967), 533.

[4] Ralph W. Conant, "Sociological and Institutional Changes in American Life: Their Implications for the Library," *ALA Bulletin*, LXI (May, 1967), 528.

[5] Francis Keppel, "Libraries: Future Unlimited," *ALA Bulletin*, LVIII (December, 1964), 994.

[6] *Webster's New International Dictionary, op. cit.*

[7] *Webster's Third New International Dictionary of the English Language* (Springfield, Mass.: G. & C. Merriam Company, Publishers, 1966).

[8] *The Random House Dictionary of the English Language* (New York: Random House, Inc., 1966), p. 826. Library science is defined as "the study of the organization and administration of a library and of its technical, informational, and reference services." Reprinted from *The Random House Dictionary of the English Language* © Copyright 1966, by Random House, Inc.

the extent of their preparation, their function, and their performance. And some progress has been made in this direction. But, for whatever reason, the word "librarian" does not yet carry with it an indication of the kind and amount of education and other preparation required nor the number and variety of responsibilities; and unlike a teacher, for example, who may be elementary, secondary, college, or kindergarten, to most laymen a librarian is a librarian. Few people outside the profession know what is required in the way of education; what a librarian *can* or *should* do; or what the differences are in the preparation for and the activities in the several types of libraries.

The librarian is perhaps the only professional person who is best known, popularly, for the lowly and onerous tasks he has to perform,[9] such as stamping and checking books; and from these kinds of activities has come the belief in some quarters that being a librarian is not very demanding. This is likely the reason that in almost any group of new library school students there will be at least one who admits that he wants to study library science because he can be a librarian when he is too old to do anything else. It is also probably a part of the reason the public has so long been complacent about the shortage of librarians. Not understanding what a library really is and what its management requires, nor that a librarian is educated for this specific function, the public has too often been satisfied with a "collection of books" and a "keeper" to whom they have given the name librarian. Librarianship may be the only profession in which the professional title is not reserved wholly for the professionals.

The suffix "-ship" denotes condition, office, or profession, and in general, dictionaries define librarianship as being the office, duties or profession of librarian. Thus it has remained for those who are librarians to define and explain the office, duties, and profession.

In 1933, when books were the main items in a library's collection, Dr. Pierce Butler of the University of Chicago Graduate Library School said that "the basic elements of librarianship consist in the accumulation of knowledge by society and its continuous

---

[9] In the absence of adequate clerical assistance.

transmission to the living generation so far as these processes are performed through the instrumentality of graphic records" and that "the fundamental phenomenon of librarianship . . . is the transmission of the accumulated experience of society to its individual members through the instrumentality of the book."[10] About three decades later, Dr. Carl White, in discussing the bases of librarianship, wrote that modern librarianship is concerned with assuring the continuance and full use of the power to retain, organize, and use the accumulated heritage of all generations of all mankind in all its forms—the written word being only one.[11]

This book is about these three subjects: libraries, librarians, and librarianship. It offers indications and suggestions about what they have been, what they are now, what they should be, and what they may become; but obviously, it does not exhaust these subjects: it only introduces them.

[10] Pierce Butler, *An Introduction to Library Science* (Chicago: The University of Chicago Press, 1933), pp. 29, 84.
[11] Carl M. White (ed.), *Bases of Modern Librarianship* (New York: The Macmillan Company, 1964), pp. 10, 11.

PART I
THE STORY OF LIBRARIES

> Whether you show the works of man's spirit and imagination in the form of pictures hung upon a wall, as plays enacted before an audience, or as books made accessible on the shelves does not really matter; the important thing is the degree to which the organization involved is larger than any individual and has the capacity to outlive change and serve the needs of the time.[1]

It is commonly believed by scholars that civilization had its beginnings in the fertile valleys of the Tigris and Euphrates Rivers. Aided by a favorable climate, rich farming lands, and his growing skill as a farmer, man gradually became able to live generation after generation in the same place. His development of agriculture has been evaluated as "perhaps the greatest stride forward that man has ever taken."[2] for in a settled agricultural economy population multiplied; nomadic tribal settlements became towns; and towns grew into cities. In the cities governmental, economic, social, and religious institutions were developed; trade, commerce, and industry expanded; and technological inventions and discoveries multiplied. It was in the complex organized life of the cities around 3500 B.C.[3] that the wonderful instrument of writing was invented, apparently as a tool for dealing with such practical day-by-day economic, social, and administrative affairs of the community as the keeping of accounts, the issuing of receipts, the recording of contracts of sale and exchange, and the making of final wills and testaments.

The length of time the first-known system of writing was used for strictly practical purposes can only be conjectured. Suffice it

[1] August Heckscher, "Libraries and the Nation's Cultural Life," *ALA Bulletin*, LVI (September, 1962), 717.
[2] Herbert J. Muller, *The Uses of the Past* (New York: Oxford University Press, 1952), p. 45.
[3] M. E. L. Mallowan, "Civilized Life Begins . . . ," *The Dawn of Civilization*, ed. Stuart Piggott (New York: McGraw-Hill Book Company, 1961), p. 83.

that the basic techniques of writing on clay, which handled commercial and related transactions adequately, in time became sufficiently flexible to express and record a variety of complicated historical and literary compositions. The library as an indispensable agency of civilized society became inevitable whenever and wherever records, of whatever sort, were inscribed on clay tablets, for with the first written works came the need for a place to keep them so that they could be protected and preserved; so that they could be used when needed; and so that they could be handed on. Here, then, in basic economic and social needs of both individuals and the community are the beginnings of the story of libraries and librarians.

Since recorded communications and their collection, organization, preservation, and utilization are so significant in the story of civilization, it is not readily understandable why cultural historians have not contributed more to library history than occasional brief descriptions, chance references to names and places, and meager discussions of contributions and services. Those who have searched fruitlessly for a longer explanation, a fuller description, a newer interpretation of an ancient library may well have thought: "One would give much to know the nature of the contents of Timgad's library in its prime."[4] Even so, from the bits and pieces of history and from surviving documents and inscriptions, a fairly satisfactory story of the library can be put together. Encouragingly, as our total knowledge of the past increases, our knowledge of recorded communications and of the library grows. With the factual and analytical materials which are now at hand it is nothing less than imperative that the serious student of librarianship commit himself to the priority effort of developing and maintaining his own historical orientation. This is a major intellectual undertaking, for just as civilization is fluid and moving, so is the story of libraries; and just as civilization is ever changing and ever becoming, so are libraries and librarianship ever becoming something different and,

[4] Sir Mortimer Wheeler, "The Vision Turns Inward: The Art and Architecture of a World Empire," *The Birth of Western Civilization: Greece and Rome*, ed. Michael Grant (New York: McGraw-Hill Book Company, 1964), p. 300.

it is hoped, something better today than they were yesterday. In a time of restless and radical change, like today, historical perspective becomes an essential tool for both the student and the practitioner of librarianship in accommodating and effectively handling the situations of decision making and problem solving with which unavoidably they must deal.

The story of the library has been told often, either wholly or in part, and with each telling certain facts of significance and importance become more clear: (1) Libraries are essential ingredients of a civilized society; (2) they come into being to meet certain recognized needs, and these needs determine their forms, purposes, functions, programs, and services; (3) certain conditions—economic, technological, scientific, geographical, cultural, or social—encourage their development, and when such conditions do not prevail, libraries decline and may disappear.

The following brief historical overview of the development of libraries up to the twentieth century[5] is designed to present certain selected facts and describe certain movements, events, and conditions which show the library as an essential part of civilized society or which point up needs which called it into being and determined its character and direction or which discouraged its development and perhaps caused it to disappear.

[5] It would not be possible to treat the broad field of comparative librarianship in the twentieth century adequately in this brief overview. Chapters 9 through 23 are devoted to the development of libraries and librarianship in the United States in the twentieth century.

CHAPTER 1
ANTIQUITY

The fertile crescent

On the basis of their present knowledge, students of the beginnings of civilization believe that the Sumerians were the first people to develop a widely usable writing system. The earliest written documents are in the Sumerian language, and since 1877, when the French began the first successful excavation at a Sumerian site, the ancient city of Lagash (Telloh), a large store of Sumerian written material has been accumulated. Professor Kramer has noted "that more than ninety-five percent of all the Sumerian tablets are economic in character"[1]—tallies, accounts, and records relating to personal property and temple business. Sir Leonard Woolley has emphasized the fact that the early Sumerian pictograms "denote things, but that is all; they cannot make statements, and they cannot convey thought."[2] The Sumerians, however, were able to make the needed transition from the pictogram to the hieroglyph to the phonetic sign, so that "there is little doubt that some time before the end of the third millennium B.C. the Sumerian men of letters actually wrote down—on clay tablets, prisms, and cylinders—many of their literary creations which until then had been current in oral form only."[3]

Thus the tool of writing, at first crude and pictographic in character, turned out to have highly significant consequences, in time being modified and molded into a phonetic system which served the Sumerians as a capable instrument for recording their

[1] Samuel Noah Kramer, *Sumerian Mythology, A Study of Spiritual and Literary Achievement in the Third Millennium*, B.C. (Rev. ed.; New York: Harper Torchbooks, Harper and Row, Publishers, Incorporated, 1961), p. 10.
[2] Sir Leonard Woolley, *History of Mankind, Cultural and Scientific Development*, Vol. I, Part 2: *The Beginnings of Civilization* (New York: Mentor Books, New American Library of World Literature, Inc., 1965), p. 364.
[3] Samuel Noah Kramer, *History Begins at Sumer* (Indian Hills, Colo.: Falcon Wing's Press, 1956), p. xix.

social, political, and philosophical thinking, for maintaining the accounts of schools and social reforms, and for preserving the form and content of their hymns, prayers, rituals, sacred legends and magic formulas. By 2700 B.C., the Sumerians had established temple, private, and government libraries in which their varied writings could be preserved and used.

Their neighbors were quick to adopt not necessarily the Sumerian system of writing but the Sumerian idea. There arose a number of scripts which, although they differed completely in form from the Sumerian, were indebted to it for the basic conception that a written sign might represent not a thing but a sound.[4] For example, Sumerian culture, including religious beliefs and practices and the Sumerian script, was readily taken over and assimilated by the Babylonians. These Semitic conquerors adapted the Sumerian script to the needs of their own language, so that in time "the Babylonian language written in the cuneiform script became the recognized diplomatic language of the middle east."[5]

Much of our knowledge of Babylonian civilization comes from the tablets of the Library of Borsippa, which were copied and then preserved in the library of King Ashurbanipal of Assyria (r. 668–626 B.C.). This library of King Ashurbanipal, one of the earliest patrons of letters, was at Nineveh; it contained tens of thousands of tablets, including many which had been copied and translated by scribes as they traveled throughout Babylonia and Assyria. In this well-organized library, the tablets were tagged for identification and arranged by subject or type in alcoves, with a list of the contents of each alcove painted or carved on the entrance to serve as a catalog. It is believed that this library was open for the use of the king's subjects.

As a vehicle for conveying thought, the Babylonian cuneiform system represented a revolutionary advance over the primitive pictographic form. It was, however, such an intricate system of ideographs and syllabic signs that the literate Babylonian or Assyrian had to spend years of study in its mastery. The alphabetic script

[4] Woolley, *op. cit.*, p. 364.
[5] *Ibid.*, p. 383.

of the Phoenicians was much more manageable in that its signs were definite in their meaning and could easily be memorized so that "a man could become literate in a matter of weeks." The main role in working out new forms of effective writing about the middle of the second millennium B.C. and of influencing the various peoples with whom they dealt "was played by the Phoenician inhabitants of the Syrian coast towns, whose commercial activities supplied them with both the need and the opportunity" for such inventive action.[6]

Antiquity—Egypt

The civilization of ancient Egypt flourished simultaneously with that of Sumer. The earliest written texts date from the last quarter of the fourth millennium B.C., as do those of Sumer, but the style of writing developed by the Egyptian scribes to suit their needs and language was hieroglyphic—a name deriving from two Greek words meaning "sacred" and "to carve." The chief purpose of their writing was to provide lasting and impressive inscriptions suitable for monuments, for writing was believed to glorify kings, and the inscriptions on monuments and on the walls of the temples were meant to impress the world. Since most of the people were illiterate, the style of writing was more or less pictorial. This elaborate, pictorial, hieroglyphic style was not practical for writing manuscripts, and a cursive style called hieratic was devised for everyday use; eventually a popular script called demotic was evolved.

The invention of a flexible writing material, made from the pith of the papyrus plant and known from ca. 3200 B.C., greatly advanced the progress of writing. In order to make a papyrus sheet, the marrow of papyrus stalks was cut into thin strips and laid flat, side by side, one layer crossways over the other. The two layers were treated with a gum solution, pressed, pounded, and smoothed until the surface was suitable for writing, and then sized to resist the ink. The form of the Egyptian book was the roll, and the instruments for writing were a brushlike pen and ink. While the hieroglyphs continued in use for the sacred carvings

[6] *Ibid.*, p. 387.

on monuments and in tombs and for inscriptions on temples, early use of the hieratic script was largely for religious purposes. Few people outside the priestly class were literate, and it was in the temple schools that scribes received their training. Examples of official literature as well as religious, philosophical, historical, and scientific writing survive.

Our knowledge of Egyptian libraries is scant, but there are references to temple libraries and records of a library which belonged to Khufu, a monarch of the Fourth Dynasty, and another to Khafre, the builder of the second pyramid. At Edfu, the library was a small chamber in the temple on the wall of which was a list of all the works which were given to the priests. The only library of any significance of which we have a record was that founded by Rameses II at Thebes about 1250 B.C. This library, in which the King took great pride, is believed to have had twenty thousand books[7] and was called "a place of Healing for the Soul."[8]

GREECE AND ROME

Greece

In the early part of the second millennium B.C., Crete became the center of a highly developed civilization which spread to the mainland of Greece and, before the end of the fifteenth century B.C., throughout the entire Aegean area. The Cretans developed the art of writing from a pictographic system to a cursive form, Linear A, and by the fifteenth century B.C. to a system now called Linear B.[9] Many scholars believe that the language of the Linear B tablets is an early form of Greek which was spoken by the Mycenaeans who occupied Knossos ca. 1460 B.C. and eventually

[7] C. L. Nichols, *The Library of Rameses the Great* (Cambridge: Cambridge University Press, 1909), p. 30.
[8] *Ibid.*, p. 10.
[9] In 1900, Sir Arthur Evans made his first discovery of clay tablets in Linear B stored in the Palace of Knossos. In 1939, over five hundred tablets were found at Pylos; many more have been found at Pylos since World War II and at Mycenae also from 1952 on. See M. S. F. Hood, "The Home of the Heroes: the Aegean Before the Greeks," Piggott, *op. cit.*, pp. 216, 220.

overthrew the Minoan Kingdom. The Mycenaeans adopted the Minoan Linear B script and improved and simplified it, but their invention was short-lived in that after 1200 B.C. the Mycenaean world ceased to exist and the script disappeared.[10] A period of illiteracy is believed to have existed from the time of the disappearance of the Linear B script until the time when the Greeks adopted the consonantal twenty-two letter alphabet of the Phoenicians; "thus the introduction of the alphabetic script in the eighth century (most probably about the middle of the century) may be regarded as representing a new birth of literacy in Greece."[11]

Early uses of the alphabetic script were for inscriptions of a practical nature, though there are some examples of verses written on pottery. Of the seventh and sixth centuries B.C., only fragments of literature remain, but in the sixth century, according to Athenaeus,[12] there were libraries in Greece, including those of Peisistratus, the tyrant of Athens, and Polycrates, the tyrant of Samos. Athenaeus refers also to the libraries of Euripides and others in the fifth century when the civilization of ancient Greece reached its golden age under Pericles—a time which saw the spread of reading as a pastime and the development of a book trade. Aristotle (384–322 B.C.) is said to have been the first person to collect, preserve, and use the culture of the past. The fate of his library is told by Strabo, who relates that Aristotle left his library to Theophrastus, who willed it to Neleus, who, in turn, took it to Scepsis and bequeathed it to his heirs. Later, when the Attalid kings of Pergamum[13] were gathering manuscripts for their library, the descendants of Neleus hid the books underground in a kind of trench, where they remained until, much later, their descendants sold them to Apellicon of Teos for a large sum of money. It was the library

[10] Woolley, *op. cit.*, pp. 385–386, *passim.*
[11] Alan J. B. Wace and Frank H. Stubbins (eds.), *A Companion to Homer* (London: Macmillan and Company, Ltd. 1963), pp. 217, 552, *passim.* Scholars are not in agreement regarding the date of the adoption of the Greek alphabet. Suggested dates range from as early as the fourteenth century B.C. to the end of the eighth century B.C. *Ibid.*, p. 554.
[12] Athenaeus, *The Deipnosophists*, with an English translation by Charles Burton Gulick (Rev. ed.; "The Loeb Classical Library"; Cambridge, Mass.: Harvard University Press, 1951), I, 11.
[13] See pp. 15–16.

of Apellicon, including that of Aristotle, which Sulla confiscated when he captured Athens in 86 B.C.[14]

The most important libraries of ancient Greece were established during the Hellenistic Age—a period which was characterized by the spread of Greek culture and learning through the conquests of Alexander and his successors, the creation of new Greek cities, and the development of monarchal governments. These libraries were located at the new city of Alexandria in Egypt and in the kingdom of Pergamum in Asia Minor.

Founded by Alexander the Great in 332 B.C. as the city which should bear his name, Alexandria was destined to become not only one of the world's most splendid cities but also the intellectual and literary center of the Hellenistic world. In the Royal Greek Center of the city, Ptolemy I (305–283 B.C.) founded the Museum, an academy of scholars under royal patronage, consecrated to the Muses and dedicated to learning. An essential part of the Museum was the library—called the Museion or the Brucheion—which had as its object to collect all Greek texts as well as manuscripts in all languages from all parts of the known world and to provide facilities for writing and copying books.

Demetrius of Phalerum, who had been largely influential in establishing both the Museum and its library, was given the task of building the collection. Manuscripts were acquired in every way possible—by private purchase or force, honestly or otherwise—and under his administration the holdings grew to 200,000 rolls. The library was greatly enlarged and enriched by succeeding Ptolemies, and by the middle of the first century B.C. it contained more than 700,000 rolls. A second library, called the Serapeum, was established by Ptolemy III in the Temple of Serapis in another section of Alexandria. To this library was allocated a collection of 42,800 carefully selected rolls; the collection was gradually enlarged until it reached more than 100,000.

The vast holdings of the two libraries were classified and organized, and, in addition, two other important tasks were carried out:

[14] *The Geography of Strabo*, with an English translation by Horace Leonard Jones ("The Loeb Classical Library"; Cambridge Mass.: Harvard University Press, 1960), VI, 111, 113.

All texts were edited, arranged into convenient form, and provided with commentaries; and a comprehensive bibliography of Greek literature was compiled.

Significantly, all the librarians of Alexandria were scholars—poets, critics, and grammarians. To Zenodotus, described as the "earliest editor of Homer," is given credit for dividing the *Iliad* and *Odyssey* into twenty-four books each. Aristophanes of Byzantium, who systematized accentuation and punctuation, produced the first collected edition of Pindar. The responsibility for compiling the bibliography of Greek literature was given to the poet Callimachus, who is said to have made lists of authors and their works which included brief biographies, dates of the production of certain dramas, and the number of lines in each work. His *Tables of All Those Who Were Eminent in Any Kind of Literature and of Their Writings* is said to have filled 120 volumes in which the works cataloged were arranged by categories: drama, legislation, history poetry, oratory, rhetoric, and miscellaneous.[15] "The scholars of Alexandria were . . . the earliest examples of the professional scholar and they deserve the gratitude of the modern world for criticising and classifying the literature of the golden age of Greece and handing it down to posterity."[16]

Although there is not complete agreement regarding the fate of the Alexandrian libraries, many historians date the destruction of the Museion from Julius Caesar's campaign in Alexandria in 47 B.C. and that of the Serapeum from the reign of Theodosius the Great (379–395), whose edicts against paganism resulted in the destruction of many pagan temples.

In northwest Asia Minor, Pergamum, like Alexandria, became a great center of learning and literary activity. In the second century B.C., Eumenes II founded a library, and, following the example of the Ptolemies, he assiduously searched the Hellenic world for manuscripts. Both cities and individuals were prevailed upon by

[15] Frederick William Hall, *A Companion to Classical Texts* (Oxford: Clarendon Press, 1913), p. 32.

[16] Sir John Edwin Sandys, *A History of Classical Scholarship*, Vol. I: *From the Sixth Century B.C. to the End of the Middle Ages* (3d ed.; Cambridge: Cambridge University Press, 1921), p. 144.

sundry means to part with their written treasures. Copies were made when originals were not obtainable, and for this copying program great quantities of papyrus were imported from Egypt. Jealous of this rival library and hoping to halt its growth, Ptolemy VII— then King of Egypt—forbade the export of papyrus to Pergamum. Consequently, of necessity, a new writing material was developed in Pergamum. This material, called parchment,[17] made it possible to continue the copying of manuscripts, and the holdings of the Pergamene library reached a total of two hundred thousand rolls. Crates of Mallos, known for his criticism of Homer, became head of the school and librarian at Pergamum and was probably responsible for making a classified listing of works in the library.[18]

Pergamum's great library remained in active use for nearly a hundred years. It is believed that Antony gave it to Cleopatra[19] (the last of the Ptolemies) and that she, in turn, added it to the collection of the Serapeum in Alexandria, making Alexandria again the site of the largest library in the world.

For centuries following Alexander the Great, the cultural ideal was kept alive by the scholarly activities of the libraries of Alexandria and Pergamum, resulting in the increased availability of books, the gradual rise and growth of a reading public, the production of literature, and the spread of learning throughout the Hellenistic world.

Rome

Greek influence over the cultural and intellectual life of the Roman people began with the capture of Tarentum by the Romans

[17] Parchment was the skin of animals, principally that of the sheep or calf, prepared for writing. Although this kind of writing material had been known to the Greeks for some time, it had not been used widely, for papyrus was cheaper and easier to write on. During the reign of Eumenes II, parchment was developed and improved. It eventually displaced papyrus and continued to be the chief writing material until the invention of printing.

[18] Crates also served as envoy to the Roman Senate. While in Rome he suffered an accident, and during the period of his recovery he gave many lectures on Greek literature and many recitations. He is said to have been the first to introduce the Romans to the scholarly study of literature. Sandys, *op. cit.*, p. 159.

[19] *Plutarch's Lives of Illustrious Men*, corrected from the Greek and revised by A. H. Clough (Boston: Little, Brown and Company, 1930), p. 674.

in 272 B.C. Among the prisoners was the dramatist Livius Androni-
cus, who became a schoolteacher and translated the works of Homer
into Latin for use in his teaching. He also wrote the first Latin
plays which were based on original Greek works. Crates of Mallos,
as was noted above, later introduced the Romans to the study of
Greek literature. Thus, by the time of the Roman conquest of
Greece in 146 B.C., the Romans read and studied Greek literature,
philosophy, and science; sent their sons to Athens to be educated;
and, at times, spoke Greek.

Private libraries became an important feature of Roman civilization when generals began to bring back entire libraries as spoils
of war from their campaigns in Greece. For example, Sulla captured
Athens in 86 B.C. and with it the library of Aristotle.[20] Another
collection which had been brought back by Lucullus twenty-three
years earlier was the basis of his library, which, according to Plutarch, he opened to all Greeks.[21]

From the time of Cicero (106–43 B.C.), who had a library
in each of his villas, private libraries were a necessity, since the
educated man required both Greek and Latin works. Manuscripts
were sought eagerly in Rome and Athens for the libraries of wealthy
collectors; and private libraries became so fashionable, numerous,
and large by the middle of the first century that Seneca spoke
out against the collecting of books "not for the sake of learning,
but to make a show."[22] The great demand for books stimulated
book production, and multiple copies were made by dictating the
text to a roomful of slaves. Bookstores occupied prominent places
on the busiest streets and often were the meeting places for scholars.

By the time of Julius Caesar, Greek influences—especially from
Alexandria and Pergamum—were widely in evidence, particularly
in the growing appreciation of literature. With the prospect of
an extended period of peace after long years of building a strong
national life, it was possible to give attention to cultivating the

---

[20] See pp. 13–14.
[21] *Ibid.*, p. 367.
[22] Seneca, "De Tranquillitate Animi," in Seneca, *Moral Essays,* with an English
translation by John W. Basore ("The Loeb Classical Library"; Cambridge,
Mass.: Harvard University Press, 1958), pp. 247, 249.

minds and talents of the people. Caesar, for example, wanted to found Greek and Latin libraries and open them to the public. His libraries would preserve books and records, serve as a means of instructing the people, and add to the cultural influence already being exerted by the private libraries, bookshops, and schools; and the nucleus of their collections would be the historical and political archives. Marcus Terentius Varro was to organize and manage them. Although these plans were interrupted by Caesar's death they were carried out by Asinius Pollio in the reign of Augustus, who began the imperial custom of establishing libraries by founding the Palatine Library in the Temple of Apollo with both Greek and Latin collections and later a second library, the Octavian, in a temple dedicated to Juno and Jupiter.

The period from A.D. 96 to 180 has been called the high point of ancient civilization. During this time of peace, prosperity, and order, not only the accumulated inheritance of art, letters, philosophy, and the science of government was handed down from generation to generation but new literary production was encouraged. More than twenty-five public libraries flourished in Rome in the second century.[23]

As a significant part of Rome's civilizing process, libraries spread throughout the Empire to important towns and cities in Italy, Greece, Asia Minor, Cyprus, and Africa. Typical of these was the one established by Emperor Trajan (r. A.D. 98–117) at Timgad in North Africa. The Ulpian Library in Rome, a scholarly collection housed in two structures—one for Greek and one for Latin works—was also founded by Trajan.[24] It was second in importance among ancient libraries only to those of Alexandria and Pergamum. The library founded by Emperor Hadrian (r. A.D. 117–138) in the Temple of Olympeium in Athens was known widely for the magnificence of its building and the quality of its collection.

At the height of the Roman Empire, a new book form came into prominence. The roll, inconvenient to write upon and to read and difficult to consult quickly, was superseded by the codex, in

[23] F. R. Cowell, "The Greece and Rome of Everyday," Grant (ed.), *op. cit.*, p. 205.
[24] The Roman Empire reached its greatest extent about A.D. 117 under Trajan.

which parchment sheets were fastened and bound together as in a modern book. Although used to some extent by the Greeks and by the Christians in the second century A.D., the codex did not come into general use until about the fourth century. The development of the codex was a highly significant step in bookmaking. In addition to providing easier access to the contents of a book, it greatly improved its chances for survival, a factor of extreme importance in long works like the Homeric poems.[25] The use of parchment in codexes, which further improved the chances for survival, also made possible the use of larger pages than had been possible with papyrus, thus providing room for illustrations or for the marginal notes and commentaries which are now so important to scholars.

By the third century the body of Christian literature had materially increased and Christian libraries had been established in many places throughout the Empire. Two important Christian centers for learning were at Alexandria, dating from about A.D. 180 and at Caesarea, where a notable library was assembled; in the western provinces, Carthage became the first center of Christian scholarship and libraries.

During the third century, barbarian invaders succeeded in making considerable inroads into the Roman Empire. Civil strife, combined with the attacks of Germanic tribes to the north and the pressure from the Persian kings to the east, threatened to disrupt the Empire and resulted in the loss of entire provinces; but before the end of the century Emperor Diocletian (284–305) had begun the task of restoring the strength and power of the imperial government and of returning the Empire to its early greatness. As a part of his plan to secure efficient administrative control over the Empire, Diocletian divided it into eastern and western spheres and established a system by which he was "supreme commander of the East with a colleague, Maximian, to govern the Western provinces."[26]

Although his reign is of great importance in the history of the Roman Empire, Diocletian is perhaps most often remembered

[25] Wace and Stubbins, *op. cit.*, p. 225.
[26] Michael Gough, "From the Ancient to the Medieval World: A Bridge of Faith," Grant (ed.), *op. cit.*, p. 329.

for his persecution of the Christians. From the beginning, Christians had suffered harassment, but the climax was reached in 303 when Diocletian instituted a persecution which raged until 313 when Constantine—who had openly accepted Christianity—issued the Edict of Milan giving Christians religious freedom and restoring their property and their civil rights. In the story of libraries, the ten-year persecution is noteworthy because during that time many churches with their libraries were razed and great numbers of books were burned.

During the fourth and fifth centuries invasions by barbarian tribes into the western parts of the Empire continued with increasing frequency; Britain, Gaul, Spain, and North Africa were conquered; and in 476 the western part of the Roman Empire fell to the invaders. At this very time, however, the eastern part of the Empire—now called the Byzantine Empire—was entering a period of vitality and progress which was to last almost a thousand years.

Of the barbarian German tribes which established kingdoms on Roman soil, the most important were the Burgundians and Franks in Gaul, the Visigoths in Spain, the Vandals in Africa, and the Ostrogoths in Italy. They all retained whatever remained of Roman administrative organization and with the help of the Roman citizens maintained some form of government and society. In Rome and other urban centers in Italy during the sixth century, classical culture was kept alive, secular letters were cultivated, and some literature was produced. The most notable scholar and writer in Italy during this century was Boethius, whose works included theological and philosophical writings and Latin translations of the works of Aristotle with commentaries. From these translations and commentaries the Western world derived its knowledge of Aristotle for the next six centuries.[27]

A final attempt to restore the former bounds of the Roman Empire and to reestablish one absolute emperor was made by Justinian, who, as emperor of the Byzantine Empire (527–565), di-

[27] M. L. W. Laistner, *Thought and Letters in Western Europe* A.D. *500 to 900* (Rev. ed.; Ithaca, N.Y.: Cornell Paperbacks, Cornell University Press, 1957), p. 87.

rected all his efforts toward these goals and succeeded in recovering Italy, North Africa, and parts of Spain. In both territorial expansion and the revival of cultural activities, some of the former grandeur of the old Roman Empire was recovered; but Justinian's successors were unable to hold together the restored empire, and as the sixth century advanced, the West again fell victim to the invading barbarians. Centralized control in Western Europe came to an end except for that of the papal state of Rome. Learning and literature continued to decline, leaving the monasteries[28] as the only repositories of culture and education in Western Europe.

[28] See pp. 23, 26ff.

CHAPTER 2
THE EARLY
MIDDLE
AGES

The period between the end of the Western Roman Empire and the emergence of medieval Europe—from ca. 500 to 1000—has traditionally been referred to as the Dark Ages, a period of barbarism and blight. But these centuries were not wholly dark, as historians increasingly emphasize, for they were also the centuries which saw the flowering of Byzantine civilization and the rise of the Muslim world in the East and, in the West, the expansion of Christian monasticism and the revival of learning under Charlemagne. Thus, although in each of the preceding periods it has been possible to discuss a people or a center of culture, in the early Middle Ages it is necessary to speak of several peoples and several centers of culture, which all influenced the preservation and transmission of learning and, therefore, the story of libraries.

THE BYZANTINE EMPIRE

Constantine the Great[1] became Emperor of both the Eastern and the Western Roman Empire in 324, at which time he chose a new capital, Byzantium (which he called Constantinople), made it the seat of his government in 330, and named Christianity the state religion. Moving the capital from Rome to Constantinople was to have far-reaching cultural as well as political and religious significance, for Constantinople—as the major center of Greek learning and scholarship—became the source of civilization to both Eastern and Western Europe.

Constantine began the establishment of the imperial library and emphasized the collecting of Latin works, since Latin was the offi-

[1] See p. 20.

cial language until about the sixth century. His successors enriched the library by the addition of Christian and pagan works, both Latin and Greek, and employed scribes to copy manuscripts. By the fifth century, the imperial library had some one hundred twenty thousand volumes, the largest book collection in Europe.[2] During that century, Theodosius II, a serious scholar and an ardent book collector, founded the University of Constantinople, which became the most important center of learning in the empire. The age of Justinian, as was noted above, produced a culture which covered in some degree almost every branch of learning; it is especially noteworthy for its contributions in mathematics, science, law, architecture, and art.

Since the church was the empire's most important institution in its early days, bishops, monks, and priests were more prominent than secular scholars and writers. Church buildings multiplied and, as a consequence of the requirement that each bishop have a library, ecclesiastical libraries and monastic collections were established widely. Monasticism, a way of life based on the Christian practice of asceticism, had originated in Egypt in the last years of the third century, and in the next century it became widespread throughout the Byzantine Empire. The Syriac language was developed from Aramaic and was used as the medium for a number of Christian writings.

The Byzantine Empire was wealthy and thickly populated by people whose heritage of civilization went back to the days of the invention of writing. Politically, intellectually, and culturally mature, enriched by Greek and Oriental learning, and influenced by the Roman tradition in government, it did not experience any "dark ages." For more than eleven centuries Constantinople survived the attacks of barbarians and the encroachments of the Arabs and became in the eighth, ninth, and tenth centuries the "most stable and cultured power in the world, and on its existence hung the future of civilisation."[3]

[2] James Westfall Thompson, *The Medieval Library* (New York: Hafner Publishing Company, Inc., 1957), p. 313.
[3] Frederic Harrison, *Byzantine History in the Early Middle Ages*, The Rede Lecture Delivered in the Senate House, Cambridge, June 12, 1900 (London: Macmillan & Co., Ltd., 1900), p. 11. By permission of Macmillan & Co., Ltd.

From the middle of the seventh to the middle of the ninth centuries very little secular literature was produced. The controversy growing out of iconoclasm, which was the ban on the representation of Christ or the saints and which lasted for over a century, resulted in the closing of the University of Constantinople and of some schools. Numerous monasteries were closed and their properties confiscated; this caused many Greek monks to seek refuge in Italy, taking with them their language and their culture, and thus made the learning of the East known in the West. During this period illumination[4] was not used in Bibles or religious works, but abstract letters and patterns were introduced into the copying of certain kinds of manuscripts.

By the second half of the ninth century the religious controversies were settled and the University of Constantinople was reopened, becoming a center for the study of ancient Greek works. The revival of interest in learning sparked great literary activity; and during the next three centuries ancient Greek texts were copied, commentaries were written, compilations and digests of Greek literature were made, and encyclopedias and lexicons were produced. While these works show little new or original thought, they are of inestimable value to the classical scholar and the cultural historian.

> The peculiar, indispensable service of Byzantine literature was the preservation of the language, philology, and archaeology of Greece. It is impossible to see how our knowledge of ancient literature or civilisation could have been recovered if Constantinople had not nursed through the early Middle Ages the vast accumulations of Greek learning in the schools of Alexandria, Athens, and Asia Minor; . . . if indefatigable copyists had not toiled in multiplying the texts of ancient Greece. . . . It is no paradox that their very merit to us is that they were never either original or brilliant. Their genius indeed would have been our loss. Dunces and pedants as they were, they servilely repeated the words of the immortals. Had they not done so, the immortals would have died long ago.[5]

[4] Illumination was the adornment of manuscripts, using ornamental letters, scrolls, or miniatures—small paintings—in color. The principal colors were red, blue, and gold; purple, yellow, and green were also used.
[5] *Ibid.,* pp. 36–37.

THE ARABS

Toward the end of the sixth century a new Oriental religion and a new political power arose in Arabia under the Prophet Mohammed. His followers, called Muslims, were a militant religious power. Bent upon world conquest, they began raiding the Byzantine Empire, and although during the seventh century they conquered most of Syria, Babylonia, Mesopotamia, Persia, and Egypt, Constantinople was able to withstand their attacks. Moving westward, the Arabs overran parts of Africa and Spain, but their attempts to invade the Frankish kingdom were checked at Tours in 732. Within two centuries they acquired an empire extending from Spain on the Atlantic to the boundaries of China. The Arabs were indeed great conquerors, but it was in the role of "adapters, preservers, and spreaders of civilization" that they contributed to the story of libraries, and it was largely through them that mathematical and scientific knowledge was transmitted to Europe.

During the eighth and ninth centuries, when the study and production of secular literature were at a standstill in Constantinople, Bagdad became the center for the study of Greek works. Through the Nestorian monks, a scholarly Christian sect which conducted a school near Bagdad, the Muslims were introduced to Aristotle's logic; and as Bagdad grew into a great city, physicians and scholars gathered there to study and to translate Greek medical, scientific, and philosophical works into Arabic, sometimes from Syriac or Aramaic versions rather than from the original Greek. The height of this translation movement was reached under the Abbasid Al-Mamum, who established in 830 "a house of wisdom," an institution of learning that combined the functions of library, academy, and translation bureau. Scholars went to Asia Minor and to Constantinople for materials, for even though hostilities existed between the Muslim and Byzantine Empires, trade and travel between them were only sporadically interrupted. Medicine, mathematics, and natural science were especially studied, as were also the works of Plato, Aristotle, Hippocrates, and Galen which were translated into Arabic. The period of translation, lasting roughly for a century and ending about 850, was followed by one of original works on astrology, alchemy, and magic.

Under the Abbasids, Bagdad rivaled Constantinople as a center of cultural activities, boasting many colleges and more than a hundred booksellers. In the course of their military conquests, the Arabs had learned the Chinese secret of papermaking, and paper was manufactured in Bagdad in the eighth century, when the Western world was still using parchment and even papyrus. Papermaking remained under the almost exclusive control of the Muslims for the next five centuries and the technique was taken by them to various parts of their empire. Since paper was cheap and plentiful and was easier to write on than parchment or papyrus, book production increased tremendously and great libraries were assembled. There were libraries in the mosques and in the colleges, and in the library of Shiraz, founded in the last half of the tenth century, books were listed in catalogs, arranged in cases, and administered by a regular staff.[6] In the eleventh century the library of the caliph of Cairo is said to have contained some one hundred fifty thousand books.[7]

When Arab culture moved to the western part of the Muslim Empire, many Arabic translations of Greek works were taken to Spain, where Spanish Muslim rulers continued the practice of patronizing scholars and founding schools and libraries. The library at Cordova, which was the center of a brilliant culture in the tenth century, contained four hundred thousand books.[8] In the libraries of Cordova, Toledo, and Seville, the Greek classics which had been translated from Syriac into Arabic were preserved until the scholars of the twelfth century came to render them into Latin and take them to the new universities in Europe.

WESTERN MONASTICISM

Christian monasticism, which had originated in Egypt in the last years of the third century, was introduced into the West by

[6] Philip K. Hitti, *The Near East in History: A 5000 Year Story* (New York: D. Van Nostrand Company, Inc., 1961), p. 271.
[7] Douglas C. McMurtrie, *The Book, the Story of Printing & Bookmaking* (New York: Oxford University Press, 1943), p. 67.
[8] R. H. Pinder-Wilson, "Islam and the Tide of Arab Conquest," *Dawn of European Civilization*, ed. David Talbot Rice (New York: McGraw-Hill Book Company, 1966), p. 62.

Athanasius and greatly advanced by the efforts of St. Martin, who founded religious settlements in Poitiers and later at Tours. Monastic foundations quickly multiplied in other parts of Gaul and in Italy, for in the midst of the disorder and confusion attending the barbarian conquests that brought an end to the Western Roman Empire, the monasteries offered a contrasting life of stability and security. Because they were looked upon as the refuge of holy men, the monasteries were often spared in war and frequently received gifts of land and such special privileges as exemptions from taxes.

Of particular importance in the story of Western monasticism is St. Benedict, who founded several religious communities near Subiaco in Italy and a larger monastery at Monte Cassino (ca. 529) and who formulated a rule for the guidance of his monks which was eventually adopted by most monasteries in the West. This Benedictine Rule was made up of moral and religious precepts and specific rules of conduct and organization, including devotional reading. Although this reading requirement suggests the existence of a library, the only kinds of mental activities encouraged in the early monasteries were those which contributed directly to spiritual growth. It was not until the last half of the sixth century that the monastery became a center for all studies and for the preservation of all writings, both religious and secular. These important developments began with Cassiodorus.

Cassiodorus, a contemporary of Boethius[9] and a distinguished official under three Ostrogothic kings, had wanted to establish in Rome a center for the study and teaching of Christian literature comparable to those in which pagan literature had been taught. This desire was not fulfilled; and when, upon his retirement, he established the monastic community of Vivarium (ca. 540 or 553), he made it a center for religious studies based on the Bible and recommended to the monks the reading and studying of secular as well as Christian authors in order to better understand the Scriptures. To support his program of studies, he set up a great library, adding to his personal collection—which he gave to the monastery—manuscripts of the great literature of the past, Greek and Latin, pagan and Christian, which he collected from many parts

[9] See p. 20.

of the world. The library was further enlarged and enriched by the products of the scriptorium which he established for the copying of Christian and secular literature and the translating of Greek authors into Latin. As patron, editor, and writer, he set high standards of achievement, and his zeal in bringing together a large and diversified library assured the preservation of much ancient writing, both sacred and profane, which otherwise would have perished in those disturbed days.[10]

In other parts of the West, continuous wars and invasions created conditions highly unfavorable to cultural activities, but in Spain the scholarly writings of Isidore, Bishop of Seville (d. 636), on a wide range of subjects indicate the breadth of his reading and reveal the extent of the library at Seville. His most extensive work, the *Etymologiae*, an encyclopedia of the arts and sciences containing much of the learning of the ancient world, became a standard reference work and was found in most monastic libraries.

Although Cassiodorus may be regarded as "the inaugurator of' the learned, compiling, commenting and transcribing functions of monasticism,"[11] the preservation and transmission of learning in the widest sense—literature, history, rhetoric, grammar, and astronomy as well as the Scriptures and the writings of the Church Fathers—began in northwestern Europe in the period of monastic expansion during the first half of the seventh century.

Ireland and Britain

After Cassiodorus, intellectual activity came to a standstill in Western Europe, but in Ireland a strong new culture was maturing—a culture which had originated and developed under the patronage of the Irish church. The beginnings of Irish Christianity are obscure. Unconquered by the Romans, Ireland's tribal, agricultural society was virtually undisturbed by outside forces until the Norsemen came late in the eighth century. But the Irish did not live in isolation; through trade and travel they were in contact

---

[10] Laistner, *op. cit.*, p. 102.
[11] Henry Osborn Taylor, *The Mediaeval Mind, A History of the Development of Thought and Emotion in the Middle Ages* (4th ed.; Cambridge, Mass.: Harvard University Press, 1925), I, 94.

with the outside world and, whatever the source, Christianity came to Ireland. In 431 a bishop was sent from Rome to organize a church, and the following year Patrick arrived on his historic Christianizing mission.

In the sixth century numerous monasteries came into existence,[12] including Clonard, Clonmacnois, and Bangor, and in all monasteries learning was encouraged from the beginning. Although Latin was the language of the church, the Irish vernacular continued to be used in ordinary speech and for written composition. Manuscripts of the Bible and of theological works and writings of secular authors had been brought into the country during the fifth and sixth centuries, and the respect which the Irish had always felt for their own national lore was extended to the new learning—both Christian and secular. In the larger monasteries there were schools which attracted many students and, from the seventh century, many foreign students. The Scriptures, writings of the Church Fathers, Latin classics, mathematics, and astronomy were studied.

In the scriptoria of the Irish monasteries a national script and a national art evolved and the first great development of manuscript books was begun—books which were characterized by superb calligraphy and illumination and fine workmanship. In fact, manuscript art attained an eminence which was never surpassed, reaching its height in the *Book of Kells,* a manuscript of the Gospels written in the eighth century representing Irish calligraphy and illumination at its best and believed to be the most richly decorated manuscript ever produced by an Irish scriptorium.[13]

Irish monks were characterized by their asceticism and their zeal for learning. They also had a strong penchant for travel and, as a result, became the greatest missionaries of the early Middle Ages, taking the Gospel and their learning and art to Scotland, northern England, and Europe and establishing many monastic centers in which learning was kept alive.

Foremost among the missionaries was St. Columba who founded several monasteries in Ireland, including Durrow and Kells,

[12] Ludwig Bieler, *Ireland, Harbinger of the Middle Ages* (London: Oxford University Press, 1963), p. 24. See map showing the major monasteries.
[13] *Ibid.,* p. 134.

and then went to the coast of north Britain, where at Iona (ca. 565) he established a monastery with a scriptorium and a library. From Iona, which became the "spiritual capital of what is now Scotland," Irish missionaries went to northern Britain to found at Lindisfarne in Northumbria (ca. 634) the first of a series of monastic houses. Lindisfarne became the center for intellectual activity on the east coast; throughout Northumbria churches and religious houses were established, and in their schools Irish teachers taught English boys not only the rudiments of knowledge but advanced learning.[14] The monastery at Iona and her dependent houses were famous for their illuminated books, notably the Book of Durrow, a copy of the Latin Gospels; and the Lindisfarne Gospels, a copy of the Vulgate text, which is the greatest surviving example of Northumbrian book production in the period of Celtic influence.

From the monastery at Bangor, another Irish monk, Columban—comparable to St. Columba both in name and in zeal for study—took Irish Christianity to the Continent, where in northern France he founded a number of monasteries, including Luxeuil, which became the greatest monastery of the time and an important writing center. His last monastery was founded in 614 at Bobbio in the Apennines and had a library and an active scriptorium. His disciples founded the Abbey of Corbie in France and the monastery of St. Gall in Switzerland, which became great writing centers in the eighth and ninth centuries. Bobbio, Corbie, and St. Gall maintained close relations with Luxeuil and continued to be strongly influenced by Irish tradition and practices.

Irish monks, teachers, and pilgrims took books with them to the Continent—not only the Scriptures and the lives of the saints but also their own Latin writings on theology and on the learned disciplines which were taught in their schools, many of which were masterpieces of illumination. These writings are known almost exclusively from copies preserved on the Continent and later in England, because great numbers of manuscripts were lost when the Vikings invaded Ireland in the eighth century and destroyed churches and monasteries and with them their libraries and schools.[15]

[14] John Godfrey, *The Church in Anglo-Saxon England* (Cambridge: Cambridge University Press, 1962), p. 106.
[15] Bieler, *op. cit.*, p. 110.

During the period of Irish missionary and cultural activity in Scotland and northern Britain and on the Continent, the church at Rome sent a mission to southern England, and in 597 the monk Augustine landed at Kent, where he founded the church at Canterbury. After 597, there were continuous relations between Britain and Italy, and pilgrims and travelers often brought back books and manuscripts. In the next century, under Theodore and Hadrian (ca. 669), the school at Canterbury became an educational center, attracting great numbers of students. Both Greek and Latin were taught, and the library, enriched by manuscripts which Theodore and Hadrian brought from Rome, had Greek and Latin works as well as many theological and secular works which had not formerly been known in Britain.[16]

In the eighth century, the joint foundation of Wearmouth and Jarrow in Northumbria, founded in the preceding century by Benedict Biscop, became the center of a "brilliant Christian culture." On numerous trips to Rome, Biscop made a point of securing great numbers of books to enrich the library, a practice which was continued by his successors. This great collection of books made possible the literary work of Bede, the most learned theologian and the most widely read and comprehensive author of the early Middle Ages.

Like the Irish church, the English church sent missionaries to the Continent. Most eminent was Boniface, who was called the Apostle to Germany and who was instrumental in the formation of many monasteries. His greatest monastery, Fulda, founded in the eighth century, was a center of learning and literature in Germany. Its library was strengthened by gifts of manuscripts from England as well as by copies of manuscripts made in its scriptorium.

For more than a century and a half after Cassiodorus, it was the Irish, first alone and later with the Anglo-Saxons, who were the chief transmitters and preservers of learning in the West and the "decisive cultural factor throughout the territory of the future Carolingian Empire."[17]

---

[16] Laistner, *op. cit.*, p. 151.
[17] Bieler, *op. cit.*, p. 104. See also map on p. VIII showing the most important centers of Irish-Christian influence.

THE CAROLINGIAN RENAISSANCE

At the mid-point between ancient and modern history stands the commanding figure of Charles the Great. The centuries of the Middle Ages which precede him record the decadence and final extinction of ancient institutions, while the nearly equal number of centuries which follow up to the time of the Renaissance and Reformation record the preparation for modern history. Thus, as finisher of the old order of things and beginner of the new, he is the central secular personage in that vast stretch of time between antiquity and the modern world, which we call the Middle Ages.[18]

The reign of Charles the Great (Charlemagne, 768–814) was marked by his efforts to raise the educational and cultural level of all his subjects, which brought to Western Europe a period of high educational and cultural growth and a revival of sacred and profane studies. Giving first attention to improving the education of the clergy, on whom his educational program would depend, Charlemagne then extended his interest to "all who were able to learn according to the capacity of each individual."[19]

Alcuin, master of the school at York in Northumbria and renowned throughout Britain for his teaching, was chosen by Charlemagne to direct his educational program. In 782, Alcuin became head of the Palace School in Aachen and began the task of establishing educational centers and of disseminating learning throughout the Frankish empire. Under his leadership, schools were founded, educational reforms were introduced, and grants for the purpose of establishing schools were made to the clergy, who were instructed to educate both the sons of freemen and those of servile origin. In his *Mind of the Middle Ages,* Henry Osborn Taylor refers to this period as "the schoolday of the Middle Ages," pointing out that "the whole period was at school . . . at school to the Church Fathers, at school to the transmitters of antique culture."[20]

Scriptoria were established in the monasteries and in many ca-

[18] Andrew Fleming West, *Alcuin and the Rise of Christian Schools* ("The Great Educators"; New York: Charles Scribner's Sons, 1892), p. 1.
[19] "Letter of Charlemagne to Abbot Baugulf, 780–800," *Basic Documents in Medieval History,* ed. Norton Downs (Princeton, N.J.: Anvil Books, D. Van Nostrand Company, Inc., 1959), p. 32.
[20] Taylor, *op. cit.,* pp. 103, 214.

thedrals; a library became a necessary part of religious institutions; and a carefully planned system of selecting, collecting, and copying scholarly literature, both religious and secular, was begun.[21] Correct Latin for literary purposes was revived, and authentic copies of the best texts were made. A new style of writing, the Caroline minuscule, was developed—a style which was adopted everywhere for manuscripts written in Latin and copied centuries later in metal types by the early printers for use in printing the Latin classics.

When Alcuin retired from the Palace School to the monastery of St. Martin at Tours, one of the oldest and wealthiest in the kingdom, he set about making it a center of learning by introducing the study of the liberal arts,[22] which he had introduced at York and later emphasized at the Palace School. To support his program of studies, he sent to York to obtain the scholarly works which he had used when he was master of the school there, for the York library was one of the most famous in Christendom and was reputed to contain whatever learning there was at that time.

In addition to his program of instruction, Alcuin supervised the copying of manuscripts in the scriptorium, giving careful attention to punctuation, spelling, and style of writing. These works served as models for copyists for many generations.

> Perceiving that the precious treasure of knowledge was then hidden in a few books, he [Alcuin] made it his care to transmit to future ages copies undisfigured by slips of the pen or mistakes of the understanding. . . . Thus, in every way that lay within his power, he endeavored to put the fortunes of learning for the times that should succeed him in a position of advantage, safeguarded by an abundance of truthfully transcribed books, interpreted by teachers of his own training, sheltered within the church, and defended by the civil power.[23]

[21] According to Einhard, Charlemagne commanded that at his death the books which he had collected in his library in great numbers be sold for fair prices and the money given to the poor. Einhard, *The Life of Charlemagne*, with a foreword by Sidney Painter (Ann Arbor, Mich.: Ann Arbor Paperbacks, University of Michigan Press, 1960), p. 66.

[22] The subjects believed to ensure a liberal education were the *trivium*: grammar, rhetoric, and dialectic; and the *quadrivium*: arithmetic, music, geometry, and astronomy. (Laistner, *op. cit.*, pp. 40–41).

[23] West, *op. cit.*, pp. 122, 123.

This revival of learning, which was sponsored by Charlemagne and inspired and directed by Alcuin, is called the Carolingian Renaissance. Out of the renewed educational activity had come new interest in all learning. Even after the partial collapse of Charlemagne's empire, interest in education and the cultivation of letters continued. "It was due to the efforts of the Carolingian scholars that the Latin past was salvaged at all. . . . anything that reached the eighth century has survived for our use today."[24]

The Carolingian Renaissance did not extend beyond the Frankish empire, but a century later King Alfred (871–899) tried to do for his kingdom of Wessex what Charlemagne had done in the Frankish empire. He brought foreign scholars to Wessex to reintroduce learning on a broad scale and organized a school attached to his household in which his own sons, the sons of noblemen, and even those from humble families were taught to read both Latin and the vernacular. Since only a few men could read Latin but many could read the vernacular, Alfred's educational plans included translating Latin works into the vernacular, and he himself undertook the translation of several works. During the latter part of the ninth and throughout the tenth century Wessex was the cultural center of England, with schools, monasteries, and scriptoria for the copying of manuscripts.

THE SCRIPTORIA[25]

The story of the libraries in which manuscripts were preserved during this period cannot be separated from the story of the scriptoria in which manuscripts were copied; and both libraries and scriptoria are a part of the story of Western monasticism, for "it was through the dissemination of Christianity that the continuity of our early European legacy was assured."[26]

Every monastery of any importance made some provision for

[24] Philip Grierson, "Charlemagne and the Carolingian Achievement," Rice (ed.), *op. cit.*, pp. 294, 295.
[25] See Thompson, *op. cit.*, pp. 594–612, and Laistner, *op. cit.*, pp. 225–237, for discussions of the scriptoria of this period.
[26] Gough, *op. cit.*, p. 329.

copying manuscripts, usually a scriptorium. Logically, the most productive scriptoria were in those monasteries and cathedrals which had sizable libraries. Library catalogs of the later eighth and ninth centuries show that most of the major monastic foundations acquired large collections of manuscripts. From the time of Charlemagne the practice of copying both religious works and the Latin classics was diligently followed, and the scriptorium of a large monastery or abbey would have a number of scribes, some of whom did ordinary copying while others who were specially trained in calligraphy or in illumination made the beautiful books for which the period is renowned. Manuscript art attracted the best artists of the period, and in addition to the scribes who lived in the monastery, secular scribes were often brought in from the outside for special tasks. In many monasteries, multiple copies of an author or of a particular work were made and some of them were distributed to other monasteries. "It was the universal multiplication of copies in the century 750–850 that enabled scholarship to survive the disasters[27] of the following century and hand on a legacy to the future."[28]

The seventh- and eighth-century scriptoria in Ireland, Britain, and on the Continent have already been noted. Some of these scriptoria became increasingly active in the ninth century, notably Bobbio, Corbie, St. Gall, and Tours, and their libraries grew correspondingly, showing large collections of both sacred and secular literature. There were many other scriptoria in the monasteries and in the cathedrals of Europe, and the frequent references to the borrowing and lending of manuscripts for copying reveal that they maintained close working relationships with each other.

Although some scriptoria declined in the tenth century, others, like St. Gall and Fleury, became more productive. The borrowing and lending of manuscripts continued, and the many extant manuscripts copied in the tenth century attest to the activity of the scriptoria and to their role in the transmission of Carolingian culture.

[27] See the Viking invasions, p. 36.
[28] Grierson, *op. cit.*, p. 295.

CHAPTER 3
THE PERIOD
OF
FEUDALISM

The breakdown of Charlemagne's empire was hastened by invasions from all sides, and the pieces out of which he and his predecessors had put together their empire fell apart along the old geographical and tribal lines. Local officials and great landholders became a law unto themselves, and the bonds which held society together were personal rather than political. From the ninth and tenth to the twelfth and thirteenth centuries the personal relationships which existed between the fighting and landholding classes and the subjugated peasantry on the land owned by these classes formed the basis of the social and political system called feudalism. Although feudalism had existed in the Frankish kingdom since the eighth century and had been encouraged by Charlemagne, it did not become widespread until the beginning of the tenth century, when the need for protection against barbarian invaders became urgent.

Most feared of the barbarians were the Vikings, who invaded by water, penetrating a country by way of its rivers, burning towns, villages, and monasteries and killing their inhabitants. The terror created by these raids led freemen to give themselves and their land to a large landholder in return for protection. Many feudal states were created, and the lord was a virtually independent sovereign. The building of castles as places of defense in this time of almost continuous warfare was widespread. Knighthood was a special military rank, and chivalry was its spirit and manners. Feudalism was most highly developed in what is now France, but it extended beyond Europe to England and even to the Byzantine Empire.

In such a time of fear and insecurity, the monastery once again became the retreat of literature and learning. Education was in the hands of the clergy, and literature was preserved in the libraries and scriptoria of the monasteries. During this period, events of particular significance in the history of libraries were the Crusades, the rise of universities, and the development of vernacular languages and literature.

THE CRUSADES

In the eleventh century, the Seljuk Turks became the ruling element in the Muslim world, and after conquering Persia they spread into Syria, Armenia, and Asia Minor. Their capture of Jerusalem in 1078 led to the Crusades, which began as religious wars aimed at the recovery of holy places which had been captured by unbelievers. Although they were preached in the name of the Church and stimulated by grant of ecclesiastical privileges, the Crusades were, nevertheless, fought by a cosmopolitan army. The First Crusade, launched in 1095 by Pope Urban to aid the Byzantines in recovering Jerusalem, resulted in its recovery in 1099. Almost a century later, Jerusalem fell again to the Turks and brought about the Third Crusade led by Philip Augustus of France, Richard the Lionhearted of England, and Frederick Barbarossa of Germany—a campaign full of adventures and celebrated in story and song but unsuccessful in accomplishing the recovery of Jerusalem. There were many other Crusades, covering more than two centuries in all. They provided an outlet for adventurers, for kings seeking glory, for both the devout and the sinful seeking penance through holy pilgrimage, and for rich merchants seeking new trade and commercial expansion.

The name and idea of the Crusades were eventually extended to expeditions other than the religious wars against the Mohammedans in the East. Such a campaign was the Fourth Crusade, directed against Egypt but diverted to Constantinople, which the Crusaders captured and sacked in 1204. Although there was a great loss of literary works in the fires which attended the capture of the city and in the destruction and loss of libraries, many manuscripts were dispersed, and from that time Greek works, including the original texts of Aristotle, found their way to Western Europe in increasing numbers.

The Crusades stimulated trade, brought goods and money into circulation, and created new activity and enterprise, and as a result, towns grew up around castles and monasteries or along waterways. The lot of the peasant gradually improved, resulting eventually in his emancipation. By the twelfth century some towns had achieved self-government and others had won a measure of freedom. The merchant class became important and, for mutual support and protection, formed guilds. Artisans and craftsmen followed the example of the merchants, and guilds became an important part of the social, political, economic, and industrial life of the time.

From the viewpoint of the student of librarianship, the most significant result of the Crusades was that twelfth-century Europe was brought into touch with the highly developed civilization of the East and exposed to new ideas, new knowledge, and new literature.

THE RISE OF THE UNIVERSITIES[1]

The economic and social changes resulting from the rise of towns, the expansion of trade and industry, and the growth of municipal institutions and individual freedom were accompanied by comparable developments and advances in art, literature, education, science, and thought.

The intellectual darkness of the century following the breakup of Charlemagne's empire was brightened by the cathedral school at Rheims and the teaching of Gerbert, the greatest scholar of the tenth century in Western Europe. Through his influence, cathedral schools were established in other French towns in the eleventh century and teaching again became important in a number of monasteries; and although the amount of knowledge then available was scant, there was a marked growth of interest in, and eagerness for, learning. The first notable increase in the knowledge of the eleventh century was in the field of medicine, when Salerno, already known throughout Europe as a school of medicine, began to receive Latin

[1] See Richard Hunt, "The Sum of Knowledge: Universities and Learning," *The Flowering of the Middle Ages*, ed. Joan Evans (New York: McGraw-Hill Book Company, 1966), pp. 179–202.

translations of the Arabic versions of Greek medical works. Early in the following century, the study of Roman law was revived at Bologna.

In northern Europe, also, the number of teachers increased, with attention being given to the study of Latin grammar and literature. Influenced by the works of Plato and Aristotle, some of which were newly available through translation, scholars showed renewed interest in astronomy, philosophy, theology, and logic. Adelard of Bath, an outstanding English scholar and traveler of this period, visited Greece, Asia Minor, and Spain to acquire wider knowledge in the fields of natural science and mathematics and became one of the first translators into Latin of the Arabic renderings of Greek and Oriental works. From the middle of the twelfth century, Spain was the center of translation from Arabic into Latin of Greek works of science, philosophy, medicine, and geography which the Arabs had preserved, as well as of recent works of the Arabs themselves. These Latin translations were transmitted to the scholars of twelfth- and thirteenth-century Europe and to the new universities which were established, thus increasing the knowledge and outlook of the learned world and further stimulating the intellectual curiosity already prevalent.

Exposure to Latin grammar and other basic subjects in the cathedral schools, the development of writing in the language of the masses, and more favorable social and economic conditions accelerated the enthusiasm for learning and set up a situation in which many students wandered from place to place to pursue more advanced studies with individual teacher-scholars. In time, a sufficient number of teachers and students congregated regularly in certain locations to form the nuclei of institutions of higher learning. In the beginning, these institutions did not own land or permanent buildings, but gradually teachers united into faculties according to their areas of scholarship and were empowered either by religious or by civil authority to grant degrees. The universities of Bologna, Paris, and Oxford are examples of permanent institutions of higher education which grew out of the wanderings of students and the instruction of individual teachers. The first universities in Italy, France, and England were followed by the establishment of institutions of higher learning in Spain and other countries of Western Europe, and thus by the close of the Middle Ages there were about eighty universities in Europe.[2]

The control over education and books, which had been maintained by the monasteries, now passed to the secular clergy and the universities. Book dealers (*stationarii*), appointed or controlled by the university to guarantee authenticity of texts, kept in stock correct editions of books used for instruction and rented them to students. As long as students could rent the required texts, there was little need for libraries; however, as the number of students increased, the universities were forced to establish libraries, and in time, gifts of books for the use of students were made by individuals. One of the most important academic libraries was the one given by Robert de Sorbon to the college which he founded in Paris in the thirteenth century for students of theology and which eventually became a part of the University of Paris.

Eventually, every college in a university had its own library. The more important books were chained to the desks, but in some libraries the chains were lengthened so that the student could take his book to a nearby table while he studied.

THE DEVELOPMENT OF VERNACULAR LANGUAGES AND LITERATURE

In addition to the scholars and students there were—in the new society which was created by the social, economic, and cultural changes of the eleventh, twelfth, and thirteenth centuries—the knights and lords who composed the feudal aristocracy, the townsmen, the Germanic and Norse invaders, and the Celts and Romans, most of whom neither spoke nor understood Latin. They, too, felt a new interest in learning, but literature intended for their use had to be written in the language of their daily life. France became the center of this vernacular literary activity, producing the *chansons de geste*, the *Fabliaux*, and the poetry of the troubadours and

[2] Rashdall Hastings, *The Universities of Europe in the Middle Ages*, ed. F. M. Powicke and A. B. Emden (New ed., 3 vols., London: Oxford University Press, 1936), I, xxiv.

the trouvères. Other examples of vernacular literature are the English epic poem, *Beowulf*, the *Eddas* of Iceland, the German *Nibelungenlied*, and Spain's *El Cid*. Medieval literature reached its height in Italy in the *Commedia* (*Divine Comedy*) of Dante, who wrote in Latin but also in Italian, thus establishing the vernacular Italian as a language suitable for literary expression.

CHAPTER 4
THE LATE
MIDDLE
AGES

The social, economic, cultural, and educational progress of the thirteenth century, which created such widespread interest in reading and then produced materials to be read, normally might have resulted in the collecting of books and the founding of many libraries had not the forces of war and of nature intervened. The Hundred Years War and the Black Death made the fourteenth century one of the most calamitous in all history. It is estimated that the Black Death alone killed one-third to one-half of the population of England and Europe. Homes and families were blotted out, agriculture ceased because of lack of tenants or lords and overseers, in many guilds there were no master craftsmen, trade diminished, few monks were left in the monasteries, and schools closed. Prices rose, taxes were increased to pay for the cost of the war, and revolts of the peasants in both France and England against the burden of taxation followed. France achieved nationality after a century of struggle but was left in a state of desolation, depopulation, and apparent ruin and for more than a century was prevented from continuing the literary activity for which she was famous in the eleventh, twelfth, and thirteenth centuries.

During this period, only royalty, nobility, the church, and the universities could afford books. Charles V (r. 1364–1380), known widely for his patronage of art and literature, built a large library which became the basis of the French Royal Library. In spite of the deprivation of the times, his brother Jean, Duke of Berry, built twenty castles and surrounded his luxurious court with the most illustrious artists of his time. His passion for collecting books resulted in the assembling of one of the most varied collections of manuscripts in history, numbering among its treasures the handsomely illuminated Books of Hours.[1] The first large private library in England, estimated at one thousand volumes, was collected during this period of war and suffering by Richard de Bury, Bishop of Durham. His library was dispersed, but his *Philobiblon*,[2] one of the first books about books, tells of his extravagant love of books and reveals some of the methods he used in collecting them.

THE RENAISSANCE

The fourteenth century was as unfortuitous for the Byzantine Empire as it was for Western Europe. The steadily advancing armies of the Ottoman Turks frightened many Byzantine Greeks into fleeing Constantinople and seeking shelter in Italy. They took with them manuscripts of the ancient writers and were welcomed by Italian scholars, who encouraged them to open schools for the study of both Greek and Latin.

The Renaissance in Italy

Petrarch (fl. 1304–1374) is credited with "preparing the soil of Italy for the reception of Greek culture" because he was the first to recognize the intellectual and cultural value of ancient Latin and Greek literature. Called the Father of Humanism,[3] Petrarch added to medieval culture a worshipful appreciation of the ancient classics. He searched neglected libraries in monasteries for old manuscripts, and many long-lost ancient Latin works were recovered, including the writings of Cicero, Quintilian, Plautus, and Lucretius. Petrarch gave his library to St. Mark's in Venice, but his wish that it be maintained by the Venetian government was never fulfilled.

Boccaccio was influenced by Petrarch to study the Latin

---

[1] *The Belles Heures of Jean, Duke of Berry, Prince of France*, with an introduction by James J. Rorimer (New York: The Cloisters, The Metropolitan Museum of Art, 1958), *passim*.

[2] Richard de Bury [Richard Aungerville], *The Philobiblon* (Berkeley, Calif.: University of California Press, 1948).

[3] Humanism stressed the study of the "more human letters" of the Greek and Latin writers in contrast with the theological letters of the medieval scholars.

classics, and he learned Greek in order to be able to read the Greek authors. Continuing the search for manuscripts, Boccaccio visited many monasteries, made copies of ancient works, and became a student of Tacitus, whose *Histories* he is believed to have found in Monte Cassino.[4] Foremost in the quest for ancient manuscripts was Poggio Bracciolini, whose searches of monasteries at Cluny, St. Gall,[5] and throughout France and Germany yielded many works of early Latin literature. The decline of monastic life following the rise of towns and the universities had led to gross neglect of the libraries. Precious manuscripts were left unprotected from dust, dirt, and the elements, and in some monasteries pages were torn out of manuscripts or portions were cut out and sold. Boccaccio is said to have "burst into tears" over the condition of manuscripts in Monte Cassino, and Poggio found many manuscripts exposed to the dampness of the church towers at St. Gall.

Constantinople, which had been menaced for more than a century by the Ottoman Turks, finally yielded to them in 1453, and the Byzantine Empire came to an end. One scholar pays proper tribute to Constantinople's contribution to culture by saying that:

> The capital of the Eastern empire had . . . proved strong enough to stand for centuries as the bulwark of Europe against the barbarians of the East, thus sheltering the nascent nations of the West, while they slowly attained the fulness of their maturity, and, at the same time, keeping the treasures of the old Greek literature in a place of safety, until those nations were sufficiently civilised to receive them.[6]

It cannot be said that the fall of Constantinople caused the Renaissance, but it is clear that it did aid greatly the revival of learning begun by Petrarch, Boccaccio, and others by dispersing to Europe many works of Greek and Latin literature.

What the word Renaissance really means is new birth to liberty— the spirit of mankind recovering consciousness and the power of

---

[4] See p. 27.
[5] See p. 30.
[6] Sandys, *op. cit.*, p. 439.

self-determination, recognizing the beauty of the outer world, and of the body through art, liberating the reason in science and the conscience in religion, restoring culture to the intelligence, and establishing the principle of political freedom. The Church was the schoolmaster of the Middle Ages. Culture was the humanizing and refining influence of the Renaissance.[7]

The Renaissance in Italy, also called the age of Humanism, was characterized by the eager and unceasing search for the manuscripts of ancient Greek and Latin authors, the intense yearning and effort to read and understand them, the aim to imitate and reproduce their style and form, and the acquisition of great libraries in which to preserve and use them. "It was an age of accumulation, of uncritical and indiscriminate enthusiasm. Manuscripts were worshiped. . . . The good, the bad, and the indifferent received an almost equal homage. Criticism had not yet begun."[8]

Florence became the center of the Italian Renaissance. For over a century, the Medici were its greatest patrons and led the rich middle class in sponsoring the most brilliant development of culture since the Golden Age of Greece. Cosimo de' Medici, who ruled until 1464, was an enthusiastic patron of manuscript collectors, copyists, and Humanists. He sent his agents throughout the known world to find classic works and was successful in bringing together most of the Latin classics. He established the library of San Marco and from his own collection founded the great Medici Library, now housed in the Laurentian Library in Florence. His grandson Lorenzo, a generous patron of the arts, writer, and lover of learning, continued the search for manuscripts, greatly enriched the Medici Library, and established the great Florentine library of Greek and Latin classics.

The age of Humanism was also a period of discovery and exploration. In an effort to open a new sea route to the East to replace the land route closed by the fall of the Byzantine Empire, Bartholomew Diaz rounded the Cape of Good Hope in 1488, Christopher Columbus set foot upon the American continent in

[7] John Addington Symonds, *Renaissance in Italy: The Age of the Despots* (New York: Henry Holt and Company, 1888), p. 28.
[8] *Ibid.* p. 21.

1492, and Vasco Da Gama reached India via the Cape of Good Hope in 1498.

After the sack of Rome in 1527,[9] when many collections of manuscripts were destroyed or scattered and many artists and scholars perished or were forced into exile, the center of the Renaissance moved to northern Europe, where a new medium for transmitting knowledge was then being developed, a medium which would make the learning of the ancients—and all learning—easily available to all men.

Printing with movable types

Sandys reminds us that:

> While we gratefully recall the preservation of Latin manuscripts in the mediaeval monasteries of the West, as well as the recovery of lost Classics by the humanists of the fourteenth and fifteenth centuries, and the transference to Italy of the treasures of Greek literature from the libraries of the East, we are bound to remember that all this would have been of little permanent avail, but for the invention of the art of printing.[10]

The zeal for learning engendered by the Renaissance brought about a demand for books which could no longer be satisfied by handwritten copies. The need for a new and faster medium for transmitting thought and knowledge was immediate and urgent. A kind of printing had been known since the time when the Babylonians and Egyptians used metal or wooden seals to print on soft clay or on wax. As early as the fifth century, the Chinese printed short mottoes and charms from seals on which the characters to be printed were carved in relief. The full-page woodcut, printed from a wooden block on which the text and illustrations had been carved, was the next step in printing, and by A.D. 868 the Chinese

---

[9] Although this was a period of intellectual and artistic supremacy for Italy, it was, politically, a period of civil strife. Italy was a divided country, and there were wars among the several states and also with France, Germany, and Spain. Rome was sacked by the mercenaries of Charles V of Spain.
[10] Sir John Edwin Sandys, *A History of Classical Scholarship*, Vol. II: *From the End of the Revival of Learning to the End of the Eighteenth Century* . . . (Cambridge: Cambridge University Press, 1908), p. 95.

had produced a complete book, *The Diamond Sutra,* in this manner. Woodcut printing in Europe, however, was delayed until the fourteenth century.

Movable types, made first of clay and then of tin, also originated in China but were never used extensively by the Chinese. It is likely that Europeans had heard of printing and may have seen samples of it during the Crusades, but "printing as it appeared in Europe, was an independent outgrowth of the times."[11]

The materials required for printing—a cheap and plentiful substance on which to print, an ink that would adhere to metal surfaces and transfer to paper, a press to bring paper and metal into contact with each other, and a general knowledge of metal technology— were all available by the second quarter of the fifteenth century, and to Johann Gutenberg is given the credit for combining these materials and for supplying the necessary technological skill which resulted in the invention of printing with movable types. This event of incalculable significance in the cultural history of mankind occurred between 1440 and 1450 in the vicinity of Mainz, Germany.

The first piece of printing which bears a date (1454) was a papal indulgence. The forty-two-line Bible, commonly called the Gutenberg Bible and generally regarded as the first printed book in Europe, was completed not more than two years later. By the end of the century, printing had been carried to all parts of Europe. Of the fifteenth-century German centers of printing, Nürnberg was the most important, and Anton Koberger was its greatest printer. His most elaborate publication was the *Liber Chronicarum,* 1493, with 1,800 woodcut illustrations. The first book printed in the English language was the *Recuyell of the Histories of Troy,* printed between 1474 and 1476 by William Caxton, who learned the art of printing in order to be able to print his own translation of this work.

About one-half of the books printed in the fifteenth century were religious works: the Bible, works of the Church Fathers, manuals for priests, and religious tracts. Other publications were

[11] McMurtrie, *op. cit.,* p. 123. See Chapters IX–XI in McMurtrie for a discussion of the invention of printing.

encyclopedias, pamphlets, calendars, epistles, handbills, and some books on mathematics and astronomy. Printed books which can be dated before the year 1501 are called incunabula.

Venice, already important for trade and commerce, became a major center of printing by the beginning of the sixteenth century. Here Nicolas Jenson became the world's first great type designer, including Greek type, and Aldus Manutius began the publication of pocket editions of the Latin and Greek classics. By 1515, all the principal Greek classics had been printed in this scholarly, compact, and inexpensive format and were easily available to all who wanted to own them.

The most important library of the fifteenth century was the Vatican Library. Pope Nicholas V (1447–1455), when he was a priest, drew up a plan for a library for Cosimo de' Medici, aided in the search for manuscripts, and copied manuscripts himself. When he became Pope, he added his own library to the approximately three hundred fifty manuscripts which then constituted the Vatican Library and began the task of collecting the works of classical authors. With his librarian, Tortelli, Pope Nicholas V planned the complete translation of Greek literature into Latin, employing many copyists. In the Vatican Library, classical, Humanist, scholastic, and patristic works stood side by side. Pope Sextus IV continued the work of Pope Nicholas V and opened a part of the library to the public.

An outstanding private library was that of the Duke of Urbino, which contained copies of all the Latin and Greek authors then discovered—all "written by hand because the Duke would have been ashamed to possess a single printed book."[12]

The outstanding contributors to the art of printing and to the spread of the Renaissance in sixteenth-century France were (1) Robert Estienne and his son, Henri, who published the Greek and Latin classics and Latin, Greek, and Hebrew dictionaries; (2) Claude Garamond, designer of Roman typefaces; and (3) Geofroy Tory, printer to the king, scholar, spelling reformer, type designer, and wood engraver.

[12] Sandys, *op. cit.*, II, 96.

Antwerp was notable in this century for the work of Christopher Plantin, whose twenty-two presses produced religious, classical, scientific, and medical works and the works of contemporary French authors. His most important publication was the Polyglot Bible, 1568–1573.

By the beginning of the sixteenth century, vernacular works outnumbered Latin works in all countries. Interest in education had been stimulated by the intellectual activity of the Renaissance and the religious upheaval which resulted in the Protestant Reformation; and among all classes of society, except the very lowest, there was an intense desire to read.

The invention of printing with movable types resulted in an inestimable increase in the supply of books, the greater diffusion of knowledge, the dissemination of classical literature, the flowering of national literature, the development of literary criticism, and the rise of publishing as a business. Libraries increased in number and in size as a natural consequence of the fact that learning, formerly confined to the monasteries or the universities, was now within reach of any person who wished to pursue it.

The foremost scholar of the sixteenth-century Renaissance in northern Europe was Erasmus, student and teacher of Latin and Greek, whose textbooks in syntax and style, translations, rescensions, and editions of Latin and Greek works contributed to the study of Latin grammar and rhetoric and the advancement of learning. Erasmus and other scholars of the sixteenth century, including the scholar-printers, had the task of criticizing, editing, and preparing for publication the manuscripts which Poggio and others had collected during the early fifteenth century.[13]

Francis I, King of France and patron of the arts, aided the development of the Renaissance in France by giving protection and encouragement to authors and scholars and by founding chairs of Latin, Greek, and Hebrew which formed the nucleus of Collège de France. He assembled the various royal libraries at Fontainebleau, appointed Guillaume Budé, learned scholar and one of the first French Humanists, as Royal Librarian, and added to the library

[13] See pp. 43–44.

by the acquisition of Greek and Oriental manuscripts and by requiring in 1537 that one copy of every Greek book published in
France be given to the Royal Library.

The most important private libraries in France were those of
Jean Grolier, which contained 3,000 volumes, and Jacques Auguste
de Thou, which reached a total of 8,000 printed works and 1,000
manuscripts. Both libraries were noted for their fine gold-tooled
bindings.

In Germany, the efforts to make Latin and Italian literature
available to more people by translating it in the vernacular encouraged reading and the practice of book collecting by individuals.

The Renaissance can be characterized as an age of elegance,
refinement, and cultural growth, of fine books with beautiful bindings, and of splendid library collections which provided books both
for education and for aesthetic enjoyment.

The Protestant Reformation

As the sixteenth century advanced, Humanism slowly but
steadily declined and the study of Latin and Greek gradually gave
way to theological and moral discussions, with the result that
religious differences between Catholics and Protestants, and among
Protestants themselves, received most of the intellectual emphasis
of the time. The Protestant Reformation, begun in 1517 to reform
certain doctrines and practices in the Roman Catholic Church, resulted in the establishment of various Protestant denominations in
central and northwest Europe.

> The whole movement of the Reformation is a phase in that acceler-
> ated action of the modern mind which at its commencement we
> call the Renaissance. . . . The Reformation exhibits in the realm
> of religious thought and national politics what the Renaissance
> displays in the sphere of culture, art, and science—the recovered
> energy and freedom of the reason.[14]

During this period of religious upheaval and controversy, many
monastic libraries disappeared and others were scattered or

[14] Symonds, *op. cit.,* p. 26.

destroyed, but in some places libraries passed from Catholic to Protestant ownership with little change.

Martin Luther encouraged the building of good libraries, and library buildings and municipal libraries in Germany date from this period. There were many church libraries and many private libraries also. It has been said that Germany in the sixteenth century "was saturated with books."[15]

Libraries in England suffered more than those of any other country in the sixteenth century, when Henry VIII dissolved the monasteries, 1535–1539, appropriating their wealth for himself and his favorites. The contents of many libraries were lost, some books were sold, and others were exported. Fortunately, some were saved by the abbots who took them to their new posts. Sir Robert Bruce Cotton, collector of manuscripts and coins, saved many works from the dissolved monasteries, including the Lindisfarne Gospels.[16] Numerous schools attached to the religious houses vanished and Oxford and Cambridge lost large numbers of students.

In Spain, an important library was established by Philip II in the monastery of San Lorenzo Del Escorial outside Madrid with his own private collection of almost two thousand volumes. It was enriched by gifts of Greek, Latin, and Arabic works, by "choice items" which the King's learned representatives brought back from Italy, Germany, and Flanders, and by the writings of eminent scholars of the time. The library was housed in a building which was reportedly as magnificent as its collections.[17]

---

[15] Alfred Hessel, *History of Libraries*, trans. Reuben Peiss (2d ed.; New York: Scarecrow Press, Inc., 1955), p. 55.

[16] See p. 30.

[17] John W. Montgomery (tr.), *A Seventeenth-Century View of European Libraries: Lomeier's De Bibliothecis, Chapter X* (Berkeley, Calif.: University of California Press, 1962), pp. 58–60.

CHAPTER 5
FROM THE
AGE OF
ENLIGHTENMENT
TO THE
TWENTIETH
CENTURY

The Renaissance, with its high artistic and literary achievement, also laid the foundations of the scientific revolution of the seventeenth century. Humanists had gradually developed a critical approach to the study and comparison of ancient manuscripts and to the interpretation of the history of the ancient past. In the revival of learning, scientific as well as philosophical, literary, and artistic works were recovered, stimulating the study of astronomy, mathematics, medicine, and physics. The discovery of America and of the new routes to the East led to the scientific construction of maps.[1] The printing press, itself a scientific achievement, provided the medium for quickly disseminating all knowledge.

Led by Galileo, Kepler, Francis Bacon, and Descartes, the new scientific era focused attention on the bases of science and on the scientific method. The practical applications of science and the increase in trade and commerce gave rise to a new moneyed class of doctors, merchants, lawyers, and other professional groups. By the end of the seventeenth century the decline in the power of the clergy was seen in the secularization of society, the emphasis on reason over faith, and in the questioning, rather than the uncritical acceptance, of authority. It was a period of exploration, territorial expansion, and colonization. The first permanent English

---

[1] The Byzantine Humanist Pletho (ca. 1355–1452) had exerted considerable influence on Renaissance geography by introducing the work of the ancient geographer Strabo to the West.

Colonies in America were established during the first three decades of this restless century.

The general spirit of inquiry and research, which was dependent upon access to materials of all kinds, stimulated the formation of libraries made up of printed works as well as hand-written manuscripts. One analyst of the times has noted that "certainly, in any listing of the factors which, at that critical period in European history contributed to a settled order in things of the mind, to the overthrow of superstition and the growth of tolerance, libraries will have to be ranked high."[2]

Some of the great national libraries[3] were founded during the seventeenth century: the Prussian State Library in Berlin (1659), the Kongelige Bibliotek in Copenhagen (1661), and the National Library of Scotland (1682).

In 1622, under Louis XIII, the first catalog of the Bibliothèque du Roi (the French Royal Library) was drawn up by Nicolas Rigault,[4] and in the reign of Louis XIV, under the direction of Colbert, the library almost doubled in size. The library of Cardinal Mazarin in Paris was collected and arranged by Gabriel Naudé in 1642. Its collection soon numbered forty thousand volumes and it was open to all who wanted to go there and study.

In 1598 Sir Thomas Bodley began the work of rebuilding the library at Oxford and opened it in 1602 with two thousand volumes. He later persuaded the Stationers' Company to deposit in it a free copy of every book published in England and left to it a considerable legacy of land and property.

That libraries were an important part of seventeenth-century life is seen in the statement of Johannes Lomeier that "one may scarcely find any moderately famous city, scarcely any community, gymnasium, university or monastery where a library has not been set apart for the public use of the studious."[5]

---

[2] Montgomery, *op. cit.*, p. 11.
[3] One of the functions of a national library is to collect and preserve for future generations the written production of that country.
[4] La Bibliothèque Nationale ("La Documentation Française Illustrée," No. 50; Paris: La Direction de la Documentation, 1951), p. 15.
[5] Montgomery, *op. cit.*, p. 12.

The scientific spirit of the age is reflected in the writings on the history, planning, organization, and administration of libraries and on the classification and arrangement of materials. In 1602, Justus Lipsius published his *De Bibliothecis Syntagma*, which Irwin describes as "the foundation of all modern histories of libraries."[6] Of the numerous treatises which were written pertaining to the systematic organization of libraries, the earliest was Naudé's *Advis Pour Dresser Une Bibliothèque*, published in 1627, in which he discussed the reasons for establishing a library, the size, quality, and arrangement of the collection, the kind of building required, and the library's basic purpose. Regarding purpose, he remarked that "in vain does he strive to carry out the preceding suggestions or go to any great expense for books who does not intend to devote them to the public use and never to withhold them from the humblest of those who may reap benefit thereby. . . ."[7]

John Durie, Keeper of the Royal Library, made the first contribution to library economy in England in 1650 with his *The Reformed Librarie Keeper*, in which he outlined a plan for expanding the Royal Library into a "truly national collection"; and in 1697 Richard Bentley added to the literature of libraries his *Proposal for Building a Royal Library*.

Principles which should govern the development of a large scholarly research library were set forth by Leibniz, who administered the library of Wolfenbüttel in Germany. His principles, which are still valid, included firm financial support with regular appropriations, continuing and systematic acquisition of all major works of learning, and classification of all works for greater accessibility.[8]

The zeal for research extended to all fields of knowledge and was reflected in the diversity of the great libraries of the time. It found expression also in the national institutions and societies which were organized to pursue research and to provide the neces-

[6] Raymond Irwin, *The Origins of the English Library* (London: George Allen & Unwin Ltd., 1958), p. 182.
[7] Gabriel Naudé, *Advice on Establishing a Library*, with an introduction by Archer Taylor (Berkeley: University of California Press, 1950), p. 74.
[8] Hessel, *op. cit.*, p. 72. See also Ernest Maass, "Leibnitz' Contribution to Librarianship," *College and Research Libraries*, IV (June, 1943), 245–249.

sary materials. A notable example is the Royal Society in London, founded in 1662 as a cooperative endeavor of scientists, historians, and philosophers.

The appearance of the parish library in the late seventeenth century is evidence of the importance which the Anglican Church attached to the continuing education of its ministers. Established by Reverend Thomas Bray and others in England, it was designed to aid the rural Anglican clergy in carrying out its educational, as well as its spiritual, mission.

The eighteenth and nineteenth centuries

The scientific thought and progress of the seventeenth century gathered momentum in the eighteenth century, bringing greater advances in both the pure and applied sciences and leading to the mechanical inventions and technological achievements which resulted in the industrial revolution and the rise of the working class. In the last quarter of the century, the Revolution of the American Colonies focused attention on the democratic concept of the worth and dignity of the individual and the French Revolution proclaimed the importance of the common man.

With the French Revolution in 1789, church libraries became national property and the libraries of the émigrés were confiscated. Great numbers of books were taken from their owners and placed in the "*dépôts littéraires*," which had been established to receive them. Many books were assigned to university libraries, but the largest share was given to the French Royal Library, which became national property and was renamed La Bibliothèque Nationale. By the time of the Revolution, in addition to being open to scholars,[9] the library was open to the public on two days a week for five hours, and during the Revolution a regulation of 25 Fructidor, An IV opened the library every day for four hours.[10] The governments

[9] As early as 1720, the library (then the French Royal Library) was open to scholars of all nations on days and hours regulated by the librarian and open to the public on one day each week for two hours. *La Bibliothèque Nationale, op. cit.*, p. 8.
[10] *Ibid.* Fructidor was the twelfth month of the Republican Calendar. 25 Fructidor, An IV was 11 September, 1796.

after the Revolution were as interested in the growth of the Bibliothèque Nationale as were the sovereigns of the Ancient Régime, and through governmental appropriations, legal deposit, gifts, and legacies the Library continued to grow. The publication of catalogs, begun in 1622, continued, and in 1897 the *Catalogue Général des Livres Imprimés: Auteurs* was begun.

During both the eighteenth and the nineteenth centuries, national libraries were established throughout Europe: La Biblioteca Nazionale Centrale in Florence, the Kungliga Biblioteket in Stockholm, the Koninklijke Bibliotheek in The Hague, the Universitetsbiblioteket in Oslo, La Bibliothèque Royale de Belgique in Brussels, Ethnike Bibliotheke tes Hellados in Athens, La Biblioteca Nacional in Madrid, The National Library of Ireland in Dublin, and La Bibliothèque Nationale Suisse in Bern.

Many private libraries were also established. The most famous private library of this period in England, and the only one to survive in its original state, was that of Samuel Pepys, with its three thousand volumes arranged in eleven carved mahogany cases. There were some eccentric book collectors, too. Thomas Rawlinson, for example, who was called a "universal scholar as far as title pages go," had his rooms so full of books that he had to sleep in the passage. Another collector, John Bagford, collected only the title pages of books.[11]

Many large libraries, rich in materials for research, were also assembled. Edward Gibbon owned a library of nearly seven thousand volumes, which he systematically collected in order to write *The Decline and Fall of the Roman Empire*. Sir Hans Sloane's library numbered more than 40,000 printed works and 3,576 manuscripts, including all fields of knowledge, and the libraries of Robert and Edward Harley, Earls of Oxford, contained thousands of printed books and pamphlets and several thousand manuscripts.

The Sloan and Harleian collections and that of Sir Robert Cotton, together with the Royal Library which had existed from the reign of Henry VII, formed the foundation of the British Museum, which was incorporated in 1753. Other collections of the

[11] Irwin, *op. cit.*, p. 183.

royal family, famous collections from many sources, and books provided by the copyright deposit law added to the size and importance of the Museum's holdings. Under the direction of Sir Anthony Panizzi, who became Keeper of the Printed Books in 1837, the British Museum became an institution for the "diffusion of culture" and a national library in the sense that it preserved all English books and most of the important foreign literature. Panizzi made sure of a large and regular yearly budget, reorganized the library, designed its new building, which included a reading room separate from the rooms used for shelving, and began the complete revision of the catalog. By 1870 the holdings had reached a million volumes.

Reading became fashionable for women in the eighteenth century; the habit of reading spread to the lowest social classes; and interest in reading for instruction, for political purposes, and for recreation was widespread. Bookshops, newspapers, magazines, pamphlets, coffeehouses, book clubs, and learned societies and institutions served some of the intellectual, literary, and social needs of the people; but to meet all the new demands for books from people who were unable to buy them, a new kind of library was developed: the lending or circulating library, begun by booksellers who loaned books on payment of a small fee. The lending library was a commercial enterprise more concerned with making money for its owner than with the education of its readers. Its chief item was the novel, and most of the patrons were women. The first lending library was opened in Edinburgh in 1726 and in London in the 1730s. In 1804, the three largest lending libraries in Dresden had a combined stock of sixty thousand volumes, and by the end of the eighteenth century lending libraries had become a common feature of every town in Western Europe.[12]

The mechanization of industry following the industrial revolution created many problems relating to the training and welfare of apprentices, and when in 1800 George Birkbeck, a Scottish teacher of philosophy, started classes and a library for the mechanics' apprentices, his example was followed by others.

[12] S. H. Steinberg, *Five Hundred Years of Printing* (2d ed.; Baltimore: Penguin Books, Inc., 1961), pp. 259, 260.

Mechanics' institutes were organized in the industrial centers and in London, providing elementary instruction and lectures for the benefit of apprentices who needed to improve their technical knowledge. Libraries were organized as a further aid to the self-education of the apprentices and for moral betterment as well as recreation; they were financed by subscriptions of the members. The management was in the hands of the members, but gifts from wealthy individuals aided the operation. By the middle of the century, mechanics' institutes and libraries had spread throughout England, providing help and encouragement to the laboring class.

In 1850 the English Parliament passed the first Public Libraries Act, allowing local councils to organize libraries and support them by taxation but limiting the amount that could be spent for that purpose. The first public library was established at Manchester with Edward Edwards as librarian. Edwards, who had been influential in securing the passage of the Public Libraries Act, set forth some general principles of library service which have been followed ever since: Library service must be given freely to any citizen who wants to use it; library service is a local responsibility and the cost is borne collectively by all who pay taxes whether they use it or not; books of all kinds and on all aspects of a question should be included in the collection. During the first twenty years of the Public Libraries Act only thirty-five new libraries were established.[13] With the passage of the 1870 Education Act and the organization of the Library Association in 1877 for the purpose of encouraging the establishment of public libraries, the public library movement was greatly accelerated.

The closing years of the nineteenth century were characterized by the expansion of public library service in Great Britain, the Scandinavian countries, and Germany and by the growth of all established libraries throughout Europe, especially the great national and university libraries.

[13] Lionel McColvin, "The British Public Library," White, *op. cit.*, pp. 57–67, passim.

CHAPTER 6
AMERICA—THROUGH
THE EARLY
NINETEENTH
CENTURY

The discovery of America was one of the early achievements of the Renaissance.[1] The colonization of America was the result of more than a century of such Renaissance influences as the spread of learning, the religious unrest following the Reformation, the growth of trade and commerce, the emergence of capitalism, the rise of the middle class, and scientific study and technological invention.

The English colonists came to the New World for various reasons—to secure religious freedom, to acquire land, to develop trade, for self-enrichment, or for the glory of England—and while they shared the same political, social, and intellectual heritage, the society which they developed took several forms, depending on the part of the New World in which it grew. Land was the principal resource in every Colony, but the basis on which it was acquired and distributed was a determining factor in the growth and development of a Colony. For example, in the Chesapeake Colonies (Virginia and Maryland) land was given directly to individuals and additional holdings were acquired through headrights for each servant or slave. Thus, great estates were acquired, and landowners settled along the waterways and at some distance from each other, rather than in villages. Communication was difficult, methods of transportation were slow, and in this society of widely scattered farmers, the maintenance of churches and schools was impossible. The family became the social and economic unit; the religious needs were ministered to by itinerant clergymen. Schoolmasters were imported from England to provide for the educational needs of those

[1] See pp. 43–51.

who made up the plantation family. The Southern Colonies (Georgia and the Carolinas), also based on large grants of land, developed a plantation system of agriculture with a few staple products and a society which was comparable to that of Virginia and Maryland. From 1670, these Colonies were strongly affected by the introduction and use of slaves.

In Massachusetts Bay and the other New England Colonies land was distributed in townships. A community was created within the township, and outside the community—but within the township—lands were allotted for farming and grazing. Even though individuals were given titles to land, "the essence of the system was the preservation of a community."[2] The population was homogeneous, the town was the center of life, and the church and school were easily accessible to all. When the Massachusetts Bay Colony expanded, it was in group migrations along the coast, and communication and trade between settlements were maintained. "New England can properly be called a section as early as the middle of the seventeenth century, whereas the Chesapeake colonies cannot be properly called a section until very late in the eighteenth or early in the nineteenth century."[3]

In the Middle Atlantic Colonies a cosmopolitan society developed. New Netherland began as a trading post, and commerce, its chief activity, attracted a heterogeneous population. A landed aristocracy was established under the Dutch patroon system, but land was looked upon primarily as an investment; the vocations were business, law, and other professions. Pennsylvania from the beginning included non-English-speaking peoples, since the Dutch and Swedish Colonies which had been established earlier became a part of William Penn's Colony in 1628. In these Colonies emphasis was on ethnic or religious groups rather than on the community as a whole.

In spite of the differences in their social and political structure, the early colonists resembled each other as well as their English

[2] Clarence L. Ver Steeg, *The Formative Years: 1607–1763* ("The Making of America"; New York: Hill and Wang, Inc., 1964), p. 55.
[3] *Ibid.*, p. 52.

contemporaries in attitudes, ambitions, and characteristics, and particularly in their interest in learning.

EARLY COLONIAL LIBRARIES

Among the valued possessions which all the early settlers brought to America or imported as necessities as soon as they were settled were books, and since the literary tastes and the special needs of the settlers influenced their choice of books, naturally the Puritans brought with them and later imported more religious works than did the Southern planters. Even so, there tended to be a similarity in the titles in all the Colonies. Theological and moral works were most numerous, but there were also textbooks for self-instruction; handbooks on medicine, law, and farming; dictionaries and encyclopedias; and some historical, political, scientific, and classical works. These books, brought or purchased for use by the settlers, constituted the collections of the first libraries in America, and although they were the private libraries of individuals, they were often shared with friends and neighbors.

The size of these libraries varied. Captain John Smith is said to have owned two books: Miles Standish, fifty; Governor Bradford, eighty; John Harvard, more than three hundred; and Elder William Brewster, four hundred. John Winthrop, Jr., Governor of Connecticut, had the largest scientific library in the colonies—over one thousand volumes—which was used freely by his neighbors. Even though a printing press was in operation in Massachusetts as early as 1639, books had to be imported from England and the Continent for many generations.

The importance of learning to the colonists is revealed in their early efforts to establish colleges, of which books and libraries were a significant part. Almost as soon as the Jamestown Colony was settled, steps were taken to establish a college for the colonists and Indians at Henrico, Virginia. Fifteen thousand acres of land were granted by the London Company toward the endowment of the College, and more than one hundred colonists were settled on the land. At the request of King James I, the English churches contributed £1,500 to aid in erecting churches and schools. Other gifts came from many sources, including a library valued at 100 marks given for the use of the college by Master Thomas Burgrave. The Indian massacre of 1622 put an end to the plans for Henrico College, and not until the last decade of the century did the Virginia colonists make another effort to establish an institution of higher education.

Efforts to found a college in the Massachusetts Bay Colony proved to be more successful than those in Virginia. In 1636, the General Court voted £400 toward the establishment of a college or school. Two years later the college came into being when John Harvard willed half of his property and all his library of more than three hundred volumes to this college. This historic reality is described in striking language in "New England's First Fruits":[4]

> After God had carried us safe to *New England,* and wee had builded our houses, provided necessaries for our liveli-hood, rear'd convenient places for Gods worship, and setled the Civill Government: One of the next things we longed for, and looked after was to advance *Learning* and perpetuate it to Posterity; dreading to leave an illiterate Ministery to the Churches, when our present Ministers shall lie in the Dust. And as wee were thinking and consulting how to effect this great Work; it pleased God to stir up the heart of one Mr. *Harvard* (a godly Gentleman, and a lover of Learning, there living amongst us) to give the one halfe of his Estate (it being in all about 1700.*l.*) towards the erecting of a Colledge: and all his Library: after him another gave 300.*l.* others after them cast in more, and the publique hand of the State added the rest: the Colledge was, by common consent, appointed to be at *Cambridge* (a place very pleasant and accommodate) and is called (according to the name of the first founder) *Harvard Colledge.*

In 1693 the Virginia colonists successfully established the second colonial college, the College of William and Mary; and in 1701

[4] "New England's First Fruits, 1643," reprinted in Samuel Eliot Morison, *The Founding of Harvard College* (Cambridge, Mass.: Harvard University Press, 1935), p. 432. This selection is found also in *American Higher Education, A Documentary History,* ed. Richard Hofstadter and Wilson Smith (Chicago: The University of Chicago Press, 1961), I, 6.

Yale College was founded in Connecticut, and eleven ministers, meeting for that purpose, gave a number of books toward its founding.

Provisions for what may be called the first public library[5] in the Colonies were made in the will of Captain Robert Keayne of Boston (d. March 23, 1655/56), who gave £300 for a public building in Boston which was to include a room for a library. Captain Keayne gave certain of his own books to begin the collection and authorized his wife and son to give others. The building, called the Town House, was erected, and the library served the people for almost a century.[6]

Toward the end of the seventeenth century another kind of library—already well known in England[7]—made its appearance in the American Colonies. When Rev. Thomas Bray was appointed by the Anglican Church in 1696 as Commissary for the Colony of Maryland to work toward the establishment of the Anglican Church there, he immediately proposed a system of parochial libraries for the Colonies similar to those he had established in England for the rural Anglican clergy, and with the approval and aid of the Anglican Church he collected money and books for these libraries before he sailed for Maryland on December 16, 1699. Rev. Bray remained in Maryland only a few months, but through his Society for Promoting Christian Knowledge and its branch, the Society for Propagating the Gospel in Foreign Parts, he established libraries in the English Colonies from Massachusetts to South Carolina. His society is said to have been responsible for founding thirty-nine libraries in the Colonies with more than thirty-four thousand volumes.[8]

These libraries were of three kinds: (1) parochial, for the sole

---

[5] The term "public library" is used in the sense that it was open to the public; it was not supported by taxes levied for that purpose.

[6] Jesse H. Shera, *Foundations of the Public Library: the Origins of the Public Library Movement in New England 1629-1855* (Chicago: The University of Chicago Press, 1949), pp. 19-24, *passim*.

[7] See p. 55.

[8] Edgar L. Pennington, *The Reverend Thomas Bray* ("The Church Historical Society Publication," No. VII; Philadelphia, 1934), p. 14. See also Bernard C. Steiner, "Rev. Thomas Bray and His American Libraries," *The American Historical Review*, II (1896), pp. 59-75.

use of the minister; (2) provincial, for the use of all types of readers; and (3) layman's, containing books to be "lent or given at the discretion of the Minister." The largest of the provincial libraries, the Annapolitan Library at Annapolis, Maryland, had a collection which totalled 1,095 volumes.

LIBRARIES OF THE PRE-REVOLUTIONARY PERIOD

Through travel and correspondence the American colonists were acquainted with the spirit of scientific inquiry which characterized the Age of Enlightenment in Europe.[9] William Byrd II of Virginia and other Americans were members of the Royal Society of London and shared the common desire of the members for wider knowledge in all areas of thought. Their need to have access to a broad range of materials for study and research led them to acquire large private libraries. Cotton Mather of Boston owned between 3,000 and 4,000 volumes before his death in 1728; Thomas Prince, Minister of the Old South Church in Boston, collected a library of 1,400 volumes; James Logan of Philadelphia acquired a library of more than 2,000 volumes, which was especially rich in both classical and scientific works; William Byrd II's library had reached 3,600 titles at his death in 1744; and William Fitzhugh, Robert Carter, Ralph Wormeley, and other Southern gentlemen assembled large and valuable collections. All these libraries included not only religious works but also works in natural science and history and a number of Greek and Roman classics.

Social Libraries

Interest in learning was not confined to the wealthy, even though they alone had the means for acquiring large libraries. The desire for self-improvement—always a characteristic of the American colonists—found a new expression in the social library, which grew out of the social club idea. Benjamin Franklin, a native Bostonian, had lived in London as a journeyman printer, and there he became familiar with the social club[10] as an organization for

[9] See pp. 52–53.
[10] See p. 57.

the encouragement of intellectual and cultural, as well as social, life. In 1727, Franklin and some of his friends in Philadelphia formed a club for "mutual improvement" which they called the Junto—also sometimes called the Leathern Apron Club because the members worked at "lowly jobs" during the day. The club members met on Friday evenings for discussions and debates, and these activities called for the use of many books. Franklin tells of his plan for meeting this need:

> About this Time [1730] our Club Meeting, not at a Tavern, but in a little Room of Mr. Grace's set apart for that Purpose; a Proposition was made by me that since our Books were often referr'd to in our Disquisitions upon the Queries, it might be convenient to us to have them all together where we met, that upon Occasion they might be consulted; and by thus clubbing our Books to a common Library, we should, while we lik'd to keep them together, have each of us the Advantage of using the Books of all the other Members which would be nearly as beneficial as if each owned the whole. It was lik'd and agreed to, and we fill'd one End of the Room with such Books as we could best spare. The Number was not so great as we expected; and tho' they had been of great Use, yet some Inconveniences occurring for want of due Care of them, the Collection after about a Year was separated, and each took his Books home again.[11]

Franklin was not discouraged by the failure of his plan for providing the books his club needed. In fact, failure stimulated him to produce another plan:[12]

> And now [1731] I set on foot my first Project of a public Nature, that for a Subscription Library. I drew up the Proposals, got them put into Form by our great Scrivener Brockden, and by the help of my Friends in the Junto, procur'd Fifty Subscribers of 40s. each to begin with and 10s. a Year for 50 Years, the Term our Company was to continue. We afterwards obtain'd a Charter, the Company being increas'd to 100. This was the Mother of all the N American Subscription Libraries now so numerous.

[11] *The Autobiography of Benjamin Franklin*, ed. W. Labaree and Others (New Haven, Conn.: Yale University Press, 1964), p. 130.
[12] *Ibid.*

Any "civil gentleman" was allowed to peruse the books in the library, but only subscribers could borrow them.

In this manner was begun the social library, a voluntary association of individuals who contributed to a common fund to be used for the purchase of books which every member had the right to use but whose ownership was retained by the group. It provided a means of self-education and self-improvement, of promoting useful learning, and of affording profitable recreation and social life for the members.

Once begun, social libraries spread rapidly. In 1733, the Book Company of Durham, Connecticut, was established, and in 1747 the Redwood Library was founded in Newport, Rhode Island, by Abraham Redwood in a building which still stands—"the oldest library structure in the United States to be used continuously as such since its erection."[13] By the middle of the century, New England had at least a dozen social libraries.

The Southern Colonies produced only two social libraries of prominence before the Revolution. In 1748, seventeen young men in Charleston, South Carolina, associated themselves for the purpose of raising a small fund to collect new magazines and pamphlets published in England. Before the close of the year, they took the name Library Society and arranged to buy books as well as pamphlets and magazines. The library suffered greatly during the Revolution and many books were lost, but the books that were saved, together with the few added from time to time, formed the nucleus of the present library of Charleston which was organized in 1790.

The only other social library south of Philadelphia which is known to have existed prior to the Revolution is that which was attached to the Winyaw Indigo Society in Georgetown, South Carolina. This society, formed about 1740 by the planters of the Georgetown District, was originally a social club which met once a month to discuss the latest news from London on the culture of indigo, the staple product of the county. The society was chartered in 1755, and out of the initiation fees and annual subscriptions, which were paid in indigo, a library was acquired and a charity school

[13] Shera, *op. cit.*, p. 38.

for the poor—attended by all classes—was established. For more than a hundred years this was the chief school for all the county lying between Charleston and the North Carolina line. Both the school and the library were destroyed in the Civil War.

The New York Society Library, incorporated in 1754 and first called The City Library, was formed by a group of men who "clubbed together" for the purpose and raised in a few days nearly £600 for seven hundred volumes of "well-chosen" books. The books were deposited in the city hall along with the remnants of two other collections: one, a small library presented in 1700 by Rev. John Sharp; and the other, a gift in 1729 of the Society for the Propagation of the Gospel in Foreign Parts. A charter was granted in 1772 under the name New York Society Library.

The importance of the social library in the years before the Revolution was pointed out by Franklin in his *Autobiography:*[14]

> It [the subscription library] is become a great thing itself, and continually increasing. These Libraries have improv'd the general Conversation of the Americans, made the Common Tradesmen and Farmers as intelligent as most Gentlemen from other Countries, and perhaps have contributed in some degree to the Stand so generally made throughout the Colonies in Defence of their Privileges.

Further evidence of the contributions of the social library to the cultural life of the colonists is given by Rev. Jacob Duché:[15]

> You would be astounded . . . at the general taste for books, which prevails among all orders and ranks of people in this city. The librarian of the Philadelphia Library Company assured me that for one person of distinction and fortune, there were twenty tradesmen that frequented this library. . . . But such is the prevailing taste for books of every kind that almost every man is a reader; and by pronouncing sentence, right or wrong, upon the various publications that come in his way, puts himself upon a level, in point of knowledge with their several authors.

[14] Franklin, *op. cit.*, pp. 130–131.
[15] Jacob Duché, *Observations on a Variety of Subjects, Literary, Moral and Religious* . . . (Philadelphia: Printed by John Dunlap, 1764), pp. 10–11. (Microfilm.)

The Philadelphia Library Company suffered little from the Revolutionary War, and both the members of the Continental Congress and British Army officers who occupied the city from 1777 to 1778 used the library.[16] Other social libraries, however, suffered greatly; some were lost completely, and others were forced to suspend operation during the war.

THE POST-REVOLUTIONARY PERIOD

At the time of the Revolution, libraries reflected the existing cultural interests and attitudes of the public, offering works on the political, economic, and social issues of the time as well as literary, historical, scientific, and theological works. They were either connected directly with institutions of higher learning or were the outgrowth of associations of persons who had common tastes and interests. After the Revolution, the growth of the social library was greatly accelerated and new forms appeared. Some were organized for a particular purpose, such as the athenaeum; others were designed to meet the special needs or reading interests of a particular clientele, such as the mechanics' apprentices, mercantile clerks, factory and mill workers, and members of the Young Men's Christian Association.

The Athenaeum

Before the nineteenth century few libraries had a reading room; in general, books were taken out of the library for use. An increasing interest in magazines, newspapers, and pamphlets—both American and foreign—led to a movement to establish and maintain by subscription reading rooms where members could have access at all times to periodical publications. Out of this movement came the form of social library called the athenaeum.[17] In 1807, the Boston

---

[16] Today, the Library Company of Philadelphia is open to the public for research and for interlibrary loan.

[17] The Athenaeum in Greek antiquity was the temple of Athena, in which professors taught their students, and orators and poets rehearsed their compositions. The meaning has evolved to that of a building or institution in which books, periodicals, and newspapers are provided for use. In 1822, it was used in the sense of a literary clubroom, reading room, and library in relation

Athenaeum opened as the Anthology Reading-Room and Library—an affiliate of the magazine *The Monthly Anthology*. The first department to be opened was a reading room, and the second, the library, was to contain outstanding scholarly works in all languages, especially those which could not easily be obtained in America.

The breadth of the intellectual and cultural aims of this kind of social library is seen in the stated objectives of the Philadelphia Athenaeum: [18]

> About the close of 1813 a number of gentlemen assembled for the purpose of establishing a reading-room in Philadelphia. Their first and immediate object was the collection, in some central place, of American and foreign periodical publications of politics, literature, and science, maps, dictionaries, and other works of reference to which access might be had at all hours of the day. Besides the purchase of all new books of merit, they contemplated the gradual acquisition of such as might lay the foundation of a large and useful public library, and of such manuscripts, medals, and coins as might be valuable for their curiosity or as tending to illustrate the history of this country. They looked forward also to the establishment of lectureships on science; and, as accessory to this desirable object, it was intended to commence the collection of mineral, botanical, and other specimens illustrative of natural history.

The Philadelphia Athenaeum was incorporated "for the promotion of literature" on April 5, 1815, and within a decade athenaeums were established in Brunswick, Salem, and Portland, Maine; in the New York Society Library; and in Frankfort, Kentucky.

Mechanics' apprentices' libraries

The growth of manufacturing in the nineteenth century greatly increased the demand for apprentices and brought many problems regarding their behavior and welfare. Boys became apprentices as early as thirteen years of age, and many came from rural sections

---

to such an institution in Manchester, England. It assumed this meaning in America.

[18] "Libraries and Historical and Scientific Societies," *History of Philadelphia, 1609–1884*, II (1884), 1206.

to the city, where they lived in rooming houses which offered neither supervision nor means of recreation or self-improvement.

William Wood, a Boston merchant, believed that much could be done for the welfare of apprentices through libraries and set about getting subscriptions, books, and a place to keep the books. In 1820, the Mechanics' Apprentices' Library was established in Boston through his philanthropy, and other libraries for mechanics' apprentices were organized, through the aid and encouragement of educators, religious leaders, social reformers, and philanthropists. In general, the motives of all the supporters of the mechanics' apprentices' libraries were similar to those of the "benevolent individuals" of Philadelphia who, in 1820,

> believing that it would promote orderly and virtuous habits, diffuse knowledge and the desire for knowledge, improve the scientific skill of our mechanics and manufacturers, increase the benefits of the system of general education which is now adopted, and advance the prosperity and happiness of the community, associated themselves under the title of "The Apprentices' Library of Philadelphia," for the purpose of establishing a library for the use of apprentices and other young persons, without charge of any kind for the use of books.[19]

The company was incorporated the following year.

Apprentices' libraries were organized in other cities, including some libraries for girls, and some of them offered courses, sponsored debates, and engaged in other educational activities. In many cities, apprentices were given access, without cost or at reduced rates, to libraries which were formed by mechanics' institutes. These institutes, here as in England,[20] were designed to help apprentices train for the new factory system which had been brought about by the industrial revolution. The mechanics' institutes were a form of adult education and provided not only library materials but also lectures and evening study courses.

[19] *Ibid.*, p. 1208. Because of the very satisfactory and beneficial results of loaning books to boys without charge (except fines for overdue books), the managers began in 1841 a separate library for girls. The two libraries were consolidated in 1882.
[20] See p. 58.

Mercantile libraries

America was quickly becoming an industrial nation in the early nineteenth century as a result of the increasing trade and commerce brought by the steamboat and railroad, and those who made up the mercantile community quite naturally were very important in the new commercial society. Unfortunately, however, the mercantile class did not have the educational background which their growing social importance demanded. This was particularly true of many of the mercantile clerks, who, like the mechanics' apprentices, were quite young—sixteen years of age or under—and had come to the cities from the rural sections, where their educational opportunities had been meager. They, too, had to live in dreary boarding houses, which offered few, if any, opportunities for self-improvement.

Soon after he had organized the apprentices' libraries, William Wood began a companion movement to provide libraries for the "young gentleman employed by the merchants," and in 1820 the Boston Mercantile Library was established. Similar libraries were organized in New York (1820) and in Philadelphia (1821).[21]

In contrast with the libraries for mechanics' apprentices, which were provided and administered free of charge to the users by interested citizens, the libraries for mercantile clerks were established by the young clerks themselves and were supported and administered by them for their intellectual improvement and wholesome recreation. In general, each one had a school or an educational department which offered classes in bookkeeping, arithmetic, writing, and debating, and some of them provided gymnasiums, museums, and exhibitions. The library collections contained, in addition to materials of practical importance in trade and commerce, literature, biography, history, travel, and popular reading matter.

Other types of social libraries

Factory or mill libraries were established by some of the larger manufacturers in New England and the Middle states for the use

---

[21] U.S., Bureau of Education, *Public Libraries in the United States of America, Their History, Condition and Management, Special Report,* Part I (Washington, D.C., U.S. Government Printing Office, 1876), pp. 928, 963. By 1875 there were fifteen mercantile libraries located in eleven states. *Ibid.,* pp. 800–01.

of employees and their families, but in most cases the employees were required to contribute to the upkeep of the libraries. In addition to books, lecture halls and facilities were provided for the cultural improvement of the workers. One of the best-known mill libraries was the Pacific Mills Library in Lawrence, Massachusetts.

In the Young Men's Christian Association libraries, which were organized as a means of self-improvement for the members, the chief emphasis at first was placed on books of a religious and moral nature; later, however, history, travel, and biography were added to the collections. This type of social library did not develop until the middle of the nineteenth century when the first one was opened in Boston in 1851.

Forms and contributions of social libraries

Two basic forms of the social library developed during its most active period of more than a century: (1) proprietary, or joint-stock, based on ownership of shares in the property of the library; (2) subscription, or association, based on payment of an annual or other fee or subscription.[22] In proprietary libraries only shareholders had library privileges; but all who paid a fee could use the subscription libraries.

The collections of social libraries were at first strongly theological and moral in content; in time, however, they emphasized history, biography, literature, and travel, and by the second decade of the nineteenth century they included a number of scientific materials.[23] It can be said that, in varying degrees, they reached every level of literate society, revealing, and to a certain extent satisfying, the desire and need of each class for educational and cultural improvement. Even so, the social library as a type of service agency inevitably declined because it served only those who could pay and was always in need of financial aid because there were too few subscribers and too few gifts to provide adequate support. Only one social library had more than one hundred members, and most of them had between twenty-five and fifty. Many social libraries

[22] Carleton Bruns Joeckel, *The Government of the American Public Library* (Chicago: The University of Chicago Press, 1935), p. 2.
[23] See Table 12 on p. 103 in *Shera, op. cit.*

suffered from the competition of the circulating libraries.[24] The final results were that some social libraries disappeared completely, not surviving long after the death of the founder; some became parts of other existing libraries; some formed the nucleus of the public libraries which followed; and some are still in existence today.

As an important factor in the evolution of the American public library, the social library cannot be overlooked. Its contributions lay not only in the influence it exerted upon the society which was to create and support the public library, but also in the fact that it pointed up, both negatively by its inadequacies and affirmatively by its contributions to literate society, the overwhelming need for libraries that would serve all the people.

Circulating or lending libraries

The practice of renting books for use dates back to the thirteenth and fourteenth centuries, when texts were rented to students at the medieval universities. Circulating libraries—or lending libraries, as they were also called—originated in Scotland in the eighteenth century, became numerous there, and then spread to England and the Continent.[25] The first attempts to open circulating libraries in the Colonies, however, met with short-lived success. William Rind of Annapolis began a circulating library in 1762, but it was abandoned two years later; John Mein opened one in Boston in 1765 which functioned until only about 1770. After the Revolution, circulating libraries operated successfully in connection with bookshops, general stores, and other kinds of shops, and before the end of the eighteenth century a bookseller and a circulating library were operating as far west as Pittsburgh.

The circulating libraries were strictly business enterprises based on payment for the use of books, either a rental fee per book borrowed or a quarterly or annual subscription; consequently, their chief purpose of making money for the owner greatly influenced and limited the kinds of reading materials they offered. In general,

[24] Oliver Garceau, *The Public Library in the Political Process: A Report of the Public Library Inquiry* . . . (New York: Columbia University Press, 1949), pp. 19–20, 21.

[25] See p. 57.

and with varying degrees of effectiveness, the social libraries provided for the needs of those who had a real interest in good literature and for those who sought moral, intellectual, or vocational self-improvement. The circulating libraries, on the other hand, arose in answer to the desire for popular reading materials, and their collections were indicators of popular reading tastes. They catered to the recreation and entertainment needs of their clients, and here, as in England,[26] the novel was their chief item. In addition to fiction, many circulating libraries offered drama, history, and travel. Although they filled an immediate need for certain kinds of reading material, the contribution of the circulating libraries to American library development was negligible.

[26] See p. 57.

CHAPTER 7
AMERICA—
THE NINETEENTH
CENTURY

The period following the Revolution was a time of extraordinary political, economic, and social change, characterized by (1) a developing sense of nationalism; (2) westward expansion and the building of towns and cities along the Ohio, the Mississippi, and the Great Lakes; (3) widespread interest in formal education and in self-education and self-improvement; and (4) the accumulation of great individual wealth. All these developments were accompanied by the establishment of libraries—their size and importance depending upon the needs they were to serve.

The influence of nationalism

The spirit of nationalism found expression in a new interest in history, particularly American history, and in the desire to preserve it. Historical societies and museums were established for this purpose, and the collection and preservation of historical materials was a major concern of the Library of Congress—established to serve the Federal government—as well as of the state and territorial libraries.

HISTORICAL SOCIETIES

Of the historical societies which were formed to collect and preserve the materials of American history, the earliest were the Massachusetts Historical Society, which was organized in 1791 and incorporated in 1794, the New York Historical Society in 1804, and the New Hampshire Historical Society in 1823. Other states, as well as associations and groups within the states, also formed historical societies, some of them emphasizing the collection of materials important only in the history of the state or locality. The basic purposes of all the historical societies and the principal means which they used in accomplishing them are illustrated in the statement of objectives of the Pennsylvania Historical Society:

> The objects of the society are to trace all the circumstances of early settlements; to collect all documents and written and printed evidence, and all traditionary information that may still be obtainable; and after having thus acquired possession of such materials, to publish such portions as may be deemed most interesting and instructive. The purpose of the society also is to form an ample library and cabinet, the collection of books, pamphlets, and manuscripts on any subject or of any date, medals, coins, or any article drawing value from historical or biographical affinities, Indian idols, ornaments, arms, utensils, etc.[1]

By the last quarter of the century there were fifty-one historical libraries in twenty-four states.[2]

THE LIBRARY OF CONGRESS

The library needs of the Continental Congress were met by the "chance researches of its members and the gratuitous use of books tendered them by the Library Company of Philadelphia."[3] but the new Capital city, Washington, did not have any library facilities, and therefore a library had to be organized to provide for the needs of the National Congress for books and information. The Library of Congress was authorized in 1800, and on April 24 of that year Congress made the first appropriation ($5,000) for books and for "fitting up a suitable apartment for containing them and placing them therein." Two years later an act providing for the organization of the Library of Congress placed the library in the Capitol building, set up regulations for operating the library, and established the office of librarian. When the Capitol was burned by the British Army in 1814, the Library of Congress was lost, and it was former President Jefferson's private library of some 6,700

---

[1] *History of Philadelphia, op. cit.,* p. 1219.
[2] U.S., Bureau of Education, *Public Libraries in the United States, op. cit.,* pp. 798–799.
[3] Ainsworth R. Spofford, "The Library of Congress, or National Library," *ibid.,* p. 253.

volumes which formed the basis for a new congressional library. Another fire in 1851 destroyed all but 20,000 volumes of the library's 55,000-volume collection, but the library was rebuilt out of fireproof materials, and from that time it entered upon a period of continuous growth, greatly strengthened by the acquisition in 1866 of the Smithsonian Institution's scientific collection of some 40,000 volumes and the Peter Force historical collection of 60,000 volumes the following year.[4]

STATE AND TERRITORIAL LIBRARIES

It was more than thirty years after the Constitution went into effect in 1789 before the states began to establish libraries to serve the state governments. In the older states, collections of laws and legislative proceedings had been preserved in one or more legislative libraries. Records of the state of Pennsylvania show that there was a library at its capital as early as 1777, though the state library was not officially established until 1816. In 1811, Massachusetts initiated the system of the annual exchange of statutes between the states, and it was these documents which constituted the basic collections of state libraries. By 1876, every state and territory had a governmental library whose purposes were (1) to collect and preserve complete sets of all publications of the state or territory and, as far as possible, of the several states and territories; and (2) to collect works in American history, especially of the state or territory.

Westward expansion

As settlers moved west they took with them the culture and ideas to which they had become accustomed in their former homes. Schools were soon established, and books were accessible through the stocks of the general merchants, which included dictionaries, grammars, spelling books, arithmetics, devotional books, and handbooks. Peddlers carried books and pamphlets to the outlying parts of the settlements, and before the close of the eighteenth century some subscription libraries were started. The "coonskin library,"

---

[4] See also Chap. 13.

so named because the subscribers paid their fees in coonskins, was begun in 1803 in Ames Township, Ohio. It is estimated that there were probably a dozen subscription libraries in Ohio before 1812.[5] By mid-century a circulating library was operating in Little Rock, having been organized in 1843. In the Far West, the gold rush brought a great influx of population to California. Many of these persons were well educated, and by the middle of the century there were fifty printers in San Francisco, at least three social libraries, and many private libraries.

Educational influences

The belief of our early national leaders that knowledge is necessary to good government grew, in the early decades of the nineteenth century, to a widespread belief that universal literacy is necessary in a democracy. Education, continuing education, and self-improvement became growing concerns of the young nation.

THE LYCEUM MOVEMENT

Interest in self-education and self-improvement in the first half of the nineteenth century, already seen in the establishment of mercantile and mechanics' apprentices' libraries, found another form of expression in the Lyceum movement. In 1826, Josiah Holbrook set forth his scheme for a "Society for Mutual Education," which became known as the American Lyceum, a system of popular lectures to improve the quality of the schools, advance the education of adults, reactivate neglected libraries, and encourage the building of libraries and museums. Beginning in Millbury, Massachusetts, the movement spread rapidly, supported and encouraged by educators; and since its program was based on continuing study and reading, the purchase of books in many fields was stimulated. Although its influence on library development may not have been extensive, the Lyceum was a means of cultural stimulation for many people and its widespread popularity indicated the extent of interest in self-improvement.

[5] Louis B. Wright, *Culture on the Moving Frontier* (Bloomington, Ind.: Indiana University Press, 1955), p. 118.

SCHOOL DISTRICT–PUBLIC LIBRARIES

A year after Holbrook initiated the Lyceum movement, Governor Dewitt Clinton of New York recommended, in his message to the legislature, the formation of school district libraries. These were not to be libraries for the schools, but free public libraries for adult readers. The libraries were to be attached to, and administered by, the school district, which was the administrative unit for the common school system.

In 1835, the New York legislature passed a law permitting the voters in any school district to levy a tax of $20 to begin a library and $10 each succeeding year to provide for its growth. Few districts, however, voted the necessary tax. Three years later legislation was enacted authorizing the state to distribute among the school districts of the state a total of $55,000 a year to buy books for libraries, requiring each school district to raise by taxation for the same purpose an amount equal to that received from the state. Some districts were so small that their share of the money was negligible, but even so, by 1853 school district–public libraries in New York contained more than 1,604,210 volumes.[6] Unfortunately, school districts began to use the appropriations for other purposes.[7] By 1875 only about one-half of the state appropriation was spent on libraries, with the result that the number of volumes decreased by almost 50 percent.

The concept of the school district–public library found wide favor, and before 1850 nine states had followed the example of New York in developing a system of public libraries administered by the school districts, and by 1876 twelve other states and territories had made similar provisions.

Regrettably, most of these libraries were ineffective. In analyzing the reasons for their eventual failure, Garceau[8] has pointed out that the school districts were artifically created by state planners and did not follow local patterns of cultural loyalties and intel-

[6] U.S., Bureau of Education, *op. cit.*, p. 40.
[7] In 1843, authority had been given to school districts to pay for school apparatus from the library fund, and later they were allowed to use the money for teachers' salaries rather than for library purposes, if they chose.
[8] Garceau, *op. cit.*, p. 25.

lectual needs; and the libraries served too small an area, were inadequately housed, were poorly supervised by school trustees, and were badly managed by elected librarians.

THE TAX-SUPPORTED FREE PUBLIC LIBRARY

Free town libraries date from Captain Robert Keayne's gift to Boston in the mid-seventeenth century.[9] They were usually established by gifts from affluent citizens or from other philanthropy. In 1803, Caleb Bingham, a Boston bookseller, founded the Bingham Library for Youth in his hometown of Salisbury, Connecticut, with a gift of 150 books—the first free library for children and young people. The vote of the citizens of the town in 1810 to give financial support to this library is believed to be the first time a municipal governing body contributed financial aid to public library service.[10] However, it is Peterborough, New Hampshire, that is given the distinction of having established the first free town library when, in 1833, the citizens voted to use for a town library funds distributed by the state to the town for free schools and other educational purposes; and they voted to maintain it by an annual appropriation.

As worthy as Peterborough's effort was, the concept of a fully tax-supported free library open for use by all who might need it was not yet established among the taxpaying public. As Scudder has pointed out, "The idea of a free public library could hardly find general acceptance until the idea of free public education had become familiar to men's minds."[11] Therefore, the educational revolution of the second quarter of the nineteenth century led by Horace Mann and Henry Barnard, which resulted in the beginning of our American system of free public education, provided a strong stimulus to the public library idea. Both Mann and Barnard supported the school district–public libraries and both saw the library as an essential contributor to the educational program of the school, an invaluable aid in continuing education and in self-improvement, and an indispensable part of the cultural life of the people.

[9] See p. 63.
[10] Shera, *op. cit.*, p. 160.
[11] Horace E. Scudder, "Public Libraries a Hundred Years Ago," U.S. Bureau of Education, *op. cit.*, p. 1E.

The second quarter of the nineteenth century was a period of scholarly and literary activity and accomplishment. Interest in American history, first seen in the establishment of historical and state libraries for its preservation, spread to the study of American history and then to the history of other countries. Historical research and investigation reached a high point in the writings of Prescott, Motley, and Parkman, in spite of the fact that the dearth of materials for research in America made it necessary for historians and scholars to go to Europe and England to carry on their investigations—a fact which was emphatically pointed out by those who worked for the establishment of publicly supported libraries. American literature broke away from its long dependence upon England and in the middle half of the century reached its peak in the works of Hawthorne, Longfellow, Emerson, Lowell, Whittier, and Holmes.

The period brought many of the changes in education that eventually led to free, universal, secular elementary and secondary schools, such as removing elementary education from the control of religious, charitable, and other private groups, abolishing tuition fees, and establishing the principle of taxation for the support of schools. The demand for practical education to meet the needs of an industrial society resulted in the addition of vocational subjects to the course of study offered by the academies, and the belief in universal educational opportunity gained widespread support, leading in 1852 to the passage by Massachusetts of the first compulsory school attendance law.

It was a time of industrial and commercial development, territorial expansion, growth of population, urbanization, and national prosperity. In this climate of literary scholarship, educational progress, and wealth and prosperity, the free public library came into being. Dr. Shera has summarized the factors that influenced the development of the American public library in this manner:

> Historical scholarship and the urge to preservation, the power of national and local pride, the growing belief in the importance of universal education, the increasing concern with vocational problems, and the contribution of religion—these, aided by economic ability and encouraged by the example of Europe, were the causal

factors in the formation of libraries that would be free to all the people.[12]

As early as 1826, George Ticknor, a trustee of the Boston Athenaeum, realizing that social libraries could no longer meet the growing needs of scholars and laymen for library materials, proposed that all libraries in the city of Boston be united with the Boston Athenaeum and that their facilities be made freely available to the public. This particular plan did not materialize, but Ticknor's efforts on behalf of a public library did not cease. In 1841, Nicolas Marie Alexandre Vattemare, a French actor and ventriloquist, gave new impetus to the idea of a free public library when he presented to the city of Boston a proposal for international exchanges of books. The people of Boston saw in this proposal a means of achieving international goodwill, but a library was needed before books could be received and exchanged.

Although the idea of a free public library was well received, little would have been accomplished had it not been for the continuous efforts of civic-minded citizens, notably George Ticknor and Edward Everett, both of whom believed that in a democracy education must be provided equally for all people and both of whom saw the public library as a means of self-education and of continuing education after high school. Financial support was offered in 1847 by Mayor Josiah Quincy in the amount of $5,000 for books if the city would provide an equal amount. The following year, the state legislature gave the city of Boston permission to levy taxes to support a library, and by 1852 the Boston Public Library was organized. When it was opened to the public in 1854, the free, public, tax-supported library became a part of American life.

The historical significance of the Boston Public Library cannot be measured, for it established the precedent for free, publicly supported library service to all citizens and set an example both in administrative organization and in objectives for other public libraries to follow. The importance which the first board of trustees, under the strong leadership of Ticknor and Everett, attached to the role of the public library in continuing education, in developing

[12] Shera, *op. cit.*, p. 243.

informed citizens, and in raising the cultural and intellectual level of the entire community is seen in their first report in 1852,[13] a document which Dr. Shera calls "the first comprehensive statement of the functions and objectives of the American public library" and "its first real credo."[14]

During the period in which the Boston Public Library was taking form, the State Legislature of New Hampshire passed permissive legislation (1849) enabling towns to levy taxes for the support of libraries. Massachusetts passed permissive legislation for the entire state in 1851, and other states followed: Maine, 1854; Vermont, 1865; Rhode Island and Connecticut, 1867; and New York, 1872. The pattern of state legislation then, as now, was permissive—not mandatory—and thus the levying of taxes for the establishment of libraries has always depended upon local interest and initiative.

The public library developed where there was a concentrated and homogeneous population with more than average education and cultural background, where there were leaders who had a deep sense of civic responsibility, and where there was adequate taxable wealth to support it. Before the Civil War, public libraries flourished in the northeastern section of the country; after the Civil War, they had their greatest growth in the West and North.

COLLEGE LIBRARIES

Before the Revolution nine colleges were founded in the Colonies, each one modeled after Oxford and Cambridge and shaped by aristocratic tradition to serve the aristocratic elements of colonial society. After the Revolution, "a commitment to the republic became the guiding obligation of the American college."[15] and in the course of westward expansion the college as a distinctive Ameri-

[13] "Report of the Trustees of the Public Library of the City of Boston, July, 1852, City Document No. 37," (Boston: J. H. Eastburn, City Printer, 1852) in Shera, *op. cit.*, pp. 267–90. See also Walter Muir Whitehill, *Boston Public Library, A Centennial History* (Cambridge, Mass.: Harvard University Press, 1956), pp. 27–34.
[14] Shera, *op. cit.*, p. 181.
[15] Frederick Rudolph, *The American College and University: A History* (New York: Alfred A. Knopf, Inc., 1962), p. 61.

can institution evolved, "shaped and adapted to the peculiar needs of an advancing people."[16]

Before the Civil War more than 500 colleges (182 of them became permanent) and 21 state universities were founded. Of these, only Yale and Harvard had library collections numbering as many as 50,000 volumes by 1850. The Land Grant College Act of 1862 gave added impetus to the establishment of institutions of higher education, and by 1875 there were 312 college libraries with a total of 1,949,105 volumes.[17]

Since the colleges of the period emphasized textbook teaching and discouraged wide reading, their libraries were open chiefly for the occasional loan of a book to a professor or a student or for the perusal of recent periodicals. Upperclassmen could use the library under certain conditions, but, in general, freshmen and sophomores were not permitted to use it at all. Literary societies formed an important part of college life, and each society had its own library which provided materials needed for the debates and discussions which the society sponsored and for recreational reading. The society library often had a larger collection than the college library and always offered a wider variety of materials. In time, many of the literary society libraries were merged with the college libraries. The importance of the society libraries is illustrated in this description of the Georgetown University Library in 1875: "The library, which now numbers 28,000 volumes, is always accessible to visitors. Books are never loaned outside of the College. Students may visit the library to consult authorities, but they rarely have the occasion to do so, as their own society libraries are well supplied with standard works, to which access can be had by them at any moment."[18]

STATE LIBRARY COMMISSIONS

Although the Tenth Amendment to the Constitution gave to the states all powers not reserved to the Federal government and

[16] Donald G. Tewksbury, *The Founding of American Colleges and Universities Before the Civil War* (New York: Bureau of Publications, Teachers College, Columbia University, 1932), p. 1.
[17] U.S. Bureau of Education, *op. cit.*, pp. 798–99.
[18] U.S. Bureau of Education, *op. cit.*, p. 72.

was interpreted as authorizing the states to establish school systems, it was not until 1837, when Massachusetts established a state board of education, that a state moved in this direction. By 1875 nearly all the states required local administrative units to tax themselves for the support of the public schools, and by 1880 every Northern state had established a state educational system. As schools improved and public high schools became common, the states began to take an interest in providing the means of continuing education after high school by aiding public library development.

In 1875, Rhode Island gave the state board of education the right to grant sums to existing libraries. Massachusetts established the first state library commission in 1890, followed by New Hampshire in 1891. Other commissions were established during the next decade, all for the purpose of extending library service within the state. Financial aid was provided by the states for the founding of libraries, boxes of books were sent to libraries, and traveling libraries—small collections of books to be sent from place to place to circulate freely—were initiated in a number of states.

COUNTY LIBRARIES

The scattered population and uneven distribution of wealth in some of the states called for a type of library organization which could provide service to rural areas. The county was the logical governmental unit to provide this service. In 1898, two county libraries were incorporated and both were opened in 1901—the County Library in Van Wert, Ohio preceding the Washington County Free Library in Maryland by a few months.[19] Under the leadership of Miss Mary L. Titcomb, the Washington County Free Library initiated book-wagon service in 1907.[20]

The influence of philanthropy

The tremendous industrial and commercial growth of the United States in the nineteenth century resulted in relative prosperity for the country as a whole and in the accumulation of great

[19] Mary Lemist Titcomb, *Story of the Washington County Free Library* (Hagerstown, Md.: n.d.), p. 7. The county library type of organization was particularly suited to the Southern states.
[20] *Ibid.*, p. 14. See also p. 179.

fortunes by certain individuals. Among the philanthropic enterprises of these individuals was the endowment of libraries. Endowed libraries—sometimes called patronymic libraries—were fully supported by private funds but were opened to the public on conditions set up by the donor.

Of major historical and cultural importance are three endowed libraries which were established in New York City in the latter half of the century. John Jacob Astor, one of the first of the great fortune makers, bequeathed $400,000 for the founding of a library for the public, and the Astor Library was organized in 1848 "for the advancement of useful knowledge." The Lenox Library, founded in 1870 by James Lenox, was "dedicated to history, literature and the fine arts." The third library was the gift of Samuel Jones Tilden, who, at his death in 1886, left about 2 million dollars and fifteen thousand books for the establishment of a library under the Tilden Trust "to serve the interests of science and popular education." These three libraries—the Astor, the Lenox, and the Tilden Trust—were consolidated in 1895 to form the New York Public Library, an institution which continues to be supported by both public funds and private philanthropy and which is the nation's outstanding public library.[21]

Other endowed libraries which were established before the end of the century and during the first quarter of the twentieth century are the Peabody Institute of Baltimore, established in 1857 and opened to the public in 1866; the Newberry Library, Chicago, 1887; the John Crerar Library, Chicago, 1894; the Henry E. Huntington Library, San Marino, California, 1919; and the Pierpont Morgan Library, New York City, 1924.

City libraries, in particular, were aided during the last quarter of the nineteenth century by the gifts of Andrew Carnegie. From 1881 to 1898, Carnegie provided the funds for fourteen municipal libraries. During the year 1899 his gifts totaled approximately 4 million dollars and were made to more than thirty libraries or localities in the United States. "These gifts make the endowment of libraries the most striking feature of the library year 1899, supple-

[21] New York Public Library, *The Many Faces of the Library: Its History, Its Services, Its Future* (New York: The New York Public Library, n.d.), *passim.*

mented as they were by gifts from other benefactors."[22] By 1917, Carnegie public library buildings numbered 1,681 and his contributions for these buildings exceeded 41 million dollars.[23]

The librarians' conference of 1853

By 1853 there were about seven hundred libraries in the United States—mercantile, society, school, and college—with total collections estimated at about 2 million volumes, but with no single collection numbering as many as a hundred thousand volumes.[24] Generally attached to institutions of learning or to social organizations, the common objective of these libraries tended to be to supply current reading materials rather than to provide collections valuable to the scholar. The inadequacy of the libraries of this country for scholarly research, making it necessary for scholars to take trips to Europe to obtain materials, has already been mentioned.[25]

Generally speaking, by mid-century librarians as a group had not made any significant contribution to library development in America. Leadership had been provided by educators, scholars, authors, religious leaders, and civic-minded citizens, but in 1853 practicing librarians made a public effort on behalf of library advancement.

On May 15, 1853, an invitation was sent by Charles C. Jewett, librarian of the Smithsonian Institution, Charles E. Norton, publisher and bookseller, and others to librarians and persons interested in bibliography "to meet in convention at New York on Thursday the Fifteenth day of September, for the purpose of conferring together upon the means of advancing the prosperity and usefulness of public libraries and for the suggestion and discussion of topics of importance to book collectors and readers."[26] In response to the invitation, eighty-two men—librarians, educators, authors, and

[22] *Library Journal*, XXV (January, 1900), 3.
[23] Florence Anderson, *Carnegie Corporation Library Programs, 1911–1961* (New York: Carnegie Corporation of New York, 1963), pp. 4, 25.
[24] George B. Utley, *The Librarians' Conference of 1853: A Chapter in American Library History*, ed. G.H. Doane (Chicago: American Library Association, 1951), pp. 113–14.
[25] See p. 81.
[26] *Norton's Literary and Educational Register for 1854* (New York: Charles B. Norton, 1854), p. 49

clergy—met in New York to share experiences, give attention to common problems and ways of solving them, and offer suggestions regarding the establishment of popular libraries. One of the most important decisions made was to organize a permanent association of librarians at the next meeting. Unfortunately, the next meeting was never called because the War between the States and the long period of Reconstruction occupied the attention of the country for the next quarter of a century. While the measurable results of the meeting were few, the convention deserves attention as the first effort toward the organization of librarians as a group.

The librarians' conference of 1876

Almost a quarter of a century later, another meeting of librarians was called to be held in Philadelphia during the Centennial Exposition of 1876. By that time, according to the U.S. Bureau of Education's published special report, *Public Libraries in the United States of America, Their History, Condition, and Management*,[27] there were 3,682 libraries of all kinds in the United States, a noticeable growing interest in library work, and a consequent increasing demand for librarians. At this meeting, the American Library Association was organized "to promote the library interests of the country."[28]

Other events of the year 1876 which were of great significance for libraries and librarians were the founding of *The American Library Journal* by F. Leypoldt and the publication of Melvil Dewey's *A Classification and Subject Index for Cataloguing and Arranging the Books and Pamphlets of a Library* and of C. A. Cutter's *Rules for Making a Dictionary Catalogue*.[29] The first formal library school program was opened at Columbia College by Melvil Dewey in 1887, and before the close of the century, four other programs for the training of librarians were established.

At the close of the nineteenth century in the United States, there was a developing interest in all libraries, in the extension of library services on local, county, state, and national levels, and in the training of persons for library positions.

[27] U.S. Bureau of Education, *op. cit.*, pp. 798–801, *passim.*
[28] *The American Library Journal*, I (March, 1877), 253.
[29] This publication constituted Part II of U.S. Bureau of Education, *op. cit.*

CHAPTER 8
THE
LIBRARY
IN
SOCIETY

In the preceding historical sketch, the library is seen as a component part of the history of civilization, its story interwoven with the story of the peoples it has served. Thus no one plan can describe the form, nature, purposes, and services of the library throughout history, for they have been determined by the needs of the people who have produced and used "the book" in its multiple forms—from the clay tablet to the original scientific report and the magnetic tape and disc of today. These needs to which libraries have responded are as diverse as the conditions out of which they have grown, but in the story of libraries certain types of needs recur frequently enough to be identified as basic, universal, and continuing, and certain periods of library development or certain specific libraries are particularly identified with each of these types of needs.

Recurring basic needs

The need to preserve government documents is as old as ancient Sumer, where such preservation began, and as current as today's *Congressional Record;* throughout history this need has been served by a kind of library called archives, established for that specific purpose. This need is served also by state and national libraries, which preserve, in addition to government documents, other kinds of materials that are necessary to the conservation and transmission of local, state, and national history.

The use of the library to support religious and moral instruction, of particular importance to the ancient Egyptians and the people of Israel and Judah, was characteristic of all early civilizations because libraries generally were connected both physically and administratively to the temples. The monastery library of the Middle Ages was established primarily for this purpose, and modern church, Sunday school, and synagogue libraries follow in this same tradition.

The need for libraries in furthering the ends of formal education recurs frequently in the story of library development. It is noted in relation to the Sumerian school, which "came to be the center of culture and learning" in the community and also the center of creative writing, in which "the literary creations of the past were studied and copied" and new literary compositions were produced.[1] Alcuin made the library an "indispensable aid to the school" in the eighth and ninth centuries, and this function has become the basic purpose of all school and academic libraries.

Literature occupied a central place in the education and in the adult life of the ancient Greeks, and Athenians took for granted that "literature deeply affects society and is something with which society must be concerned."[2] It is not surprising then that libraries both supported and were supported by the educational and the cultural endeavors of the Greeks, reaching in Alexandria and Pergamum the high point of their participation in scholarly activities. When interest in scholarly research and in the exploration of new fields of knowledge during the period of the Enlightenment called for the establishment of large collections of research materials, both the private and national libraries of Europe responded; and in colonial America private libraries of appreciable size, containing valuable scholarly materials, were accumulated by William Byrd II, James Logan, and others. This practice of providing the materials and facilities for serious scholarship is continued today at an accelerated pace and on an expanded scale in national libraries throughout the world, in the great universities and independent research organizations and institutions, and in large public library systems. Whenever and wherever literate and cultured people strive to stimulate educational growth and cultural achievement, libraries become both the source and the center of these activities.

[1] Samuel Noah Kramer, *op. cit.*, pp. 2, 3.
[2] H. D. Baldry, "The Voice of Greece," Grant (ed.), *op. cit.*, p. 99.

When mention is made of the dependence of a democratic society on an informed citizenry, the American public library usually comes quickly to mind as the instrument which has had as its fundamental purpose the serving of this crucial need. One should remember, however, that as early as the first century B.C. Julius Caesar proposed the establishment of public libraries to educate the people for intelligent participation in the affairs of state, and his proposal, carried out after his death, resulted in the eventual establishment of some twenty-nine public libraries in Rome.

The desire and need for some means of self-improvement and self-education prompted the founding of social libraries, which flourished for more than a century preceding the public library movement of the mid-eighteenth century. Self-education of a practical nature was made possible by specific types of social libraries, such as the mechanics' apprentices' libraries and the mercantile libraries, and both self-education and self-improvement are today integral parts of the program of the American public library.

Many types of libraries provide materials for recreational reading, but at least one type of library was organized specifically for this purpose—the lending library. A creation of the late eighteenth century to cater to the light-reading needs of its clientele, the lending library—or rental library as it is often called—still provides materials at small cost not only for recreational enjoyment but for cultural and educational improvement as well.

Of the efforts put forth in certain periods of history to preserve the recorded cultural heritage of the past for future ages, those of the Byzantines and the Arabs are perhaps most noteworthy because they utilized libraries primarily for this purpose. However, the libraries of the medieval monasteries, although not established for the purpose of protecting and preserving the recorded "word," contributed immeasurably to that important result.

From the time of Rameses the Great to the present day, libraries have brought personal pride and satisfaction to their owners, and during the Renaissance they were the source of both spiritual and intellectual sustenance for the Humanist collectors. Many of the treasures collected by booklovers for their personal enjoyment have been given to the rare-book collections of our libraries, where they strengthen our cultural heritage, provide invaluable resources for the scholar, and afford aesthetic enjoyment to all who see them. In every civilization, persons of wealth have seen libraries as suitable and proper expressions of their generosity and benevolence. Their gifts have resulted in some of our most splendid libraries; they have supported many of our most worthy programs of library development and continue to provide buildings and resources as well as support for programs and services.

Conditions favorable to library development

Just as the story of the library reflects the social, economic, cultural, and educational needs to which libraries have responded, so does it also point up the fact that the many conditions which affected these societies also affected the development of their libraries. It seems clear that libraries have tended to prosper:

1. In societies of political and cultural maturity which recognize the necessity of preserving, transmitting, and enlarging the body of knowledge

2. During periods of relative peace and tranquillity which afford time to plan and pursue cultural and intellectual activities

3. When individuals have both the leisure and the means to "cultivate the finer arts and improve the common stock of knowledge"

4. In periods of intellectual creativity and scholarly activity, when large and varied collections of materials are required for study and research

5. When there is large societal emphasis on self-improvement and a well-informed citizenry

6. During revivals of learning which center around and depend upon accumulations of graphic materials and access to them

7. When institutional stability and security of tenure offer permanence and continuity

8. In areas with concentrated population and especially in an urban environment which can provide the leadership,

the financial means to support libraries, and the cultural and intellectual interest to stimulate their use

9. When economic prosperity provides sizable individual and corporate wealth and encourages philanthropic giving

10. In times when, as in recent decades, economic growth and national power and status are considered to be dependent upon the wide dissemination and use of information and knowledge which have utilitarian value

From the beginning, the library has been an agency for the collection, preservation, use, and transmission of recorded information and knowledge; and from the beginning, librarianship has been concerned with assuring the continuing accumulation, preservation, organization, and use of recorded materials by the living and the transmission to future generations of those materials which have more than momentary significance.

Many of the basic needs which are served by libraries today—such as, education, research, information, civic responsibility, aesthetic appreciation, and recreation—are also served by other agencies and groups; but the library, in a collective sense, is the only agency devoted solely to the purpose of collecting, making available, and securing the widest and most effective use of the record of civilization by the society of which it is a part. Since the library is intertwined in purpose and function with society's needs, any piece or item of recorded material is a potential library acquisition and no part of the social structure, regardless of the stage of its development, is outside the scope of the library's generic concern. The need of any highly industrial and technical society for knowledge and for dependable and timely information is almost without limit, and in such a society, in such a day as this when fast and radical changes are taking place throughout the world, the need for the library is also almost without limit.

Librarianship embraces all fields of human knowledge and all the forms in which it is recorded. It is made up of the people to whom the collection, preservation, use, and transmission of knowledge are entrusted and the programs, activities, and services which they devise to carry out these tasks. It is concerned with their preparation—their education, skills, abilities, attitudes, resources, and professional growth—and with the quality of their performance. It is concerned also with the needs of the societies they serve, the plans and efforts which they develop and make to meet these needs, and the results of these plans and efforts.

Although the basic functions of the library from antiquity to the present time have remained the same, there have been changes in the activities designed to carry them out; in the purposes for which they were performed; in the conditions which influenced them; in the forms, content, and volume of available materials; and in the ways of making them accessible and of encouraging their use.

It is the librarian's responsibility to use his knowledge of recorded materials and of the principles and techniques of selection, organization, and arrangement as well as his knowledge of the needs of the clientele he serves to plan and execute a program within his own library for accumulating, preserving, using, and disseminating recorded knowledge.

PART II
LIBRARIANSHIP AS A PROFESSION

Professionalization seeks to clothe a given area with standards of excellence, to establish rules of conduct, to develop a sense of responsibility, to set criteria for recruitment and training, to ensure a measure of protection for members, to establish collective control over the area, and to elevate it to a position of dignity and social standing in the society.[1]

One of the much-discussed but still unanswered questions pertaining to librarianship concerns its professional status. Such discussions, among both librarians and nonlibrarians, usually involve an examination of the essential elements of a profession as delineated by students of this subject and an analysis of the extent to which librarianship possesses these elements. A sampling of the definitions of a profession will reveal some of the ingredients which are usually used as bases of comparison.

1. *The Oxford English Dictionary* defines a profession as "a vocation in which a professed knowledge of some department of learning or science is used in its application to the affairs of others or in the practice of an art founded upon it."[2]

2. *A Dictionary of the Social Sciences*[3] says that "the term professions denotes occupations which demand a highly specialized knowledge and skill acquired at least in part by courses of a more or less theoretical nature and not by practice alone, tested by some form of examination either at a university or some other authorized institution,

[1] Herbert Blumer, "Preface," *Professionalization*, ed. Howard M. Vollmer and Donald L. Mills (Englewood Cliffs, N.J.: Prentice-Hall, Inc., 1966), p. xi.
[2] *The Oxford English Dictionary*, VIII, 1427. By permission of the Clarendon Press, Oxford.
[3] N. Elias, "Professions," *A Dictionary of the Social Sciences*, ed. Julius Gould and William L. Kolb, compiled under the auspices of the United Nations Educational, Scientific and Cultural Organization (New York: The Free Press of Glencoe, 1964), p. 542.

and conveying to the persons who possess them considerable authority in relation to 'clients.' . . . At present the term usually denotes certain occupations whose members give service rather than engage in the production and distribution of goods. . . ."

3. The eminent social scientists, A. M. Carr-Saunders and P. A. Wilson, writing on the subject of professions, said "we recognize a profession as a vocation founded upon a prolonged and specialized intellectual training which enables a particular service to be rendered"[4] and, in another work, pointed out that "special competence, acquired as the result of intellectual training, is the chief distinguishing feature of the professions."[5]

Among the essential elements of a profession which are generally agreed upon by analysts of the subject are:[6]

1. A systematic theory which delineates and supports the skills that characterize the profession

2. A level of authority which comes from extensive education in the systematic theory

3. Community sanction and approval of this authority as expressed in the conferring on the profession of such powers as accreditation, formulation of standards of performance, and establishment of rules for admission into the profession

4. A code of ethics which regulates relations of professional persons with clients and colleagues

5. A professional culture sustained by formal associations, consisting of its values, norms, and symbols and having at its center the career concept

6. A service orientation

[4] A. M. Carr-Saunders and P. A. Wilson, "Professions," *Encyclopaedia of the Social Sciences*, XI-XII (1933), 478.
[5] A. M. Carr-Saunders and P. A. Wilson, *The Professions* (London: Oxford University Press, 1933; second impression published by Frank Cass & Co., Ltd., 1964), p. 307. By permission of the Clarendon Press, Oxford.
[6] See Ernest Greenwood, "Attributes of a Profession," *Social Work*, II (July, 1957), 44–55.

Librarianship is, certainly, an occupation which demands specialized knowledge and skills which are acquired at least in part by courses of a more or less theoretical nature and are tested by an examination at a university or other authorized institution. Implicit in this requirement for specialized knowledge and skills is the availability of a body of literature to be used in acquiring them, and librarianship has produced such a body of literature and is continually adding to it. The persons who satisfactorily complete these courses develop a sense of responsibility for their technique, which they reveal in their concern for the competence and performance of the practitioners as a whole, and they are given considerable authority in the formulation of standards of performance, in the power of accreditation, and in the establishing of rules for admission into the profession. Librarianship has its professional organizations which promote excellence in the work of the members, influence public sentiment and support, and endeavor to raise it to a position of dignity and social standing. It has at its center the career concept; and from the beginning it has rendered a service.

In view of these actualities, the student might well assume that there is agreement among librarians that librarianship qualifies as a profession. This is not the fact; there is not unanimity of opinion. While acknowledging that librarianship has many of the ingredients that characterize a profession, those who do not believe that it has achieved professional status question, for example, the intellectual content of its knowledge base, the rigor of its educational requirements, the extent of its authority, and the strength of its code of ethics.[7]

Every student of librarianship should accept the opportunity and assume the responsibility to examine the question and should be aware of the ideology, the processes, and the activities by which an occupation moves toward becoming a profession. Every practicing librarian should prod himself into an examination of his own activities and attitudes in order to decide how professionalized his

[7] See William Goode, "The Librarian: From Occupation to Profession?" *The Library Quarterly*, XXXI (October, 1961), 306–18 for the views of a nonlibrarian.

individual librarianship is and to what extent he is contributing to the professionalization of the occupation.

It is not the purpose of the chapters in Part II to attempt to answer the question, Is librarianship a profession? but rather to present three of the major steps which librarians have taken toward the professionalization of their occupation and toward making of themselves professional people. The three steps which will be considered in this section are, in this order, (1) the establishment of professional associations which, according to Carr-Saunders and Wilson, usually occurs as soon as a profession emerges, for as they also state, "a profession can only be said to exist when there are bonds between the practitioners, and these bonds can take but one shape—that of formal association";[8] (2) the development of educational programs to provide the specialized intellectual study and training necessary for providing skilled service; and (3) the production of a body of literature, part of which delineates and supports the skills that characterize the profession.

[8] Carr-Saunders and Wilson, *The Professions, op. cit.,* p. 298.

CHAPTER 9
PROFESSIONAL
ORGANIZATIONS

It was observed in Chapter 1 that the basic social, economic, and administrative needs of early urban life called forth the production of recorded materials, which in turn called forth the establishment of the library as an agency designed to preserve, arrange, and make these materials available for use.

The student of librarianship should keep in mind the fact that it was in a historical context of high importance that the library was born and that the significance of the library's functions in the ongoing of civilization implied from the beginning knowledgeability and competency on the part of those who performed those functions. As would be expected in any field, not all who have committed themselves to the purposes and services of libraries have possessed these characteristics, but the requirement for knowledgeability and competency has always existed, and in general the performance of librarians throughout the ages has been one of high quality and efficient and indispensable service in behalf of some of the most central needs of civilized peoples.

From the days of the first-known library catalog—probably produced by the graduate of a Sumerian scribal school as he arranged literary tablets on the shelves of the "library-room" of the tablet-house[1]—some of the most creative minds and most reputable scholars, scientists, teachers, and administrators of their day have invested their time and talents in the promotion, organization, and operation of libraries. Throughout the largest part of library history many of those who have had a significant part in the making of that history have had competencies and reputations in other fields of knowledge and action before they became concerned with library purposes and operations. Historians have commented that the Alexandrian libraries would have been considerably less important in

[1] Kramer, *History Begins at Sumer*, p. 219.

the impact which they made on the life of their times if their directors had not been teachers and scholars as well as librarians.[2] It is logical that men who had previously committed their lives to a belief in the efficacy and high place of knowledge and intellect in the life of a society, and thus were already engaged professionally in intellectual pursuits of some kind, should be the first to devote themselves to the nurture and growth of libraries not only in the days of Alexandria's glory but also in pioneer America and later in the days of industrial America's growth.

It is not a simple task to isolate clearly the beginnings of librarianship as a self-conscious occupation. Some library historians date this beginning from the seventeenth century, when writings which dealt seriously with major library problems and functions appeared for the first time. The seventeenth century was a propitious time for such writings. After the invention of printing, libraries began to be faced with multitudes of books on all known subjects and in various sizes which had to be added to their traditional collections of handwritten manuscripts and codexes, which dealt with a more limited number of subjects. The inquiring and productive minds of philosophers, scientists, and mathematicians, such as Bacon, Galileo, Descartes, and Kepler, stimulated greatly the growth of recorded knowledge, and thus by the middle of the seventeenth century the great quantities of library materials included such new forms as periodicals, broadsides, newspapers, news pamphlets, reference books, maps, globes. charts, and printed books in various sizes, as well as the remaining collections of handwritten books. Certainly not at any time before, and perhaps not again until the middle of the current century, did the volume and multiplicity of form of recorded knowledge create so many problems of organization and administration for librarians in comparison with what had gone before.

Gabriel Naudé, a liberal scholar and author and also a gifted librarian, contributed to the need for guidance in the establishment and operation of libraries by offering in his *Advis Pour Dresser Une Bibliothèque* such sound principles of selection, arrangement, and use of materials that they are still considered to be basic in

[2] See pp. 14–15.

building library collections. Some of the writings of Leibniz, noted mathematician and philosopher, were concerned with systematic acquisition of materials, financial support, and the need for bibliographic access to a library collection through an ordered system of classification. Contributions to the general history of libraries by Justus Lipsius and Johannes Lomeier and to the history of national libraries by Durie and Bentley, when added to the writings of Naudé and Leibniz, constituted a sizable body of what could be considered professional literature.[3]

Although these writings indicated clearly that special knowledge, techniques, and principles are required in the effective organization and administration of a library, they did not inspire any organized movement toward the professionalization of librarianship. Hessel has noted that realization of the new duties and responsibilities which devolved upon libraries as a result of printing and the scientific and scholarly approach and ferment of the day "seems to have dawned quite gradually. The need of the time for usable public institutions was materially undermined by the great abundance of private collections."[4] National, private, and church libraries, some of which had very large collections, continued to be established throughout the seventeenth and eighteenth centuries, and writings on the classification of knowledge, inventories and catalogs of library collections—both national and private—charters of purpose, and other materials relevant to library organization and operation were produced. It was not, however, until school district libraries and the subsequent public library movement—triggered and sustained by the concept of democracy—began to take hold in nineteenth-century America that a fruitful self-consciousness regarding the importance and distinctiveness of their activities and purposes emerged among those who were devoting themselves in a practicing or supporting capacity to the establishment and operation of libraries.

Professional organization: background

In 1853, a group of men—librarians, scholars, teachers, and clergymen—"believing that the knowledge of Books, and the foun-

[3] See pp. 51n, 53–54.
[4] Hessel, *op. cit.*, p. 52.

dation and management of collections of them for public use"[5] could be promoted by consultation among librarians and others interested in bibliographical activities, met in New York for that purpose. This first known meeting of its kind in library history called public attention to the specialized requirements for organizing and administering libraries. Some library historians choose to date the emergence of the "library profession" from this convention, which was held more than two centuries after Naudé wrote his monograph on the "setting up" of a library and argued for public use of materials.

In his presidential address to the Librarians' Convention, as it was called, Charles Coffin Jewett, librarian of the Smithsonian Institution, pointed out that their interest was in conferring together for the purpose of seeking mutual instruction and encouragement and exchanging information regarding the best means of collecting books for private culture, public enlightenment, and learned investigations and of increasing the efficiency of such collections. He added, "We meet to provide for the diffusion of a knowledge of good books, and for enlarging the means of public access to them. Our wishes are for the public, not for ourselves."[6]

This conference brought to the attention of the public the fact that the special distinctive function of the library is to collect, organize, and promote the use of books and that special methods are required in carrying out this function; it pointed up the need of librarians as a group to confer together; and it emphasized that service is the primary motivation and aim of the library. Another meeting was planned, but because of unfavorable social and political conditions it was never held.

"Taking the hint from the meeting of 1853, a few library devotees in May 1876 proposed a like gathering in connection with the great Exhibition"[7] in Philadelphia that year and the announcement of such a meeting, to be held in October, was sent to the leading libraries of this country and to the leading librarians abroad.

In the meantime, on September 30, 1876, the first issue of *The American Library Journal* appeared. Published by F. Leypoldt, with

[5] *Norton's Literary and Educational Register for 1854* (New York: Charles B. Norton, 1854), p. 49.
[6] *Ibid.*, p. 57.
[7] *The American Library Journal*, I (September 30, 1876), 13.

Melvil Dewey as managing editor and with twenty-one leading librarians as associate editors, the new publication was planned as a "journalistic medium of exchanging thought and experience on topics of interest to librarians."[8] It carried the program of the October conference, numerous items of practical interest to librarians, and articles by a number of notable librarians, including Melvil Dewey's now classic statement, "The Profession."[9]

THE AMERICAN LIBRARY ASSOCIATION— ORGANIZATION AND EARLY DEVELOPMENT

On October 4, 1876, a large number of librarians from all over the United States, as well as librarians from Canada and the United Kingdom, convened in Philadelphia and a permanent organization of librarians was effected, with Justin Winsor of the Boston Public Library as president; Ainsworth R. Spofford of the Library of Congress, William F. Poole of the Chicago Public Library, and Henry A. Homes of the New York State Library as vice-presidents; and Melvil Dewey as secretary. The object of the newly formed American Library Association, as stated in its constitution, was "to promote the library interests of the country by exchanging views, reaching conclusions, and inducing co-operation in all departments of bibliothecal science and economy; by disposing the public mind to the founding and improving of libraries; and by cultivating good-will among its own members."[10] The February 28, 1877 issue of *The American Library Journal* carried on the title page, "Official Journal of the American Library Association."

The early activity of the association was restricted largely to holding annual meetings and to committee work, and it was not until World War I that the American Library Association gained national prominence and stature as a result of its contribution to the war effort, which included supplying library materials for the armed forces; building, equipping, and operating camp libraries here and abroad; and carrying on a national campaign for magazines and books for these purposes.

[8] *Ibid.*
[9] *Ibid.*, p. 5. See Appendix I, pp. 359–61.
[10] *The American Library Journal*, I (March, 1877), 253.

As early as 1902 the American Library Association had received an initial endowment from Andrew Carnegie, and since 1924 the Carnegie Corporation has played a significant role in the development of the association and many of its programs. From 1924 to 1926 the corporation provided $549,000 toward its general support and in 1926 gave 2 million dollars as an endowment for the association.[11] Since that time, the ALA has been the recipient of many other grants from the Carnegie Corporation for specific purposes, such as the creation and publication of teaching materials to be used in library schools; the preparation of reading courses; making studies of adult education, public library needs, and such library activities as circulation, reference, book selection, and library services for children; and the development of standards for library service.

State and regional associations of librarians appeared soon after the ALA was organized: the New York State Library Association in 1909 and within a decade the Pacific Northwest Library Association, followed in 1922 by the Southeastern Library Association and the Southwestern Library Association. There are, at the present time, fifty-eight state, regional, and territorial library organizations which are chapters of the American Library Association and twelve library associations which are affiliated with the ALA. Other national library associations, with which the ALA works cooperatively, are Association of Jewish Libraries, Bibliographical Society of America, Council of National Library Associations, and Special Libraries Association.

The American Library Association—organization

According to its latest constitution, the object of the American Library Association is "to promote library service and librarianship."[12] To carry out this purpose, its organization is composed of:[13]

---

[11] Anderson, *op. cit.*, p. 89.
[12] "Constitution and Bylaws," *ALA Bulletin*, LXI (November, 1967), 1239.
[13] For the specific purposes and responsibilities of the divisions, chapter, and affiliated organizations, see the "ALA Organization and Information" issue of the *ALA Bulletin* published in November of each year.

1. Five type-of-library divisions: American Association of School Librarians, American Association of State Libraries, Association of College and Research Libraries, Association of Hospital and Institution Libraries, and the Public Library Association
2. Nine type-of-activity divisions: Adult Services Division, American Library Trustee Association, Children's Services Division, Library Administration Division, Library Education Division, Reference Services Division, Resources and Technical Services Division, Young Adult Services Division, and Information Science and Automation Division
3. Fifty-eight state, regional, and territorial chapters
4. Twelve affiliated organizations: American Association of Law Libraries, American Documentation Institute, American Merchant Marine Library Association, American Theological Library Association, Association of American Library Schools, Association of Research Libraries, Canadian Library Association—Association Canadienne des Bibliothèques, Library Society of Puerto Rico—Sociedad de Bibliotecarios de Puerto Rico, Medical Library Association, Music Library Association, Theatre Library Association, and Catholic Library Association

The membership of more than thirty-five thousand librarians, library trustees, libraries, and friends of libraries governs the association through a body of elected representatives called the council which determines all official policies.

THE ALA WASHINGTON OFFICE

In the interest of securing Federal legislation which would benefit libraries, the ALA Washington Office was opened in 1945. In 1949 it took over the functions of the former ALA National Relations Office and International Relations Office.[14]

The first major piece of library legislation to which the office

[14] See pp. 175–76 for a discussion of the Public Library Demonstration Bill.

gave its attention was the Public Library Demonstration Bill which was introduced in 1948 and in 1949, and defeated in 1950. Prior to and following the passage of the Library Construction Act in 1956,[15] the legislative activity of the ALA Washington Office increased. Since that time, it has played a highly significant role in the activities which have led to the passage of major Federal legislation for libraries. Its continuing program of activities on behalf of needed legislation for libraries includes: keeping up with congressional opinion concerning libraries; advising with state and local library officials regarding library needs; organizing national, state, and local support for favorable legislation as well as against unfavorable legislative action; providing information and witnesses for congressional committees; and reporting regularly and systematically to the profession concerning the status of legislation—both pending and enacted.

In addition to its work in securing support for library legislation, the ALA Washington Office engages in other activities: It cooperates with ALA committees, the Library of Congress and other government departments and agencies, and national professional groups in furthering library programs; with international organizations like the Pan American Union and the United Nations Educational, Scientific, and Cultural Organization (UNESCO) in implementing library aspects of their educational and cultural programs; and with the Department of State in an advisory capacity on problems connected with overseas information libraries and exchange-of-person programs.

The American Library Association—activities

The activities of the association are carried on by a headquarters staff under the direction of the executive director, by appointed committees whose members volunteer their services, by the fourteen divisions and their functional sections, and by round-table groups which are devoted to areas and facets of librarianship not within the scope of any division. Cooperative activities with other organizations are carried on by joint committees established for the specific

---

[15] See pp. 176–77, 187–88.

purpose, such as the Joint Committee of the ALA and the American Book Publishers Council's Committee on Reading Development and the Joint Committee of the ALA and the National Education Association.

All the activities of the ALA are directed to the achievement of its objective of promoting library service and librarianship; and its policies, programs, and activities are still permeated with the same desire to serve the public interest which was expressed by Mr. Jewett at the 1853 Librarians' Convention. In carrying out this desire, the association conducts programs to educate the American public in the important contributions which the library makes to our cultural, social, and educational life; provides leadership in planning for the extension and improvement of library services and in securing public and financial support on national, state, and local levels; maintains a constant watch over our freedom to read; establishes and encourages the adoption of standards to improve the quality of library service and to ensure the provision of qualified personnel; and strives to maintain equal access to materials, facilities, and services.

In addition to its activities for the public, which result in benefits for the profession as well, the ALA serves its members directly by giving them the means and the opportunity to discuss their ideas and beliefs, to formulate objectives and purposes, and to develop policies and programs and by providing the media for publicizing and promoting them throughout the profession. It establishes standards of support and welfare as well as standards of service and education, protects their professional status by accrediting library education programs, provides guides for their professional performance and opportunities for continuing self-improvement, and, in general, strives continually to improve the status of librarianship as a profession. It creates, publishes, and encourages the publication of professional literature by other publishers. It is receptive to new trends and new knowledge, and encourages the use of new technology to improve library facilities and library techniques.[16]

---

[16] See "ALA Goals for Action, 1967," *ALA Bulletin*, XLI (September, 1967), 951–954.

STANDARDS

Standards are criteria which are established by authority or by general consent as a measure or test of the quantity or quality of a given thing. They point out a condition or degree or level which must be attained if a desired goal is to be realized and are designed to set and maintain a high level of professional performance.

Early standards in librarianship were quantitative, measuring such tangible elements as physical facilities, staff, budgets, and collections. Now they measure the quality of library service first in terms of the library's functions, purposes, and services and then in terms of the material resources which are needed to carry out the programs. Some standards are established to serve as general guides for those who are developing library programs or an aspect of a program; others are designed to be used for purposes of accreditation. They may set goals, they may explain how certain activities should be carried on, or they may be actual units of measurement. Standards formulated by national associations to apply to all states must, of course, be general, for library development and the conditions affecting it vary from state to state and within a state. Therefore, they cannot offer the specific quantitative criteria which are often needed by a particular library.

Some libraries have already reached a very high stage of development, and standards which provide goals for these libraries will appear to be impossible of achievement for the small, just-beginning, or struggling library. In any case, they can serve as goals to be aspired to, as instruments for continuous self-study and self-evaluation, and as guides in developing specific criteria for a given situation.

Although standards for all aspects of library service have not yet been formulated, the American Library Association, through its divisions, has developed standards for state, public, school, junior college, and college libraries; for graduate and undergraduate programs of library education; for service to children, young people, and to the blind; and for bookmobile service.[17] They have been

---

[17] The American Library Association accredits only graduate library schools. See p. 119. Standards formulated by the ALA as well as those established by national, state, and regional groups are discussed in the appropriate chapters.

a significant factor in the development of libraries and library services and in the professional growth of librarians.

GUIDES FOR PROFESSIONAL PERFORMANCE

In addition to formulating standards to raise the level of library service and to ensure the professional competency of librarians, the American Library Association has established principles to guide its members in the performance of their professional duties. Principles of ethical behavior are set forth in the document, "Code of Ethics for Librarians,"[18] adopted by the association in 1938, which defines the duties and obligations of the professional librarian in relation to the governing authority of his library, to the library constituency, to his staff, to his profession, and to society in general.

Since 1939 the American Library Association has "consciously promoted the concept of man's freedom to seek the truth where and how he will."[19] During that year the "ALA Bill of Rights" was adopted, and in 1940 the Committee on Intellectual Freedom to Safeguard the Rights of Library Users to Freedom of Inquiry— later changed to ALA Intellectual Freedom Committee—was created to recommend necessary steps to safeguard the rights of library users in accordance with the Bill of Rights of the United States and the "Library Bill of Rights." In 1948, the ALA Council reaffirmed the revised "Library Bill of Rights," amended it in 1951 to include all media of communication collected or used by libraries, and in 1961 broadened it to include the statement that the right of an individual to use libraries should not be denied because of race, religion, national origin, or political views. In 1967 it was further revised to strengthen and clarify its content.[20] This official statement of the American Library Association regarding free inquiry sets forth basic policies which govern the librarian in his selection of library materials, his attitude toward the censorship of library materials and the right of free access to ideas and freedom of expression, and his efforts to make library facilities equally available to all groups. The purpose of the "Library Bill of Rights" is

[18] See Appendix I, pp. 362–65. The "Code of Ethics" is presently being revised.
[19] David K. Berninghausen, "The History of the ALA Intellectual Freedom Committee," *Wilson Library Bulletin*, XXVII (June, 1953), 813.
[20] See Appendix I, pp. 373–74.

not "to protect librarians, but to preserve the right of *every citizen* to read whatever he wishes, forming his own private judgments."[21]

"The School Library Bill of Rights," endorsed by the American Library Association in 1955, reaffirms the principles of the "Library Bill of Rights" and defines the responsibilities of the school library in its selection of materials.[22]

Other statements by the American Library Association regarding its steadfast belief in free access to ideas and its opposition to all attempts to restrict that right are[23] the "ALA Statement on Labeling," presented by the Committee on Intellectual Freedom to the ALA Council in 1951 and adopted at that time, and "Freedom to Read," drawn up in collaboration with the American Book Publishers Council in 1953.

American Library Association—advances and problems

The growth of the ALA, in both size and influence, has been accelerated in the past decade and many major advances have been made, including:

1. Higher standards of education for librarians and stronger standards in all areas of library service
2. Federal legislation to aid in the extension and improvement of library service to both rural and urban areas and to strengthen libraries of all kinds
3. Increased interest on the part of philanthropic foundations and industry as evidenced by their gifts for demonstrations, studies, and research
4. New library buildings and new and improved equipment and facilities
5. Higher salaries and improved welfare measures for professional librarians
6. Increased efforts to assist foreign countries in planning library service
7. Rising public interest in and attention to libraries

[21] Berninghausen, *loc. cit.*, p. 817.
[22] See pp. 248–49.
[23] See Appendix I, pp. 366–72.

Obviously, the American Library Association is not solely responsible for these gains and much credit must be given to educational and cultural organizations, to other library associations, to individuals, to public officials, and to educational, sociological, and technological changes which have played a significant role; but, as Mr. Ralph Munn said at the dedication of the association's new headquarters building, "At the core of the library world is the ALA . . . and to a greater or lesser degree, ALA influence has been present in virtually every advancement in recent years."[24]

In spite of the gains mentioned above, the nation's libraries still do not meet the basic criteria for materials and staff established by the American Library Association. To these basic deficiencies are added the difficulties and problems created by the greatest demands in history for library service—demands resulting from such social factors as the rise in both general and school-age population, early retirement, increasing leisure time, widespread prosperity, and accelerating requirements for formal education and a better informed citizenry and from such factors within the profession as the overwhelming number of publications in multiple forms with which libraries must deal, the upheaval in librarianship growing out of the scientific and technological revolution of communication and information processes, the serious shortage of librarians, and the inadequacy of financial support for even minimum library service in a large number of instances. These are problems facing the American Library Association and all its affiliated organizations in the coming years in their continuing efforts to promote library service and librarianship. In fact, these are problems of American society and are problems which are shared, in varying degrees, by all free countries of the world.

The individual librarian: privileges and obligations

Membership in the profession of librarianship, as in any profession, carries with it certain privileges and certain obligations. There is the privilege of being a part of a profession devoted to a high and worthy purpose whose services are completely indispensable in an advanced scientific and technological society, the privilege

[24] Ralph Munn, "Th New ALA Headquarters: A Symbol of Accomplishment," *ALA Bulletin*, LVII (September, 1963), 731–32.

of sharing the benefits of every advance which the profession makes, the privilege of enjoying the recognition and the prestige which each achievement brings, the privilege of having the protection and support which come from a unified body, and the privilege of participating in its programs. Of course, participation is not just a privilege: it is also a prime responsibility, for with the assumption of librarianship there is automatically assumption of the obligation to support, to aid, and to further it. A profession grows in strength, importance, and influence with and through its members; and the principal vehicles for growth are the professional organizations— local, state, and national—which are formed by its members for that purpose and organized and directed by them to that end. Thus an individual librarian's responsibility extends beyond the boundaries of his immediate job description and his membership on a given library staff to include membership in his professional organizations and participation in their programs.

There are several ways of participating in a professional organization. Some of them are enrolling and paying dues to help finance the programs and services of the organization, attending and participating in its meetings, taking part in programs, serving on its committees, making contributions to professional literature, conducting and reporting the results of studies and research, and supporting and seeking support for its activities.

Participation in professional activities is one of the hallmarks of a professional person. The everyday tasks in a library often demand so much attention that librarianship seems to be reduced to a series of routines and the librarian to a mere performer of these routines. It is here that a librarian's personal attitudes toward his duties are vitally important—his constant concern for the excellence of his own particular work, whatever it may be; his ready willingness and effort to adjust and change as he faces new conditions and needs; and his continuous recognition that he must always be a learner. Emphasis on the professional aspects of librarianship and participation in the professional activities within the library and its supporting institution as well as those initiated by local, state, and national organizations help to keep the librarian at a professional level.

CHAPTER 10
LIBRARY
EDUCATION

In his annual report for 1869, Mr. Justin Winsor, superintendent of the Boston Public Library, spoke about the current status of library education:

> We have no schools of bibliographical or bibliothecal training whose graduates can guide the formation of, and assume management within, the fast increasing libraries of our country; and the demand may perhaps never warrant their establishment: but every library with a fair experience can afford inestimable instruction to another in its novitiate; and there have been no duties of my office to which I have given more hearty attention than those that have led to the granting of what we could from our experience to the repesentatives of other libraries whether coming with inquiries fitting a collection as large as Cincinnati is to establish or merely seeking such matters as concern the establishment of a village library.[1]

The report on American libraries made by Charles C. Jewett in 1850 had listed 10,640 libraries of one kind and another in the United States,[2] and according to Mr .Winsor's own statement nineteen years later, libraries were increasing rapidly; yet the demand for persons with special library training to fill positions in these libraries was not great enough to justify the establishment of schools for the preparation of librarians.

However, the professional development of librarians was not

---

[1] Justin Winsor, "A Word to Starters of Libraries," *The American Library Journal,* I (September 30, 1876), 1.

[2] C. C. Jewett, "Second Annual Report of the Assistant Secretary of the Smithsonian Institution, Relative to the Library—Presented Jan. 2, 1850," *Fourth Annual Report to the Board of Regents of the Smithsonian Institution* . . . (Washington, D.C.: Printed by the Printers to the Senate, 1850), p. 38.

completely neglected, thanks to the aid and instruction given by experienced librarians and to the additional help which was available in the reports, rules, and catalogs of libraries and in such publications as *Norton's Literary Gazette* and *Norton's Literary Almanac*, which carried statistical information and news items about American libraries as well as notices of publications of interest to them.

In 1876 the U.S. Bureau of Education published its report *Public Libraries in the United States of America, Their History, Condition, and Management.* This publication proved to be a veritable library of helpful aids for librarians, containing historical and statistical information, discussions of numerous matters pertaining to library economy and management, and as a special bonus, the *Rules for Making a Dictionary Catalogue* by C. A. Cutter. It was soon followed by the publication of *The American Library Journal* which was "intended to cover the entire field of library and bibliographical interests" and "to collate for the librarian every view or fact which may be of use or interest in his work, to the saving of time, money, and effort for him, and . . . to the advancement of his honorable profession."[3] This journal became the official organ of the newly organized American Library Association. During that same year, Melvil Dewey's publications, *Library Notes and A Classification and Subject Index for Cataloging and Arranging the Books and Pamphlets of a Library*, were added to the literature and other aids which librarians and aspiring librarians had available for their self-education and improvement.

Early library training agencies[4]

Even after the American Library Association was established, for several years little attention was given to the matter of training librarians. Dewey's proposals to train prospective librarians by apprenticeship and a later proposal to establish a school of library economy were not endorsed by the association, but in 1887 he was successful in opening the first school for librarians, the School of

[3] *The American Library Journal,* I (September 30, 1876), 12, 13.
[4] See Sarah K. Vann, *Training for Librarianship Before 1923, Education for Librarianship Prior to the Publication of Williamson's Report on Training for Library Service* (Chicago: American Library Association, 1961).

Library Economy at Columbia College. When it was transferred to the New York State Library at Albany in 1889, becoming the New York State Library School, Dewey continued as its head. The curriculum which he developed was based on the routine and typical day-by-day activities of a library and thus was essentially technical and clerical in content.

Once the idea of formal library training had taken original shape, other training programs for librarians were established: Pratt Institute, 1890; Drexel Institute, 1892; and Armour Institute in Chicago, 1893, which was transferred to the University of Illinois in 1897 and became the University of Illinois Library School. Apprentice classes were conducted in the Los Angeles Public Library in 1891 and later in the public libraries in Denver and Cleveland; summer courses were offered at Amherst College and by some of the state library commissions; and in 1900 a training program for children's librarians was established at the Carnegie Library of Pittsburgh, the first effort to offer training in a particular area of library operations and service.

In the first two decades of the twentieth century, the rapid growth of public and special libraries and of the number of services which they offered, the growing importance of the university library in scholarly research, and the emphasis placed on academic and school libraries by accrediting agencies brought added demands for trained librarians. The programs designed to prepare them took several forms: (1) library schools which offered one- and two-year programs; (2) colleges which gave summer courses only; (3) libraries which provided apprentice and in-service training; (4) colleges and normal schools which offered courses in bibliography or library economy; (5) institutions of various kinds which offered courses by correspondence. In all these programs, the courses which received the greatest emphasis were cataloging, book selection, reference work, and classification.[5]

With the growth in the number and kinds of programs came the recognition on the part of the established library schools of

[5] Charles Clarence Williamson, *Training for Library Service* (New York: Carnegie Corporation of New York, 1923), p. 21.

the need to establish and maintain standards of instruction, entrance requirements, and curriculum; and in 1915 the Association of American Library Schools was organized for this purpose.

In 1915 a study of selected Carnegie libraries made by Alvin S. Johnson for the Carnegie Corporation showed that many of these libraries were not providing good service because they lacked trained personnel, and Johnson recommended that the corporation turn its attention to the preparation of librarians before giving more money for buildings. In 1919 the trustees commissioned C. C. Williamson, head of the Division of Economics and Sociology of the New York Public Library, to conduct a study of library training programs. This study, published in 1923, marks the turning point in education for librarianship.

Prior to the Williamson report, Mr. Carnegie and the Carnegie Corporation had contributed to the training of librarians by making grants for endowment and/or support of the library schools at Western Reserve University and Hampton Institute and to the schools operated by the Carnegie Institute in Pittsburgh, the Carnegie Library of Atlanta, and to the New York Public Library.

In criticizing the emphasis which was then being placed on the clerical and routine aspects of library work to the neglect of general education, Mr. Williamson pointed out that "no amount of training in library technique can make a successful librarian of a person who lacks a good general education."[6] He explained that two types of training are required: (1) thorough preparation for professional service, represented by a full college course providing a broad general education and at least one year of graduate study in a library school properly organized to give professional preparation; (2) training for clerical and routine work by completion of a four-year high school course followed by a course of instruction designed to provide an understanding of the mechanics and routine operations of a library.

In addition to the need to differentiate between the professional

[6] *Ibid.,* p. 6.

and the clerical types of library work and to provide the kind of training required for each, Mr. Williamson pointed out, among other things, the need for:[7]

1.   Standards regarding the scope and content of courses, the accrediting of library schools, and the certification of librarians, and an authoritative body to formulate and enforce them

2.   Entrance requirements based on a college education or its full equivalent, thus placing library schools on the graduate level

3.   Adequate budgets to support library education programs,[8] including higher salaries to attract better qualified faculty and to ensure higher standards of instruction

4.   Provision of textbooks, handbooks, treatises, and other professional literature in all areas of library practice

5.   A better grade of student and the provision of fellowships and scholarships to attract them

6.   The establishment of the professional library school as a department of a university

7.   Specialized training for certain types of libraries and in certain areas of librarianship

8.   Opportunities for librarians to continue their professional and educational growth

As a result of the Williamson report, the Carnegie Corporation began a considerable expansion of its library program with emphasis on improving library education and in 1926 launched a ten-year "Library Service Program."[9] Grants for the endowment and support of existing library schools and the establishment of a new school for graduate training in librarianship at the University of Chicago totaled more than 3 million dollars.[10] Additional grants were made to these schools for conferences, studies, publishing, and other

[7] *Ibid.*, p. 136–44., *passim.*
[8] Mr. Williamson pointed out that only four schools had a total expenditure in 1920–1921 of more than $10,000. (Williamson, *op. cit.*, p. 140).
[9] Anderson, *op. cit.*, p. 7.
[10] *Ibid.*, p. 10.

projects. The major contribution of this period was the establishment at the University of Chicago of the first graduate library school offering a curriculum leading to the Ph.D. degree; a million dollars was given for its endowment in 1926 and grants totaling $462,750 were made toward its support between 1925 and 1942.[11] The Board of Education for Librarianship, established by the ALA in 1924 to formulate standards and to evaluate and accredit programs of library education—and partly supported by Carnegie funds— aided the corporation in distributing the funds for the development of library education programs.

Between 1928 and 1930 the corporation further promoted the cause of library training with funds for fellowships, some of which were given directly to individuals; others were administered by the American Library Association. After World War II, grants were made by the corporation for specific purposes rather than for the general support of library schools, such as training in library administration and in the administering of audio-visual materials, developing teaching materials for library schools, and developing a curriculum in librarianship at Western Reserve University.

Development of standards

In 1926, following the recommendations of the Williamson study, the Board of Education for Librarianship formulated minimum standards[12] for advanced graduate library schools, graduate library schools, junior and senior undergraduate library schools, summer courses, library apprentice and training classes, and the curriculum in school library work. The first list of accredited library schools, which was published in 1925-1926, included fourteen schools, of which only six were organized within a college or university. In 1932 the standards for training and apprentice classes and for summer schools which were not a part of the regular curriculum of accredited schools were discontinued, and new qualitative standards, "Minimum Requirements for Library Schools,"[13]

---

[11] *Ibid.,* p. 11.
[12] "The Second Annual Report of the Board of Education for Librarianship," *ALA Bulletin,* XX (1926), 405-73.
[13] *ALA Bulletin,* XXVII (December 15, 1933), 610-13.

adopted by the American Library Association in 1933, recognized three classes of library schools: Type I, first year graduate and advanced graduate work—the master's degree program; Type II, those which offered only the first year of graduate work—the second bachelor's degree; and Type III, those which gave a full year of library science without the degree requirement for admission. The next year, additional standards, "Minimum Requirements for Teacher-Librarian Training Agencies," were formulated to aid institutions in developing programs for teacher-librarians. Since 1939, all accredited library schools have been a part of degree-granting institutions.

The decade of the forties, particularly the latter half, was a period of experimentation in library education, sparked by surveys and studies including the Public Library Inquiry, [14] which offered some of the same criticisms which Williamson had made as well as similar recommendations relating to the accrediting of library schools and the necessity for having the library school as a part of a university.

When new standards for accrediting library schools were prepared in 1951 by the Board of Education for Librarianship[15] with the assistance of the ALA Library Education Division and the Association of American Library Schools, they provided qualitative bases for evaluating the basic professional program of education for librarianship, consisting of five years of study beyond the secondary school and leading to a master's degree. Since that time, the American Library Association has accredited only this type of program, using the 1951 standards, and their accrediting activities have been limited to the maintenance and implementation of these standards. Accreditation by the American Library Association is not compulsory, and the ALA Committee on Accreditation visits a library school only upon invitation from the school.

Toward the end of the forties, increasing recognition on the part of educational leaders, school administrators, librarians, and teachers of the importance of the school library in the entire educa-

[14] See pp. 198–99.
[15] In 1956 the Board of Education for Librarianship was replaced by the ALA Committee on Accreditation.

tional program was seen in the new policies and criteria relating
to school libraries which were included in state and regional accreditation requirements. One of the requirements had to do with
the educational preparation of school librarians. The requirements
ranged from four semester hours of library science in some states
to twenty-four or more semester hours in others, and to help librarians and teacher-librarians meet these requirements, colleges—
chiefly teacher-training and state-supported institutions—added library science courses to their curricula. In order to provide guidance
in the establishment of these programs, the American Library Association formulated "Standards for Library Science Programs in
Teacher Education Institutions" in 1952. Two years later, when
the National Council for the Accreditation of Teacher Education
was established, the American Library Association began to work
with the council in the area of undergraduate library education.
As a result of a lengthy study, the ALA Committee on Accreditation drew up new guidelines, "Standards for Undergraduate Library
Science Programs,"[16] which were adopted by the ALA Council in
1959 to be used for advisory purposes by a library education program engaged in a self-study, by the National Council for the
Accreditation of Teacher Education, or by a regional accrediting
association whenever such an association might be engaged in
evaluating an institution of higher education offering an undergraduate library science program.

Influences in the development of library education

In addition to the influence of early library leaders, the Williamson report and other studies, and the standards established from
time to time by the Board of Education for Librarianship and its
successor, the ALA Committee on Accreditation, contributions to
the development of library education have been made—and are

---

[16] American Library Association, Committee on Accreditation, "Standards
and Guide for Undergraduate Library Science Programs," *ALA Bulletin*,
XLII (October, 1958), 696–700. The American Library Association does not
accredit undergraduate library education programs. These standards are used
only as general guidelines. The accreditation of a graduate or undergraduate
library education program is included in the accreditation of the parent institution by national, state, or regional accrediting agencies. See pp. 262–65.

being made continually—by the Library Education Division of the ALA, the Library Services Branch of the Office of Education, state departments of education, state library commissions, and new Federal legislation.

The Library Education Division, a type-of-activity division of the ALA, is engaged in studying the changing needs for library education; planning programs of study and research to improve education throughout the profession; developing educational programs including programs for the continuing education of library personnel; and encouraging the preparation, publication, dissemination, and use of materials needed in library education.

The Library Services Branch of the U.S. Office of Education, and particularly the Library Education Specialist, contributes to library education by making surveys and compiling statistics relating to enrollment, degrees, faculty, financial status, and costs of library education; reporting on new developments in library education; publicizing conferences, workshops, institutes, short courses, and other forms of continuing education for librarians; planning programs under new Federal legislation, such as institutes under the National Defense Education Act and the Higher Education Act; and cooperating with the Library Education Division, the ALA Committee on Accreditation, and library schools in planning and improving library education throughout the profession.

It is the responsibility of state departments of education to formulate the basic program for the education of professional personnel in the field of education as a prerequisite for certification, and since school librarians are part of the public school's professional personnel and are certified as both teachers and librarians, their professional preparation is closely related to the professional preparation of teachers. State departments of education may assist in developing programs for the education of school librarians in state institutions of higher education, set standards for these programs, and accredit them. They evaluate the credentials of candidates for school library positions and certify them as school librarians. State departments of education also provide information regarding the professional qualifications for school librarianship to appropriate authorities, such as the state directors of teacher education and certification, institutions of higher education, local boards of education, and school administrators. The required number of hours of library science for certification varies from state to state and may be based on school enrollment or on the amount of time given to the library, when the position is a part-time one.

In a number of states, state library extension agencies have the responsibility for certifying librarians for positions in public libraries and have worked with library schools in developing programs to satisfy the certification requirements for both professional and nonprofessional library positions. Since the passage of the Library Services Act in 1956 and the Library Services and Construction Act in 1964, more than 500 graduate library school scholarships have been provided by states receiving aid under the provisions of these acts as a means of recruiting public library personnel.[17] As a part of their program for the continuing education of public library personnel, the state library extension agencies conduct conferences, workshops, institutes, and short courses.

Several new Federal programs, established through recent legislation, contribute to professional library education. The National Defense Education Act of 1958, as amended in 1964, provided for short-term or regular session institutes for advanced study by library personnel in the elementary or secondary schools or by supervisors of such personnel. In 1965, twenty-six institutes for school librarians were held and were attended by approximately one-thousand persons[18] who were to hold school library positions in the fall of 1965. Beginning July 1, 1967, institutes for school librarians became a part of the library training program authorized by the Higher Education Act of 1965, which includes training for all librarians and provides fellowships in library and information science. Funds for the construction of new buildings or new facilities for library schools are available under the Higher Education Facilities Act of 1963.

---

[17] *The Federal Government and Public Libraries, A Ten-Year Partnership, 1957–1966* (Washington, D.C.: U.S. Government Printing Office, 1966), p. 11. See pp. 176–77, 187–88 for a discussion of these acts.
[18] Sarah R. Reed, "The Federal Government and Professional Library Education," *ALA Bulletin,* LX (February, 1966), 163.

Present status of library education

Preparation for librarianship requires a mastery of the body of knowledge and techniques utilized in library operation and service which constitute what is called library science. This involves an understanding of the historic and current functions of the library to collect, preserve, organize, and transmit for both immediate and continuing use the record of civilization; an appreciation of the social, educational, cultural, and utilitarian roles of libraries in a civilized society; a knowledge of the contents, characteristics, purposes, and uses of recorded materials; and the ability to apply knowledge, techniques, understanding, and appreciation to planning and executing an effective program of library service for a given clientele at a given time, in a given situation, and in productive relationships with other libraries and agencies which have the same or similar aims.

The structure of library education includes (1) undergraduate programs, the majority of which are designed to enable school librarians to meet certification requirements; and (2) graduate programs, including the master's degree program, which is the basic professional program; the intermediate program, that is, a nondegree second year of professional education; and the doctoral program. Although there is not a prelibrary undergraduate curriculum comparable to premedicine, prelaw, or preengineering, there may be certain undergraduate prerequisites. In general, the student who is preparing for graduate study in librarianship is encouraged to emphasize broad general education in the humanities, social sciences, and natural sciences and to study one or more foreign languages. Library education is concerned in varying degrees with the whole range of human knowledge, but there is a certain body of knowledge which all professional librarians are assumed to possess, including the history of books and libraries; the place of the library in society; general library objectives and functions; and the basic principles and procedures of classification, cataloging, reference, selection of materials, and other services. The majority of accredited library schools include in their basic professional curriculum a core of courses which includes a general introduction to librarianship, selection of materials, cataloging and classification, and reference materials and services. These courses may be prerequisite to the master's program or they may be a part of that program.

According to the "Standards for Accreditation,"[19] the basic professional program, that is, the master's degree program, includes "(*a*) general education which comprises a systematic survey of the various fields of knowledge, concentration in one or more subject fields, background courses of special value in library service, and (*b*) study of professional principles and methods common to the several kinds of libraries and library service." Admission to the graduate library program is based on graduation from an approved college or university with an adequate background in general education and some subject specialization, scholarship as required for graduate study in the institution, and personal characteristics indicating aptitude and suitability for library service.

Types of library curricula include college and university librarianship, public librarianship, school librarianship, special librarianship, and information science. Within these broad areas of specialization by types of agencies, further specialization by functions may be possible, such as cataloging and classification, administration, reference, and subject bibliography.

The undergraduate library science program, if it meets the ALA guidelines as they are set forth in "Standards for Undergraduate Library Science Programs,"[20] is an instructional unit within a college or university which is approved by the appropriate accrediting association. On the assumption that the full basic program of professional education for librarianship is a minimum of five years study beyond the secondary school, culminating in the master's degree, the undergraduate program offers introductory preparation for library personnel for positions on the level of their preparation and provides a foundation for graduate study in the field of librarianship. It may also provide in-service training opportunities for librarians. The undergraduate program of not fewer than twelve and not more than eighteen semester hours is planned in relation to the institution's program of general and professional education,

[19] American Library Association, Board of Education for Librarianship, "Standards for Accreditation," *ALA Bulletin*, XL (February, 1952), 49.
[20] American Library Association, Committee on Accreditation, *loc. cit.*

the specific needs of the geographical area, and the types of libraries to be served. It should begin to develop in students an understanding of the library as a social, cultural, and educational agency and a knowledge of the content, evaluation, organization, and use of materials as well as of the principles, practices, and techniques of library organization and administration. Admission to the undergraduate library science program should be based on high standards of scholarship and aptitude and on personality characteristics appropriate for library service.

According to the *Library Education Directory 1964–65*, there were at that time 102 library education programs in the United States which offered graduate work and 217 programs which offered undergraduate courses.[21] By 1967 forty-two graduate library programs were accredited by the American Library Association—thirty-nine in the United States and three in Canada.

Problems and needs

It is always true that in a time of change in any vital part of life, the agencies whose policies and programs importantly affect that area of life are subject to and receive criticism—both from within and from without the agencies. This is true in exaggerated fashion in times like the present, when changes in the needs, interests, and values of people around the world are rapid, major, and of far-reaching significance. It is not surprising, therefore, that in recent years education—which is universally recognized as being crucial in the nation's future—has been undergoing an unprecedented amount of evaluation and criticism from educators and laymen alike. Correspondingly, it is neither surprising nor inappropriate that libraries, librarians, and library education are receiving widespread critical attention.

Libraries must respond to the needs and demands of a society in which recorded information and knowledge are growing in volume and complexity and appearing in many diverse forms and in

[21] Sarah R. Reed and Willie P. Toye (eds.), *Library Education Directory 1964–65* (Washington, D.C.: Bureau of Educational Research and Development, 1965), p. 1. See also footnote 16, p. 120.

which more and more persons of all ages and occupations are becoming increasingly dependent upon efficient access to these materials. Librarianship is today undergoing significant changes in outlook, in functions, in range and types of service, and in methods and techniques. It follows that these changes in librarianship and the societal conditions and requirements which make them necessary should affect materially the scope and nature of library education. The kinds of criticism leveled at traditional library education are varied. It is not necessary to air them all, but the student of librarianship should be aware of some of them.

For example, there is considerable concern, particularly among library educators, regarding some of the new programs of library education at the undergraduate level which have been established to try to meet the increasing demand for librarians—particularly school librarians—which the graduate library schools have not been able to satisfy. Lacking adequate financial support, a sizable number of these programs are substandard in staff, facilities, and learning resources.

Some critics charge that the admission standards of some library schools as well as of undergraduate library programs are too low; that their faculties are not characterized by the high level of leadership, scholarship, and experience which characterizes the faculties of certain other professional schools; and that much of the curriculum of library schools is less rigorous in its intellectual demands than that of other graduate departments. Others complain of the wide gap which exists between what students are given the opportunity to learn and what they actually do as practitioners of librarianship. These critics are saying, among other things, that there is too much emphasis on the acquisition of techniques and skills and not enough on broad-gauged education or—at the other extreme—that there is too much emphasis on the more intellectual and professional aspects of librarianship, when in actual fact, the tasks that many of their students will perform as librarians are largely repetitive and clerical. Some suggest that too many teachers are out of touch with actual library situations and thus send students out poorly prepared to deal intelligently with such important realities as management; budget making; planning quarters; evaluating objectives, materials, equipment, and services; public relations; and local, state, and Federal legislation.

There are also those who are critical of much of library education at all levels because they are inclined to discount librarianship as a significant force in contemporary society, saying that librarians are merely archivists and that new agencies are needed to handle efficiently the organizing and disseminating of specialized utilitarian information; and consequently, new types of educational and training programs must be created for those who are to man these agencies.

To the library educator, the most pressing problem today is the severe shortage of competent, experienced library school faculty—a shortage which results in the employment of a large number of part-time faculty members and in the inability to provide the needed new kinds of training and specializations for the responsibilities of contemporary librarianship. A second major problem, and a contributing factor to the shortage of capable faculty, is inadequate financial support. For the fiscal year 1967 ALA-accredited library schools budgeted an average of $1239 per student, which was less than half of the $2500 per student established by the U.S. Office of Education as the amount of institutional support required to administer its fellowship programs.[22] The dual problems of too many part-time students and too few graduates result in a third major concern of library educators; the growing shortage of qualified personnel for all types of libraries.

Some other easily identifiable and immediate needs in library education are:

1. A greater emphasis on the increasing importance of the library to the educational, social, economic, and/or utilitarian needs of society, and the preparation of librarians to serve these needs in the most efficient way possible and with the most effective tools and procedures, always encouraging open-mindedness and receptivity to new ideas, methods, and materials

[22] Henry T. Drennan and Sarah R. Reed, "Library Manpower," *ALA Bulletin,* XLI (September, 1967), 962.

2. A greater awareness of the changing patterns in librarianship and library use, such as the system concept of library service, and education for participating in planning these services and for bringing them into being

3. Provision not only of broad general education and education for specific kinds of librarianship, but more experiences in the kinds of activities which the practitioner will have to perform

4. A clear definition of the boundaries of professional, subprofessional, and clerical work, and a determination of what levels of training are needed, who should offer the several kinds of training, and what the several curricula should be

5. An assessment of the effects of training programs for nonprofessionals upon the traditional library school curriculum, and a determination of what new avenues are opened for the professional librarian and what new responsibilities he can assume, having been freed from nonprofessional tasks

6. More opportunities for the continuing education of librarians in new areas such as data processing and information science, new types of materials, new services, new procedures, and new legislation

7. Research into the problems and needs of the profession, and the development of new teaching materials and new methods of teaching

8. Identification and recruitment of potential library school teachers and the provision of both the incentive and the opportunity to teach

9. Budgets which will provide the salaries that will attract qualified faculties and provide the facilities, equipment, and resources necessary in carrying on a program of quality education

10. Higher standards of performance by undergraduate library science programs and their organization as instructional units within the academic framework of the institu-

tion rather than as adjuncts to the library, and more effective articulation between graduate and undergraduate programs to provide an adequate basis for graduate study

11. A determination of the common characteristics of, and the relationship between, librarians, documentalists, information scientists, educational media specialists, and other related groups in the light of needed curriculum changes

12. A national inventory of the personnel needs of libraries—both nonprofessional and professional—which can be used to develop realistic programs of education and recruitment[23]

Perhaps the most basic need of library education today, granting that librarianship has changed in the last half of the twentieth century, is to determine what librarianship now is and what it most urgently requires, for these facts and judgments must determine the nature and direction of library education.

Trends

The library profession is continually seeking and planning effective ways of meeting the needs and solving the problems which face library education. To the efforts of the profession—and particularly of the Library Education Division of the ALA—are added the assistance of the Division of Library Services and Educational Facilities, Library Services Branch, of the U.S. Office of Education, the cooperation of the institutions having library schools, the National Education Association, state and local library agencies, philanthrophic organizations, and the Federal government. Some noteworthy developments and trends are:

1. The American Library Association Commission on a National Plan for Library Education. This commission, a part

---

[23] The School of Library and Information Services of the University of Maryland has begun a national study of the problems of selecting, recruiting, training, and utilizing manpower in the library and information professions. A grant of about four hundred thousand dollars, provided by the Office of Education, the National Science Foundation, and the National Library of Medicine will support the first eighteen months of a projected three-year study.

of the Library Education Division, was established in 1962 composed of representatives from the several national library associations, from the principal fields of librarianship, and from related agencies dealing with information. Its object has been "to reassess the needs of American libraries and related institutions for professional personnel in the years immediately ahead and to make recommendations appropriate to these needs for the selection, education, and utilization of professional personnel."[24] In its recently published report,[25] the commission proposes "to concern itself with the whole field of responsibility for conserving, organizing, and disseminating knowledge and information," giving attention to "present and probable future personnel requirements of school, college, university, public, and special libraries; of educational and research agencies requiring specialized personnel for handling audio and visual media; and of agencies engaged in providing specialized technical and scientific information *regardless of the means through which such information is acquired, organized, and disseminated or the degree of analysis to which it is subjected.*" It recommends that the American Library Association seek funds for the establishment of an office or center for research and experimentation in library education and personnel administration and suggests as a program for the center a study of (1) the character of librarianship—now and in the foreseeable future; (2) the program of professional education needed to fulfill the requirements for such librarianship; and (3) the kind of action program throughout the profession that will be necessary to implement these findings.

2. Research and curriculum revision and expansion. Library schools are undertaking or sponsoring research into the new problems created by the overwhelming number of publica-

---

[24] "Restatement of the Program of the Commission," *ALA Bulletin*, LVII (April, 1963), 317.
[25] "A Report From the Commission on a National Plan for Library Education," *ALA Bulletin*, LXI (April, 1967), 419–22.

tions in all subject fields and are cooperating with other agencies which are conducting such research;[26] they are holding special institutes, conferences, and workshops to study these problems and explore ways of solving them; and they are introducing new courses into the existing curricula and launching new programs which are planned to produce subject specialists or specialists in the field of mechanization.[27]

3. The organization of new programs. Undergraduate programs are being organized or expanded to meet the rising need for school librarians; the number of schools offering graduate work leading to a postbaccalaureate degree is increasing; several master's degree programs in information science have been initiated either by existing schools or by schools organized for that purpose; and the intermediate or sixth-year program—offering thirty hours beyond the master's degree—has been introduced.

4. Programs of continuing education. These programs have become necessary in order to keep the profession abreast of the changing social, educational, and cultural needs of its varied clientele and of developments within the profession. In 1966–1967, library schools offered 288 continuing education programs in the form of workshops, institutes, and short courses, compared with 259 the previous year.[28]

5. Training of nonprofessional staff. Programs for the training

[26] See pp. 159, 167–68, 295–96.

[27] At the time of a study conducted by Alan M. Rees and Dorothy Manfredt of Western Reserve University, seventeen ALA accredited library schools were offering a total of twenty-five courses in the area of data processing and library automation; nineteen offer a total of thirty-nine courses in the area of documentation and information storage, retrieval and dissemination; and six offer a total of thirteen courses in the area of information science research methodology. (Alan M. Rees and Dorothy Manfredt, "Information Science in Library School Curricula," paper presented at the International Conference on Education for Scientific Information Work, sponsored by FID, OSTI, the Institute of Information Scientists and ASLIB, Queen Elizabeth College, London, April 3–7, 1967.)

[28] Sarah R. Reed (ed.), *Continuing Education for Librarians—Conferences, Workshops, and Short Courses, 1966–67* (Washington, D.C.: U.S. Department of Health, Education, and Welfare, 1966), p. 1.

of library technicians, aides, and other nonprofessional library staff are increasing. At least twenty-four of these programs were in operation in 1965[29] and others were in the planning stage; most of them are in junior colleges.

6. Scholarships, fellowships, assistantships. These kinds of assistance to students preparing to begin or continue their work in library schools are being offered in increasing numbers by state and other library associations, library schools, state library commissions, and philanthropic foundations.

7. Federal legislation. Under recent Federal legislation, funds are available for scholarships, graduate fellowships, and the training of librarians. In 1965 and 1966, under the National Defense Education Act, fifty-eight institutes for school library personnel were conducted for 2,047 persons. During the summer of 1967, eighteen institutes were planned for some five-hundred-seventy-five persons in school librarianship.[30] Beginning July 1, 1967, institutes for the training of librarians—public, academic, and special as well as school—were included in Title II, Part B, of the Higher Education Act, which authorizes the U.S. Commissioner of Education to make grants to institutions of higher education to assist them in training persons in librarianship. Fellowships in library and information science are also authorized under this act.

8. The Office for Library Education. Aided by a grant of $75,000 from The H. W. Wilson Foundation, the ALA established on September 1, 1966 the Office for Library Education, to study the problems of library education, to aid in developing and carrying out programs of library education, and to identify and stimulate needed research in this and related fields.

[29] See John L. Martinson, *Vocational Training for Library Technicians: A Survey of Experience to Date* (Washington, D.C.: Communication Service Corporation, 1965).

[30] *LED Newsletter*, No. 61 (March, 1967), 18.

CHAPTER 11
THE
LITERATURE
OF
LIBRARIANSHIP

Library science may be defined in simple terms as the body of organized knowledge—in whatever form—which is concerned with the purposes, objectives, and functions of libraries and the principles, theories, methods, organization, and techniques employed in performing library service. Librarianship may be defined as the application of this knowledge in the collection, organization, preservation, and use of books and other materials in libraries and in the continuous improvement and extension of library service.

Like other subject fields, librarianship has a body of literature specifically its own. The specialized literature of librarianship treats of:

1. The bases of librarianship, that is, (*a*) the factual and interpretative history and development of libraries and librarianship—their economic, social, educational, and cultural foundations and functions and their underlying principles, theories, and philosophies; (*b*) the history of the book and its forms, of printing, publishing, copyright, and the distribution of recorded materials; and (*c*) the story of the lives of men and women who were a part of each trend, movement, or period

2. Library functions, techniques, and activities and the principles underlying them, including (*a*) the administration and management of the library; (*b*) the selection and acquisition of materials; (*c*) the provision of physical and bibliographical access to recorded materials; and (*d*) the service to users through circulation of materials, provision of informa-

tion and reference services, reading guidance and aid in research, and instruction in the use of materials and facilities

3. The library profession—the purposes, activities, and services of professional organizations; the professional preparation for librarianship; and the extension of library service in all its geographical, sociological, economic, and legal aspects

The forms of the literature vary according to the purposes and uses they serve. Some of the forms are:

1. Histories
   a. Of libraries or book production in general
   b. Of a particular kind of library or a particular library
   c. Of a given aspect, area, period, or kind of librarianship or book production
2. Essays
   a. On the meaning of library science or librarianship
   b. On the theories and principles underlying library functions or activities
3. Monographs on a given area of libraries, librarianship, or book production
4. Biographies
   a. Of an individual library leader
   b. Of several individuals
5. Reports
   a. Of the results of research
   b. Of the findings of studies and surveys
   c. Of meetings on special problems
   d. Of the professional associations
6. Case studies
   a. In personnel administration
   b. In reference work
   c. In other specific areas
7. Theses and dissertations for advanced degrees
8. Legislation
   a. Individual statutes
   b. Compilations of library laws
9. Standards and guidelines

10. Instructional materials
    a. Textbooks
    b. Syllabi
    c. Problems
    d. Audio-visual and other non-book materials
    e. Programmed materials
    f. Collections of readings
11. Proceedings
    a. Of meetings of professional organizations
    b. Of conferences, institutes, and workshops
12. Statistical compilations
13. Reference books[1]
    a. Bibliographies
    b. Dictionaries
    c. Encyclopedias
    d. Directories
    e. Manuals
    f. Indexes
    g. Yearbooks and annuals
14. Professional journals

Broad knowledge and understanding of the literature of librarianship is basic to preparation for a library career. The student will find that many of the materials which he studied in library school are also his indispensable tools in the practice of librarianship. Of particular usefulness to the librarian in the performance of his work are manuals, which give him instruction and aid in performing essential activities and professional journals, which contribute to his continuing education and professional growth.

Manuals

Manuals provide instruction on, or guidance in, the performance of certain activities, such as classifying and cataloging library materials and maintaining the card catalogs. Some examples are:

---

[1] See Constance M. Winchell, *Guide to Reference Books* (8th ed.; Chicago: American Library Association, 1967), pp. 65–77.

ALA Cataloging Rules for Author and Title Entries. 2d ed. Chicago: American Library Association, 1949.

Anglo-American Cataloging Rules. Chicago: American Library Association, 1967.

ALA Rules for Filing Catalog Cards. Chicago: American Library Association, 1942.

Dewey, Melvil. *Dewey Decimal Classification and Relative Index.* 17th ed., 2 vols. Lake Placid Club, N.Y.: Forest Press, Inc., 1965.

————. *Dewey Decimal Classification and Relative Index.* 9th abridged ed. Lake Placid Club, N.Y.: Forest Press, Inc., 1965.

Sears List of Subject Headings. Edited by Bertha M. Frick. 8th ed. New York: The H. W. Wilson Company, 1959.

U.S. Library of Congress. *Library of Congress Classification, Class D: History: General and Old World.* 2d ed. Washington, D.C.: U.S. Government Printing Office, 1959.

————. *Subject Headings Used in the Dictionary Catalogs of the Library of Congress.* 7th ed. Washington, D.C.: U.S. Government Printing Office, 1966.

Professional journals

The most recent material on problems, trends, and new developments in librarianship will be found in periodical publications; and subjects which are too new or even too obscure or too temporary to be covered by books are treated in journals. The trend of interest or opinion at any given period can be traced easily in periodical literature, the current issues giving contemporary information and the back issues giving a record of past ideas, problems, and accomplishments. Professional journals provide articles on topics of current interest, essays, book reviews, news, announcements, and other types of material of interest to librarians. Some major sources of professional journals in librarianship, with examples of titles, are:[2]

[2] For a comprehensive list, see "Library Periodicals," *Ulrich's International Periodicals Directory, 1965–66* (11th ed.; New York: R. R. Bowker Company, 1966), II, 752–60.

1. They are published by the national association, by one of its divisions, or by an affiliated association.

   ALA Bulletin. Chicago: American Library Association, 1907– . Monthly. The official organ of the American Library Association.

   College and Research Libraries. Chicago: American Library Association, 1939– . Bimonthly. The official journal of the Association of College and Research Libraries.

   Journal of Education for Librarianship. Urbana, Ill.: University of Illinois, 1960– . Quarterly. The official journal of the Association of American Library Schools.

   Library Resources and Technical Services. Chicago: American Library Association, 1957– . Quarterly. The official journal of the Resources and Technical Services Division of the ALA.

   RQ. Chicago: American Library Association, 1961– . Quarterly. The official journal of the Reference Services Division of the ALA.

   School Libraries. Chicago: American Library Association, 1952– . Quarterly. The official publication of the American Association of School Librarians.

   Top of the News. Chicago: American Library Association, 1942– . Quarterly. The official organ of the Children's Services Division and the Young Adult Services Division of the American Library Association.

2. They are published by other library associations.

   Catholic Library World. Villanova, Pa.: Villanova University, 1929– . Monthly, October–May. The official journal of the Catholic Library Association.

   Library Association Record. London: Library Association, 1899– . Monthly. The official journal of the British Library Association.

   Special Libraries. New York: Special Libraries Association, 1910– . Monthly, September–April; bimonthly, May–August. The official journal of the Special Libraries Association.

3. They are published by graduate library schools.

Library Quarterly. Chicago: University of Chicago Press, 1930– . Sponsored by the Graduate Library School of the University of Chicago.

Library Trends. Urbana, Ill.: University of Illinois Graduate School of Library Science, 1952– . Quarterly.

4. They are published by state and regional library associations and by state library commissions.

California Librarian. Berkeley: California Library Association, 1939– . Quarterly.

Florida Libraries. Miami: Florida Library Association, 1949– . Quarterly.

Illinois Libraries. Springfield, Ill.: Illinois State Library, 1919– . Monthly, September–June.

Kansas Library Bulletin. Topeka: Kansas Traveling Libraries Commission, 1932– . Quarterly.

5. They are published by libraries.

Huntington Library Quarterly. San Marino, Calif.: Henry E. Huntington Library and Art Gallery, 1937– . Quarterly.

New York Public Library Bulletin. New York: New York Public Library, 1897– . Ten times a year.

6. They are published by commercial firms:

Library Journal. New York: R. R., Bowker Company, 1876– . Semimonthly. The issue of the fifteenth of each month, September through May, includes a section Children's and Young People's Libraries, which is available as a separate publication under the title *School Library Journal*.

Wilson Library Bulletin. New York: The H. W. Wilson Company, 1914– . Monthly, September–June.

Abstract journals

An abstract journal lists and provides digests or summaries of periodical articles and other literature. Abstracts may be in the original language in which the article appeared or they may be translated into English or another language. Abstract journals in all fields are bibliographical aids in identifying, selecting, and locating materials. In the field of library science, the principal abstracting service is the publication, *Library Science Abstracts*. International in scope, it provides classified abstracts from some one-hundred-twenty-five periodicals.

> *Library Science Abstracts*. London: Library Association, 1950– .
> Quarterly; annual index by author, title, and subject.

An important aid in the use of professional journals and other professional literature in the field of librarianship is the index *Library Literature*, which indexes journals, books, pamphlets, and other materials in library science, including library school theses and dissertations.

> *Library Literature*. New York: The H. W. Wilson Company, 1921– . Quarterly; annual and permanent three-year cumulations.

This brief discussion of the literature of librarianship is designed to introduce the student to some of the kinds of materials which will aid him in carrying on his developing professional activities and assist him in broadening his perspective and his skills. The titles listed will lead him to other titles which serve similar purposes as well as to later editions of—or supplements to—the titles listed above. In this day, when the growing volume of recorded materials makes it impossible for the librarian to know all that is being produced, it is essential that he keep up with the aids, devices, and techniques—mechanized or other—and with the developing cooperative efforts, such as union catalogs and union lists, which will enable him to be knowledgeable about his own collection as well as about other available resources in order to better serve his clientele.[3]

---

[3] See Winchell, *op. cit.*, for titles of bibliographies, guides, indexes, and other bibliographical aids in both the general and the subject fields.

PART III
KINDS OF LIBRARIES
AND LIBRARY SERVICES

It was noted in Chapter 8 that no one plan can describe all libraries, for the purposes, form, collection, and program of each library are determined by the specific needs of its clientele, influenced of course by the availability of funds, facilities, equipment, and number and quality of personnel. Over the years, however, libraries which have the same general types of objectives and functions have come to be identified as a group or as a kind of library service, such as national, state, municipal, public, county, school, academic, research, and special.

In the following chapters, each of these major types of library service is considered, and the kinds of activities and programs which are discussed are those which, in general, are developed by a particular *type* of library to serve the needs of a particular *type* of clientele. Attention is given also to certain specific types of libraries within the large categories, such as the elementary school, the junior high school, and the high school library in the school library category and the junior college, the college, and the university library in the academic group.

It is important to remember that individual libraries within any given category will differ in terms of their specific objectives and programs, which grow out of the specific needs of their users.

CHAPTER 12
ACTIVITIES
CARRIED
ON IN
LIBRARIES

Libraries of all kinds have developed numerous activities and programs to meet the needs of their users. Some of these activities and programs are peculiar to a given type of library,[1] but others are performed in all libraries and are considered to be basic to the operation of any library. The activities which are common to all libraries have to do with (1) administering the library; (2) building the collection; (3) making it accessible for use; and (4) serving the users.[2] The number and variety of these activities and the ways of performing them will vary according to the size, purposes, and clientele of the library, the adequacy of financial support, and the availability of personnel.

Administering the library

The administrator is responsible for defining the objectives of the library, developing the policies and programs needed to achieve them, providing the organization, staff, and facilities needed to execute them, and exercising direction and control over them. Administrative activities include formulating and administering policies, rules, and regulations; making and administering the budget; planning and maintaining buildings and equipment; preparing salary schedules; making recommendations regarding appointments, promotions, transfers, and dismissal of personnel; assigning activities and delegating responsibility; supervising the work of the staff; mak-

---

[1] See Chapters 13–22.
[2] Additional categories of activities are given in American Library Association, Subcommittee of the ALA Board on Personnel Administration, *Descriptive List of Professional and Nonprofessional Duties in Libraries* (Chicago: American Library Association, 1948).

ing surveys and studies; preparing and analyzing reports, statistics, and records; and engaging in public relations activities.

Building the collection

The size, nature, and content of the library collection depend upon the objectives of the library and the needs of the clientele, and with these factors in mind, the librarian selects and acquires the materials required to carry on the library's program in keeping with established policies and procedures. The selection of materials depends upon wide knowledge of available materials and the ability to evaluate them and to choose those which will contribute most effectively to the achievement of the library's purposes. Aid in performing this function is found in published bibliographies and lists of books, such as *Cumulative Book Index, Books in Print, American Book Publishing Record, Book Review Digest, Book Review Index,* and *Technical Book Review Index;* in book-review sections of professional journals and newspapers; in evaluative book-reviewing media prepared for all libraries, such as *Booklist and Subscription Books Bulletin;* and in publications prepared specifically for a given type of library, such as *Choice: Books for College Libraries, Children's Catalog, Junior High School Library Catalog, Standard Catalog for High School Libraries,* and *Standard Catalog for Public Libraries.*[3]

Selection means maintaining a live, balanced, up-to-date collection both in subject content and in kinds of materials, and it involves

---

[3] *Cumulative Book Index,* (New York: The H. W. Wilson Company, 1898- . Monthly); *Books in Print* (New York: R. R. Bowker Company, 1948- . Annual); *American Book Publishing Record* (New York: R. R. Bowker Company, 1960- . Monthly); *Book Review Digest* (New York: The H. W. Wilson Company, 1905- . Monthly); *Book Review Index* (Detroit: Gale Research Company, 1965- . Monthly); *Technical Book Review Index* (New York: Special Libraries Association, 1935- . Monthly); *The Booklist and Subscription Books Bulletin: A Guide to Current Books* (Chicago: The American Library Association, 1905- . Semimonthly); *Choice: Books for College Libraries* (Chicago: American Library Association, 1964- . Monthly); *Children's Catalog* (11th ed.; New York: The H. W. Wilson Company, 1967); *Junior High School Library Catalog* (New York: The H. W. Wilson Company, 1966); *Standard Catalog for High School Libraries* (8th ed.; New York: The H. W. Wilson Company, 1962); *Standard Catalog for Public Libraries* (4th ed.; New York: The H. W. Wilson Company, 1958).

withdrawing materials which are little used or obsolete as well as adding new materials.

The acquisition of materials requires a knowledge of publishers; the sources of hard-to-find and out-of-print materials; the comparative advantages of buying directly from publishers or through a dealer; and an understanding of ordering policies and procedures and of practices and policies regarding gifts and exchanges. It includes setting up and maintaining accounts and records and corresponding with publishers and/or dealers.

Making the collection accessible for use—classification and cataloging

Throughout the history of libraries the most satisfactory basis for organizing materials for quick and easy accessibility has been subject classification. In addition to providing a basis for organizing materials so that they can be found quickly and easily by those persons who use the library, classification provides a means of bringing books on the same subject together in one place—an additional aid to ease of use.

The most commonly used system of classification is the Dewey Decimal Classification. Devised by Melvil Dewey and first published in 1876, it is now in its seventeenth edition and is used in libraries throughout the world. The basic plan of the Dewey Decimal Classification is to assign into ten decimal classes the whole of recorded human knowledge. The ten classes are divided into ten divisions and each division into ten sections; and Arabic numerals are used decimally to signify the various classes of subjects. The ten classes are:[4]

000	Generalities	600	Technology (Applied
100	Philosophy & related		sciences)
	disciplines	700	The arts
200	Religion	800	Literature & rhetoric
300	The social sciences	900	General geography, his-
400	Language		tory, etc.
500	Pure sciences		

[4] Melvil Dewey, *Dewey Decimal Classification and Relative Index* (17th ed.; Lake Placid Club, N.Y.: Forest Press, Inc., 1965), I, 109.

In the process of classification, a book is classified according to its subject matter and is given the number in the classification schedule which stands for that subject. It is further identified by an author number, using the first letter of the author's last name plus Arabic numerals. The table from which the author number is taken was developed by Charles A. Cutter about the time that Dewey was devising his classification system. The Cutter Table assigns certain numerals, used decimally, to letters of the alphabet in the order of the alphabet. The title of the book may also be represented by placing the first letter of the title, excluding articles, immediately following the author number. Symbols may be added to indicate that the book is a certain kind of material, as Ref for reference, or J for juvenile. Classification number, author number, and symbol—if any—make the call number of the book. The call number indicates the subject matter of the book and its physical location in the library.

The Library of Congress Classification System combines the letters of the alphabet and Arabic numerals. It provides twenty-six main classes compared to ten main classes in the Dewey Decimal Classification System. Main classes are designated by capital letters, subclasses (except Z and E-F) by two capital letters, and further divisions and subdivisions by integral numbers in ordinary sequence. Further expansion is possible through the use of decimal numbers and letters. The letters I, O, W, X, and Y are not used at the present time but are reserved for future expansion of the system. The use of letters, numbers, and decimal numbers and letters makes possible the most minute classification. Arrangement within each glass is generally alphabetical by author and title. Author numbers are taken from a simplified Cutter Table. The main classes of the Library of Congress Classification System are:[5]

A   General Works—Polygraphy

B   Philosophy—Religion

[5] From The Library of Congress, Subject Cataloging Division, *Outline of the Library of Congress Classification* (revised and enlarged ed. of "Outline Scheme of Classes"; Washington, D.C.: U.S. Government Printing Office, 1942. Reprinted 1965).

C	History—Auxiliary Sciences
D	History and Topography (except America)
E-F	America
G	Geography—Anthropology
H	Social Sciences
J	Political Science
K	Law
L	Education
M	Music
N	Fine Arts
P	Language and Literature
Q	Science
R	Medicine
S	Agriculture—Plant and Animal Industry
T	Technology
U	Military Science
V	Naval Science
Z	Bibliography and Library Science

Other systems of classification are *Bibliographic Classification*, edited by Henry E. Bliss; *Colon Classification*, by S. R. Ranganathan; and the *Universal Decimal Classification*, which is an expansion of the Dewey Decimal Classification. Other systems or adaptations of these systems are in use; in general, they are all based on classifying by subject.

The purpose of cataloging is to make all library resources completely accessible to the users. The catalog points out the location of each item of material by giving the location symbol or call number. It lists in one place, in alphabetical order, all books by a particular author or on a particular subject regardless of their locations in the library. And it provides several ways of finding materials, listing them by author, title, and subject; by coauthor, translator, or illustrator, if there is one; and often by series, if the book belongs to a series. An entry, which is a single listing of a publication, may be an author entry, a title entry, a subject entry, an added entry (coauthor, illustrator, translator, series), or an analytical entry (used to analyze by author and title the contents of a yearbook, an anthology, or other collected work). The catalog is the index to the materials in the library and is the reader's chief means of discovering and locating materials. There may be an author catalog and a subject catalog, but in general, all kinds of cards are filed together in one alphabet and constitute a dictionary catalog.[6]

The process of cataloging involves the systematic description of a publication by author, title, place of publication, publisher, date, collation, and subject matter. Notes concerning bibliography, series, and other points may be included and the call number is given. The subject matter of a publication is indicated by the subject headings, and because all materials on the same subject must be given the same subject headings it is necessary to follow an established list. To ensure consistency in the subject headings used in the card catalog, many libraries follow those given in *Subject Headings Used in the Dictionary Catalogs of the Library of Congress*, 7th edition. School libraries follow those in *Sears List of Subject Headings*. Another tool for the cataloger is the *Anglo-American Cataloging Rules*, published in 1967 by the American Library Association, which offers rules for the descriptive cataloging of both books and nonbook materials.

In 1901, the Library of Congress, as a service to libraries, began the practice of selling them copies of the printed cards which are used in the Library of Congress card catalogs. Most libraries—except school libraries—use these cards. However, since printed cards are not available for all titles, libraries have to do much original cataloging. The H. W. Wilson Company prepares and prints cards for school libraries.

Other activities connected with the cataloging of materials include setting up and maintaining such needed catalogs and files as the catalog for public use, the master file of authors and/or subjects, and the shelf list—a file of the library's holdings arranged according to call number; withdrawing cards from the catalog for discarded or lost materials; recataloging, that is, changing from one classification system to another or changing the classification number

[6] Indexes to periodical and other literature, bibliographies, and catalogs of special materials supplement the card catalog in providing access to all the materials in the library.

for one reason or another; making cross references for the catalogs; and routine activities such as opening books, collating, stamping, pasting, lettering, typing, and mending.

Service to users

All activities of the library are performed for the purpose of serving the clientele, but it is in the circulation and reference departments that the public is served directly.

The activities of the circulation department involve giving assistance to readers in using the catalog; issuing and receiving books; maintaining borrowers records; keeping records and statistics; making studies of the use of library materials; collecting fines; and formulating policies and procedures for these activities.

The purpose of reference service varies according to the kind of library which gives it. Reference work in the public library emphasizes facts, information, ideas, interpretation, and personal aid. It provides, in person and by telephone, practical information to be used immediately, and it provides resources and aid in study and research. In the school library, reference work is closely allied to the curriculum, and students are encouraged and guided to learn to do the work themselves. In the college or university library, the object of reference work is to help students understand the usefulness of basic reference works and develop a facility for using all library resources independently. It has been said that "reference service is the special library's mode of existence" and that the desired information must be provided regardless of where and in what form it may be available, using photocopies if necessary.

The reference function of the library, depending upon the kind of library, includes giving information and answering factual questions; answering complex reference questions by literature searching, compiling bibliographies, and making annotations or abstracts when necessary; maintaining information and other files as required; borrowing and lending materials on interlibrary loan; and giving instruction in the use of the library by conducting formal classes and by giving instruction to individuals or groups on one or more kinds of materials.

In all libraries, the encouragement of reading is a primary objective and a continuing activity. Stimulation of reading and guidance of the reader in choosing the materials which are most suitable for his needs take several forms, varying according to the type of library and the nature and needs of the user. They include direct assistance in the form of planned reading programs, book talks and book reviews, book lists and specialized bibliographies, displays and exhibits, browsing areas and other means of easy access, and teaching the use of specific library tools.

Library positions

Library activities which depend upon a general body of knowledge, attitudes, and skills and involve making decisions and judgments, communicating knowledge and ideas, and working with the public in an official capacity are considered to be professional activities. Nonprofessional jobs, by contrast, are concerned with repetitive procedures and activities, such as clerical work, shelving, lettering, and operating equipment. Out of the library activities which have been described above have come such traditional positions as chief librarian or library director, circulation librarian, catalog librarian, reference librarian, acquisitions librarian, readers' adviser, and children's librarian. An examination of any current list of positions now open to librarians will show that, in addition to these postions, many new ones have come into being. Some of them are:

Administrative or systems analyst
Adult services librarian
Archivist
Area or subject bibliographer
Audio-visual division chief
Book selection specialist—for a language, a subject, or a region
Coordinator of library services
County extension supervisor
Curator of rare book collection
District library consultant
Editor of publications
Field services librarian
Head of films division
Information scientist or documentalist

Paleographer
Map librarian
Personnel manager
Photographic specialist
School liaison librarian

Many of the activities that librarians will perform in their productive years as yet have neither a name nor a classification. In the rapidly expanding field of librarianship the need for a strong foundation of general education with several subject specializations and facility in one or more foreign languages becomes increasingly important; and continuous education to keep abreast of new ideas, trends, and opportunities in the field and of ways of improving and extending library service is no longer merely desirable: it has become imperative.

CHAPTER 13
LIBRARIES
AND
LIBRARY
SERVICES
OF THE
FEDERAL
GOVERNMENT

The growth of the library system of the Federal government has been a logical one; it has grown in size and in range of interests and activities as the government itself has expanded the scope of its activities and increased the intensity of its concerns for the general welfare and for the security, economic growth, and intellectual and cultural strength of the nation.

During the second third of this century in particular there has been a growing recognition that the running of a modern national government requires up-to-date knowledge and intellectual training along with practical political experience, and thus administrators and managers of the Federal government's activities cannot allow themselves to become separated from the main body of the national intellectual, scientific, technological, and cultural community. The result is that some of the most forward-looking steps in the field of librarianship and information transmission are being taken by professionals and innovators identified directly or indirectly with the Federal government.

When the government was located in Philadelphia, government officials and members of Congress made use of the available proprietary libraries. It was not until the Library of Congress was established in Washington in 1800 that a specific library for the Federal government came into being. As the business of the new government grew and expanded, departments were formed and functional divisions and offices were organized within the departments. A library was authorized for each department and, in general, for each major functional part of the department. Independent agencies, offices, commissions, and institutions of many varieties have been established in the course of time, and almost without exception, library and information resources and personnel have been authorized for them. Today all libraries of the Federal government, except the Library of Congress and the National Archives, are integral parts of the agencies they serve and their legal basis is in the Congressional act which creates the agency.

Currently, the Federal government owns and operates many thousands of libraries in this country and abroad—more, in fact, than any other body in the Western Hemisphere.[1] They include government agency, institutional, military, college, university, school, public,[2] special, and highly specialized technical and scientific research libraries. In 1965, a Federal Library Committee of twelve permanent and six rotating members was established to examine and evaluate Federal library programs and resources; consider problems of budget, education, recruitment, training, acquisition, preservation, and bibliographic access; and study ways of providing more effective service to the nation as a whole, including the need and potential of technological innovation in library practices. The statement of the Federal library mission, as delineated by this committee, reads, in part:[3]

> Federal libraries support the missions and programs of the Federal Government by providing bibliographically related information services. To achieve this objective they have a minimum of four responsibilities:
>
>   *a.*   To collect and organize pertinent recorded information, in whatever form required, on the basis of its utility in meet-

[1] *Ninth Annual Report,* for the year ending June 30, 1965 (Washington, D.C.: Council on Library Resources, Inc., 1965), p. 12.
[2] The government, for example, operates school libraries in connection with schools on military posts and bases; college and university libraries at West Point, the Air Force Academy, the Naval Academy, the National War College, the Industrial College of the Armed Forces, the Air University, and Howard University; and public libraries in the District of Columbia.
[3] The Federal Library Committee, *The Federal Library Mission: A Statement of Principles and Guidelines for Their Implementation* (Washington, D.C.: The Federal Library Committee, October, 1966), p. 4.

ing the research, management, educational, informational,
or other program responsibilities;

b. To provide ready access to their materials and to assist
users in locating required information;

c. To disseminate pertinent information from their collections on a selective basis;

d. To make their collections and services known to present
and potential users.

To discharge these basic responsibilities, Federal libraries perform
in varying degrees, a range of tasks including assistance to users
through counseling, literature searching, reference service, bibliographical work, lending and borrowing materials, and supporting
functions such as selecting, acquiring, cataloging, indexing, and
abstraction. . . .

The collections of Federal libraries constitute an important
resource for providing information needed in daily operation of
the government and in the conduct of agency research programs,
both within and outside the government. Interlibrary lending,
inter-agency reference assistance, cooperative cataloging, literature
searching and other forms of cooperation promote the full and
efficient use of this resource.

Increasingly, a community of interest has developed among
Federal and non-Federal library users. Federal libraries support
those missions of their agencies that relate to non-Governmental
groups by extending their library services to scholarly and other
libraries, research institutions, and the general public.

Of the many and varied types of libraries, those which serve
the nation as a whole, as well as specific clienteles, are the National
Archives; the National Libraries—the Library of Congress, the National Library of Medicine, and the National Agricultural Library;
and the libraries operated by the United States Information Agency.

The National Archives

The National Archives "holds in trust the records of our national life and symbolizes our faith in the permanency of our national institutions."[4]

"Records become 'archives' after the original function for

[4] Exterior inscription, National Archives Building, Washington, D.C.

which they were intended (usually administrative) has been fulfilled."[5] They cover all the military and diplomatic as well as the domestic activities of the Federal government and date from around 1770 to the present time. The National Archives arranges and describes these records; prepares and publishes guides to their use; provides reference service concerning them in person and through correspondence; furnishes authentic copies of records to appropriate persons, agencies, institutions, and libraries; offers for sale facsimiles of historic documents and thousands of microfilms; and keeps on public display the original copies of the Declaration of Independence, the Constitution of the United States, and the Bill of Rights.

Although many types of people—such as historians, economists, political scientists, and lawyers—make use of these materials, the National Archives exists primarily "to serve the government by preserving and making available records that are essential for the effective administration of the public business."[6]

The Library of Congress

The Library of Congress, created in 1800 for the purpose of serving the Congress, is supported by congressional appropriations and by the gifts of individuals and foundations. The Librarian of Congress is appointed by the President with the consent of the Senate.

In 1876, Ainsworth R. Spofford, Librarian of Congress, wrote: "As the library of the American people, supported and constantly enlarged by taxation, it is eminently fitting that this library should not only be freely accessible to the whole people, but that it should furnish the fullest possible stores of information in every department of human knowledge."[7] Mr. Spofford served as Librarian of Congress from 1864 to 1897 and under his administration the Library

[5] Herman Kahn, "The Functions of National Archives," *Proceedings of the Third Assembly on the Library Functions of the States, Held November 13–15, 1963*, ed. Mary A. McKenzie (Washington, D.C.: Library of Congress, 1964), p. 88.
[6] *The National Archives* ("National Archives Publication No. 66-1"; Washington, D.C.: U.S. Government Printing Office, 1965), [7].
[7] A. R. Spofford, "The Library of Congress or National Library," U.S. Bureau of Education, *op. cit.,* p. 258.

began a period of spectacular growth: Beginning in 1865 the Library received a copy of each publication copyrighted in the United States; acquisition of the Smithsonian Institution's scientific collection in 1866 laid the foundation for its now unsurpassed scientific collection; and the Peter Force historical library, acquired in 1867, added to both the size and the importance of the Library. Herbert Putnam, Librarian from 1899 to 1939, continued to enlarge the holdings of the Library, developed better ways of access to these collections through cataloging and classification, and provided many new and special services, such as printed catalog cards and interlibrary loan.

In size, the collections today are perhaps the largest in the world; in scope, they are definitely universal. As David Mearns has said, "From every region of the earth, from every age, by every means of transportation they have been brought together; and although statistics may suggest their magnitude, enumeration cannot elucidate their lively resourcefulness. To be understood, they must be experienced, they must be used, they must be tested and tried."[8]

This collection, numbering more than 44 million items, includes Federal and state documents; books and pamphlets in many languages; professional journals, periodicals, newspapers, and broadsides; manuscripts relating to American history and civilization, including the personal papers of most of the Presidents; maps and views; sheet music, music scores, and phonographic recordings of music, speeches, poetry, and readings; photographic negatives, photostats, prints, slides, films, filmstrips, and microfilm; and prints and reproductions of art. Also, although it does not serve children, the Library has an extensive collection of children's books for the use of teachers and other interested adults.

The Library of Congress serves members of Congress, agencies of the executive and judicial branches of the Federal structure, scholars, students, libraries throughout the world, and the general public. Although it is not considered a public library, it is open to the adult public and provides service within the Library in two

[8] David C. Mearns, "The Answers: A Fog-laden Panorama of LC's Collections," *Library Journal*, XC (April 1, 1965), 1601.

general reading rooms—the Main Reading Room[9] and the Thomas Jefferson Room in the Annex—and in fifteen special reading rooms. Materials are loaned only to members of Congress, their staffs, high officers of the Federal government, and diplomatic representatives of other governments.

In addition to its services to the members of Congress, to government agencies, and to other libraries through interlibrary loan, the Library of Congress provides photocopies of materials for research; compiles and maintains the *National Union Catalog*, which gives information about the location of books in more than seven hundred libraries in the United States and Canada; provides reading materials for the blind; maintains the copyright office and registers all claims to copyright protection; prints catalog cards for the books, films, periodicals, and other materials in its own collection and sells them to libraries; publishes bibliographies, guides, catalogs, and other materials of interest to libraries;[10] sponsors such cultural events as chamber-music concerts, literary readings, and lectures; microfilms more than eight hundred daily newspapers in many languages and sells copies at cost to some one thousand libraries; maintains a catalog of newspapers on microfilm; and offers cultural, educational, and informational exhibits.[11]

The Library of Congress is organized into six departments, each of which has a number of divisions:[12]

1. The administrative department has responsibility for the maintenance and preservation of the collections and the

---

[9] The Main Reading Room, opened to readers in 1897, when the Library of Congress was moved from the United States Capitol to its own building, was closed for the first time in 1964–1965 for renovation and restoration.

[10] *The Library of Congress Publications in Print April 1967* lists 330 titles which are published by the Library of Congress or which it produces for publication by other publishers. Current publications are announced in its weekly *Information Bulletin*, its *Annual Report*, and in the Superintendent of Documents' *Monthly Catalog of United States Government Publications* and *Price List 83, Library of Congress*. The Library of Congress exchanges publications with some 25,000 foreign libraries and educational organizations.

[11] For a detailed account of each year's activities, see the *Annual Report of the Librarian of Congress*.

[12] See *Annual Report of the Librarian of Congress for the Fiscal Year Ending June 30, 1966* (Washington, D.C.: U.S. Government Printing Office, 1967), p. XIII *et passim*.

buildings and grounds; for fiscal services; and for protective services

2. The Copyright Office (since 1870) registers all claims for copyright protection and receives the copies of books and other materials which are deposited with the application for copyright

3. The Law Library provides legal reference and circulates legal materials to the members of Congress

4. The Legislative Reference Service uses the Library's holdings for legislative purposes, fulfilling the information and research needs of the members of Congress

5. The processing department, which includes the descriptive and subject cataloging divisions, the Decimal Classification Office, and the card division, also administers the sale of printed cards, bibliographies, and other aids to librarians and scholars

6. The Reference Department is in charge of and gives service on the Library's general and specialized collections (except the collections of the Law Library). Among its seventeen divisions are the Division for the Blind and Handicapped and the Rare Book Division, which has a collection numbering more than 300,000 items, including some 2400 volumes from Thomas Jefferson's private library which was purchased by Congress in 1815 to replace the Library of Congress which was destroyed when the British burned the Capitol in 1814.

Among the special projects of the Library of Congress are (1) the *National Union Catalog*; (2) the *Union List of Serials*; (3) the *National Union Catalog of Manuscript Collections*; (4) the *Monthly Index of Russian Accessions*; (5) Editing the *Dewey Decimal Classification*; (6) the Center for the Coordination of Foreign Manuscript Copying; and (7) the National Referral Center for Science and Technology.[13]

---

[13] This center is located at the Library of Congress but is supported by the National Science Foundation. It maintains an up-to-date inventory of organizations, institutions, and individual specialists who will provide informa-

In his testimony before the Education Subcommittee of the Senate Committee on Labor and Public Welfare in support of the Higher Education Act of 1965,[14] Mr. L. Quincy Mumford, the present Librarian of Congress, pointed out that for more than half a century the Library of Congress has conducted research in library technology in an effort to find the most efficient and economical way to organize and administer its collection. The results of this research have been made available to libraries throughout the nation. At the present time, the Library is carrying on studies relating to the application of computer technology to library operations, especially to the production of machine-readable catalog-card copy and to the automation of the entire bibliographical record. Looking to the future, Mr. Mumford spoke of the Library of Congress as the main store of information for a national computer-based information system which would serve all the country's great research libraries.

Under a grant from the Council on Library Resources, the Library of Congress made studies leading to the inauguration in the fall of 1966 of a pilot program for the distribution of cataloging data in machine-readable form to sixteen participating libraries—university, research, public, government, and school—which are now receiving the equivalent of catalog cards in machine-readable form, that is, on magnetic tape. Catalog cards, book catalogs, reading lists, and other bibliographical materials can be automatically produced from the magnetic tape at a local computer facility. Another purpose of the project is to examine the feasibility of a national communications network in which machine-readable data would be transmitted electrically from library to library. Participants in the Machine-Readable Cataloging Pilot Project (MARC) receive tapes on a weekly basis. The input is now limited to 1966 and 1967 English-language monographs, but later the Library of Con-

---

tion in all fields of science and technology, and provides free referral service to direct those who need specialized information to those who can provide it.

[14] "Testimony of L. Quincy Mumford, Librarian of Congress, Higher Education Act of 1965, Education Subcommittee, Senate Committee on Labor and Public Welfare, May 19, 1965," pp. 2, 6. (Processed.)

gress plans to include some foreign-language materials. According to Mr. Mumford, as the Library of Congress automates its own bibliographical record, cataloging information will be made available in some machine-readable form which libraries around the world can order just as they now order printed catalog cards.[15]

Some legislative measures of immediate and long-range significance for the Library of Congress and for all libraries are:

1. Provision for a new building—to be called the James Madison Memorial Building—to provide space and facilities for added and improved services.

2. Public Law 480 (the Agricultural Trade Development and Assistance Act of 1954, amended 1958), which authorized the Librarian of Congress to use United States-owned foreign currencies for the purchase of foreign publications; for cataloging, indexing, abstracting, and related activities; and for depositing them in libraries and research centers in the United States.[16]

3. Title II, Part C, of the Higher Education Act of 1965, which authorizes a five-year centralized cataloging program at the Library of Congress (the National Program for Acquisitions and Cataloging) and enables the Librarian of Congress to acquire the maximum number of library materials published all over the world which are of value to scholarship and to provide cataloging information promptly after receipt by printed catalog cards or other means. With the cooperation of national libraries abroad and more than ninety libraries in the United States, it has become known as the Shared Cataloging Program. The descriptive entry of each national bibliography is accepted as the basis for Library of Congress cataloging. Shared cataloging offices have been opened in London, Oslo, Weisbaden, Vienna,

---

[15] L. Quincy Mumford, "International Breakthrough, An Account of the Operational Beginnings of the Shared Cataloging Program," *Library Journal*, XCII (January 1, 1967), p. 81. See also U.S. Library of Congress, Information Systems Office, *A Preliminary Report on the MARC (Machine-Readable Catalog) Pilot Project* (Washington, D.C.: Library of Congress, 1966).

[16] See *Annual Report of the Librarian of Congress for the Fiscal Year Ending June 30, 1966, op. cit.*, pp. 34–37. See also pp. 305–06.

Paris, Nairobi, and Rio de Janeiro, and others are planned. The catalog cards for these materials will be included in Library of Congress catalogs, and the national bibliography which supplied the cataloging information will be indicated. In this manner, Library of Congress catalogs will become increasingly international guides to materials of value to scholarship published throughout the world.[17]

4. Legislation which made the United States a member of the Florence Agreement and the Beirut Agreement. Under the Florence Agreement, drawn up in 1950 at the UNESCO Conference in Florence, participating nations remove tariffs on books and ease restrictions on the exchange of scientific apparatus and cultural objects. Under the Beirut Agreement, adopted by the UNESCO Conference in Beirut in 1948, tariff and other controls on educational, scientific, and cultural audio-visual materials are removed.

The National Library of Medicine

The National Library of Medicine dates from 1836, when its predecessor the Library of the Surgeon General's Office, was established. Under the direction of John Shaw Billings, who served as librarian from 1855 to 1895, the collection grew from fewer than 3,000 volumes to more than 300,000 books and pamphlets.[18] Billings also developed a system for large-scale indexing of current medical-journal literature, which resulted in the first issue of *Index Medicus* in 1879. The National Library of Medicine is now the world's leading institution for the collection and dissemination of biomedical knowledge. In order to provide more rapid and efficient bibliographical access to the great volume of medical literature, the National Library of Medicine has adopted the Medical Literature Analysis and Retrieval System (MEDLARS), a high-speed data-processing facility, to perform various functions of literature analysis and retrieval, including the preparation of the monthly *Index*

[17] Mumford, *loc. cit.* See also *Annual Report of the Librarian of Congress for the Year Ending June 30, 1966, op. cit.,* pp. 25–34.
[18] William Grigg, "Medical Library to Salute Index Originator," *The Evening Star* (Washington, D.C.), June 16, 1965, sec. C, p. 1.

Medicus, the annual *Cumulated Index Medicus,* and other similar compilations as well as for servicing requests for special bibliographies on demand.

MEDLARS has three major subdivisions: an input subsystem, a retrieval subsystem, and a publication subsystem.

The input subsystem combines the skills of professional literature analysts and the processing and storage capabilities of the computer. The Library's literature specialists analyze articles from biomedical journals and, according to the subject matter, prepare bibliographic citations using standard medical subject headings. The citation (basic unit-record) consists of the article title, author names, journal reference, and subject headings assigned by the indexer. The citations are then punched on paper tape, fed into the computer (MEDLARS), and transferred to magnetic tapes for storage and retrieval.

Through the retrieval subsystem, citations which have been stored in the computer, are recovered. Requests for bibliographic citations from scientists, physicians, librarians, and others are given to a staff of specialists who analyze the requests and formulate them into search statements, based upon subject headings or other elements. The formulated search requests are then punched into paper tape and entered into the computer.

The publication subsystem provides recurring bibliographies by processing citations for eventual printing from photopositive film. The magnetic-tape files of retrieved citations are used for preparation of print copy by a computer-driven phototypesetter (Graphic Arts Composing Equipment, referred to as GRACE).

MEDLARS has three principal products: (1) *Index Medicus,* a comprehensive monthly subject and author index to articles from approximately twenty-five hundred of the world's biomedical journals;[19] (2) recurring bibliographies—data taken from the computer from time to time to produce bibliographies in specific fields; (3) demand bibliographies, data resulting from machine searches of the computer file in response to complex questions which cannot be answered from traditional printed indexes or catalogs.

---

[19] "Decentralization of MEDLARS," (Washington, D.C.: National Library of Medicine, February, 1966), p. 2. (Processed.)

MEDLARS, which has been in operation since January, 1964, is the only library-based computerized system now in operation for the retrieval of references to published medical literature.[20] As a means of sharing MEDLARS's retrieval capacity with other libraries, additional centers have been established or are becoming operational at the University of California at Los Angeles, the University of Colorado Medical Center in Denver, the University of Alabama, the University of Michigan, Harvard University, and Ohio State University. Other MEDLARS research centers are located in Sweden and England.

The National Agricultural Library

The National Agricultural Library, founded as part of the Department of Agriculture in 1862 and designated a national library in 1962, now has over 1.5 million volumes, including journals, books, pamphlets, and reports in more than fifty languages from over two hundred countries, many of which are on highly technical and scientific aspects of agricultural and allied sciences. Bibliographical access to these materials is gained through the card catalog of more than 2 million author, title, and subject cards, supplemented by bibliographies, abstract journals, and indexes. The Library provides individual loan, reference, photocopying, and bibliographical service to Washington-based and field employees of the Department of Agriculture and gives interlibrary loan service to government and other libraries

It compiles and publishes monthly the *Bibliography of Agriculture*, an index to the world's agricultural literature received in the National Agricultural Library and compiles bibliographies on special subjects for the use of the Department and for public use. It houses and services the reserve collection of the Department of Agriculture Graduate School, which includes in its offerings courses in library science.

The United States Information Agency

The United States Information Agency, in carrying out its basic purpose of explaining the United States abroad, makes use

[20] *Ibid.*

of all the techniques and tools of modern mass communication, including libraries. The United States Information Service (the name it carries overseas) operates 168 libraries, maintains 58 reading rooms, and supports 142 binational centers, which make books available in scores of foreign countries.[21] In some countries traveling libraries and bookmobiles are used to take books to the people. The USIS libraries endeavor to make a reality of President Johnson's statement that "the library is the best training ground for enlightenment that rational man has ever conceived."

Attracting millions of visitors annually, the USIS libraries provide, in addition to reference and other library services, such programs as lectures, concerts, seminars, exhibits, documentary film showings, and special activities for children.

The collection in all libraries contains certain basic reference books, but each collection is developed with the reading interests and abilities of the local patrons in mind and about 30 percent of the books are in the local language. The library materials must provide information about the United States—its people, culture, institutions, policies, problems, and achievements—and must present diverse views on national and international issues.[22] Considerable emphasis is placed on publications in the sciences and the social sciences, but attention is also given to the classics which have influenced American life and thought, especially those which are not easily available locally.

USIS libraries do not replace local or national libraries; they supplement them. In many instances, they have served as a demonstration of the value of public library service to a community and have introduced into the community such library practices as free use of books and open-shelf access to materials. They encourage and assist local librarians who are trying to improve their own library service by providing useful study and reference materials in library science; giving advice on problems related to cataloging,

[21] *Facts about the USIA* (Washington, D.C.: U.S. Government Printing Office, 1965), p. 4.
[22] George V. Allen, "Books and the American Image," *The Atlantic Monthly*, CCVII (May, 1961), 78. Copyright © 1961 by *The Atlantic Monthly*, Boston, Mass. 02116. Reprinted with permission.

reference work, and book selection; and often by sponsoring workshops and short courses in library subjects. They give information and advice to the large number of librarians who annually come to the United States to study library methods and practices on State Department grants, under the auspices of foreign governments, or at their own expense.[23]

Other Federal libraries

In addition to the libraries noted above both in the text and in footnotes, there are other major libraries which serve various branches of the Federal government, such as the Supreme Court; the Departments of State, Commerce, and the Interior; the Central Intelligence Agency; the Federal Bureau of Investigation; and the Bureau of the Budget. These libraries serve not only the personnel of their own agencies but also the staffs of other government agencies, members of the Congress, and—under particularized rules and regulations—the general public.

Of the thousands of libraries supported by the government in this country and around the world, most are parts of systems, such as those in the hospitals of the Veterans Administration, those maintained on the research installations of the National Aeronautics and Space Administration, and those operated by the armed services on shipboard and Naval stations, and on army posts and Air Force bases. Wherever armed-forces personnel are stationed, in this country and throughout the world, collections of general materials are maintained. Usually they are under the management of professional civilian librarians when outside of combat zones and where the size of the collection makes the use of a professional staff feasible.

Beginning primarily as a service to provide recreational reading

[23] Mr. Allen, in his article, "Books and the American Image," p. 77, relates that the Mexican foreign minister once said to him, "The United States has done many fine things for Mexico; you spent fifty million dollars helping us eradicate hoof-and-mouth disease; you have constructed sewage systems in each of our towns along the border; and you have helped us build health clinics and other public works throughout the country. But the finest single thing you have ever done for us, in my opinion, was the establishment of the Benjamin Franklin Library." (The Benjamin Franklin Library in Mexico City is a USIS library.)

materials, the library programs of the Army, the Navy, and the Air Force have come to be in recent years broad gauged in their purpose and mission and thoroughly serious in their efforts to achieve professional standards in their selection of materials, in their provision of services, and in their recruitment of trained personnel. General nonfiction works and various kinds of reference materials along with current periodicals, professional journals, and special materials on international relations, world political affairs, area economics, and foreign languages now constitute the greater part of the holdings of nonresearch military libraries. In most instances there is a close coordination of effort between the library staff and those who manage the off-duty education program, particularly in those cases where a degree-granting local college or university offers credit courses for military personnel on the installation or in convenient nearby facilities.

Recruitment for library positions in overseas installations is centralized for the three armed services in a special recruitment office in Washington.[24]

Assistance to libraries

Notice has been taken previously of the several important activities of the Federal government in service to libraries throughout the country, which center in the Library of Congress. In addition to these valuable services, assistance to libraries is provided by other government offices and agencies as a regular part of their program. For example, the Smithsonian Institution in Washington receives the official publications of foreign governments and distributes them to libraries in the United States. The Smithsonian Institution also maintains a Science Information Exchange, which receives notices of current research projects from scientists supported by the Federal government and invites privately employed scientists to submit similar reports. These notices are classified, duplicated, filed, and placed on computer tape. When a scientist makes

[24] An article by Shirley Havens, "A Day with the Army," *Library Journal* XCI (February 15, 1966), 894–900, although devoted specifically to an exposition of the Army's library program, is helpful in understanding the largely comparable programs of the Navy and the Air Force.

an inquiry, the exchange's resident scientists retrieve relevant notices and send them to the inquirer. He can then check directly with the scientist who is carrying on the research project.[25]

The U.S. Department of Commerce maintains a Clearinghouse for Federal Scientific and Technical Information which indexes and makes available to the public unclassified technical reports and translations generated by all government agencies. The Clearinghouse is a part of the Institute for Applied Technology in the National Bureau of Standards, an agency of the Department of Commerce. The National Science Foundation, largely through its Office of Science Information Service, is aggressively interested in expanding and improving ways by which current scientific material can be made available to the interested citizen as well as to the professional scientist.[26] The Defense Documentation Center (formerly known as the Armed Services Technical Information Agency) is also a valuable center for the distribution of scientific publications and abstracts and reports on technical matters.

In 1895, Congress enacted legislation which provided for the designation of 637 libraries, both academic and public, as depositories to receive free-of-charge publications issued by the Federal government. This legislation also required that the designated libraries make their depository materials available to anyone who might want to see them. The Depository Library Act of 1962 permits the designation of additional depository libraries and extends the kinds of publications to be distributed to include those printed by the executive departments as well as those printed by the U.S. Government Printing Office. Today most departments and agencies of the Federal government have publications which they make available to all libraries.

Throughout the years the U.S. Office of Education has made

---

[25] The results of a survey made by exchange officials are illustrative of a significant problem attendant upon the continuing proliferation of scientific research projects. The survey revealed that more than 90 percent of all scientists making inquiries of the exchange were unaware that other investigators were working on the same problem in which they were interested.
[26] See footnote 13, p. 158, for reference to one of the projects which the foundation supports at the Library of Congress.

statistical studies and reports on libraries, beginning with the highly significant report of 1876, *Public Libraries in the United States. . .* Creation of the Library Services Branch in the U.S. Office of Education in 1937 represented the first action to assign to an agency of the Federal government specific responsibilities in the field of libraries and librarianship which went beyond the making of statistical studies and reports. Pursuant to its legislatively authorized purpose, this agency works closely with professional library associations and groups, state agencies and officials, individual librarians and educational leaders, and citizen groups and organizations in their continuing efforts to improve and extend the facilities, resources, and services of all types of libraries.

The year 1956 was a turning point in Federal assistance to libraries, bringing both new legislation and increased services. The Library Services Act of 1956 was followed by new depository library legislation in 1962 (Public Law 87-579), the Higher Education Facilities Act of 1963, the Library Services and Construction Act of 1964, the Elementary and Secondary Education Act of 1965, the Higher Education Act of 1965, and a number of programs in other areas which gave indirect aid to libraries.[27] Of this series of legislative enactments, Frank Keppel, then Commissioner of Education, said, "Congress has reflected the people's great expectations in the boldest sequence of acts for education in the nation's history. From the second session of the 88th Congress through the first session of the 89th, twenty-four major education measures were enacted." Much of this legislation included specific provisions for the improvement and expansion of library facilities and services; other measures aided libraries indirectly by providing funds, personnel, or materials for institutions which libraries serve; and still other measures offered aid to libraries which choose to participate voluntarily in the numerous programs for social, educational, and economic betterment.

In terms of the organization of the Federal administrative structure, this mass of legislation has resulted in the creation of the Office of Assistant Secretary of Health, Education, and Welfare

[27] See pp. 176–77, 187–88, 200, 243–44, 269, 270, 304–05.

in charge of coordinating all Federal educational programs; in the functional reorganization of the Office of Education; and specifically in the assignment of broad responsibilities to the Division of Library Services and Educational Facilities.

The burgeoning interest of the Federal government in a better-informed and socially competent citizenry and in the extension of more adequate study and learning opportunities to all segments of the national society portends an increasingly constructive and helpful partnership in the future between the government and library leaders.

Of major significance was the creation by President Johnson, through Presidential executive order of September 2, 1966, of the National Advisory Commission on Libraries, consisting of outstanding educators, librarians, industrialists, and other recognized leaders appointed to review and critically judge the role and adequacy of our libraries "now and in the future, as sources for scholarly research, as centers for the distribution of knowledge, and as links in our nation's rapidly evolving communications networks." Through the same executive order the President's Committee on Libraries was established, consisting of the Secretary of the Department of Health, Education, and Welfare, the Secretary of the Department of Agriculture, the Director of the Office of Science and Technology, and the Librarian of Congress, to evaluate the potential role of libraries as components of a network of information exchange and to develop recommendations for action. In the development of these recommendations, the Committee will work closely with the National Advisory Commission and will rely heavily on its report.[29]

---

[29] Activities of the National Advisory Commission on Libraries and the President's Committee on Libraries will be reported in current library journals. The President's Committee on Libraries is not to be confused with the Federal Library Committee discussed on pp. 153–54.

CHAPTER 14
STATE
RESPONSIBILITY
FOR
LIBRARY
SERVICE

In the first quarter of the nineteenth century there was a general trend toward establishing libraries as a part of the state government,[1] and by 1876 every state and territory had a library which was located at the seat of government and maintained at public expense primarily for the use of the legislature, state officers, and the courts.

From the beginning of the establishment of state-supported colleges and universities, the states had recognized their responsibility to provide some library services in these institutions. This responsibility assumed greater proportions and began to receive stronger emphasis in the first decade of the twentieth century, when accrediting agencies included the library as an area to be evaluated in granting accreditation to an institution.[2] The state's responsibility for library service in the public schools is a part of its total obligation for providing public education since the public school library is part of the public school system; and this responsibility is carried out by its central educational agency, the state department of education.[3]

Toward the end of the nineteenth century the concept of state responsibility for library service was broadened to include free public library service for the people of the state as well as for its officials, and in 1890 a specific agency, called the state library com-

[1] See p. 77.
[2] See pp. 262–65.
[3] See pp. 212–16.

mission, was established by the state of Massachusetts for the purpose of extending library service within the state. The example of Massachusetts was followed by New Hampshire in 1891, and by the close of the century many states[4] had established or designated specific agencies—referred to as library extension agencies—to be responsible for developing and extending library services throughout the state.

Thus, historically, the state's responsibility for library services includes:

1. The provision of library service for the state government

2. The provision of library service in state–supported educational institutions—the public schools, colleges, and universities

3. The improvement and extension of public library service throughout the state

The legal basis for library service at the state level is found in the statutes which set up the general conditions under which library services are to be provided, authorizing governmental units to establish libraries, vote taxes, and/or use public funds for their maintenance. State law may also establish specific libraries and define their responsibilities and composition. In general, the state provides by law for specific agencies to carry out its responsibilities for library service. These agencies may operate the libraries, as in the case of the state governmental library, thus performing the service directly; or they may, as the state library commissions do, plan and direct a statewide program of services, providing leadership and supervision in its execution.

The state agencies which provide library services vary from state to state, depending upon the political, administrative, and fiscal structure of the state government. In most states, there are several state-level agencies which offer library service exclusively or as a part of their responsibilities. Some of the state agencies which perform library functions either as their sole mission or as one of their responsibilities are:

[4] Garceau, *op. cit.*, p. 39.

1. The state governmental library
2. The state library extension agency
3. The state department of education[5]

THE STATE GOVERNMENTAL LIBRARY

The state governmental library exists primarily for the use of state officials, and its function is to provide the best possible resources, legal and otherwise, for the operation of the state government and the administration of justice. It may be organized into separate units, such as historical collections, archives,[6] legislative reference service, law collections, or combinations of these. It may be controlled by the executive, legislative, or judicial department, or by a commission or a board.

The complete body of laws and official papers constitute the basic collection of the state governmental library, but it also includes books; research and information reports; trade, industrial and professional journals; files of state newspapers and major newspapers from other states; maps; statements of public policies; a complete collection of the documents of the state government and those of other states; and extensive collections of both local and Federal documents. The library contains, or has access to, regional, state, and local historical materials, such as biographies and papers of the state's eminent citizens and local histories, directories, guides, and archives of the state's own records and the records of local government.

[5] In forty-eight states, the state department of education has legal responsibility for school libraries, and all state departments of education perform some services for them. See pp. 212–16.
[6] The place of the state archives in the state's program of library services has received attention in a study underwritten by the Council on Library Resources and conducted by Dr. Ernst Posner. The study, which showed that few state archives are adequate, proposed standards relating to their legal authority, budget, personnel, facilities, and function. It has resulted in legislation in several states creating or improving archival programs, the addition of professional personnel, new facilities, new methods of preserving records, and increased interest in archival administration as a career. See Ernst Posner, *American State Archives* (Chicago: The University of Chicago Press, 1964).

The services performed by the state governmental library include:

1. Information and reference service for governmental agencies and the courts in the form of bibliographical searches, abstracting, and quick information either by telephone or in person
2. Legislative reference and information service to the legislative branch of government, providing information on laws and government to the legislature, supreme court, and other state officials and, in some cases, to the public
3. Setting up libraries in some of the divisions and agencies of the state government
4. Reference, bibliographical, and interlibrary loan services to its own clientele and to other libraries

It is generally conceded that the staff of the state governmental library should be appointed on the basis of merit and that the personnel should meet both the professional requirements of education and training and the specific qualifications established by the appropriate state agencies.

STATE LIBRARY EXTENSION AGENCIES

The term "library extension" means extending public library service throughout the state by grants-in-aid or subsidies in order to aid, improve, and extend existing library service or to aid in establishing libraries in areas which do not have them; and by such other means as branch libraries, mobile units, deposit stations, or traveling libraries. The state agency which performs this function may be called the state library, the state library commission, the public library commission, or the division of library extension of the state department of education. It may be made up of a lay board with a professional director or secretary; it may be the state library under the direction of the executive, legislative, or judicial department; it may be a library department of the state government with or without a board and with library extension as one function; or it may be a division of the state department of education under the supervision of the state board of education. Whatever its title and control, the primary objective of the state library extension agency is to expand and improve library service within the state.

Unfortunately, the acts creating state library extension agencies have not always included the funds for providing the staff, quarters, and the central collection of books and other materials required for planning and carrying out a program designed to improve and extend library service throughout the state. In the early twenties, some assistance came in the form of books from the World War I libraries collected by the American Library Association and made available to the public at the close of the war. During this period, individuals, clubs, associations, book publishers, and such philanthropic foundations as the Rosenwald Foundation provided funds for salaries, services, and additional materials for the central collection. When state aid was provided it was often for books only. Funds for personnel, quarters, and services were to be supplied by the counties.

Early efforts of state library extension agencies to carry out their responsibility for improving and extending library service throughout the state included shipping traveling libraries to communities without library service; lending collections of books to public libraries; making loans of books by mail to individuals who did not have access to free public library service; answering reference questions by mail; visiting schools, communities, and institutions of higher education to give instruction and advice on library matters; providing schools with collections of books for long periods; classifying books in school libraries; and compiling lists of books for the use of school librarians and teachers. These efforts were designed to meet the immediate needs for books and to create library-minded communities which would want to organize their own libraries.

During the Depression of the 1930s, state library extension service was sometimes the first state program to be reduced. But under the Works Progress Administration, Federal funds were made available for the establishment of libraries under the operation and supervision of certified workers on the Federal relief rolls. Some of these libraries, which were established to provide employment, later were absorbed into county libraries. Clerks and bookbinders and menders were employed in the state agency's central library headquarters and in libraries in the counties. Without these workers, library services during this decade would have been severely curtailed and many libraries would have been forced to close.

Although Professor Joeckel noted in the late thirties that the state's contribution to library service was "the weakest link in the chain of library development,"[7] he pointed out also that indications of improvement could be seen in the new library legislation enacted in some states; in the new programs of state aid to libraries for salaries, books, and equipment; in the increased number of states requiring certification; and in the development of stronger state library extension agencies. In some states, financial aid was granted for multicounty demonstrations to show the advantage of larger units of service.

The transition from a peacetime to a war economy in the early forties brought many new problems and duties to the state library extension agency. Withdrawal of WPA funds in 1943 and the subsequent decrease in personnel led to the curtailment of a number of services. In some states, civic-minded citizens and educational and cultural organizations helped to keep the libraries open. Library extension was greatly hampered by wartime restrictions, which resulted in a shortage of books and other library materials, staff, and transportation facilities. The state library agency was called upon to extend new and additional services to government, hospitals, and military camps and installations and to disseminate informational and educational materials relating to the war. At the close of the war, interest in the expansion and improvement of library services was revived; and national, state, and local library associations and groups renewed their efforts to secure adequate financial support on all levels.

In 1948, under the sponsorship of the American Library Association and supported by many state and national organizations,

[7] Carleton Bruns Joeckel, *Library Service* ("Staff Study, Number 11"; Washington D.C.: U.S. Government Printing Office, 1938), p. 20.

the Public Library Demonstration Bill was introduced in Congress to provide for the demonstration of public library service in areas without such service or with inadequate facilities. Designed to stimulate state and local interest in improving library service to rural areas, the bill called for a five-year period in which the Federal government would aid in introducing and demonstrating the advantages of public library service in neglected areas. The program, under the supervision of the state library extension agency, was designed to aid the estimated 33 million people in the United States without access to free public library service, about 90 percent of whom lived in rural areas.[8] The bill, reintroduced in 1949 and 1950, failed to pass by three votes.

Although the Public Library Demonstration Bill failed to pass, it pointed up the great inadequacy of public library service, gave to the state library extension agencies a stronger awareness of their responsibility for providing library service for all the people, encouraged them to study their needs and to begin statewide planning, and called attention to the advantage of larger units of library service.

In 1956, Federal aid for libraries became a reality in the Library Services Act. At that time, in spite of more than a half century of effort on the part of state library extension agencies, national and state organizations, civic leaders, and private organizations, some 25 million people were still without local public library service and another 87 million had inadequate library service as measured by state standards. Twenty-nine states had a total of three hundred nineteen counties without local public library service—slightly over 10 percent of all counties in the United States.[9]

The purpose of the Library Services Act was to promote the further extension by the states of public library services to strictly rural[10] areas without such services or with inadequate services.

---

[8] U.S., *Congressional Record*, 81st Cong., 2d Sess., 1950, XCVI, Part 3, 3119.
[9] Wilfred L. Morin and Nathan M. Cohen, *State Library Extension Services* ("Misc. No. 37, OE-15009"; Washington, D.C.: U.S. Department of Health, Education, and Welfare, 1960), pp. 4, 23.
[10] In the Library Services Act, "rural area" refers to any place of 10,000 population or less, according to the latest United States census.

Funds, allocated on the basis of the per capita income, were to be spent for books and other library materials, library equipment, salaries, and other operating expenses but not for erecting buildings or purchasing land. The state library extension agency was designated as the administrative unit for the act at the state level, with responsibility for preparing and submitting to the U.S. Commissioner of Education a plan for using the funds to maximum advantage in extending and developing public library service to rural areas and for administering the plan upon its approval. Originally meant as a five-year program, the Library Services Act was amended in 1960 to extend to June 30, 1966.[11]

Congress extended Federal aid to urban as well as to rural public libraries in the Library Services and Construction Act of 1964, which provided funds for grants to states on a matching basis to extend public library service to all areas without such service or with inadequate service and to construct public library buildings. This law, like the Library Services Act, is administered in accordance with the state plan which is submitted to the U.S. Commissioner of Education by the state library extension agency.

The state library extension agency has thus risen to a new position of importance and leadership in planning, administering, and coordinating the state's program of library services, and with this stronger status have come new duties as a part of its new legal responsibilities as well as increased demands for the services it has traditionally performed.

The state library extension agency has responsibility for:[12]

1. Keeping state library laws up to date
2. Gathering and publishing annual statistics on all libraries in the state
3. Conducting research to determine public library needs
4. Providing direct library service to sparsely settled areas

---

[11] The Library Services Act was amended in 1964 and named the Library Services and Construction Act. In 1966 Congress extended the Library Services and Construction Act for five years. See p. 188 for details.

[12] See American Association of State Libraries, Survey and Standards Committee, *Standards for Library Functions at the State Level* (Chicago: American Library Association, 1963).

5. Determining needed financial support for the agency's proposed program
6. Providing reference and bibliographical service to all public libraries
7. Providing consultants for all aspects of library service
8. Interpreting library service to all units of government within the state and to the public
9. Certifying personnel, when required
10. Participating in the development of all types of libraries
11. Establishing branches of the state library (regional centers) over the state to supplement library resources of the area
12. Encouraging the development of library systems
13. Formulating standards to establish eligibility for grants-in-aid
14. Administering state and Federal grants-in-aid

The state library extension agency builds and maintains a central collection of materials for the use of both government and citizen.[13] To the basic collections of books, periodicals, pamphlets, newspapers, and audio-visual materials are added research and information reports; the laws and official documents of the state and a collection of those of other states, of the Federal government, and of local governments; historical and archival materials; and reading materials for the blind and the visually handicapped. The collection should be large enough in number of copies to supply the needs of the individuals, the organizations and agencies, and the libraries which it serves.

The librarians who direct the rapidly developing and potentially powerful state library extension agencies must have strong leadership, organizational, and management ability; political know-how; experience and skill in working with groups—both governmental and civic—and with individuals; general and specialized backgrounds; and training and experience in all the highly specialized areas of the state agency's program.

---

[13] The state library extension agency may also be the state governmental library; if it is not, it must be able to supplement its resources.

LIBRARY EXTENSION THROUGH
LARGE UNITS OF SERVICE

Public libraries began in the city and have always been stronger in urban environments, for small communities and rural areas have never been able to provide the financial support necessary for adequate library service. As has been noted, state library agencies early extended service to these areas by means of boxes of books and traveling libraries, but it was not until the county—rather than the municipality—was seen as the unit of support and service that rural communities were able to have libraries of their own.

County, multicounty, and regional libraries

The first county libraries were established in 1898 in Van Wert County, Ohio, and in Washington County, Maryland, and both were opened to the public in 1901, Ohio preceding Maryland by some seven months. According to Miss Mary Titcomb, librarian of the Washington County Library, boxes of books were first transported by wagon between branch stations in her county by the janitor, and the first book wagon—designed for that specific purpose—started its run in April, 1907.[14] Branches and bookmobiles continue to be two significant features of modern public library systems.

A county library law was passed by California in 1909 under the leadership of James L. Gillis and was revised in 1911 to enable counties to create and maintain their own independent libraries. By 1920, twenty-six other states had enacted similar legislation, and a decade later a multicounty unit was established in Vermont. At the present time (1967) all states permit the establishment of county or multicounty libraries voluntarily or on petition of a required number of citizens.

In spite of the long tradition of county library service, however, development of county libraries has been slow, and as was noted previously, in 1956—just prior to the passage of the Library Services

---

[14] There are variations in library literature regarding these dates. This information comes from Mary Lemist Titcomb, *Story of the Washington County Free Library* (Hagerstown, Md.: n.d.), pp. 7, 14. See also p. 85.

Act—319 counties in twenty-nine states did not have local public library service[15] and only 29 percent of the state grants-in-aid to libraries went to county or multicounty libraries.

The county library may be (1) a department of the county government with or without its own board; (2) a library service provided by contract with an existing public library—that is, an established library in a city is paid by the county to provide library service for the remainder of the county; or (3) a joint city-county system which serves both city and county under the county government. County libraries are financed with taxes voted by the county and with state and Federal aid.[16] A county library may serve an entire county or only the part which does not already have library service.

A multicounty library is established by vote of the participating counties, it is supported by local taxes voted by each of the counties for that purpose, and it is supervised by a library board composed of members from each of the participating counties. A multicounty library district may be created by vote of the people in the counties concerned, in which case, a district library board is established and a specific tax is levied in each county for the support of the library district.

Regional libraries may be formed (1) by several counties or parts of counties or other governmental units which cooperate to maintain library service; or (2) by areas defined by geographical, sociological, cultural, economic, or other factors within the same county.[17] They are supported by public funds from the different governmental or geographic units which they serve, and their boards are made up of members who represent these units.

The objective of the county, the multicounty, and the regional library is to provide free library service to their constituency on equal terms. Each kind of library maintains a central collection[18]

[15] Morin and Cohen, *op. cit.*, p. 4.
[16] Under the Library Services Act and the Library Services and Construction Act, grants are made by the Federal government to the states for the extension and improvement of rural public library service. See pp. 176–77, 187–88.
[17] Montgomery County, Maryland, for example, has three regional libraries.
[18] The multicounty and the regional library maintain a central collection at one place and establish branches in the other counties or areas.

and extends service through branch collections, deposit stations, and bookmobile service. The collection, consisting of books, periodcals, newspapers, pamphlets, and audio-visual materials is planned to meet the needs of the people it is to serve and is supplemented by materials provided by the state library extension agency.

To the traditional services of reference, information, circulation privileges, and reader guidance, the county, multicounty, and regional libraries add:

1. Special services to children and youth through bookmobile service to schools, school service by mail, visits of classes to the library for instruction in the use of library materials or for book talks and story hours, and the provision of reading lists
2. Special services to government employees of the counties and other governmental units served and to welfare institutions, hospitals, and penal institutions
3. Special services to adults in the form of adult education programs
4. Special services to the aged
5. Special services to minority groups

The passage of the Library Services Act in 1956 greatly accelerated the organization of county, multicounty, and regional libraries, for the early efforts of the state library extension agencies under this act were directed to demonstrating the value of larger units of service by developing pilot projects of county or regional library service. These projects were organized to provide efficient and economical service to all residents of the area Cooperative activities such as centralized processing, cooperative use of audio-visual materials, and centralized reference services were features of these projects.

Other types of cooperation as well as of methods of extending and improving services are (1) voluntary arrangements by libraries to provide cooperative services in certain specialized areas, such as making union catalogs and lists or sharing certain resources; (2) contract service, in which one governmental unit contracts with another to provide certain kinds of library service for pay; and (3) public library systems, in which libraries cooperate with the state library extension agency on a voluntary basis in grouping themselves into regional systems in order to make available to their users a wider range of resources.

Library systems

In 1923, C. C. Williamson recommended "a change from a fundamentally unsound system of small isolated, independent libraries to a system in which the administrative unit is large enough to make it economically possible to command the services of an educated professionally trained and skilled librarian . . . the so-called county library system" and stated that "the main effort of all concerned should be directed toward the extension and improvement of the county library system."[19] Recommendations for the organization of larger units, serving more people and able to provide greater financial support, were also made in *A National Plan for Library Service* in 1948.[20] The Public Library Inquiry, in 1950, broadened the concept to one of library systems and called for "the organization of larger units of public library service by consolidation, federation, or confederation of smaller units into library systems serving cities, counties, multicounty or other districts of 100,000 or more people, with total expenditures within each system of $100,000 or more"; a system of state financial aid to support these library systems, and "a state-administered program of compulsory certification of professional librarians to hold positions in public libraries."[21]

During the past decade several factors have strongly influenced the pattern of public library development and particularly the organization of larger units of service, or systems.[22] Standards for public libraries, adopted by the American Library Association in 1956,

---

[19] Williamson, *op. cit.*, p. 146.

[20] American Library Association, Committee on Postwar Planning, *A National Plan for Library Service* (Chicago: American Library Association, 1948).

[21] Alice Bryan, *The Public Librarian* (New York: Columbia University Press, 1952), pp. 445, 446.

[22] The word "system" is used in several ways; it may be a single large library—municipal, county, or regional—with its branches, or it may be a group of independent member libraries working cooperatively. See pp. 183–84.

defined the areas of responsibility of the state agency in providing a program of supplementary services to back up individual libraries and library systems within the state; all standards were based on the systems idea of library service.[23] That same year, the Library Services Act was passed by Congress to aid in the extension of library services to rural areas.[24] In 1963, *Standards for Library Functions at the State Level*[25] gave further stress to the necessity for larger units of service.

LIBRARY SYSTEMS—ORGANIZATION

An important part of the activities of state library agencies under both the Library Services Act and the Library Services and Construction Act has been devoted to the organization and development of library systems as a means of providing efficient and economical library service. The Public Library Association describes three main types of systems and the ways in which they are organized:[26]

1. A consolidated system: a single library board and administrator direct all libraries in an area as a single autonomous unit, usually a municipal public library system with a central library and branch libraries.

2. A federated system: one or more county boards of trustees appoint a system board of trustees to direct and control the activities of the system library. Local libraries within each county retain their autonomy and contract with the system for services and other assistance.

3. A cooperative system: the trustees of a group of local libraries establish a system by electing a board to have jurisdiction over the system and to represent them in directing

[23] American Library Association, Public Libraries Division, Coordinating Committee on Revision of Public Library Standards, *Public Library Service, A Guide to Evaluation with Minimum Standards* (Chicago: American Library Association, 1956), pp. 9, 17–18.

[24] See pp. 176–77.

[25] American Association of State Libraries, Survey and Standards Committee, *op. cit.*

[26] American Library Association, Public Library Association, *A Primer About Library Systems* (Chicago: American Library Association, n.d.), unpaged.

the activities of the system. The system board establishes a headquarters unit, designates a central library to house the interlibrary loan collection, and determines what services the system will provide to its users. The member libraries continue to have complete autonomy and local library boards function as usual, operating their own libraries within the system.

Of these types, the cooperative system is becoming most common. The boundaries of such a system have, in general, followed those of the natural trading area and include an area large enough to ensure adequate financial resources for the needed materials and services. The state assumes a share of the financial responsibility through a program of state aid administered under state agency regulations. The resources of all the libraries in the system are available to member libraries through interlibrary loan, and a union catalog aids them in locating needed materials; an extensive reference collection is maintained, and each system designates a central library to provide interlibrary reference for all members; quick reference service is provided users by means of teletypewriter, photocopy, and other modern methods; rotating collections of books and other materials supplement the collections of individual libraries; service is extended to residents of the system area by means of bookmobile; and a system-wide card is honored at any local library in the system. Central purchasing and processing and other cooperative practices result in substantial savings for member libraries.

The importance of the systems concept in the thinking and planning of public library leaders today[27] and the extent of services and resources which this form of organization can offer can be seen in the new *Minimum Standards for Public Library Systems, 1966.*[28] The concept of public library service, as expressed in these standards, is based on the belief that "every individual has a right to benefit from the record of what is known whether he lives in

[27] See also the amendments to the Library Services and Construction Act, p. 188.
[28] American Library Association, Public Library Association, Standards Committee, *Minimum Standards for Public Library Systems, 1966* (Chicago: American Library Association, 1967.)

a big city, a suburban community, a small town, an unincorporated area, or a rural district" and that the structure of such service should "provide a flexible, operative library network, effectively linking the libraries of the states and nation"[29] and should include three levels: (1) the community library, working jointly with the school library, the college library, and the special resource libraries in the area; (2) the system headquarters, supplying resources in depth and specialized personnel; and (3) the state library agency, using its own resources and those of universities, bibliographical centers, and Federal libraries.[30] Thus, a system would "provide *accessibility* of service through branches, cooperating libraries, and bookmobile stops, plus a *pool of resources and services* in depth and variety, used in common by all the outlets."[31] The concept of systems is no longer limited to public libraries in a natural trade area but embraces school, academic, and special libraries which have an appropriate part to play in making resources available to all people.[32]

Current library literature offers many examples of cooperative library activities and of public library systems. Some recent and dramatic examples of the system concept in action are:[33]

1. Hawaii's single consolidated statewide system of public libraries under the Division of Library Services: thirty-four public libraries form a network of branch libraries with the state library serving as the central library.

2. New York State's twenty-two public library systems which serve 98 percent of the state. In addition to these regional systems, a statewide information and reference and research library program was begun in January, 1967, in which

---

[29] *Ibid.*, p. 15.
[30] *Ibid.*, p. 12.
[31] *Ibid.*, p. 11.
[32] *Ibid.*
[33] See "Library Cooperation for Reference and Research," *ALA Bulletin* LX (December, 1966), 1133–55. See also Public Library Association, *Interlibrary Cooperation, a Sampling of Interlibrary Cooperation Programs* ("Public Library Reporter No. 12"; Chicago: American Library Association, 1967). For an extensive bibliography on cooperative reference service, see Julia Schwartz, "A Bibliography of Cooperative Reference Service," *RQ*, VI (Winter, 1966), 73–81.

twelve libraries are linked in an experimental state-financed telefacsimile network; twenty-five research libraries will eventually be included.

3. New Jersey's state plan for library service, which includes three levels: local community libraries, twenty-two area reference libraries—using already-established public libraries to serve as reference centers for designated regions, and a network of four major research libraries to provide highly specialized reference materials and services.

4. Massachusetts' Eastern Regional Public Library System, which began operation in October of 1966 with more than two hundred public libraries in one hundred eighty cities participating cooperatively. The Boston Public Library, with special state support, will serve as the regional library center of the system. This system is in addition to two regional systems already in operation.

Interstate library compact

The most recent development in larger units of public library service is the interstate library compact, which provides for an interstate library district governed by its own board made up of representatives of participating libraries. The rights, duties, and obligations of each member are set forth in "an interlocking series of agreements." The first interstate library compact was enacted by Wisconsin in 1955.[34] In 1962, the Council of State Governments, at the request of the state librarians in New England, formulated for that area an interstate library compact which is designed to authorize two different kinds of cooperation: (1) cooperation by communities on either side of a state boundary in creating a joint library or in sharing certain library resources or services; and (2) cooperative activities among state libraries. Maine, New Hampshire, Vermont, Massachusetts, and New York joined the compact as soon as it was enacted.[35]

[34] Michelle R. Vale, "The Interstate Library Compact," *Library Journal*, XCI (May 15, 1966), 2420.
[35] Mitchell Wendell, "An Interstate Compact for Libraries," *Proceedings of the Third Assembly on the Library Functions of the States Held November 13–15*, ed. Mary A. McKenzie (Washington, D.C.: Library of Congress, 1964), p. 44.

In addition to Wisconsin, Maine, New Hampshire, Rhode Island, Vermont, Massachusetts, and New York, six other states have enacted interstate library compact legislation. They are Idaho, Illinois, Iowa, Oregon, Washington, and Wyoming. Nine other states have such legislation under consideration.[36]

TRENDS AND PROBLEMS

Trends

At the time of the passage of the Library Services Act in 1956, not all states had library extension agencies; some states which had established an extension agency had not made appropriations for it, and a number of states were not able to meet the requirements of the act during the first year for financial or other reasons.[37] By 1960, however, all states were participating in the Library Services Act, which meant that they all had developed a plan acceptable to the U.S. Commissioner of Education for extending and improving library service throughout their respective states. These plans included:

1. Strengthening and improving existing county and regional libraries and establishing new ones
2. Setting up demonstration county and regional programs
3. Developing cooperative undertakings such as centralized purchasing, processing, and pooling of certain types of materials
4. Making surveys and studies of rural library problems
5. Recruiting personnel for the profession
6. Establishing scholarships for students attending library schools

Statistics for the period of the Library Services Act, 1957 to 1964, show marked progress in the extension of library services:[38]

---

[36] Vale, *loc. cit.*
[37] Thirty-six states participated the first year, 1957. U.S. Office of Education, *State Plans under the Library Services Act, Supplement 2*, p. 4.
[38] Paxton P. Price and Herbert A. Carl, "Washington Report: From the Library Services Branch," *ALA Bulletin*, LIX (September, 1965), 699.

1. 2.4 million people were receiving new service
2. 38.3 million people were receiving improved service
3. 377 bookmobiles were purchased
4. 160.6 million dollars was spent for the extension of rural library services

The Library Services and Construction Act, enacted in 1964, made possible further improvement of public library facilities and services to both rural and urban areas:

1. In fiscal 1965, the first year of Title II (construction) of the Library Services and Construction Act, 359 public library construction projects were approved, including 228 new building projects and 131 additions or renovations. Population served by these local project libraries totaled 11 million.[39]

2. Amendments to the Library Services and Construction Act in 1966 included two new titles: Title III, Interlibrary Cooperation, which provides financial assistance from the Federal government for establishing and maintaining local, regional, state, or interstate cooperative networks of libraries for the systematic and effective coordination of the resources of public school, academic, and special libraries and special information centers. One hundred percent Federal support is authorized for the first year with a 50:50 matching basis thereafter.

   Title IV, Specialized State Library Services, is divided into Part A, providing Federal grant assistance for establishing and improving state institutional library services and Part B, providing Federal financial assistance for establishing and improving library services to the physically handicapped who are unable to read or to use conventional printed materials.[40]

---

[39] Paxton P. Price and Herbert A. Carl, "Washington Report: From the Library Services Branch, Office of Education," *ALA Bulletin,* LXI (January, 1967), 27–29, *passim.*

[40] Paxton P. Price and Herbert A. Carl, "Washington Report: From the Library Services Branch of the Office of Education," *ALA Bulletin* (September, 1966), 773–74.

Public library extension has received support on the state and local level in the form of legislation:[41]
1. Providing additional state aid
2. Authorizing the establishment of library systems
3. Permitting the establishment of regional or district libraries
4. Empowering the state library agency to grant scholarships
5. Allowing the use of state aid for the construction of library buildings
6. Setting up new or revised certification requirements for public library personnel
7. Providing for full-time recruiting personnel

Problems

One of the major problems which faces the state library extension agencies in extending free public library service is the critical shortage of trained and experienced personnel. The deluge of Federal money, bringing with it vast new opportunity and equally vast responsibility, found the state extension agencies understaffed and ill equipped for the many and varied new demands, such as providing financial advice and advice on building plans, interpreting legislation, organizing and carrying out demonstration projects, developing statewide plans for effective library service, giving reference service and research assistance, and developing collections to support these programs and services. Since the consultant service is a major part of the state's program, the need for specially trained personnel in this area is crucial. A study of state consultant services conducted in 1965 revealed that, in general, consultants lacked special preparation for and experience in consulting work and spent the major part of their time doing work for local librarians rather than in studying problems and offering suggestions for solving them.[42] In this area, primary needs are for a careful defini-

---

[41] Alex Ladenson, "Twenty Years of Library Legislation," *ALA Bulletin,* LIX (February, 1965), 125–31, *passim.* See also Alex Ladenson (ed.), *American Library Laws* (3d ed.; Chicago: American Library Association, 1964). *First Supplement* (1965); *Second Supplement* (1967).
[42] Marie Ann Long, *The State Library Consultant at Work* ("Research Series No. 6"; Springfield, Ill.: Illinois State Library, 1965), pp. 78–80, *passim.*

tion of objectives and duties; recognition of the specialized techniques peculiar to consulting and programs of education which offer this preparation; more training in administration, public finance, law, and public relations as well as in basic library methods and practices; and more opportunities for personnel to continue and to upgrade their education.[43]

Other problems in the extension of public library service are:

1. Insufficient funds to support adequate library programs. The state must provide a sound foundation of financial support to supplement Federal and local funds.

2. The difficulties involved in serving large sparsely settled areas. Small population means inadequate local tax support as well as too few users to justify more than a minimum program of resources and services. Larger units of service and cooperative activities are essential.

3. Indifference toward library improvement. In some situations, both library boards and citizens are complacent about the inadequacy of library service. This attitude indicates a lack of understanding and appreciation of the importance of library service, which is itself a problem and must be met through education, public relations, and demonstrations of the value of library service.

4. Inadequate salaries. The position of leadership in which the state library agency now finds itself calls for the most talented and the best qualified personnel which the profession can offer. Salaries commensurate with the responsibilities of the position must be offered in order to attract this kind of personnel.

5. Suspicion and/or hostility toward cooperative activities which seem to threaten local autonomy. This problem, involving personal attitudes and prejudices, is not an easy one to overcome. It requires careful explanations, effective public relations, and skillful leadership.

[43] Marie Ann Long, "Action vs Advice: Conflict in Consulting," *ALA Bulletin,* LX (April, 1966), 356–61.

CHAPTER 15
THE
MUNICIPAL
PUBLIC
LIBRARY

Accurate and precise definition of the term "public library" is almost surprisingly difficult. The use of any limiting clauses in the definition immediately excludes numerous institutions which are generally considered to be public libraries. If the limitation of government control is imposed, scores of well-known libraries which are in no way officially a part of government must be omitted. Again, if limitations of ownership or of financial support by local governmental units are made, numerous libraries which are essentially public do not fit the definition. Many public libraries are not owned by any unit of government, and some receive no support whatever from public funds. The only really essential requirement in the definition of a public library is that its use should be free to all residents of the community on equal terms.[1]

As a public agency, the public library is authorized by state law; supported from general public funds or from special taxes voted for the purpose; and administered for the benefit of the citizens of the city, town, county, or region which maintains it on the basis of equal access to all. Voluntary gifts may supplement public financial support. Public library service is not mandatory in any state, but all states have a general permissive legal authorization for the establishment and maintenance of public libraries.[2]

[1] Carleton Bruns Joeckel, *The Government of the American Public Library* ("The University of Chicago Studies in Library Science"; Chicago: The University of Chicago Press, 1935), p. x.
[2] With the exception of the state of Michigan, where the constitution provides for the establishment and support of a library in each township, the legal provision for municipal libraries is found in the library laws enacted by the state legislature.

Other kinds of state laws relating to public libraries are:[3]

1. General laws relating to municipalities, which may include sections relating to the establishment of libraries
2. Separate acts for each kind of public library—municipal, county, regional, or multicounty
3. Special legislation concerning particular cities, which may include sections relating to libraries if a commission or city-manager form of government is established
4. Special state legislation concerning a particular library, such as that which established the Boston Public Library

In the preceding chapter, state, county, multicounty, and regional public libraries were discussed.[4] The remainder of this chapter will be devoted to the municipal public library, which is supported and controlled by the public.

Municipal public libraries, in terms of their control, are of several kinds:[5]

1. Those administered by a board which is appointed by the mayor, the city council, the city manager, or the city commission or which is elected by the people
2. Those administered as a department of the city government by the city government
3. Those attached to the school district as the legal entity and administered either by separate boards or by the board of education[6]

Most municipal public libraries are administered by a board which determines the policies of the library; employs a librarian; gives advice in the preparation of the budget and works for the necessary funds; provides buildings and facilities; develops and works for needed new library legislation; stimulates interest in, use of, and support for the library; and works with public officials,

---

[3] Joeckel, *op. cit.,* pp. 53–59, *passim.* See also Ladenson, *op. cit.*
[4] See pp. 172–74, 179–82.
[5] Libraries not controlled by the public but which are called public libraries because they are free to all residents of the community may be (1) corporation or association libraries or (2) privately endowed libraries.
[6] Notable examples of school-district public libraries are the Cleveland Public Library and the Kansas City Public Library.

other libraries, library associations, and citizens in providing quality library service.[7]

Perhaps the most significant feature of the free public library throughout its history is that it has been financed from local tax revenues or by a local tax for the specific purpose of maintaining it. This has been its weakness as well as its civic strength. As competition for local tax dollars has increased, many municipal libraries have not been able to maintain a program of services adequate to the demands made upon them by their users. In 1965, for example, twenty-five states were operating grants-in-aid programs to public libraries to supplement the inadequate amounts available from local taxes and to help equalize the tax burden among communities with different abilities to support even minimum library programs.

DEVELOPMENT OF THE MUNICIPAL PUBLIC LIBRARY SINCE 1876

The tax-supported free public library, which came into being with the establishment of the Boston Public Library in 1852, had its most vigorous growth in Massachusetts, where there was "wealth and a concentrated urban population that inherited the habit of communal cultural activity."[8] These same conditions—wealth, a concentrated urban population, and cultural activity—have continued to be vital forces in the development and growth of public libraries.

The last quarter of the nineteenth century was characterized by the rapid establishment of town and city libraries, and the great increase in the number of libraries created an urgent need for trained personnel. Some large libraries set up training or apprentice classes: The Los Angeles Public Library began a training program in 1891, and similar programs were established in the Denver and Cleveland Public Libraries. In 1900, the Carnegie Library of Pittsburgh began a program for training children's librarians.

The last decade of the nineteenth century and the first two

---

[7] See Virginia G. Young (ed.), *The Library Trustee, A Practical Guide-book* (New York: R. R. Bowker Company, 1964).
[8] Garceau, *op. cit.*, p. 38. See also pp. 82–83.

decades of the twentieth constituted a period of marked and constructive effort in the municipal public library's program. Such activities as children's departments, open shelves, cooperation with the public schools, extended hours of service, subject departmentalization, and the establishment of branch libraries—resulting from the work of such pioneering leaders as Caroline M. Hewins, William Brett, Arthur Bostwick, Samuel S. Green, William Foster, and John Shaw Billings—enabled the public library to extend its services and increase the accessibility of its resources.

Branch libraries date from 1870, when the East Boston Branch of the Boston Public Library was established;[9] and during the last decade of the nineteenth century the trend toward branches was well established, aided by the Carnegie program which provided for branches as well as for the central library.[10] "A branch public library is usually defined as an agency in its own building or rooms, with a substantial and permanent book stock, with paid staff members, and open to the public on a regular schedule of hours."[11] Branches have, in general, been either small versions of the central library, offering most of the same services on a limited scale, or distribution centers for the circulation of popular books at the neighborhood level. The purpose of a branch library is to "give as much service to as many citizens in its area as possible."[12]

The first world war gave the public library the opportunity to make a significant contribution to the community and the nation, and it responded by serving as an agency of war publicity for the government; aiding in the Americanization of aliens; and providing library facilities for soldier's hospitals, the handicapped, and the blind. The emphasis on democracy during and immediately following the war focused attention again upon the essentiality of an informed electorate in a democratic society and gave new importance to the educational role of the public library—a role which assumed greater proportions in the face of the educational and infor-

[9] Whitehill, *op. cit.*, p. 85.
[10] See pp. 86–87.
[11] Joseph L. Wheeler and Herbert Goldhor, *Practical Administration of Public Libraries* (New York: Harper & Row, Publishers, Incorporated, 1962), p. 411.
[12] *Ibid.*, p. 420.

mational requirements of the great numbers of foreign born in the population and of the needs created by the enfranchisement of women in 1920. Early efforts to meet these needs included reading guidance and the provision of special materials and services to factory workers and to national and racial groups. These services grew gradually into a planned program of adult education, offering advisory service in terms of reading programs and reading lists designed to encourage purposeful use of the library's materials by both individuals and groups; informational and educational services to business, to community organizations and agencies, and to special groups, such as labor, immigrants, and migratory workers; and library-sponsored group programs on books or films, forums, lectures, and the "Great Books." For more than thirty years, emphasis on adult education was a major factor in planning the program of the public library, and by 1955 the adult education activities developed during that thirty-year period were accepted parts of the public library's service to adults.[13]

The Depression of the 1930s called for additional resources and services on the part of the municipal public library. In response, vocational and occupational readjustment and guidance as well as adult training classes were added to the program. The public library participated in the Federal Emergency Programs of the times—the Works Progress Administration and the National Youth Administration—by providing the unemployed with jobs and training in clerical work, bookbinding and repair, and other nonprofessional activities. The library benefited, in turn, because these workers could perform routine tasks and release professional librarians for other duties. In many instances, library services which otherwise would have been curtailed or dropped completely were maintained because of these emergency programs of the Federal government. In addition to providing funds for training and employing clerical and other nonprofessional workers in existing libraries, the Federal government aided in extending free public library service to sections of the country without such service by making available funds for the

[13] Margaret Ellen Monroe, *Library Adult Education, the Biography of an Idea* (New York: Scarecrow Press, Inc., 1963), pp. 10, 12.

establishment of branch libraries in towns, including physical quarters, books, equipment, and some personnel. Donations from the local community, civic organizations, and individuals supplemented Federal funds and helped to provide books and other library materials.

The program of service of the public library to the public schools, begun before the end of the nineteenth century, was greatly expanded during the late 1930s and 1940s.[14] In addition to opening its own collections and facilities for the use of school students and teachers, the many services to the public schools have included lending boxes of books, setting up school libraries wholly by the public library and the public librarian, instructing students in the use of library materials, giving book talks and holding story hours for children, and assisting teachers in the evaluation and selection of materials to supplement the curriculum. As late as the 1960–1961 school year, more than 5,000 schools with over 950,000 pupils were totally dependent upon public library loan collections or public library bookmobile service for library materials.[15]

During World War II the public library led the community in planning programs and disseminating materials to inform and educate the citizens on the issues involved; extended new services to government, business, and industry; sponsored programs for both recreational and cultural growth; provided services to transient groups of workers; and served as a clearinghouse of information relating to the war effort.

The interest in science and technology, stimulated by the Russian Sputnik in 1957, called for new library materials—both popular and technical—for all levels of readers and brought great numbers of new readers to the library. This interest in scientific and technological information—and in all fields of knowledge and information—continues to grow, bringing to the public library not only new readers but vast amounts of new materials in many forms, requiring new and expanded services, facilities, and programs.

---

[14] See p. 221.
[15] Mahar and Holladay, *op. cit.*, p. 38. Some of these services were provided by the state library extension agency and by county and regional libraries.

Influences on the municipal public library

Called "an organ of social democracy and an instrument of personal self-realization,"[16] the American public library from the beginning has been characterized by its commitment to the goals of promoting an enlightened citizenry; providing the opportunity, the materials, the encouragement, and stimulation for continuing self-education; and serving the community inside and outside the library walls. These basic goals distinguish the free municipal public library from all other types of libraries and have determined the nature and extent of its program.

A number of factors outside the community have influenced the public library in developing programs and services to meet these objectives. Some of these influences have been noted: philanthropy, the adult education movement, war, economic depression, and scientific and technical advances. Some other factors which influence the municipal public library are the state library extension agencies, surveys and studies, professional organizations, and the Federal government through the Library Services Branch of the Office of Education and through Federal legislation.

STATE LIBRARY EXTENSION AGENCIES

State library agencies, created to stimulate and aid in establishing public libraries on the local level, have aided in their development by:

1. Supplementing their resources with loans of special collections of books and other materials
2. Making grants-in-aid for salaries and/or books or other purposes
3. Giving advice and technical assistance
4. Providing consultative services in planning local programs and expanding services
5. Giving reference service

[16] Lowell Martin, "Potential Role of the American Public Library," *A National Plan for Public Library Service*, ed. Carleton B. Joeckel and Amy Winslow ("Planning for Libraries," No. 3; Chicago: American Library Association, 1948), pp. 1–2.

6. Making studies and reports and preparing statistics relating to municipal library programs and resources
7. Providing supervision in states where it is required
8. Certifying personnel in states where it is required

SURVEYS

An effective public library program grows out of an understanding of the community it serves: the educational and cultural level of the people; their occupational, avocational, and recreational interests; the governmental organization; the economic, social, and geographical characteristics of the area involved; and the nature and number of educational, social, and cultural institutions which the community supports. These kinds of information can be obtained by community surveys, which have become necessary aids in planning library service to a given community. On national and state levels the survey has been used frequently and successfully to determine the strengths and weaknesses of public library service in given areas and to guide in planning national or state programs.

Among the most significant and far reaching of the many studies which have been made was The Public Library Inquiry, which resulted from the proposal of the American Library Association in 1946 that the Social Science Research Council conduct a sociological rather than a professional study of the American public library to determine its potential and actual contribution to American society. In 1947, under a grant of $200,000 from the Carnegie Corporation of New York and with Dr. Robert D. Leigh as director, the study was begun "to make an appraisal in sociological, cultural, and human terms of the extent to which libraries are achieving their objectives and an assessment of the public library's actual and potential contribution to American society."[17] The many aspects of the public library which were studied and analyzed are indicated by the titles of the published reports: *The Library's Public, The Public Librarian, The Public Library in the Political Process, The Public Library in the United States, Government Pub-*

[17] Lester Asheim (ed.), *A Forum on the Public Library Inquiry* . . . (New York: Columbia University Press, 1950), p. 242.

lications for the Citizen, The Book Industry, Work Measurements in Public Libraries, and *The Information Film.*[18] The results, proposals, and recommendations of The Public Library Inquiry and the goals which it set played a major role in shaping the program of the public library in the fifties and continue to influence public library thinking and planning at all levels.

The study Access to Public Libraries proposed by the Intellectual Freedom Committee and the Library Administration Division of the ALA and supported by contributions from The H. W. Wilson Foundation, the New World Foundation, the R. R. Bowker Company, the Virginia Library Association, and Dorothy E. Bendix was prepared by the International Research Associates of New York. Its purpose was to help the library profession and the nation understand the extent of the problem of free and equal access to library buildings, resources, and services; give a valid basis for working toward improvement; and point up the accomplishments of many libraries in this area. The report of the study, covering the areas of restrictions on race, student use, foreign-language resources, and regional distribution of library resources, was presented to the American Library Association in 1963.[19] According to the Library Administration Division, the most useful parts of the study are the sections on segregation and on regional distribution of library resources. Many areas requiring further study were revealed by the report, including library service to such groups as the poorly educated, cultural and racial minorities, foreign-language readers,

---

[18] Bernard Berelson, *The Library's Public* (New York: Columbia University Press, 1950); Alice Bryan, *The Public Librarian* (New York: Columbia University Press, 1952); Oliver Garceau, *The Public Library in the Political Process* (New York: Columbia University Press, 1949); Robert D. Leigh, *The Public Library in the United States* (New York: Columbia University Press, 1950); James L. Macamy, *Government Publications for the Citizen* (New York: Columbia University Press, 1950); William Miller, *The Book Industry* (New York: Columbia University Press, 1949); Watson Pierce, *Work Measurements in Public Libraries* (New York: Social Science Research Council, 1949); Gloria Waldron, *The Information Film* (New York: Columbia University Press, 1949).

[19] "The Access to Public Libraries Study," *ALA Bulletin,* LVII (September, 1963), 742–45.

and the economically deprived; branch library service; and discriminatory practices in employment and promotion of personnel.[20]

INFLUENCE OF THE FEDERAL GOVERNMENT

The Library Services Branch of the U.S. Office of Education includes the Public Libraries Division with specialists in both adult services and services for children and young people. This division has as its responsibility assembling and analyzing statistical information relating to all areas of public library services, conducting studies, and organizing and holding conferences and workshops.

With the exception of the legislation relating to despository libraries in 1895, which included public libraries, Federal legislation of benefit to municipal public libraries is of recent date. The most significant legislation for the municipal public library is the Library Services and Construction Act of 1964, which provides Federal funds on a matching basis for both urban and rural areas which lack public libraries or have inadequate facilities and services. It covers funds for construction of buildings and other purposes, such as salaries, books and other library materials, equipment, and general operating expense.[21] Other programs of the Federal government provide funds directly or indirectly for municipal public libraries for research, dissemination of information, demonstration of library service, work training programs for clerical workers, materials, and equipment.

PROFESSIONAL ASSOCIATIONS

The Public Library Association, a type-of-activity division of the American Library Association, has specific responsibility for planning programs of study and service for the public library; establishing, evaluating, and promoting standards for public libraries; and formulating policies for selecting materials.

General standards for public libraries were drawn up in 1933, describing the purposes and setting forth standards for reasonably

[20] "Report on the Study of Access to Public Libraries by the Library Administration Division to the ALA Council at the Midwinter Meeting," *ALA Bulletin*, LVIII (April, 1964), 299–303.
[21] The Library Services and Construction Act was amended in 1966 and extended for five years. See pp. 176–77, 188.

adequate service in terms of buildings, staff, collection, and special services. *Postwar Standards for Public Libraries* followed in 1943. Both the *National Plan for Public Library Service*, 1948, and The Public Library Inquiry, 1950, made recommendations concerning standards for public libraries. In 1956, *Public Library Service: A Guide to Evaluation with Minimum Standards*, covering all major aspects of the public library program, was published by the American Library Association. Other standards published by the American Library Association relating to public libraries which serve as aids in evaluating present services and facilities and guides for future progress are *Young Adult Services in the Public Library* (1960), *Standards for Quality Bookmobile Service* (1963), *Interim Standards for Small Public Libraries* (1963),[22] *Costs of Public Library Service: Supplement to Public Library Service* (1963), *Standards for Children's Services in Public Libraries* (1963), and *Minimum Standards for Public Library Systems, 1966* (1967).[23]

THE PROGRAM OF THE
MUNICIPAL PUBLIC LIBRARY

Function

It is the function of the municipal public library to provide the printed and nonprinted materials to meet the individual and group needs of its constituency for information, education, self-realization, recreation, and cultural growth and for assistance in carrying out their duties as citizens and members of the community. The municipal public library organizes, interprets, and guides citizens in the use of these materials and makes them easily, freely, and equally available to all citizens.[24]

---

[22] *Interim Standards for Small Public Libraries* is designed to provide interim goals for libraries which serve populations under 50,000 until they can meet the goals of *Public Library Service* and/or *Minimum Standards for Public Library Systems, 1966.*
[23] See pp. 184–85.
[24] American Library Association, *Public Library Service, a Guide to Evaluation with Minimum Standards, passim.* See also: American Library Association, *Minimum Standards for Public Library Systems, 1966,* pp. 8, 9, 27.

Collection

The collection of materials, "sufficient in supply to make the library a dependable source for most people most of the time," and selected on the basis of the needs and interests of the constituency, should include books, periodicals, pamphlets, newspapers, pictures, slides, films, music scores, maps, disc and tape recordings, the various microforms and archival materials which relate to the local community. In addition to these materials, it should provide the equipment for using audio-visual materials, microreproductions, and recordings.[25]

Services

The services of the municipal public library are designed to facilitate and invite use of resources and satisfy the reading goals of individuals of all ages and groups. These services include organizing materials for ease of access and convenient use through cataloging, classification, and shelf arrangement; lending procedures that make possible the use of materials in the time and place suited to each individual; guidance to the user in finding the materials he needs and in the use of library resources; and stimulation of use of materials through publicity, display, reading lists, story hours, book and film discussions, and planned reading programs. Other services include providing information service, both to persons who come to the library and to those who telephone; giving assistance to cultural, civic, and educational organizations in finding and using materials; sponsoring cultural programs in the library for children, young people, and adults; collecting special materials of interest to the community; borrowing materials on interlibrary loan; extending library services to all points of the community through branches, deposit stations, and bookmobiles; organizing the library for easier access and specialized service into subject departments and departments for age levels; and coordinating the library program with other educational and cultural services in the community.

The variety and number of library services to meet the needs and demands of its supporting community are, in fact, limited only

[25] *Ibid.*, pp. 3–4.

by the budget of the library and the initiative and imagination of the staff. Services range from the basic types named above to such services as providing equipment for photographic reproduction of materials; short-term loans of paintings and other art forms; and vending machines with pencils and other stationery supplies. At least one study has been made of the feasibility of providing home-delivery service of library materials.[26] Large public libraries issue publications, annotated bibliographies, and reading lists.

Staff

The staff of the municipal public library should be "comparable in intellectual caliber, education, and personal qualifications with other social and educational leaders in the community."[27] This cogently stated challenge, apt when it was made sixteen years ago, is even more appropriate today and will become more appropriate tomorrow as the public library's function of "providing the printed and nonprinted materials needed to conduct the individual and group life of its constituency" calls for increasing cooperation in library planning and library activities in which all leaders of the community must participate and for which the public librarian must provide leadership. A broad general education, some subject specialization, and professional education should be combined with an understanding of the public library's objectives; ability to study the community and determine what is required in terms of buildings, personnel, and materials to develop a program to meet its needs; political acumen; and ability to work with people.

Organization

The organization of the municipal public library varies according to the size of the library; the nature of the community and the needs of the residents; the objectives and purposes of the library; and the availability of physical facilities, staff and financial sup-

[26] "Study Conducted by the Citizens' Library of Washington, Pennsylvania," reported in *Sixth Annual Report for the Period Ending June 30, 1962* (Washington, D.C.: Council on Library Resources, Inc., 1962), p. 32.
[27] Alice Bryan, *The Public Librarian* (New York: Columbia University Press, 1952), p. 6.

port. In general, the municipal public library—regardless of size—will have, in addition to the traditional departments of acquisition, technical processing, circulation, reference, and administration, a department which serves children and young people. The large municipal public library will be organized into many departments which serve highly specialized purposes: subject departments, including literature, education, sociology, history; an extension department, including bookmobiles and deposit stations; departments serving special groups, such as the foreign born or the disadvantaged; departments concerned with a particular kind of material, such as audio-visual materials or government documents; and branch libraries.[28]

PROBLEMS AND TRENDS

Problems

Considerable attention is given in these pages to the social, educational, and economic changes which affect all aspects of our society and to the problems they create and the questions that must be answered in seeking solutions to these problems. The public library, which is a component part of this society—devoted to serving its educational, cultural, economic, and utilitarian needs—shares its problems and must find answers to these questions as they affect its continuing efforts to "serve the needs of the time."

Some of the public library's major problems derive from:

1. The growth of large metropolitan areas. The shift in population from rural areas to the cities has increased the use of the central library's facilities, bringing demands for more materials and services to meet the needs of the new and unpracticed library user as well as those of the habitual user. At the same time, the shift of population from the inner city to the suburbs has created the need for more and better branch services, making necessary the resolution

[28] See p. 194.

of such questions as: When is a branch needed? Where should it be located? And what type of services should it offer?

2. Greater use of the public library by the student population. The tremendous increase in the size of school enrollments and the inability of school libraries to provide the materials needed for study and research have combined to make a student-use problem for the public library. In 1963, the American Library Association held a conference to inquire into the problems attending the tremendous use of public libraries by students and to explore possible solutions.[29] Of particular interest in this regard is the program developed for students by the Enoch Pratt Free Library of Baltimore as a result of studies conducted by Dr. Lowell A. Martin.[30] These studies, revealing that almost 55 percent of Pratt's patrons were students, resulted in the creation of a new position at Pratt, School Liaison Librarian, to develop an experimental program with the schools.[31]

Another aspect of the use of public libraries by students has to do with the role of the public library when and if school and academic libraries approach self-sufficiency and are able to provide the necessary materials and services to adequately support the instructional program. Will the public library need to find other types of users, or will it concentrate on emphasizing continuing education and be ready to offer sophisticated materials and services to support it? If increased educational opportunities and improved school and academic libraries develop in students the spirit of inquiry and motivate them to carry on their own education—as they are expected to do—what demands on public libraries will these people make as profes-

[29] *Student Use of Libraries: An Inquiry Into the Needs of Students, Libraries, and the Educational Process.* Papers of the Conference within a Conference. (Chicago: American Library Association, 1963).
[30] Lowell A. Martin, *Students and the Pratt Library: Challenge and Opportunity* (Baltimore: Enoch Pratt Free Library, 1963).
[31] Janet R. T. Stevens, "Pratt's Service to Students," *Wilson Library Bulletin,* XXXIX (January, 1965), 384–88.

sional and vocational workers and as housewives and citizens?

3. Automation. With the spread of automation in business and industry, many individuals are faced with a necessary kind of continuing education: retraining in order to secure and hold jobs. The public library is called upon to provide materials and facilities to aid the process of retraining and to provide guidance in their use.

4. Increased leisure time. Shorter work weeks, longer vacations, earlier retirement, and automation are increasing the amount of leisure time of many citizens. What programs, materials, and services can the public library offer to help these people make productive and satisfying use of their new leisure? How can these programs be made known to all who would benefit from them?

5. Increase in the Federal government's commitment to education. Federal programs which provide financial assistance for educating all the people are sending to the public library more and new types of users: the disadvantaged, the potential dropout, the nonreader, the handicapped, and others. Appropriate materials, both printed and nonprinted, as well as aid in using them must be made available for each kind of user on his level.

6. The Federal government's commitment to libraries. In addition to bringing new users and more materials to the library, the availability of Federal financial assistance calls for a reassessment of needs in order to make the most effective use of available funds and a determination of what is most needed to ensure an efficient library program for all citizens: materials, services, buildings, equipment, facilities, or branches.

7. The mass of publications and the rising cost of materials. The municipal public library, like all other libraries, has the problem of knowing what to select, what to keep, what to microfilm, what to store, and how and where to store it.

8. The trend toward cooperation. The traditional concept of the independent public library receiving its support from its immediate governmental unit and serving only the residents of that unit is rapidly being superseded by the concept of systems made up of libraries from several governmental units, supported by the several units, and serving the entire population of all the supporting units. The small public library—or any single library—faces a choice between continuing the level of service it is able to provide from the support of its governmental unit or joining cooperatively with other libraries to offer a wider range of materials and services. When to cooperate, to what extent, with what libraries, and how to enlist the financial and moral support of the community are aspects of this problem.

Some of the long-time and continuing problems of the municipal public library are:

1. Shortage of personnel. It is currently estimated that 6,400 professional librarians are needed to meet minimum ALA standards.[32]
2. Inadequate library resources. *The National Inventory of Library Needs* has estimated that more than 100 million volumes are needed to meet minimum ALA standards.[33]
3. Inadequate financial support to meet standards for a program of minimum adequacy. The current financial assistance of the Federal government cannot overcome years of inadequate support on the local level. A sound and continuing basis of financial support must be established at the state and local levels.
4. Censorship. Censorship may be practiced by individuals and/or groups who attempt to remove books from libraries, to prevent libraries from acquiring certain titles, and in some cases, to force libraries to acquire specific publications. Censorship may relate to so-called immoral or obscene sub-

[32] *National Inventory of Library Needs* (Chicago: American Library Association, 1965), p. 5.
[33] *Ibid.*

jects, to the contents of school textbooks and other materials used in the public schools, to religious problems, to political questions, or to racial matters.[34]

Trends

Increased financial support from local, state, and Federal sources is making it possible for the municipal public library to offer improved and expanded services and a broader and more diversified program, including:

1. Expanded reference, informational, advisory, and guidance services to persons of all ages
2. Subject departmentalization, especially in larger libraries, allowing for specialization by members of the staff in given areas; for provision of a greater depth of reference service than is possible when all staff members are attempting to cover all topics; and for an easier and more convenient means of access for users
3. Extensive use of all media of communication in carrying out the library's informational and educational function
4. More systematic study of the community and the library's relationship to it as the basis for developing the library's program
5. Increased cooperation with other libraries and participation in library systems to provide better service and a wider range of materials[35]
6. Greater involvement in the programs and problems of the community and more conscious effort to seek opportunities to cooperate with professional groups and agencies in planning new community programs and in providing library materials and services to support them

---

[34] Martha Boaz, "The Situation We Face," *ALA Bulletin*, LIX (June 1965), 470–71. See also pp. 109, 110 and Appendix I, pp. 366–74.

The importance of the problem of censorship is evidenced by the wide coverage it is given in library and other literature. Recent information relating to this problem can be found in current issues of the *ALA Bulletin, Library Journal, School Library Journal, Wilson Library Bulletin,* and other professional journals.

[35] See pp. 183–86.

7. A recognition of the necessity for helping the out-of-school adult learn how to use the library in order to be better able to pursue his own program of continuing and/or self-education

8. The provision of new and/or improved physical facilities with the financial assistance provided in the Library Services and Construction Act—facilities designed to be attractive, inviting, comfortable, and convenient to users as well as economical and efficient in operation

9. The use of advanced mechanization in the performance of certain library activities[36]

[36] See Chapter 23.

CHAPTER 16
THE
SCHOOL
LIBRARY

As it has been noted before, the history, objectives, services, and problems of libraries cannot be separated from those of the institutions of which they are vital parts. Therefore, in any discussion of the school library, it is relevant to review briefly some of the significant features and parts of the public school system.

The American colonists early showed their interest in education for children and young people. The unsuccessful efforts of the Jamestown Colony to establish schools for both the Indians and the colonists were followed by the successful establishment of the Boston Latin School in 1635 and Harvard College in 1636.[1] The first steps toward the establishment of permanent schools for the common people were made in colonial New England, when in 1642 Massachusetts gave town officials "power to take account from time to time" of the ability of the children "to read and understand the principles of religion and the capital laws of the country." The principle of public responsibility for education was given further form in 1647, when Massachusetts passed a law requiring towns to establish and maintain schools.

The Latin grammar schools with their narrow curricula gave way in 1751 to a new kind of school, the academy, which had as its purpose the teaching of practical and vocational subjects. The academy was not a free school and the realization of a tax-supported nonsectarian free school system had to await the efforts of Horace Mann, Henry Barnard, and others in the first half of the nineteenth century. But even before the Constitution was ratified, the foundations for the public school system were laid in the Land Ordinance of 1785, which "reserved the lot No. 16, of every town-

[1] See p. 62.

ship, for the maintenance of public schools within the said township." The Northwest Ordinance of 1787 declared that "religion, morality, and knowledge being necessary to good government and the happiness of mankind, schools and the means of education shall forever be encouraged."[2]

[2] "The Land Ordinance of 1785, May 20, 1785," and "The Northwest Ordinance, July 13, 1787" can be found in *Documents of American History*, ed. Henry Steele Commager (7th ed.; New York: Appleton-Century-Crofts, 1963), pp. 123–24 and 128–32.

A. OUR EDUCATIONAL SYSTEM

There is not a national system of education in the United States in the sense of a unified system with an official of the Federal government as director. Under Article I, Section 8 of the Constitution—the general welfare section—the Federal government expresses its interest in education in a number of ways: Congress enacts laws which provide financial support for various educational programs; the Supreme Court protects against unconstitutional laws and practices relating to education; the United States Office of Education, representing the executive branch of the Federal government, renders important advisory, consultative, and research services.[3]

Although the Constitution of the United States does not mention education, Article X, which provides that "powers not delegated to the United States by the Constitution, nor prohibited by it to the states, are reserved to the states respectively or to the people," implies that control of education shall be in the hands of the states. Nor has the responsibility of the states to provide for the educational needs of the people resulted in state systems of education operated by a designated agency of the state government, for the states have created local administrative units called school districts and have delegated to them the authority to organize and operate public elementary and secondary schools. The state, however, retains certain important regulatory and leadership functions.

State responsibility for education

Each state has made constitutional and statutory provisions for a system of public education, and although these provisions vary from state to state, in general, each state constitution provides for the creation of a central educational agency and gives to the legislature the power to establish the agency, describe its functions, and assign its responsibilities in carrying out the provisions of the constitution. The central educational agency usually consists of a state

---

[3] See pp. 243–44 for other contributions of the Federal government.

board of education and a chief state school officer, who, with a staff under his direction, comprise the state department of education. In states that do not have a state board of education, the chief state school officer develops and administers the authorized educational program.[4]

The functions of the state department of education have grown rapidly in recent years to meet the many new and expanding educational needs of the people. In addition to its regulatory and leadership responsibilities in the areas of school organization and administration, school plant services, finance, transportation, records, reports, and research, the state department of education has a basic major responsibility for the development and improvement of the instructional program of the schools. According to the Council of Chief State School Officers, instruction "embraces curriculum, supervision, teacher education, facilities and materials of instruction, pupil personnel services, accreditation of schools, and other related areas of service as they contribute to efficiency in the learning process."[5] The council states further that it is "the generally accepted premise . . . that school library services are a part of instruction and are thought of as applying to all schools for which the state department of education has responsibility."[6]

In forty-eight states the state department of education is given legal responsibility for school libraries, either by specific state laws relating to school libraries or under state board of education regulations as authorized by law, and in all the state departments of education some services are performed for school libraries and librarians.[7]

[4] Council of Chief State School Officers, *The State Department of Education: A Policy Statement of Guiding Principles for Its Legal Functions and the Organization of Its Service Areas.* (Rev. ed.; Washington, D.C.: Council of Chief State School Officers, 1963), p. 3, *et passim.*

[5] Council of Chief State School Officers, *Responsibilities of State Departments of Education for Instruction: A Policy Statement* (Washington, D.C.: Council of Chief State School Officers, 1958), pp. 2-3.

[6] Council of Chief State School Officers, *Responsibilities of State Departments of Education for School Library Services* (Washington, D.C.: Council of Chief State School Officers, 1961), Foreword.

[7] Mary Helen Mahar, *State Department of Education Responsibilities for School Libraries* (Washington, D.C.: U.S. Government Printing Office, 1960), p. 1.

In several states, the state library extension agency, in addition to the state department of education, has certain responsibilities for school libaries, such as providing loans of library materials.

In addition to providing consultative services on library equipment, quarters, and materials; compiling statistics; and making reports on school libraries—which are all a part of its leadership and regulatory services in the overall school program—the state department of education establishes standards for evaluating the effectiveness of the school library; formulates requirements and programs for the education and certification of school librarians; provides for the supervision of school libraries; and may provide state aid for books, equipment, and salaries.

STANDARDS

Standards are criteria which are formulated by the state department of education to be used in judging the quality of a school. They are designed "to give guidance and direction to the state's educational program, to encourage continuous improvement in the quality of education, and to inform the public of the quality of its schools."[8] They may be minimum standards, which must be met before a school can be accredited, that is, officially recognized as having met the criteria of quality established by the state, or they may be guides to be used in a school's self-study or in its long-range planning. They may be both quantitative and qualitative, including the library as an area to be evaluated and defining minimum standards for the quality and scope of the library program; the quality and quantity of the collection; and the staff, quarters, and budget. Some standards are applicable to both secondary and elementary schools; however, some states have separate standards for secondary school libraries, and others have formulated standards specifically for elementary and for junior high school libraries.

In addition to the state departments of education, there are regional, national, and professional, organizations which formulate standards for school library programs.[9]

[8] See Council of Chief State School Officers, *Responsibilities of State Departments of Education for Approval and Accreditation of Public Schools* (Washington, D.C.: Council of Chief State School Officers, 1960), p. 5.
[9] See pp. 224–27, 234. See also Richard L. Darling, *Survey of School Library Standards* (Washington, D.C.: U.S. Government Printing Office, 1964).

CERTIFICATION

Certification requirements are closely coordinated with the educational program for school librarians, which is planned under the leadership of the state department of education. In general, states require a minimum of a bachelor's degree, including a specific number of semester hours and specific courses in library science, ranging from six semester hours in some states to thirty semester hours as a part of a five-year program of study in other states. The educational requirement may vary depending on the school enrollment, and certification is usually given for grade levels—elementary or secondary—or it is based on the amount of service which the librarian gives, either as part time or full time.

The librarian has been described as "a teacher whose special competence is professional knowledge about the materials of instruction."[10] That school librarians are regarded as teachers is evident in the fact that they are required to meet teacher certification requirements in all states.

SUPERVISION

The primary concern of state school library supervision is to develop, improve, expand, and interpret the program of school library service. To achieve this goal, the state school library supervisor:[11]

1. Works with the chief state school officer and with the several divisions of the state department of education in planning the state's program for developing school library services, cooperating closely with divisions in the areas of certification, curriculum development, school plant, research, and teacher education

2. Interprets the functions and importance of the educational program of the school library and describes the resources and services needed for an effective program

[10] J. Lloyd Trump, "Changing Concepts of Instruction and the School Library as a Materials Center," *The School Library as a Materials Center*, ed. Mary Helen Mahar (Washington, D.C.: U.S. Government Printing Office, 1964), p. 6.
[11] See American Association of School Librarians, *Standards for School Library Programs* (Chicago: American Library Association, 1960), pp. 37–42.

3. Keeps the state department of education informed about the status of libraries—local, state, and national—and advises on needed legislation and legislative changes
4. Conducts studies and collects and interprets statistics and other factual data
5. Visits the schools and holds conferences with librarians, teachers, and administrators on various aspects of library service
6. Participates in the evaluation of school libraries and recommends changes in standards when needed
7. Assists in developing programs of library education in state institutions
8. Promotes and directs meetings and workshops for the continuing education of librarians
9. Participates in state, regional, and national professional organizations and conferences
10. Gives consultative service on school libraries to professional and lay groups
11. Coordinates library services with other educational services

STATE AID TO SCHOOL LIBRARIES

All states provide financial aid for the schools under their jurisdiction. This aid, granted on the basis of formulas fixed by law or by regulation, may be given for a specific purpose, such as transportation, or it may be given to strengthen the entire school program, allowing the local board to determine the areas in which it is most needed. Such aid may be used to improve the school library program. Some states provide direct state aid to school libraries for materials, salaries, or both.

Local responsibility for education

The strong belief in local control of education, held by our colonial forebears, increased in the nineteenth century as state and legislative bodies delegated more and more duties and powers to local school officials. This belief continues to be held by the American people today.

Through the local school districts, created by the state as the governmental units for educational purposes and governed by boards of citizens chosen by the people for the purpose of managing their schools, the American people have been able to keep the schools close to the community, fashioning them according to community desires and interests, which are limited only by the Federal Constitution—which they must not contradict; by the constitutional, statutory, and regulatory mandates of the state; and by the amount of local financial and moral support which they can muster.

In each local situation, there are many different and often conflicting desires and interests; some are given active and vigorous support, and some are only timidly voiced. In general, the school board has the aid and advice of the administrative and teaching staff and perhaps of a citizens committee in deciding which of these interests and preferences should be considered in planning the school program, but responsibility for the final decision regarding the nature and direction of the school program resides in the board.

In general, board members are not paid for their services. By tradition, and even by law in some states, they are not professional educators; they have their own occupations, and thus for most of them, their time and opportunity to keep up with current educational thought and practice are limited. Lacking this kind of information, boards of education frequently have given the major part of their attention to the tangible elements of the school program, such as buildings, equipment, and finance.

Although the school board has the legal authority and responsibility for planning and operating the educational program, the actual administration of the school is delegated to the chief local school officer—usually the superintendent of schools—who is employed to carry out the policies and regulations of the board.

In the financing of public schools, state and Federal funds supplement local funds, and the amount of money which is required for schools each year is determined by the school board of each district. The financial plan of a school district, showing the services, activities, and materials of the school program in dollars and cents, is the budget, which is annually submitted to the board by the superintendent. When it is adopted in its final form by the board, the budget reflects the areas of a school program which the board has chosen to support and the relative importance it has given to each area, such as buildings, equipment, teachers' salaries, transportation, and libraries.

The responsibilities of the local school board are summarized in this statement of the National Council of Chief State School Officers:

> Within its legal authority, the local administrative unit should exercise all functions necessary for the satisfactory operation of schools, among which are to select and employ properly qualified teachers and administrative staff, to determine the nature and scope of the curriculum, to locate, construct, and equip functional school buildings, to supply instructional materials, to provide certain special services such as school lunches, transportation, and health and recreation services, and to prepare the budget and exercise fiscal functions necessary to carry out the program.[12]

Thus, the school library, a vital part of that program, is dependent upon the local board of education, which authorizes it, provides for it, controls it, and admisisters it through its duly constituted agent, the chief local school officer, who delegates immediate responsibility to the librarian.

[12] The National Council of Chief State School Officers, *Our System of Education, A Statement of Some Desirable Policies, Programs and Administrative Relationships in Education* (Washington, D.C.: The National Council of Chief State School Officers, 1951), p. 14.

B. THE DEVELOPMENT OF THE
SCHOOL LIBRARY TO 1960

Although the basic purposes and concepts of school library service are applicable to all levels of school libraries and thus one can, in general, speak of "the school library," it is important to recognize that there are, in practice, the secondary school library, the junior high school library, and the elementary school library. They began at different times, in different ways, and for different reasons, and they have not developed concurrently nor at the same rate. For example, in 1960–1961 only 31.2 percent of all elementary schools had centralized libraries, but 94.2 percent of all high schools had such libraries.[13] Some parts of the school library story apply to the three types of libraries; others are specifically concerned with the secondary, the junior high school, or the elementary level. The following presentation is divided into (1) a general background of the school library to 1960; (2) an account of the development of the secondary school library during this period; (3) a discussion of influences affecting the elementary school library; and (4) the emergence of the junior high school library.

The school library—general background

The school library, like all other kinds of libraries, came into being when there was a need for its resources and services. When that need was limited and meager, the resources and services of the library were limited and meager. When the need grew, the library endeavored to grow but in only a relatively small measure has it succeeded thus far in being recognized by educators, school board members, parents, and political leaders as an integral and indispensable part of the formal teaching-learning process. As the need for the school library becomes overwhelmingly urgent in the late 1960s and as strong efforts are being made to bring it to its

---

[13] Mary Helen Mahar and Doris C. Holladay (eds.), *Statistics of Public School Libraries, 1960–61*, Part I: *Basic Tables* (Washington, D.C.: U.S. Government Printing Office, 1964), p. 3.

required stature, a look at its history may shed some light on why it has grown as it has and why its current status is what it is.

In the nineteenth century and the early part of the twentieth, when the mastery of subject matter was the primary goal and the textbook and the recitation were the methods used to achieve it, small need for library materials was recognized. The school libraries which first appeared were used little, and their contribution to the teaching-learning process was minimal. Even when the demand for free schools and the resulting compulsory school attendance legislation led to curriculum changes, both in the revision of content and in the addition of such new subjects as chemistry, physics, and physical geography, increased library services were not considered necessary. But in the 1920s and 1930s the emphasis in education shifted from the subject matter to the learner, and in the child-centered schools which resulted the ambitious goal was established of giving to each child the opportunity to develop all his potentialities. Materials to meet the differences in learning ability, interests, and needs of each child were required in order to organize the activities and experiences which would provide this opportunity. Libraries were organized in some high schools, and in some elementary schools a room was set aside as the library with a teacher serving as part-time librarian. The holdings of school libraries increased impressively during this period. In the late thirties, the U.S. Office of Education reported a total of 27,800 centralized school libraries with a total of 28,300,000 volumes, but more than 33,000 schools were still served by classroom collections which were usually supplied by the public library.[14]

Although state departments of education included specific requirements concerning high school library facilities in their standards for accrediting schools, a school could operate without being accredited. Regional accrediting associations also included the library in evaluating the secondary school, but membership in these associations was voluntary then as it is now, and the accreditation of a high school was not dependent upon accrediting the elementary school in the system. Thus, the existence of standards and criteria

---

[14] Carleton Bruns Joeckel, *Library Service* ("Staff Study Number 11"; Washington, D.C.: U.S. Government Printing Office, 1938), p. 21.

for the accreditation of schools encouraged but did not guarantee the development of school libraries.

With the 1940s came the concept of education for life adjustment, which emphasized educating all American youth, preparing them for future occupations and for their roles as homemakers and citizens, with attention to the importance of effective health habits and profitable use of leisure time. Enrichment of the curriculum and the project method of teaching, which were introduced to meet these new goals, called for a greater number and diversity of library materials than were then available. Much of this need for books was filled by two public library agencies: the state library extension agency with traveling libraries and boxes of books and the local public libraries with materials and services which they provided both in the school and in the public library.

Long experienced in providing library services for children and youth, the public library performed many of the services now normally performed by the school library:

1. The public librarian visited the school and assisted teachers by giving lectures on books and book selection, aiding them in selecting materials, and allowing them special privileges in the use of the library.

2. The public librarian attended teachers' meetings to keep up to date on curriculum trends.

3. The public librarian gave instruction to students in the use of the library and helped with reading problems by conducting story-telling hours and preparing reading lists.

4. The public library provided classroom collections of books and even housed branch libraries in the school to serve as the school library.

5. It organized children's libraries and provided the books for them.

6. It gave reference service to school children and maintained a separate collection of reference materials for their use.

In some communities, the public library provided the school library materials with little or no help from the local board of education; in other communities, these materials were controlled jointly by the public library and the local board of education.

Added to the boxes of books sent out by the state library

agency and the services provided by the local public library was the aid given—in many schools—by such organizations as the Parent Teacher Association, which often provided the only available funds for the school library. They were used for the purchase of such materials as an encyclopedia, books for supplementary or recreational reading, pictures, and equipment. In many schools the enterprising teachers provided funds for libraries by holding school festivals and other programs, using the proceeds to buy books.

However, library service to schools by public libraries and state agencies did not constitute *school library* service, and in 1941 a statement of principles developed by the Joint Committee of the National Education Association and the American Library Association, *Schools and Public Libraries Working Together in Library Service*, emphasized the belief that the local board of education is basically responsible for providing a school library in every school and that school library service is part of the school program. When the American Library Association published in 1945 the first compilation of national standards for school libraries, *School Libraries for Today and Tomorrow*,[15] it reiterated this belief in the responsibility of the board of education to provide school library service. These standards, both quantitative and qualitative, covered services to students and faculty, library personnel, and book collections.

The American Library Association had early shown its interest in school libraries by forming the School Library Section in 1914. The School and Children's Library Division was established in 1936, and in 1951 the American Association of School Librarians was formed as a division of the ALA. In 1960, it became also a department of the National Education Association. "Planning programs of study and service for the improvement and extension of library services in elementary and secondary schools as a means of strengthening the educational program" has been one of this division's stated purposes. State and local associations of school librarians have also worked toward this goal.

In 1937 the Library Services Branch of the U.S. Office of Education was established with a school library specialist on its staff.

[15] See p. 227.

This Federal agency has contributed to the development of school libraries through statistical and research studies, conferences, and institutes, which have pointed up the needs of school libraries and served as guides to those who were endeavoring to develop and improve school library service.

In the mid-1950s, the program of the public school was severely criticized; the objectives of education were questioned; and the content of the curriculum and the methods of teaching were investigated by parents, school boards, and interested laymen. A return to the idea of subject mastery and intellectual achievement was demanded. Reading ability, individual instruction, independent study, and the necessity for developing each student to the maximum of his ability were emphasized. Science, mathematics, and modern foreign languages were given precedence in the curriculum, and increased efforts were made to identify and educate the gifted student. New instructional materials, media, and services were urgently needed. The school library was the logical source of these materials, media, and services, but in too many instances, either there was not a library or it was unable to provide them. An examination of the status of school libraries as late as 1964 reveals an estimated shortage of more than 200 million volumes in schools with centralized libraries when measured by ALA standards.[16]

Secondary school libraries

Several important factors contributed to the development of the high school library but for one reason or another did not aid the growth of elementary school libraries.

Among the factors which have contributed strongly to the development of high school libraries are (1) college admission requirements; (2) the insistence on higher standards of secondary school library service by regional accrediting associations, national professional organizations, and state departments of education; and (3) studies which have underscored the very great necessity for quality library service in the secondary school program.

The influence of the regional accrediting associations began

[16] *National Inventory of Library Needs, op. cit.,* p. 24.

early in the story of secondary education. The period following the Civil War was characterized by the tremendous expansion of secondary education to meet the changing needs of a growing nation. "Between 1870 and 1890 the number of high schools quintupled. Twenty years later the 2,500 high schools existing in 1890 had become 10,000 and in another two decades, 24,000."[17] Because of geographic differences and distances, schools developed independently and the number of offerings changed constantly. The length of the high school course and the nature and content of the curriculum were matters of great concern to educators, and the definition of secondary school and college had to be made clear.

Toward the end of the nineteenth century, groups of colleges began to form regional associations to improve the quality of education in both the secondary schools and the colleges. The New England Association of Colleges and Secondary Schools was founded in 1885; the Middle States Association of Colleges and Secondary Schools, in 1889; and the North Central Association of Colleges and Secondary Schools and the Southern Association of Colleges and Secondary Schools in 1895.[18] Some secondary schools were brought into membership in these organizations.

One of the greatest problems claiming the attention of educators was the standardization of college entrance requirements. At the first meeting of the North Central Association, in 1896, it was established that a secondary school, in order to receive recognition, should have at least three things:[19] (1) well-arranged courses of study, the last four years of which would be devoted chiefly to Latin, Greek, French, German, history, algebra, geometry, and science; (2) a sufficient number of well-trained teachers; and (3) sufficient equipment consisting of a library, suitable rooms, and a laboratory or laboratories.

In 1900 the Middle States Association organized the College

[17] John S. Brubacher and Willis Rudy, *Higher Education in Transition, An American History: 1635–1956* (New York: Harper & Row, Publishers, Incorporated, 1958), p. 359.
[18] The Northwest Association of Colleges and Higher Schools was established in 1917 and the Western Association of Colleges in 1924. (See also pp. 262–63).
[19] Richard J. Jesse, "What Constitutes a College and What Constitutes a High School," *Proceedings of the First Annual Meeting of the North Central Association* (Chicago: The Association, 1896), p. 26.

Entrance Examination Board to secure uniformity in the requirements and examinations for college admission, and the first examinations were given in 1901. That same year the North Central Association established a Commission on Accredited Schools and began
to work on standards for secondary schools. The standards, agreed
upon in 1902, included the statement that "library facilities should
be adequate to the needs of instruction."[20] Since that time the library
has been included in the areas to be evaluated in the accrediting
of a secondary school for admission to membership in the association,
the criteria for the library showing a trend toward better facilities
with each revision of the standards.[21] The first list of accredited
secondary schools was published by the North Central Association
in 1904.

The Southern Association began the accrediting of secondary
schools in 1912, the Northwest Association in 1918, the Middle
States Association in 1921, and the New England Association in
1952.[22] The Western College Association does not admit secondary
schools to membership, and only the Southern Association admits
elementary schools.

Other educational agencies became interested in high school
libraries, and in 1915 the Library Committee of the Department
of Secondary Education of the National Education Association was
formed to investigate actual conditions of high school libraries. The
final report of this committee, "Standard Library Organization and
Equipment for Secondary Schools of Different Sizes,"[23] giving practical working standards for both junior high schools and high
schools, was presented by the chairman, C. C. Certain, to the National Education Association at its annual meeting in 1918 and

[20] William E. McVey, "Origin and Development of Criteria for the Accreditation of Secondary Schools in the North Central Territory," *The North
Central Association Quarterly*, XVII (April, 1944), 286.
[21] *Ibid.*, p. 291.
[22] John R. Mayor and Willis G. Swartz, *Accreditation in Teacher Education:
Its Influence on Higher Education* (Washington, D.C.: National Commission
on Accrediting, 1965), p. 36.
[23] "Standard Library Organization and Equipment for Secondary School Libraries of Different Sizes, Report of the Certain Committee on Library Organization and Equipment," National Education Association of the United States,
Addresses and Proceedings of the 56th Annual Meeting (Washington, D.C.:
National Education Association, 1918), pp. 691–719.

adopted at that time as its official standards for high school library development. It was approved also by the education committee of the American Library Association. The Certain Report, or the Certain Standards—as they were called—included recommendations regarding quarters, staff, collection, budget, and supervision. They continued to influence all school library standards for more than twenty years.[24]

Further progress in the matter of standards was made in 1933 with the organization of the Cooperative Study of Secondary School Standards. Its Executive Committee formulated in the following year a concise statement of desirable principles for secondary schools and included library service. These principles emphasized that the library should be an educational center, not just a collection of books; that it should provide the reading and reference facilities needed for an effective library program; and that books and other materials should be chosen in light of the specific aims and purposes of the school.[25]

Interest in the principles relating to school libraries was so great that they were published separately in 1939 under the title *Evaluation of a Secondary School Library*, sponsored jointly by the American Library Association and the Cooperative Study of Secondary School Standards. Specific quantitative measures were given; and services for teachers, administrators, and students were enumerated. In 1940, the Cooperative Study of Secondary School Standards published *Evaluative Criteria*. These criteria, which were revised in 1950 and 1960, are based on the principle that a school should be evaluated in terms of its philosophy and objectives. They provide material for a school's self-study and include the library as an area to be evaluated. Since 1940 the regional accrediting associations have used *Evaluative Criteria*. Both the Middle States Association

---

[24] See Frances Lander Spain, "The Application of School Library Standards," National Society for the Study of Education, *Forty-Second Yearbook, Part II: The Library in General Education* (Chicago: The Department of Education, University of Chicago, 1943), pp. 269–92.
[25] Cooperative Study of Secondary School Standards, *Evaluation of Secondary Schools: General Report* (Washington, D.C.: Cooperative Study of Secondary School Standards, 1939), pp. 45–46. (In 1959 the Cooperative Study of Secondary School Standards became the National Study of Secondary School Evaluation.) See also footnote 35, p. 231 and footnote 43, p. 236.

and the Southern Association require schools seeking membership to conduct a self-study using *Evaluative Criteria*, and other associations recommend them for the institution's self-study and self-evaluation.

In 1945, the American Library Association's standards for school libraries, *School Libraries for Today and Tomorrow*,[26] were added to those of the state departments of education and the regional associations in an effort to further improve the quality of school library resources and services.

Additional aid to high schools in studying their programs and in long-range planning was given by a self-study instrument, *A Planning Guide for the High School Library*,[27] published in 1951 by the ALA, which provided a means of measuring the adequacy of each area of the school library program.

In 1958, the National Education Association conducted a study to determine to what extent high school teachers were making use of the school library, the contribution of the library to the instructional program, the types of library users, and the areas needing development. The findings of this study, *The Secondary School Teacher and Library Services*, showed that "the school library has attained a position of widely acknowledged usefulness and respect among secondary school teachers" and that they "believe that acquisition of skill in the use of the library should be a fundamental part of education for American youth."[28]

The elementary school library

Efforts on behalf of elementary school libraries have always been fewer and less successful than those for secondary school libraries. Even though the state departments of education included library materials and services in their criteria for a quality elemen-

---

[26] American Library Association, Committee on Postwar Planning, *School Libraries for Today and Tomorrow; Functions and Standards* (Chicago: American Library Association, 1945).

[27] Frances Henne and Others, *A Planning Guide for the High School Library Program* (Chicago: American Library Association, 1951).

[28] National Education Association of the United States, Research Division, *The Secondary-School Teacher and Library Services* ("Research Monograph #MI"; Washington, D.C.: National Education Association of the United States, 1958), p. 24.

tary school, it was the responsibility of the local board of education to provide them. But lacking a motivation of comparable urgency to that of meeting college admission requirements, local school boards too often failed to find a place in the budget for the elementary school library. The services provided by the traveling libraries or the boxes of books sent out by the state library agency or the public libraries were, in too many instances, considered adequate to the needs of the elementary school.

Interest in libraries for elementary schools grew, however, in spite of limited local funds and support; and in 1925 a Joint Committee of the Department of Elementary School Principals of the National Education Association and the School Libraries Section of the ALA, under the chairmanship of C. C. Certain, made a study of the conditions of elementary school libraries and drew up standards for them. The "Report of the Joint Committee on Elementary School Library Standards"[29] defined the purposes of, and established standards for, the organization and maintenance of a library in elementary schools with minimum enrollments of 500 or maximum enrollments of 2,000. These standards relating to the aim, scope, collection, staff, use, organization, and supervision of elementary school libraries were circulated widely and were very helpful in arousing interest and support for elementary school libraries and in providing guidance for those who were planning to establish them. The ALA standards, *School Libraries for Today and Tomorrow*, recognized the importance of the elementary school library by presenting both quantitative and qualitative standards for elementary as well as secondary school library programs.

The need for library materials to meet the demands of the new methods of teaching in the forties stimulated increasing recognition on the part of educational leaders, school administrators, librarians, and teachers of the importance of the elementary school library in the whole educational program and produced a long-de-

[29] "Report of the Joint Committee on Elementary School Library Standards," National Education Association of the United States, Department of Elementary School Principals, *The Elementary School Principalship—A Study of Its Instructional and Administrative Aspects* ("Its Fourth Yearbook"; Washington, D.C.: National Education Association, 1922), pp. 326–59.

layed interest in improving these libraries. In some states new policies, regulations, and criteria for accrediting high schools were drawn up, requiring that elementary schools in the same system have the same letter rating as that given to the high school. Educational organizations and teachers' groups prepared documents to be used by elementary schools in studying and improving their library situations, covering books, selection aids, pupil use of the library, and the librarian's training.

The regional accrediting associations had only an indirect influence on the elementary school library. Some associations required that a high school have the highest accreditation granted by the state agency before it could apply for membership in the regional association, but this condition benefited the elementary school and its library only if the state agency required the same accreditation for both the elementary and the high school. During the period from 1948 to 1951, the Southern Association of Colleges and Secondary Schools conducted "The Cooperative Study in Elementary Education," and in 1952 the association created the Cooperative Program in Elementary Education as a service project, an action which provided for the affiliation of elementary schools with the association through membership in the cooperative program.[30]

In spite of the efforts of many educators, librarians, and professional organizations to improve the conditions of the elementary school library, the beginning of the 1960s found it still the most neglected part of the educational program, with more than 9,860,000 elementary school children attending schools which did not have centralized libraries.[31]

The junior high school library

The strictly localized approach to school development in the Colonies and emphasis on the same approach later in the states re-

[30] "Committee on Elementary Education, Cooperative Program in Elementary Education," *Proceedings of the Sixty-Ninth Annual Meeting of the Southern Association of Colleges and Schools, November 30–December 3, 1964* (Atlanta, Ga.: Southern Association of Colleges and Schools, 1965), p. 236.
[31] Mahar and Holladay, *op. cit.*, p. 8. 83.8 percent of all elementary schools—including those with centralized libraries—were not served by school librarians. *Ibid.*, p. 43.

sulted in greatly varying forms of school organization. In general, grades one to six have belonged to the elementary school and grades nine to twelve to the high school; but grades seven and eight, not having a fixed place in the administrative organization, have been sometimes a part of the elementary school and sometimes a part of the high school. Library facilities for these grades have been those of the school to which they were attached, and from the above discussions, it would seem to be clear that those attached to high schools have had more and better library advantages than those attached to elementary schools. The library story of the separate junior high school—and the library facilities and services provided for the unique program of the junior high school, regardless of whether or not it is a separate administrative unit—deserves attention; and it is, of course, a part of the story of the separate junior high school which it serves.

At the turn of the century while secondary school organization and curriculum were being studied, questions were raised regarding the nature of the individual being educated; his needs at various stages of his physical, educational, and social development; and the wide range of differences and interests among individual pupils in the adolescent years. Educators became increasingly interested in the nature of adolescence and in the problems of individual differences as they affected the educational program. Some school systems developed before 1900 various plans of organization to take care of the junior high school years, but it was not until 1909–1910 that separate three-year junior high schools appeared. By the end of the second decade of the twentieth century, some eight-hundred junior high schools had been organized; however, not all included grades seven to nine. Even though educators were honestly concerned about the problems of preadolescence, generally the first junior high schools were established as a result of overcrowded conditions and not in response to the needs of the early adolescent years.

In the first two decades of the twentieth century, the major functions of the junior high school were to keep pupils in school and to enable college-bound students to take courses earlier and thus qualify for college earlier. In the 1930s, the importance of the particular needs of the period of early adolescence for the junior high school program grew steadily, and by 1940 early adolescence became the focal point around which to develop the junior high school educational program. The number of separate junior high schools continued to grow rapidly, and during the next two decades the emphasis came to be placed on the educational function rather than on the organizational pattern. Thus, the junior high school was seen as an educational program, with organization, administration, buildings, and other features being considered important only to the extent to which they contributed to that program.[32] By 1963, approximately 60 percent of boys and girls in grades seven, eight, and nine were in junior high schools.[33]

State departments of education have evaluated and accredited the junior high school for many years, at first as a part of a six-year high school, but more recently as a separate unit. Of the regional accrediting associations, thus far only the Southern Association of Colleges and Schools accredits the separate junior high school. This program of accreditation began in 1954, and in 1958 the association published *The Junior High School Program*[34] to provide basic information to school boards, school administrators, college professors, and college students about a junior high school program based on the unique needs of preadolescence and early adolescence. All the systems for judging the quality of junior high schools which have been developed by individual schools, state educational associations, and state departments of education include the library as an area to be evaluated. In 1963, to meet the specific needs of the junior high school, the National Study of Secondary School Evaluation published the *Evaluative Criteria for Junior High Schools*,[35] of which the section on "Instructional Materials—Library and Audio-

[32] Nelson L. Bossing and Roscoe V. Cramer, *The Junior High School*, (Boston: Houghton Mifflin Company, 1965), p. 14.

[33] Calvin Grieder and Stephen Romine, *American Education; An Introduction to the Teaching Profession* (3d ed.; New York: The Ronald Press Company, 1965), p. 292.

[34] The Southern Association of Colleges and Secondary Schools, *The Junior High School Program* (Atlanta, Ga.: The Southern Association of Colleges and Secondary Schools, 1958).

[35] National Study of Secondary School Evaluation, *Evaluative Criteria for Junior High Schools* (Washington, D.C.: National Study of Secondary School Evaluation, 1963). See pp. 226–27 regarding the wide use of this agency's *Evaluative Criteria* for secondary school evaluation.

Visual" provides criteria for evaluating staff, organization and management, materials, physical facilities, and services.

It is generally agreed by educators that the primary function of the junior high school is to offer an educational program which will provide for the unique physical, social, emotional, and intellectual needs of the early adolescent age group it serves. Such a program should offer exploratory experiences both in courses of instruction and in extraclass activities, give attention to individual differences and interests, offer experiences which aid the early adolescent in making the transition from childhood to young adulthood, help develop problem-solving skills, and provide articulation with the elementary and the secondary school. Brimm, in *The Junior High School*, states that:

> The very nature of the junior high school program makes the library essential. It would be rather difficult to conceive of a program of transition that did not provide adequate facilities for the young student to explore his wide range of interests in a well-stocked library. . . . An instructional program can be broad only if its resources are broad. . . . If individual differences are to be met in the classroom, there must be a wide range of books to provide opportunities for their various levels of ability.[36]

Efforts to develop the junior high school into a distinctly different school have not always been successful. Even after its functions were clearly defined and found to be different from the elementary and the secondary school, officials have been reluctant to change the program from one patterned after the senior high school college-oriented program. Its purpose has not always been understood by the public, it has been handicapped by a lack of specially prepared teachers, and it is often improperly and inadequately housed in an old elementary or high school building. Even so in the past two decades, the junior high school has begun to achieve new importance and stature. The enormous growth in school enrollment and the trend toward consolidation of school districts have

[36] R. P. Brimm, *The Junior High School* ("The Library of Education"; Washington, D.C.: The Center for Applied Research in Education, Inc., 1963), p. 47.

provided both the need and the opportunity to reorganize the school program. New research in the growth and development of preadolescents and adolescents, increased attention in professional literature to junior high school education, and a stronger emphasis on the special preparation of professional personnel point to a growing acceptance of the unique function of the junior high school program. Such instruments of evaluation as *Evaluative Criteria for Junior High Schools* are evidence that attention is finally being given to a critical appraisal of the junior high school's functions and achievements in relation to the needs of the early adolescent years it is supposed to serve.[37]

There is, however, a wide gap between what ought to be and what actually is. For example, of 5,705 separate junior high schools reported in *Statistics of Public School Libraries, 1960–61*, 86.4 percent had centralized libraries; but 27.4 percent of these libraries were not served by a school librarian, and the total number of volumes per pupil was only 4.93[38] compared with the minimum of 10 volumes per pupil recommended in the *Standards for School Library Programs*.

[37] Bossing and Cramer, *op. cit.*, p. 433.
[38] Mahar and Holladay, *op. cit.*, pp. 3, 32, 43. In the 1,645 school districts with enrollments of from 600–2,999, the percentage of junior high schools served by a school librarian was only 51.1. *Ibid.*, p. 47.

C. THE DEVELOPMENT OF SCHOOL LIBRARIES IN THE 1960s

A new era for all school libraries opened in 1960 with the publication by the American Association of School Librarians of the *Standards for School Library Programs*,[39] a cooperative effort of twenty educational and professional organizations and the result of several years of deliberation, investigation, and planning. As successors to the 1945 *School Libraries for Today and Tomorrow*, the new standards were based on "good" programs already in operation and were designed to serve as guides for school board members, administrators, teachers, librarians, and others interested in developing and expanding school library programs. They offer recommendations for school library services in individual schools, in district or regional materials centers, and in state agencies; and they consist of "(1) principles of policy and practice that make the library program an educational force in the school; (2) principles of administration and organization that make the school library an efficient tool; and (3) specifications for the staff, materials, collection, funds, quarters, and equipment required for the translation of principles into action."[40]

The concept of the school library as an instructional materials center

The printed word, contained in the book and other convenient forms, has long been considered the primary means for recording and transmitting knowledge; and libraries have been the accepted agencies for making these forms accessible and for encouraging their use. During the past two decades, many new ways of recording and communicating knowledge and ideas have been developed, and many of these are making an important contribution to the teaching-learning process. Films, filmstrips, disc, and tape recordings, prints, transparencies, and a variety of other audio-visual materials

[39] American Association of School Librarians, *Standards for School Library Programs, op. cit.*
[40] *Ibid.*, pp. 6–7.

and resources are now available to students and teachers along with books and other printed materials. In some schools the newer media are administered by a unit which has been organized for that particular purpose. In many other schools, the traditional functions and services of the school library and the newer functions and services of the audio-visual media are provided by an integrated administrative unit called the instructional materials center.[41]

As early as 1956, the American Association of School Librarians set forth its philosophy of the school library as an instructional materials center in a statement which reads in part:[42]

> The American Association of School Librarians believes that the school library, in addition to doing its vital work of individual reading guidance and development of the school curriculum, should serve the school as a center for instructional materials. Instructional materials include books—the literature of children, young people, and adults—other printed materials, films, recordings, and newer media developed to aid learning. . . . The function of an instructional materials center is to locate, gather, provide and coordinate a school's materials for learning and the equipment required for use of these materials. . . . trained school librarians must be ready to cooperate with others and themselves serve as coordinators, consultants, and supervisors of instructional materials service on each level of school administration. . . .

The concept of the school library as an instructional materials center has been of major importance in planning and developing school libraries during the past decade. Its wide acceptance in national and regional groups and in state departments of education is seen in the following statements:

1. The National Study of Secondary School Evaluation expanded the 1960 edition of *Evaluative Criteria* to provide means of evaluating the school library as an instructional materials center. The title of this section was changed to "Instructional Materials Services—Library and Audio-

---

[41] Other names for this unit are materials center, instructional resources center, and learning center.

[42] American Association of School Librarians, *op. cit.*, pp. 11, 12.

visual,"[43] and the major purpose of the instructional materials center as defined in this section is "to serve the established aims of the total educational program by (1) providing a rich variety of materials, including books and other printed materials, recordings, still and motion pictures, filmstrips, and other audio-visual materials and resources, for use by teachers and students as individuals and in groups; (2) offering leadership in developing techniques for the use of various materials by teachers and students; (3) making available facilities, services, and equipment necessary for the selection, organization, and use of instructional materials; and (4) furnishing facilities for, and assistance in, the production of instructional materials and displays."

2. The National Committee of the National Education Association Project on Instruction, *Schools for the Sixties*, states that "in each school system there should be one or more well-planned instructional materials and resources centers . . . staffed by persons who are adequately prepared in curriculum and instruction, in library service, and in audio-visual education."[44]

3. The North Central Association of Colleges and Secondary Schools requires that: "The library shall be organized as a resource center of instructional material for the entire educational program. The number and kind of library and reference books, periodicals, newspapers, pamphlets, information files, audio-visual materials, and other learning aids shall be adequate for the number of pupils and the needs of instruction in all courses."[45]

4. The Northwest Association of Secondary and Higher

[43] National Study of Secondary School Evaluation. *Manual for Evaluative Criteria* (Washington, D.C.: National Study of Secondary School Evaluation, 1960), p. 257. *Evaluative Criteria for Junior High Schools* repeats these purposes. See p. 213.

[44] National Education Association, Project on Instruction, *Schools for the Sixties* (New York: McGraw-Hill Book Company, 1963), p. 98.

[45] The North Central Association of Colleges and Secondary Schools, *Policies and Criteria for the Approval of Secondary Schools* (Chicago: The North Central Association of Colleges and Secondary Schools, 1965), p. 19.

Schools says of the library: "It is the instructional materials center. . . ."[46]

5. The Council of Chief State School Officers, in its publication *Responsibilities of State Departments of Education for School Library Services* takes the position that "the good school library in elementary and secondary schools is a center for all instructional materials—books, periodicals, pamphlets, audio-visual materials and professional materials for teachers. It serves also as a center of information on community resources. . . . The state department of education should foster the concept of the library as an integrated instructional materials center . . . and give guidance in recommending financing and staff necessary to develop this broadened concept."[47]

It has been noted that neither the standards nor the statements of national and state groups guarantee the development of school libraries. The school library is a part of the school and exists only to help the school achieve its objectives. When the school's objectives have not called for the use of library materials and services, the role of the library has been limited or even nonexistent. The broader the objectives, the richer the offerings, and the more diversified the instructional methods of the schools, the greater are the needs for the library.

In the late 1960s, the curriculum is viewed more broadly than ever before as the growing need for all kinds of education becomes apparent and the desired level of educational achievement rises. Learning is no longer only for children and youth; it is a lifelong process, and the school must prepare lifetime learners. A student should not learn just a set of facts, many of which may soon be outdated; he should develop an effective mode of inquiry which will serve him through life. Long-term child and social growth as well as immediate subject-matter mastery are major objectives of

[46] The Northwest Association of Secondary and Higher Schools, Commission on Secondary Schools, *Manual of Accrediting Secondary Schools* (Eugene, Ore.: The Northwest Association of Secondary and Higher Schools, 1962), p. 7.
[47] Council of Chief State School Officers, *Responsibilities of State Departments of Education for School Library Services*, pp. 4, 7.

modern education. The school program, developed in the light of current conditions and needs, must also anticipate changes which are taking place in the various aspects of our national and local life as a result of such societal changes as scientific and technological advances, rapid growth of population, expansion of knowledge, urbanization, and the Federal government's increasing fiscal support of education. Such a program of education calls for high quality and diversity of materials and methods of instruction appropriate to the age and ability of the learner as well as to the changing objectives of education.

Since individual growth and development are major concerns of education and since the individual's growth and development are very greatly conditioned by experiences that can be organized as a basis for his behavior, the school must provide the materials, resources, and facilities which will make possible the organization of the kinds of learning activities and situations that are needed. In the past decade the school has introduced many curricular and instructional changes. In fact, it is said that "the spirit of innovation is perhaps the most outstanding characteristic of today's educational scene."[48] Among the important curricular changes are new and expanded offerings in the social studies, the sciences, mathematics, the communication arts, citizenship education, vocational education, the fine arts, and the humanities. Innovations in methods of instruction include independent study; advanced placement; accelerated programs; greater interrelation of subjects; team teaching; special attention to the culturally and economically deprived; the track system or ability sectioning; selective instruction to curtail dropouts; ungraded elementary schools and high schools; greater use of a wide range of materials, including audio-visual and other new media, on all grade levels and in all subjects; and large-block periods for both large- and small-group instruction to enable students to study a subject or subjects in depth.

Thus, in a time when the school program calls for broad curricular offerings, attention to individual differences, and indepen-

[48] Bernard Z. Friedlander, "Today's Innovations in Teaching," *NEA Journal*, LV (March, 1966), 11.

dent study and inquiry, all supported by a wide variety of resources, the library becomes the natural center for learning. The school's emphasis on diversified learning materials—both printed and non-printed—for all subjects and levels of ability is giving increasing actuality to the concept of the library as an instructional materials center. And basic to the implementation of this concept is the availability of school library personnel who understand teaching methods and curriculum developments and are specially trained in the evaluation, selection, and organization of instructional materials and in their effective use in the teaching-learning process.

Contributions of philanthropy

Philanthropic foundations have played a vital role in the development of school libraries in recent years. For example, in 1962 the School Library Development Project, under a grant of $100,000 from the Council on Library Resources,[49] began the task of implementing the *Standards for School Library Programs*. Direct grants were made to twenty-one states for intrastate training projects, consultant services were provided in these and other states, and materials were developed and produced to aid in planning school library development.

The School Library Development Project showed that an effective school library demonstration program would be a great stimulus to the development of school libraries by giving administrators, teachers, librarians, parents, and other interested citizens an opportunity to see a good school library program in action. An article appearing in *This Week* magazine for the 1962 National Library Week brought the problem of school libraries and the idea for a demonstration program to the attention of the president of the Knapp Foundation, Inc., who invited the American Association of School Librarians to submit to the foundation a proposal for demonstrating the educational value of school library services. The result was a grant of $1,130,000 made by the Knapp Foundation, Inc. to the American Library Association to support a five-year project

[49] The Council on Library Resources was established by the Ford Foundation. See also pp. 268–69.

for the establishment of a given number of school libraries which would serve as examples of the kind of library recommended in the *Standards for School Library Programs*. These demonstrations would be carried out in cooperation with teacher education institutions, and provisions would be made for planned visits by groups of observers made up of administrators, board members, teachers, and librarians. The Knapp School Libraries Project, planned in three phases, provided for:[50]

Phase I.   Two programs in elementary schools with "existing provisions for library service"

Phase II. Three programs in elementary schools in different geographical areas which have less adequate library service

Phase III. Three programs in secondary schools which have average or above-average provisions for library service

The schools which are participating in the project have drawn hundreds of visitors from all over the country, and the project has produced materials of benefit to all schools in planning their library programs, among them the filmstrips "Living School Libraries" and "Three for Tomorrow" and the film ". . . And Something More." Schools trying to qualify for inclusion in the project have improved their libraries; and some states have initiated plans to set up demonstration centers comparable to those in the Knapp Project. Through the participation of teacher education institutions, students can observe a school library in action, learn firsthand the value of school library service, and begin early in their career to practice the principles of school librarianship.

In 1963, the Encyclopaedia Britannica School Library Awards were initiated to "highlight the importance of good elementary

[50] Phase I schools (1963) were Central Park Road Elementary School, Plainview, N.Y., and Marcus Whitman Elementary School, Richland, Wash.; Phase II schools (1964), The Allisonville School, Indianapolis, Ind., Mount Royal School, Baltimore, Md., and Casis School, Austin, Tex.; Phase III schools (1965), Roosevelt High School, Portland, Ore., Oak Park and River Forest High School, Oak Park, Ill., and Farrer Junior High School, Provo, Utah.

school libraries to quality education and to encourage citizen planning for their development." Cash awards totaling $2,500 are given each year to three school systems which have shown significant improvement in their elementary school library programs.

Regional accrediting associations

The program begun in 1952 by the Southern Association of Colleges and Schools for the affiliation of elementary schools resulted in the preparation of standards for admitting them to membership in the association. In 1961, the Committee on Elementary Education was created as a standing committee of the association, and elementary schools were accredited by this committee for the first time in 1963.[51] Their standards for elementary schools include evaluation of school libraries in the areas of effective use of the library or materials center, the number of books per child, the annual expenditure per child for library books and magazines and the annual expenditure for instructional materials and equipment, and the size of the staff.[52] Evaluative criteria developed for the junior high school by state and national groups emphasize the unique character of the junior high school library, which must support a program that is different in purpose and organization from that of any other school level and which must be administered by librarians who have special preparation and aptitudes for this kind of library service.

Research studies

A number of research studies have focused attention on the importance of the school library. As an example, Project Talent, a study covering almost a half million high school students, indicated that the number of books in the school library is one of the four most important factors closely and uniquely associated with such

[51] "Committee on Elementary Education, Cooperative Program in Elementary Education," *loc. cit.*

[52] "Policies, Principles and Standards of Accreditation of Elementary Schools," *Proceedings of the Sixty-Ninth Annual Meeting of the Southern Association of Colleges and Schools, November 30–December 3, 1964* (Atlanta, Ga.: The Southern Association of Colleges and Schools, 1965), pp. 241, 243, 244.

school outcomes as achievement, staying in school, and going to college.[53] A similar study, made by Miss Mary V. Gaver of Rutgers University, *Effectiveness of Centralized Library Service in Elementary Schools*, resulted in comparable findings for elementary school pupils, indicating "that definite advantages accrue in schools that have school libraries manned by professional library staff."[54] A more recent study, *Evaluation of Urban Centralized Elementary School Libraries*,[55] relating to measurable differences among sixth grade students in regard to reading abilities, achievement scores in academic areas, and ability to use library tools in schools with and without centralized libraries, shows that the nature and extent of library activity do have a measurable effect upon the learning of students in these areas.

National library week

Of more than passing significance in the development of school libraries has been National Library Week, the annual observance of a year-round program which calls attention to libraries, books, and reading. Launched by the National Book Committee in cooperation with the American Library Association in 1958, National Library Week has as its purpose the focusing of public attention on the importance of reading in our national life and as a source of personal fulfillment and on libraries, "which if used fully and supported properly, can make reading materials accessible to everybody." The message of National Library Week is carried in numerous newspaper and magazine articles and editorials; radio and television programs and announcements; and programs sponsored by libraries, library associations, and civic groups. Among its tangible results are the Knapp School Libraries Project and the Encyclopaedia Britannica Awards.

[53] J. C. Flanagan and Others, *Studies of the American High School,* Technical Report to the U.S. Office of Education, Cooperative Research Project No. 226 (Pittsburgh: Project Talent Office, University of Pittsburgh, 1962), Chap. 11, p. 10.
[54] Mary V. Gaver, *Effectiveness of Centralized Library Service in Elementary Schools* (New Brunswick, N.J.: Rutgers University Press, 1963), p. 127.
[55] Ella Jean Willson, *Evaluation of Urban Centralized Elementary School Libraries* (Ed.D. Dissertation; Detroit: Wayne State University Press, 1965).

Federal legislation

The concerted efforts of librarians, educators, citizens groups, professional organizations, and news media have resulted in alerting large blocks of the public to the important place of the school library in the educational program, to its deficiencies, and to what is needed to bring it to an adequate level of efficiency. One of the most far-reaching results of these efforts has been a growing sentiment for education in the United States Congress, expressing itself most dramatically in the Elementary and Secondary Education Act of 1965. Prior to the passage of this act, Federal legislation affecting school libraries included:

1. The National Defense Education Act of 1958, which authorized Federal aid for strengthening instruction in science, mathematics, and modern foreign languages, providing printed and nonprinted materials and audio-visual materials and equipment. In some state departments of education, state library supervisors were employed to aid in carrying out the provisions of this act.

2. The National Defense Education Act of 1958, as amended in 1964, which included English, reading, history, geography, and civics as critical subjects and provided financial aid to schools in improving their programs in these areas. Libraries were strengthened, directly or indirectly, as some of the materials became a part of the collection.[56]

3. The Vocational Education Act of 1963, which was designed to aid institutions, including high schools or departments of high schools, offering vocational and technical programs. Funds were made available for librarians' salaries, books, materials, and supplies, and—in some instances—for construction or remodeling facilities.

The main features of the Elementary and Secondary Education Act of 1965 with regard to programs for the school library are:

1. A five-year program of grants for the acquisition of school library resources, textbooks, and other instructional materials for the use of students and teachers in public and private elementary, junior high, and high schools

[56] See pp. 122, 132 for the contribution of this act to the education of librarians.

2. Financial assistance in establishing supplementary education centers to stimulate and assist in providing needed educational services and in developing and establishing exemplary elementary and secondary school programs, such as a model elementary school instructional materials center
3. Expanded research in elementary school library problems and relationships
4. The strengthening of state departments of education, thus strengthening school library supervision

These legislative provisions make it clear that the Federal commitment to school libraries is a large and incomparably important one, and there is the strong belief in both legislative and educational quarters that this commitment will grow. These provisions make possible the most important steps thus far taken to meet the shortage of library materials, which affects directly more than 10 million public school students throughout the country.

D. THE SCHOOL LIBRARY PROGRAM

The purposes of the school library, delineated in *School Libraries for Today and Tomorrow* and reiterated in the current *Standards for School Library Programs*, are: [57]

1. Participate effectively in the school program as it strives to meet the needs of pupils, teachers, parents, and other community members
2. Provide boys and girls with the library materials and services most appropriate and most meaningful in their growth and development as individuals
3. Stimulate and guide pupils in all phases of their reading, so that they may find increasing enjoyment and satisfaction and may grow in critical judgment and appreciation
4. Provide an opportunity through library experiences for boys and girls to develop helpful interests, to make satisfactory personal adjustments, and to acquire desirable social attitudes
5. Help children and young people to become skillful and discriminating users of libraries and of printed and audio-visual materials
6. Introduce pupils to community libraries as early as possible and cooperate with those libraries in their efforts to encourage continuing education and cultural growth
7. Work with teachers in the selection and use of all types of library materials which contribute to the teaching program
8. Participate with teachers and administrators in programs for continuing professional and cultural growth of the school staff
9. Cooperate with other librarians and community leaders in planning and developing an overall library program for the community or area

---

[57] American Library Association, Committee on Post-War Planning, *op. cit.*, pp. 9–10, quoted in *Standards for School Library Programs*, pp. 8–9.

The form and direction of the school library program are determined by the objectives, curricula, and methods of instruction of the school of which it is a part. Each school is different; therefore each school library is different from all others. To guide the librarian in planning a program of instruction, service, and activities for children and young people, the American Association of School Librarians has provided the following basic principles: [58]

1. The school library program reflects the philosophy of the school and enriches all parts of its educational program.

2. For the individual student, the library program offers valuable experiences and instruction that start with kindergarten and, expanding in breadth and depth, continue through the secondary school. This continuity of the library program provides for the student a cumulative growth in library skills and in the development of reading, listening, and viewing abilities and tastes.

3. The true concept of a school library program means instruction, service, and activity throughout the school rather than merely within the four walls of the library quarters. All phases of the school program are enriched by means of library materials and services. The degree to which teachers and pupils can and do depend on the services, materials, and staff of the library measures the extent to which the library program is successful.

4. Every boy and girl within the school is reached by the library program according to his individual needs.

5. Through varied types of materials, the collections of the library provide for the many kinds of interests that its users have, for the different levels of maturity and ability of the student population, and for the wide range of demands evoked by the curriculum and the services of the modern school.

6. The library is a laboratory for research and study, where students learn to work alone and in groups under the guidance of librarians and teachers. Thus it contributes to the

[58] *Ibid.,* pp. 14–15.

growth and development of youth in independent thinking; in abilities to study effectively; and in desirable attitudes toward reading, toward other media of communication, and toward all learning and research.

7. The library forms one facet of an overall guidance program in the school by making important contributions through its teaching, materials, and services to the personal, social, and vocational guidance of students.

8. School library experiences serve as stepping stones to the use of other library resources in the community and to the formation of lifetime habits of library usage, as well as to pride in the ownership of books.

The collection

The nature and size of the library collection of a particular school will depend upon many factors which have been noted, but one of the most basic factors will be the philosophy of education held by those responsible for the school and the consequent specific objectives and programs of that school. If the school's role is conceived to be that of indoctrination,

> "few books are needed. If its role is to teach, that is, to help students make up their own minds about the basic assumptions of their culture after having examined and analyzed the relevant facts, an extensive library is required. It is not enough to offer students books that are programed to give the answers. They need to learn questions as well as answers. They need to gain experience from source material. They need to learn how to draw sound conclusions from raw evidence. And they also need to learn that there are some questions to which there are no answers."[59]

Since no two schools will have the same philosophy, objectives, program of instruction, or pupil needs and interests, their library collections will not be the same. However, all library/instructional materials centers should provide materials for all areas included in the curriculum and in the school program and for recreation. These

[59] Ralph E. Ellsworth and Hobart D. Wagener, *The School Library: Facilities for Independent Study in the Secondary School* (New York: Educational Facilities Laboratories, Inc., 1963), p. 76.

materials should be in sufficient quantity to enable teachers to find the materials required in the teaching-learning process and to provide the student with resources adequate for his class assignments; for independent research and inquiry; for reading, listening, or viewing; and for personal enjoyment. The collection, selected cooperatively by teacher and librarian in relation to school organization and classroom activity, should include books, magazines, newspapers, pamphlets, films, filmstrips, pictures, slides, transparencies, maps, globes, disc and tape recordings, displays, models, exhibits, and microforms and the equipment needed to use them. The collection should be organized for efficient use and easy accessibility to students and teachers in the library and the classroom and for home use.

The school library should also provide an extensive, up-to-date, and functional collection of professional books, magazines, pamphlets, curriculum guides, resource units, audio-visual, and other instructional and professional materials for the use of faculty members and administrators both for reference and for general professional reading. The *Standards for School Library Programs* recommend that the professional collection—selected cooperatively by administrators, teachers, and librarians—be housed in a special room for teachers in the school library quarters and that it be administered by the head school librarian.[60] "The professional library at its best . . . is an integral part of a larger program—that of the school library—and an organic part of the school, changing, growing, and developing with the whole school program."[61]

A guide in the selection of materials for the school library is the "School Library Bill of Rights":[62]

School libraries are concerned with generating understanding of American freedoms and with the preservation of these freedoms

---

[60] American Association of School Librarians, *op. cit.*, pp. 85, 86. See also *The Teachers' Library: How to Organize It and What To Include* (Washington, D.C.: National Education Association, 1966).

[61] Imogene J. McCarthy, "The Professional Library in the School: A Tool for Supervisors," *The Elementary School Journal*, LXIII (December, 1962), 161. Published by The University of Chicago Press with the Department of Education of the University of Chicago.

[62] Endorsed by the Council of the American Library Association, July, 1955.

through the development of informed and responsible citizens. To this end the American Association of School Librarians reaffirms the "Library Bill of Rights" of the American Library Association and asserts that the responsibility of the school library is:

> To provide materials that will enrich and support the curriculum, taking into consideration the varied interests, abilities, and maturity levels of the pupils served
>
> To provide materials that will stimulate growth in factual knowledge, literary appreciation, aesthetic values, and ethical standards
>
> To provide a background of information which will enable pupils to make intelligent judgments in their daily life
>
> To provide materials on opposing sides of controversial issues so that young citizens may develop under guidance the practice of critical reading and thinking
>
> To provide materials representative of the many religious, ethnic, and cultural groups and their contributions to our American heritage
>
> To place principle above personal opinion and reason above prejudice in the selection of materials of the highest quality in order to assure a comprehensive collection appropriate for the users of the library

The staff

The school librarian directs the school library program. In the performance of this responsibility:

1. He selects materials; orders, classifies, catalogs, and processes them; and organizes them for use.
2. He supervises the library staff.
3. He advises and works closely with teachers in selecting materials and in planning for their effective use.
4. He gives instruction in using the library and guides individual pupils in selecting and using library materials.
5. He prepares special materials for the use of students and for the faculty and administration.
6. He participates in curriculum planning and development and in guidance and cocurricular programs.

7. He provides library services and materials throughout the school as well as in the library.
8. He interprets the school library program to administrators, faculty, and community.

The school librarian must have a broad background of general education and graduate level training in both librarianship and education. In addition to the basic areas of administration, cataloging, classification, and selection, the school librarian must have special training in school library organization and management in order to be able to administer his library in the framework of the administrative organization of the school and to use the principles of scientific management to achieve greater returns for his budget allocations for professional and clerical personnel, facilities and equipment, materials and quarters, and services. He must have a wide knowledge of literature, with special emphasis on the level of library user he serves—children, adolescents, or young adults; he must know materials for the gifted, for special areas, for special purposes, and on all topics of current importance and of current interest to children and young people. He must have knowledge of all types of communication media—their production, equipment, and use. For all materials—printed and nonprinted—the librarian must know the criteria for evaluating and selecting and be able to organize them for ease of use. He must know the function of each type, be able to determine which is best for a given purpose, and know how to guide students in using them. He must know the curriculum, modern methods of teaching, and educational psychology and keep abreast of developments in these areas as well as in all aspects of school librarianship. He must be able to work with administrators, teachers, students, and citizens in the development and operation of an effective school library program.

The basic educational requirements for school librarians—including preparation in education and in library science—are set by the certification agencies in the several states. Meeting the basic requirements, however, does not conclude the education of the school librarian. The necessity for keeping up to date in both education and librarianship calls for continuing education throughout his library career through conferences, workshops, and institutes as well as in advanced formal courses.

THE SCHOOL LIBRARY SUPERVISOR

The school library supervisor for a city, county, or district system is appointed by the local board of education and works with the chief school officer of the administrative unit in planning and developing the school library program in each school as to quarters, collections, acquisitions, organization, staff, and use. The supervisor:

1. Conducts a continuous program of evaluation
2. Coordinates the program of library services in the schools of the system
3. Provides advisory and consultative service, guidance, and leadership in the professional growth of librarians through workshops, meetings, and conferences
4. Interprets school library service to administrators, teachers, and the public
5. Participates in professional educational and library organizations
6. Helps the school library define its place in the instructional program and adapt to new or experimental methods of instruction
7. Helps the school library select, prepare, and use instructional and professional materials
8. Initiates, conducts, and coordinates research
9. Disseminates effective practices

The school library supervisor must have a special competence for working with people—administrators, boards of education, teachers, librarians, and the public—a broad educational background, administrative and organizational ability, and knowledge of trends in education and in librarianship. Desirable qualifications include a master's degree in library education and basic education and experience both as a teacher and a school librarian.[63]

School library quarters

Since the school library serves the school, its physical design will be influenced by the school's educational philosophy and objectives; the breadth of the immediate school program as well as the

---

[63] See American Association of School Librarians, *op. cit.*, pp. 42, 46, *passim*.

projected plans for the future; the size of enrollment; the type of school organization; the nature of the curriculum; the methods of instruction, especially the emphasis placed upon the use of many types of media and the extent to which independent study, team teaching, large-group and small-group instruction, and closed-circuit television are emphasized; and the place which the school assigns to the library in the total school program. These factors determine the size and diversity of library resources, the various ways they should be made accessible, and the program of services and activities which must be provided; and these factors, in turn, determine the size, location, and equipment of the school library quarters.

The library, located for maximum accessibility to the instructional areas, must be flexible in design, so that it can be adapted to new changes and emphases in the curriculum and new concepts of service, including the use of technological devices; it must be functional in design and arrangement, to allow for the most effective use of materials and facilities; it must be attractive and inviting in appearance, with careful attention given to proper lighting, heat, sound control, and use of color; it must be equipped with comfortable furnishings, planned to encourage and promote efficient use and suited to the physical stature of those who will use the library; and it must be large enough to accommodate the collection of materials and the program of services required to meet the needs of students and teachers, allowing adequate space for:[64]

1. Office requirements
2. Seating requirements
3. Rooms or areas for reading, browsing, viewing, listening, and conferring
4. Shelving and storage of both print and nonprint materials and for the equipment needed to use them
5. Workrooms for the preparation and/or production of both print and nonprint materials
6. Special-purpose rooms or areas for carrels for independent

[64] See American Association of School Librarians, *op. cit.*, pp. 91–94, 119–28 for policies and specifications regarding library quarters and equipment.

study, library classes, storytelling, and professional materials for the faculty

The organization and arrangement of the school library varies depending upon the organization and program of the school. A twelve-grade school may have a large central library which serves the entire school, it may have a central library with branches in the elementary and the junior high school, or it may have separate libraries for each of the schools.

A secondary school library may be a central library which serves all grades from one location, it may be a central library with branches or resource centers in the other buildings which serve the school, it may be a central library which gives book-truck service to all classrooms and laboratories, it may be a decentralized system based on subject grouping with a central library and library areas adjacent to each of the departments,[65] or it may be one part of a larger learning resource center.[66]

An elementary school library, like the high school library, may be a centralized unit giving all service from one location; it may provide classroom collections from the central library for long or short loan periods; it may be decentralized, that is, with a central library and resource centers located in the departmental areas; or it may be a central library which extends its services by means of book trucks which take materials to the classrooms for special use.

The junior high school library may be a centralized unit; it may be departmentalized, with a central library and departmental collections in or near the instructional areas; or it may be a central library with mobile services to classrooms and laboratories.

Problems

It is clear from the preceding discussions that the problems facing education in general—and specifically elementary and secon-

[65] See Ray Tidwell and Edward Wiseblood, "The Oregon Plan," *Library Journal*, XC (September 15, 1965), 3686–89.
[66] See J. Lloyd Trump, "Independent Study Centers—Their Relation to the Central Library," *The Bulletin of the National Association of Secondary-School Principals*, L (January, 1966), 45–52.

dary education—are shared by school libraries as integral parts of the educational program. Some of the problems of education which influence the objectives, programs, and services of school libraries are those which grow out of the continuous efforts of educators to find better answers to such questions as these:

1. What are the bases, functions, and purposes of education?
2. Who shall be educated and how much education for whom?
3. How can the educational needs of those who are not typical be met most effectively?
4. What knowledge is of the greatest value and who shall decide?
5. How shall the schools be organized and administered to ensure the most efficient operation?
6. What buildings, equipment, and facilities are needed?
7. How can adequate financial and community support be guaranteed?
8. How can qualified personnel be secured and retained?
9. What should be the length of the school day and the school term?
10. What is the proper role of automation?
11. How can Federal and state financial support be used to the best advantage for all?
12. What extra-subject services and activities shall the school provide?

The approach of each school to these and related questions will determine the objectives of its library; the nature and size of the instructional and learning materials collection, and the bases and methods of selecting these materials; the ways the library is organized and administered; the nature of the quarters, and the kinds of equipment and facilities that are needed; the size and qualifications of the staff; and the number and kinds of library services.

The most pressing general problem is the critical need for more and better libraries and more qualified librarians. The *National Inventory of Library Needs* estimates that eighty-seven thousand school librarians (with fifteen semester hours of library training) and approximately a quarter of a billion volumes are needed to meet minimum ALA standards in these two areas.[67] Approximately 60 percent of America's elementary schools, which enroll some 10 million children, still do not have school libraries. The steadily increasing demands for library materials and services result from the existing inadequacy of school libraries; from the requirements of rapidly increasing school enrollments; from such curricular innovations as independent study and honors programs; and from the needs of special groups, such as the talented student, the disadvantaged, and the reluctant learner.

Other problems of concern to school librarians are:

1. What materials should be acquired? The rapid expansion of knowledge, which is recorded and transmitted in diverse forms, creates the serious problem of knowing what to select out of the multitude of materials which are now available. Another serious problem relating to the selection of materials grows out of the pressures exerted by the ever-present censors, who may demand the removal of materials to which they object or who may demand that certain materials be included in the collection.[68]

2. How can librarians gain acceptance by administrators and teachers as active participants in the instructional program? In spite of the fact that educators, when questioned, willingly acknowledge the essentiality of the school library to the school program at all grade levels, an examination of current books on modern American education will reveal few references to the school library or the school librarian. This meager consideration in professional educational literature points up two problems: (*a*) How can administrators be made to see the library as a real part of the school program—an *every day* essential, not just an essential at accreditation time or when some national or state requirement must be met; (*b*) How can the school librarian be-

[67] *National Inventory of Library Needs, op. cit.,* pp. 4, 27.

[68] See "School Library Bill of Rights," pp. 248–49. See also current issues of professional journals in librarianship and the *Newsletter on Intellectual Freedom,* published bimonthly by the Intellectual Freedom Committee of the American Library Association.

come recognized and accepted as an educator, as an actual leader and participant in the instructional program—a real teammate of curriculum planners, classroom teachers, and educational specialists—thus proving to administrators, school board, and community as well as to the teaching staff that his indispensableness is real and not merely theoretical?

3. How can the school library achieve autonomy? Although school libraries have more important status today than at any time before, there remains the question of how the library can secure the support—financial, administrative, and community—which will enable it to achieve autonomy in the sense of being able to provide the needed library materials and services *itself* without being dependent upon library agencies outside the school for them. This does not mean cutting itself off from other libraries—far from it; but it does mean using other libraries to complement the school library collection—not to substitute for it.

4. How can professional personnel be used more efficiently? In a time of severe shortage of trained librarians, how can school libraries make more efficient use of professional personnel, eliminating the waste that occurs when professional librarians are required to give their attention to tasks that can be performed by nonprofessionals, clerks, and volunteer workers?

5. How can the instructional materials center concept be made a fact? With the remarkable increase in materials for learning—both printed and nonprinted—how can all librarians be convinced of the value of new kinds of resources and new methods and of the necessity for using both the new and the old; in short, how can the library/instructional materials center become a reality instead of just a generally accepted idea with rather limited application?

6. What is the proper place of mechanization in the school library? In the effort to cope with the increase in information and knowledge, both in selecting materials and in making them quickly and easily accessible, what types of analy-

ses can the librarian use to determine when, for what purposes, and to what extent the new technology can be used to advantage in the school library?

Education for school librarianship also faces some important problems and decisions in this time of accelerated library growth. Some of the questions which grow out of these problems are:

1. Is library education preparing school librarians for the variety of tasks they now have to perform, both administrative and instructional, as well as giving them the educational background which will enable them to adapt to new patterns of school organization, new objectives, new curricular demands, and new technology?

2. Are library schools preparing school librarians to make budgets; plan quarters; select equipment; and work with administrators, school boards, architects, and the general public in planning for an era of school library expansion?

3. What changes should be made and what new emphases introduced in the basic library education courses, such as administration, cataloging and classification, and selection, in the light of the new administrative responsibilities mentioned above; the growing need for librarians who are specially trained for each level of school librarianship; the trend toward central processing for a school system, processing by commercial firms, and computer-prepared catalogs; and the tremendous increase in the number and kinds of materials for the several school levels—both printed and nonprinted?

Trends

Many of the curricular and instructional trends in education which affect school libraries have already been noted. Other educational trends which influence them are:

1. The increased financial support of schools by Federal and state governments, which makes possible the strengthening and the expansion of all school services

2. The reorganization of school districts (usually consolidation), which results in more efficient use of school funds

for better programs, better teachers, better libraries, and better laboratories and other facilities

3. The introduction of system-wide practices, such as purchasing and processing of library materials, which result in a saving of both time and money for the librarian

4. The introduction of automation into certain areas of school administration, offering the possibility of the effective and timesaving use of certain forms of the new technology in library operations

5. The practice of many school boards to use certain of their regular meetings for the purpose of learning about the school program directly from teachers, principals, and—it is hoped—from librarians

6. The growing interest in year-round schools, which offer increased opportunities for school libraries to contribute to the continuing education of pupils and parents

Some significant developments in school library programs and services include:

1. The growth in size and scope of library collections to include more reference materials, a wide selection of paperbacks, newspapers on microfilm, microreaders, programmed materials, teaching machines, individual projectors for viewing slides and filmstrips, television equipment, and equipment for the production and reproduction of materials

2. Wide intellectual acceptance of the concept of the library as an instructional materials center—an agency which stimulates and coordinates the use of all kinds of learning materials throughout the school

3. New concepts of service, such as extended hours of service—on Saturdays, holidays, and the year around; flexible circulation policies allowing circulation of all types of library materials, including reference and audio-visual materials and equipment for overnight use; participation in team teaching; aid in developing techniques of teaching with new media; and assisting in closed-circuit television programs

4. New organizational patterns, such as multiple libraries di-

vided by grade level; a multiple library system departmentalized by subject; or library resource centers for each
area of the curriculum, such as the social sciences, the arts,
or the sciences

5. New library positions, such as school library specialist with
   responsibility for developing all libraries in a school system
   or librarian of a curriculum laboratory, a district materials
   center, or a technical processing center

6. Plans to revise *Standards for School Library Programs*,[69]
   indicating that schools are already meeting these standards
   and are ready for a higher set of goals

Other possibilities for school library services can be seen in
some of the kinds of projects which are eligible for Federal funds
under the Elementary and Secondary Education Act, for example:

1. The use of prefabricated library units, which can be attached to existing elementary school buildings to provide
   quarters for a school library

2. The operation of mobile reference centers, that is, bookmobiles stocked with carefully selected reference materials
   which travel from school to school—especially schools
   which do not have a central library

3. The development of large collections of materials and resources to aid in remedial teaching of the retarded or the
   disadvantaged

4. The establishment of a comprehensive learning materials
   examination center where all adults who work with children and youth can examine—before buying—books and
   other library materials

5. The provision of centralized educational and library services, including specialized books and audio-visual materials
   that supplement local collections; centralized reference and
   research service; and centralized ordering and processing
   of materials for a school system or for a group of schools

[69] The $25,000 J. Morris Jones-World Book Encyclopedia—ALA Goals for
Action Award for 1966 was given to the American Association of School
Librarians to be used in revising the 1960 *Standards for School Library
programs*.

6. The establishment of a school library system, modeled after a public library cooperative system, for all school libraries in an area—public and private—in order to pool resources; provide bibliographical control through a union catalog; and provide such centralized services as selection, acquisition, and processing

Some promising trends in the education of school librarians are the increasing number of conferences, workshops, and short courses for school library personnel, including the institutes provided under the National Defense Education Act and the Higher Education Act;[70] the in-service courses offered by library schools for school librarians, school library supervisors, and media specialists; and programs for the training of nonprofessional personnel, such as library aides and library technicians, to provide subprofessional and clerical personnel for school libraries.

Perhaps the most encouraging trends of all are the unprecedented public interest in school libraries and the campaign now being waged on their behalf by librarians, educators, professional associations, regional accrediting associations, state and Federal education departments, local civic groups, industry, philanthropy, and the news media—a campaign which has resulted in a barrage of magazine, journal, and newspaper articles; pamphlets; leaflets; fact sheets; and films and filmstrips describing the state of the school library, enumerating its needs, and stressing its importance in the school program.

[70] See p. 132.

CHAPTER 17
GENERAL CHARACTERISTICS OF ACADEMIC LIBRARIES

Whatever level of quality the nation's institutions of higher learning now possess or aspire to will be determined by the character of their libraries—by the adequacy of their collections of books, periodicals, and research materials.[1]

Libraries in institutions of higher learning—academic libraries—are as varied and distinctive as the institutions which they serve. There are the libraries in junior colleges; in four-year liberal arts colleges; teachers colleges; agricultural and mechanical colleges; men's colleges; women's colleges; technical schools; and schools of theology, religion, law, and other professions; and there are the central libraries in the universities and the more specialized libraries in the colleges within the universities.

The legal bases for institutions of higher education is found in the charters granted by special acts of the state legislatures for the establishment of specific institutions or in the articles of incorporation granted under the educational or corporation laws of the states. Public institutions are controlled by state or local government; private institutions are usually governed by a corporation. Both public and private institutions of higher education are administered by a board. The legal status of the library in academic institutions may be determined by the charter or by the articles of incorporation, but, in general, it is established by the bylaws of the board.

---

[1] "Statement by Francis Keppel, Commissioner of Education, before the Subcommittee on Education of the Committee on Labor and Public Welfare, United States Senate, Tuesday, March 16, 1965," p. 13. (Processed.)

SOME FORCES IN THE DEVELOPMENT OF ALL ACADEMIC LIBRARIES

Among the forces which have played vital roles in the development of institutions of higher learning and thus of the libraries in these institutions are the regional, state, and professional accrediting agencies; professional organizations; private philanthropy; Friends of the Library groups; and Federal legislative programs.

Accrediting agencies

Ever since there have been schools, there have been standards of some kind which were prescribed by or for a given institution or by an appropriate agency for the institutions in a given state or area. As early as 1784 the Board of Regents of the State of New York was given responsibility for maintaining standards in institutions of higher education in that state. The state department of education, the state university, or some other state agency is usually given the responsibility by the state legislature for developing standards and criteria for evaluating junior colleges, four-year colleges, and colleges of teacher education. A number of state agencies either accept the accreditation of regional or national agencies as the basis for their approval of institutions or adapt the criteria developed by these agencies to their own use.[2]

A major influence in the development of higher education has been that of the nongovernmental accrediting agencies, the regional associations of schools and colleges. An accrediting association is "the cooperative venture of a large number of institutions who are earnestly seeking first to ascertain what are the best standards of college work and, second, effective ways and means of bringing these standards to the attention of the institutions within its constituency."[3]

Regional associations of educational institutions began to appear during the last two decades of the nineteenth century to combat

[2] Theresa Birch Wilkins, "Accreditation in the States," *Accreditation in Higher Education*, ed. Lloyd E. Blauch (Washington, D.C.: U.S. Government Printing Office, 1959), p. 41.
[3] G. F. Zook and M. F. Haggerty, *The Evaluation of Higher Institutions*, Vol. I: *Principles of Accrediting Higher Institutions* (Chicago: The University of Chicago Press, 1936), p. 15.

certain critical problems facing both secondary and higher education. Standards were needed on the college level for admission, program, facilities, graduation requirements, transfer of students, and preparation of faculty. On the high school level, the nature, content, and length of the high school course had to be established. Six regional associations have been formed:[4] the New England Association of Colleges and Secondary Schools, 1885; the Middle States Association of Colleges and Secondary Schools, 1889; the North Central Association of Colleges and Secondary Schools, 1895; the Southern Association of Colleges and Secondary Schools, 1895;[5] the Northwest Association of Secondary and Higher Schools, 1917; and the Western College Association, 1924. These associations did not begin to accredit colleges immediately. The North Central Association initiated accrediting procedures for institutions of higher education in 1910, the Southern Association in 1917, the Middle States Association in 1921, the Northwest Association in 1921, the Western Association in 1949, and the New England Association in 1952.[6]

Accreditation, "a phenomenon peculiar to the United States,"[7] is the recognition accorded to an educational institution that meets the standards or criteria established by a competent agency or association. The process of accreditation includes:[8]

1. The establishing of minimum standards or criteria by the accrediting agency which an institution must meet in order to be accredited

2. Examination of the institution by the agency to determine whether it has met the standards or criteria

3. Publication of a list of institutions which meet the standards and are therefore accredited

4. Periodic reviews to ascertain whether the accredited institution continues to meet the standards or criteria

---

[4] Mayor and Swartz, *op. cit.*, p. 36. See pp. 223–25 for a discussion of the influence of regional accrediting associations on the development of secondary schools.
[5] The name was changed in 1963 to Southern Association of Colleges and Schools, when elementary schools were admitted to membership.
[6] Mayor and Swartz, *op. cit.*, p. 36.
[7] *Ibid.*, p. 11.
[8] Blauch, *op. cit.*, p. 3.

Since accreditation is supposed to be a guarantee of educational respectability and since respectability is a quality, not a quantity, the first problem of accreditation is to discover how to appraise the quality of educational opportunity.[9] Standards are established, therefore, in areas relating to purposes and objectives, program, faculty, library, plant, equipment, physical facilities, teacher load, admission requirements, and graduation requirements; and educational institutions seeking accreditation and membership are examined in these areas.

The influence of the regional associations upon the development of academic libraries has been of major importance, for they have always included the library as a major area to be considered in the accreditation of an institution.[10] Early criteria for evaluating the library were quantitative, measuring such aspects as the number of books in the library and the amount of reading space per student. Although these quantitative standards were opposed by many educators and librarians, they did succeed in drawing the attention of college administrators to the substandard condition of their libraries and in forcing them to provide financial support of at least minimum adequacy for the improvement of their libraries so that accreditation would be granted.

New criteria adopted in 1934 by the North Central Association—and later by other associations—stressed the importance of evaluating an institution in terms of its own objectives, with emphasis upon qualitative rather than quantitative standards. According to the Middle States Association,

> The emphasis in evaluating a library [an academic library] should be on the appropriateness of the collection for the instructional

---

[9] John F. Nevins, *A Study of the Organization and Operation of Voluntary Accrediting Agencies* ("The Catholic University of America Educational Research Monographs," Vol. XXII, No. 3, Washington, D.C.: The Catholic University of America Press, 1959), p. 91.

[10] At the first annual meeting of the North Central Association in 1896, five "elements" needed by an institution in order to be recognized as a college were set forth, and among them was "a good library" (Richard J. Jesse, "What Constitutes a College," *Proceedings of the First Annual Meeting of the North Central Association*, p. 26).

and research programs of the students and faculty, its adequacy in breadth, depth, and variety to stimulate both students and faculty, its accessibility, including proper cataloging, the competence and interest of the staff, and above all what happens in the reading and reference rooms.[11]

With the rise of the accrediting movement it has become a practical necessity for an educational institution, particularly those of higher learning, to be approved by an agency of this type. . . . So great and widespread has been the public acceptance of accreditation by regional associations, that a college which lacks this approval or which loses it, is considered inferior. . . . Attendance may drop and in the eyes of the public the prestige of the institution suffers.[12]

Approximately 85 percent of the degree-granting institutions are now regionally accredited.[13]

Other accrediting agencies, in addition to state agencies and the regional associations, are the national associations or councils made up of institutions and/or organizations which are related in purpose or interests, such as the National Council for Accreditation of Teacher Education; associations of schools which prepare for a particular profession, such as the Association of American Law Schools; and organizations of members of a profession, such as the American Library Association.

Professional organizations

The Association of College and Research Libraries, representing the libraries of higher education, independent research libraries, and specialized libraries, became a division of the American Library Association in 1938. This agency provides leadership and guidance in the areas of selection, evaluation, publication, study, and review of library materials and professional literature; the formulation of

[11] Middle States Association of Colleges and Secondary Schools, Commission on Institutions of Higher Education, *Evaluating the Library, Suggestions for the Use of Faculties and Evaluating Teams* (Document No. 4.81; New York: Middle States Association of Colleges and Secondary Schools, 1957), p. 2.
[12] Nevins, *op. cit.*, p. 91.
[13] Mayor and Swartz, *op. cit.*, p. 21.

standards for the use of some of the types of libraries it represents;[14] the professional growth of librarians; and the development and interpretation of libraries and library service in the kinds of institutions it represents. It helps academic librarians to keep up to date through its bimonthly publication, *College and Research Libraries.*

Of the other professional organizations[15] and groups—national, regional, and state—which contribute directly or indirectly to the advancement of academic libraries, notable examples are the Association of Research Libraries,[16] an organization of the largest research libraries in the United States, the majority of which are university libraries; the Special Libraries Association,[17] which includes certain aspects of academic librarianship in its range of concerns; regional professional groups, such as the Midwest Academic Librarians Conference and the Conference of Eastern College Librarians; and the college and research sections of the several state library associations.

Private philanthropy

At the same time that Andrew Carnegie and later the Carnegie Corporation were making grants for public library buildings,[18] they were also financing library buildings on college campuses. After 1917 the emphasis in the Carnegie Corporation's program for the development of academic libraries moved from buildings to the improvement of services, and between 1921 and 1935 endowment grants were made to eleven institutions for general library uses or for salaries for librarians. Eventually grants totaling $667,500 were made to twenty-one colleges and universities for library development.[19]

The major program of the Carnegie Corporation of New York for the development of college libraries began in 1928 with the

[14] "Standards for College Libraries" was adopted by the American Library Association in 1959; "ALA Standards for Junior College Libraries," in 1960. These standards are to be used as guidelines, not for accrediting purposes. See pp. 119, 120.
[15] See p. 104.
[16] See p. 299.
[17] See pp. 308–09.
[18] See pp. 86–87.
[19] Anderson, *op. cit.,* pp. 5, 12.

organization of the Advisory Group on College Libraries, which had as its purpose "to upgrade the libraries of the average good colleges by focusing the attention of administrators on the inadequacies of libraries in their institutions, setting standards for improvement and providing the wherewithal to get started."[20] With William Warner Bishop as chairman, this advisory group collected specific data on the libraries of some two hundred liberal arts colleges, formulated standards for these libraries, and selected eighty-three of them to receive grants totaling over one million dollars for the purchase of books for undergraduate reading. As a result of similar studies, grants—chiefly for books—were also made to selected teachers colleges, Negro colleges, land-grant colleges, and technological colleges.[21]

A program for junior colleges was begun in 1934, when the Carnegie Advisory Group on Junior Colleges was appointed, also under the chairmanship of William Warner Bishop. Three years later this group reported on the inadequacy of junior college libraries as to housing and equipment, lack of trained personnel, and the neglected condition of books and card catalogs. As a result of this study, ninety-two junior colleges were given grants by the Carnegie Corporation ranging from $1,500 to $6,000.[22]

An additional and significant result of these studies was the production of a body of library literature, which included Randall's *The College Library*, Shaw's *A List of Books for College Libraries*, Gerould's *The College Library Building*, and Mohrhardt's *A List of Books for Junior College Libraries*.[23]

Another Carnegie Corporation study of major importance in

[20] *Ibid.*, p. 14.
[21] *Ibid.*, p. 13.
[22] *Ibid.*
[23] William M. Randall, *The College Library* (Chicago: American Library Association and The University of Chicago Press, 1932); Charles B. Shaw (ed.), *A List of Books for College Libraries* (Chicago: American Library Association, 1931); Charles B. Shaw (ed.), *A List of Books for College Libraries, 1931–1938* (Chicago: American Library Association, 1940); James T. Gerould, *The College Library Building, Its Planning and Equipment* (New York: Charles Scribner's Sons, 1932); Foster E. Mohrhardt (comp.), *A List of Books for Junior College Libraries* (Chicago: American Library Association, 1937).

the development of college libraries and college library service was conducted by Dr. Harvie Branscomb for the purpose of determining the place of the library in college teaching. The published study, *Teaching with Books*,[24] pointed up the importance of library use in college teaching and influenced libraries to become teaching instruments, providing easier access to materials through open shelves, carrels for individual use, longer hours of service, more attention to instruction and guidance in the use of materials, and greater efforts to encourage student use of library materials.

Since World War II, the attention of the Carnegie Corporation has been directed largely toward developing university centers for foreign area studies and encouraging the development of undergraduate courses in non-Western civilizations. In general, grants made to institutions for these purposes have included funds to enable their libraries to purchase the books needed to support these new programs of study.

In addition to the Carnegie Corporation, other philanthropic organizations aided in the development of college libraries in the first half of the twentieth century, notably the Rosenwald Foundation, which contributed to the improvement of facilities in libraries of Negro colleges in the South, and the General Education Board, which made grants to libraries of small colleges—especially in the South—for library materials, equipment, and personnel.

Funds provided by philanthropic foundations for scholarships, fellowships, research, and overall library development contribute both directly and indirectly to the growth of libraries in institutions of higher learning. Outstanding contributions for these purposes are being made by the General Education Board of the Rockefeller Fund, the United States Steel Foundation, and the Ford Foundation.

A significant contribution of the Ford Foundation to all libraries was the establishment in 1956 of the Council on Library Resources to aid in the solution of library problems and to conduct research

---

[24] Harvie Branscomb, *Teaching with Books: A Study of College Libraries* (Chicago: Association of American Colleges and American Library Association, 1940).

in, develop, and demonstrate new techniques and methods for the improvement of library organization and service.

Friends of the library groups[25]

Since the beginning of academic libraries there have been individuals and groups who have aided them by giving money, books, and effort toward furthering the library's aims and programs. These Friends of the Library Groups—as they are usually called—are made up of alumni and friends of the institution who continue to work on behalf of the academic library by making individual or group gifts and donations; bequests; memorials in the form of endowment, buildings, equipment, and special collections and who influence interested individuals, organizations, and foundations to make contributions. Friends of the Library groups may be formally organized, and they may issue promotional and informational publications.

Federal legislation[26]

The distribution free of charge of Federal government publications to designated libraries was authorized by act of Congress, February 5, 1895. This law provides for one depository library for each congressional district in the United States and for two depositories at large for each state. The libraries of land-grant colleges and universities are named Federal depositories. Government publications in depository libraries are permanent and are available to the public, at least for reference use. The Depository Library Act of 1962 reinforces and expands the original act, permitting the designation of additional depository libraries. The Superintendent of Documents is required to distribute the publications produced by the executive departments on their own printing equipment as well as those printed by the U.S. Government Printing Office.

[25] See Sarah Wallace (ed.), *Friends of the Library: Organization and Activities* (Chicago: American Library Association, 1962), for information concerning Friends groups in all types of libraries.
[26] See also pp. 303–06.

The Morrill Act of 1862, called the Land Grant Act, provided for a grant of 30,000 acres of land for each representative and senator in Congress to be used for the "endowment, support, and maintenance of at least one college . . . in each state" and resulted in the establishment of colleges and universities geared to the teaching of vocational subjects. The Second Morrill Act of 1890 provided annual appropriations to these institutions.

The National Defense Education Act of 1958 provided a four-year program designed to improve the teaching of science, mathematics, and modern foreign languages; to identify and educate more talented young people; and to encourage more college students to enter teaching. New programs to train modern foreign language teachers and counseling and guidance personnel at summer or academic year institutes on college campuses were among the provisions. This act was amended in 1964 to enable the Commissioner of Education to arrange through grants or contracts with institutions of higher education to operate short-term or regular-session institutes for teachers of English, reading, history, and geography; for school librarians and school library supervisors; for educational-media specialists; and for teachers of disadvantaged youth.

The Higher Education Facilities Act of 1963 authorized Federal grants and loans to institutions of higher education for the construction of various facilities, including libraries.

The Higher Education Act of 1965 provided financial aid to libraries for the acquisition of materials; for research projects and demonstrations relating to libraries and the training of librarians; for the acquisition of special equipment, including audio-visual materials and equipment; and for the operation of workshops or institutes for training librarians preparing to use educational media in institutions of higher education.

The Vocational Education Act of 1963 made available funds for salaries for librarians, library books and other materials, construction, and equipment for departments or divisions of a junior college or university which offers courses in vocational education.

A number of programs which are administered by the Department of Defense; the Department of Health, Education, and Welfare; the National Science Foundation; and the National Aeronautics and Space Administration provide funds for higher education to support research; to aid in training programs, institutes, and seminars for faculty development and for visiting scholars; to offer graduate and undergraduate scholarships; and to add to the physical plants. These programs affect academic libraries directly or indirectly by encouraging or aiding them in increasing resources, staff, and equipment to enable them to carry out their responsibilities in the several programs.

THE ACADEMIC LIBRARY PROGRAM

Academic libraries differ from each other in many respects,[27] but all are alike in certain fundamentals: They have the same basic function and organization; they carry on some of the same activities; their collections contain some of the same kinds of materials; and they share some of the same problems.

Function of academic libraries[28]

The basic function of the academic library is to aid the institution in carrying out its program. "The primary characteristic of a good academic library is its complete identification with its own institution. The measure of its excellence is the extent to which its resources and services support the institution's objectives."[29] The nature of the institution determines its objectives and program, and the library contributes to the realization of these objectives by acquiring and making available the books, materials, and services needed in the instructional program.

Kinds of materials provided by the academic library[30]

The quantity and diversity of library materials will vary according to the size, purpose, and program of the institution, but in most academic libraries the basic materials will include:

[27] See Chaps. 18–21.
[28] See also pp. 277, 282.
[29] Middle States Association of Colleges and Secondary Schools, Commission on Institutions of Higher Education, *Evaluating the Library. . .* , p. 1.
[30] See also pp. 277, 283, 291, 301.

1. Reference books of a general nature and reference books in the subject fields, with emphasis on the subject areas included in the instructional program. These reference books include dictionaries, encyclopedias, indexes, yearbooks, handbooks, atlases, gazetteers, bibliographies, and certain collected works
2. A collection containing:

   a. Books which relate to and supplement each curriculum offered, such as history, education, and foreign languages, including those books which cover the entire field and those which relate to the specific courses offered in that field

   b. Important general books not relating to a specific subject area and important books in subject fields not included in the curricula

   c. Books for voluntary and recreational reading

   d. Professional and research materials for both the faculty and certain students who require them
3. Periodicals and newspapers in foreign languages—current issues, bound volumes, and those on microfilm, microcards, and other microforms
4. Pamphlets and clippings
5. Audio-visual materials, including pictures, motion-picture films, slides, filmstrips, transparencies, music, phonograph records, tape and wire recordings, maps and globes
6. Programmed materials
7. Government publications
8. Archival materials pertaining to the institution
9. Equipment for the use of these materials, such as micro-readers and listening and viewing equipment

The academic library is administered and staffed by professional librarians who must have an understanding of the educational philosophy and teaching methods of the institution in order to be able to work with the faculty in curriculum planning and curriculum development and in selecting and evaluating materials to support the instructional program. The academic library staff should provide the necessary reference, instructional, and bibliographical services to enable students and faculty to take full advantage of the library's resources.

Problems[31]

Because academic libraries have many common characteristics, they have many of the same problems. Among the most pressing of these are:

1. The tremendous growth in student enrollments which, by 1970, are expected to double those of 1960.[32] Larger enrollments place many additional demands for materials, services, and facilities on already overburdened library staffs.

2. The rapid expansion of knowledge, which has resulted in a deluge of new publications in many new forms and has produced problems of selecting the most useful materials from the great numbers which are available.

3. The need for quicker and more effective means of bibliographical access to these publications.

4. The increasing cost of library materials—an estimated average increase during the last decade of 31 percent for books and 35 percent for periodicals[33]—without comparable increases in library budgets.

5. The many new course offerings and the resulting need for new kinds of materials and for the equipment for using them.

6. The growing emphasis on high quality in education and on the fostering of independent study and inquiry, which has brought forth new programs and methods of instruction calling for heavy use of library materials.

7. The urgent need for larger staffs of professional librarians as well as for nonprofessional supporting staff.

8. The need for more and better physical facilities.

9. The inadequacy of library resources to meet the needs of current programs—50 percent of the four-year institutions and 82 percent of the two-year colleges fall below accepted

[31] See also pp. 278–80, 287, 294–95, 306–07, and Chap. 24.
[32] "Statement by Francis Keppel . . . ," p. 14.
[33] *Ibid.*, p. 16.

minimum standards in the number of volumes in their libraries.[34]

It has been noted that each kind of academic library—the junior college, the college, and the university—in addition to the characteristics which it shares with all academic libraries, serves certain purposes and has certain features and problems peculiarly its own, which grow out of the particular character and scope of the institution of which it is a part. In each kind of institution, the nature of the library—its purposes, staff, holdings, program of services, equipment and physical facilities—is determined by the extent and nature of the curriculum, the size of the faculty and student body, the methods of instruction, the variety of graduate offerings, the needs of the faculty and graduate students for specific professional and advanced research materials, and the demands of the total academic community for learning and teaching materials of whatever sort. Other major determinants of the library's nature are the dependability and amount of its financial support; the quantity and quality of its personnel and their relationship with the faculty and the administration; and whether or not it is a part of an area, state, or regional cooperative system in which certain materials, equipment, and services may be shared.

[34] *Ibid.,* p. 13.

CHAPTER 18
THE
JUNIOR
COLLEGE
LIBRARY

The American junior college had its beginnings in the small two-year private colleges, in the two-year curricula of the normal schools and four-year colleges, in the one- or two-year technical and business institutes, and in the two-year extensions—the thirteenth and fourteenth grades—of the public secondary school. It has had various names: city college, technical institute, business school or college, junior college, and—more recently—community college. Some junior colleges are privately endowed and controlled; but more than two thirds are maintained and controlled by the public.

GROWTH OF THE JUNIOR COLLEGE

Called "strictly an American institution" and "the big discovery of the age," the junior college had grown in number to 837 in 1966, with an enrollment of 1,464,099, of which more than 1,316,980 were in the 565 publicly supported institutions.[1] Some of the factors which have contributed to this surging growth are (1) the tremendous increase in the number of high school graduates,[2] and the desire and need to provide advanced educational opportunities for all of them; (2) general acceptance of the belief that extended education increases one's earning capacity; and (3) advances in

[1] American Association of Junior Colleges, *1967 Junior College Directory* (Washington, D.C.: American Association of Junior Colleges, 1967), *passim.* Enrollment figures are for October, 1966.
[2] 2.5 million in 1964-65, compared with 1.3 million twenty years ago. *ALA Bulletin,* LX (February, 1966), 129.

technology, which have created many new jobs requiring specialized training as well as the necessity for new training in old jobs.

Purposes and programs of the junior college

The public junior college has been "specifically designed and developed to provide an open door to post-high school education," and to bring it "within commuting distance of every secondary school graduate and at a cost that will not discriminate against the children of low-income families."[3] Less expensive and more convenient than the four-year college or the university, it meets the needs of the high school graduate who cannot go to a four-year college but must have additional education and training to fit him for a vocation, to update his occupational skills, or to acquire new skills. It provides also for the needs of the student who will continue his formal education at a four-year institution. The private junior college as well as the public junior college provides a preparatory base for those who plan to transfer to the junior year of a four-year college or university.

To achieve its major goals of "effective teaching, counseling, general education, and community services,"[4] the junior college— whether public or private—must provide a great variety of programs, both terminal and preparatory, to fit the wide range of abilities, interests, and aptitudes of its diverse student body. These programs include broad general education for all students; two-year programs to prepare for semiprofessional and technical occupations; programs of continuing education, which will enable individuals to retain and upgrade their skills, keep abreast of technological, social, and economic developments, and meet their new needs and interests; and college-parallel curricula for students who will transfer to four-year colleges and to universities in their third year. In addition to the basic college curricula and its vocational-technical programs, the junior college offers adult education opportunities in the form of institutes, conferences, short courses, concerts,

[3] Howard A. Campion, "Financing the Public Junior College," *NEA Journal*, XIII (October, 1964), 67.
[4] Charles E. Chapman, "Aligning Priorities in Junior and Community Colleges," *Current Issues in Higher Education*, ed. G. Kerry Smith (Washington, D.C.: National Education Association, 1965), p. 168.

forums, clinics, and exhibits, which are all related to the needs of the community it serves.

The public junior college is becoming increasingly an institution in its own right, not just an extension of the high school nor merely the first two years of the baccalaureate program. As an institution of higher learning within commuting distance of potential students, it is rapidly becoming a community college, using the history, traditions, personnel, problems, assets, and liabilities of the community as an extension of classroom and laboratory.[5]

THE JUNIOR COLLEGE LIBRARY PROGRAM[6]

The junior college library exists to serve the needs of this multipurpose institution, and because these needs are many and varied, the responsibilities of the library correspond. It must try to provide the materials and services to support each of the programs offered—general education, vocational-technical, semiprofessional, and adult education—and serve the needs of the widely different students who enroll in these courses and the demands and needs of the faculty who teach them.

The development of an appropriate and adequate collection[7] of materials to serve these purposes becomes a most difficult task. The collection should be as broad in coverage as the course offerings, providing books, periodical publications, pamphlets, and audio-visual and other educational resources and materials in each area of emphasis in the several curricula. It should include professional and other materials for faculty use; and it should also include recreational materials for reading, viewing, or listening for both students and faculty.

The junior college library serves students and faculty by mak-

---

[5] Edmund J. Gleazer, *A New Social Invention: The Community College— What It Is* (Washington, D.C.: American Association of Junior Colleges), unpaged.

[6] See also pp. 271–72.

[7] The present ALA standards call for a minimum of 20,000 volumes, exclusive of duplicates and textbooks, for a junior college with an enrollment of 1,000 students. See the Association of College and Research Libraries, "ALA Standards for Junior College Libraries," *College and Research Libraries*, XXI (May, 1960), 203. These standards are being revised.

ing available materials for assigned and voluntary reading and study for library or home use; by giving formal and informal instruction in the use of the library; by encouraging wide reading through easy accessibility of materials, reader guidance, displays, and book discussions; by enlisting the cooperation of the faculty in making the library a study center; and by providing bibliographical information and special materials for the faculty. It also promotes cultural activities for the entire community and often serves as a center for community affairs.

An adequate and effective program of library services for such a varied clientele and instructional program calls for a staff which understands and supports the purposes and objectives of the junior college idea in general and those of their own institution in particular. A broad educational background, an acquaintance with the literature of the subject fields, and an ability to identify and appraise resources for the diversity of course offerings are desirable qualifications of staff members.

Problems

The junior (community) college has become an important institution in American life, occupying a significant position in the educational career of a growing number of college-age students and in the vocational and citizenship activities of both students and adults. Its developing significance in the life of the country is indicated in the fact that enrollments increased 22 percent in 1965 over 1964[8] and is even more dramatically suggested in the prediction that junior colleges may be responsible for 50 percent of all college students by 1975.[9]

The importance of adequate and effective library services in such an institution is tremendous. For all students—both those who have learned basic library skills and those who have been denied adequate library services in high school—the junior college library must provide the resources and opportunity to acquire efficiency in using library materials which they need immediately and those

[8] American Association of Junior Colleges, *Junior College Directory*, p. 5.
[9] Chapman, *op. cit.*, p. 168.

which they will require in continuing their formal education or in pursuing their own self-motivated education after college.

The ability of the junior college library to achieve its goal of adequate and effective library service to all students and all programs is currently not an encouraging one. The executive director of the American Association of Junior Colleges has said that "of all aspects of junior college development, less attention has been given to the junior college library than to any other part of the instructional program."[10] In 1965, 82 percent of the two-year institutions fell below the American Library Association standards in number of volumes.[11] Although quantity of holdings is far from being an exhaustive test of the adequacy and efficiency of library services, experience has shown that it is a measurable indication of the importance which administrators, teachers, and supporters of a particular institution attach to its library.

There are some at least partial explanations for this state of affairs. For one thing, the rapid growth of junior (or community) colleges in the past ten to fifteen years, with too many of them opening and continuing to operate with insufficient funds, has frequently resulted in inadequate administrative and teaching staff and across-the-board inadequacy of programs and facilities, including libraries. In those which began as extensions of the high school program, the library was frequently a part of the high school library, or it was inadequately and inconveniently housed in such inaccessible places as the basement or hallway. Other junior colleges have opened with only a few hundred volumes, provided by public donation, which may not have been related to the teaching program. Another part of the explanation is that membership in the regional associations is not mandatory and accreditation by the state accrediting agency is not always a requirement for operating a two-year college. As a consequence, many junior colleges have opened and operated under generally substandard conditions.

To those who are trying to secure belated recognition of the significance of the junior college library, it is clear that the most

[10] Edmund J. Gleazer, Jr., "The Stake of the Junior College in Its Libraries," *College and Research Libraries*, XXVII (July, 1966), 266.
[11] "Statement by Francis Keppel . . . ," p. 13.

pressing need is for funds to pay higher salaries in order to attract better-trained and more efficient personnel; to build up a collection of book and nonbook materials in line with a growing and changing instructional program, designed to meet more realistically the needs of a technologically advanced society; and to replace temporary facilities with new, permanent, and more functional buildings and equipment. A more immediate problem is that of bringing the junior college library program of services up to at least the minimum level described in the "ALA Standards for Junior College Libraries."

A recent significant development has been the creation of a national committee on junior college libraries. In cooperation with the Association of Junior Colleges, the Council on Library Resources held a meeting in 1964 of junior college presidents and librarians and of other interested persons to inquire into the needs of libraries in two-year institutions. The result of this conference was the establishment of a national committee on junior college libraries, composed of representatives from the American Association of Junior Colleges and the American Library Association. This committee has initiated a ten-point program for improving libraries in junior colleges, covering recruitment and preparation of personnel, research into library needs, provision of consultant services, establishment of demonstration libraries, and the dissemination of information on the junior college library.

CHAPTER 19
THE
COLLEGE
LIBRARY[1]

In general, the name "college" is given to an institution of higher learning which offers a four-year curriculum leading to a bachelor's degree in arts and sciences, which requires for admission graduation from an accredited secondary school or its equivalent, and which is not divided into separate schools and faculties. This definition does not indicate the wide variation among colleges as to control, purposes, programs, and size. There are liberal arts colleges, many of which emphasize specializations in given fields rather than liberal education; there are colleges for the preparation of teachers, technical colleges, and agricultural colleges. Some colleges offer a fifth year leading to the master's degree, and some call themselves universities before they have developed a sufficient number of professional schools or faculties with a quality of advanced teaching and study to merit the title. Colleges may be under state, muncipal, or denominational control; or they may be privately endowed and controlled. Enrollments range from fewer than five hundred students to more than ten thousand.

At the turn of the century, college libraries entered upon a period of growth and after World War I expanded rapidly, but their major concern in most cases was to acquire and to preserve materials rather than to encourage and facilitate their use, for at that time, the textbook was the chief method of instruction. As more knowledge—both general and specialized—became available, dissatisfaction with the textbook as the core of the teaching process became widespread, and increasingly in the thirties the college li-

[1] The basic textbook in this area is Guy R. Lyle, *The Administration of the College Library* (3d ed.; New York: The H. W. Wilson Company, 1961).

brary was given the requirement and the opportunity to concern itself with selecting and evaluating learning materiais to support the teaching program and with aiding students in their use.

In the forties and fifties, such educational emphases as eaucation for democratic living; education for world affairs; specialization; the teaching of science, mathematics, and foreign languages; and the importance of using a variety of materials called for new courses and new methods of instruction. The library endeavored to support the new curricular and instructional programs by longer hours of service, larger collections, open stacks, flexible circulation polices, new attention to instruction in library use, acquisition of various kinds of print and nonprint materials, and the provision of carrels and listening and viewing facilities.

In the past decade, public pressure for higher education for all coupled with the enormous increase in high school graduates has resulted in tremendous growth in college enrollments. New curricula, new areas of specilization, and new methods of instruction have been introduced in an effort to meet the needs of the great number of students. Advances in science and technology have called for additional specializations and additional innovations in curriculum and in the methods of instruction.

THE COLLEGE LIBRARY PROGRAM[2]

Function

Since it is the basic function of the college library to serve to the fullest extent possible the program of the parent institution, implementing the purposes of the college's general program and supporting its specific educational objectives with the needed resources, facilities, and services, each college library is in some ways different. The basic common efforts of all college libraries, however, should be to meet the legitimate needs and demands of all their patrons "from the senior professor engaged in advanced research to the freshman just entering"; to stimulate and encourage students to

[2] See also pp. 271–72.

develop lifelong habits of good reading, study, and research; and to be in fact as well as in theory the central intellectual resource of their academic communities.[3]

The collection

The college library should provide a live and growing collection of books, periodicals, pamphlets, newspapers, audio-visual materials and microforms in both English and foreign languages, planned and selected for depth as well as breadth of coverage. The collection should give full support to the general education program and to the subject majors and provide for the needs of the graduate programs (if any) and for the professional and scholarly research needs of the faculty.[4] The collection should be selected and developed on the basis of the educational philosophy and objectives of the institution, the extent and nature of the curriculum, the methods of instruction, the size and nature of the student body, the size of the faculty and their needs for research materials, and the range of services required by the library's users.[5] If the college offers graduate work, the number and character of graduate programs and students will obviously influence the selection process. The collection must support not only the traditional programs but such new programs as independent study, tutorial and seminar-type experiences, programs of study abroad and education for world affairs, residence-hall libraries, year-round study, and off-campus courses. The library's collection may also contain the equipment needed in the use of materials, such as microreaders, viewing and listening facilities, and photocopying equipment.

Services and staff

The library serves the reading, reference, and research needs of the members of the college community by providing materials

[3] See Association of College and Research Libraries, "Standards for College Libraries," *College and Research Libraries*, XX (July, 1959).
[4] *Ibid.*
[5] A minimum of 50,000 carefully chosen volumes is considered to give effective support to the instructional program of a college having an enrollment of 600 students; steady growth based on enrollment and curriculum needs is essential. (*Ibid.*, p. 278.)

adequate for their various needs and purposes; making them easily accessible physically through open shelves or other efficient means, and bibliographically through catalogs, bibliographies, and indexes; making them available for library use and home use through reasonable loan periods; giving special assistance in the use of specific materials as well as formal instruction in library resources and use; borrowing needed materials on interlibrary loan from other libraries; providing adequate and comfortable physical facilities for study, including carrels for work on special study projects; and by extending the hours of service to meet the needs of the users.[6]

In order to be able to offer such a program of services, the staff of professional librarians must be broadly educated and have some subject specialization as well as some language proficiency. They must keep up with trends in higher education, curriculum developments, methods of teaching, and new materials and new sources of materials in order to be able to participate actively in the instructional program of the college. Active participation is not limited to teaching the use of the library; it involves working closely with faculty members in planning new courses and in determining the nature of library resources for their needs and in advising them on bibliographical matters. In addition to their teaching and counseling activities in connection with developing the collection, providing bibliographical access to it through cataloging and classification, and providing reference and circulation services, the professional staff may conduct literature searches, prepare reading lists and bibliographies, teach a course in their subject specialty, and participate in team teaching.

The college library is organized and administered by the director or chief librarian. The organization should be suitable to the needs and programs of the institution; and thus it will be influenced by the size of the staff, the size of the student body, the extent to which the college encourages and provides for independent study and other individualized programs, and the number and variety

---

[6] "Statement of Service to Library Users," *ACRL News, A Supplement to College and Research Libraries*, Vol. XXVII, No. 2 (April, 1966), 21, 22. See footnote 11, p. 293, regarding interlibrary loan.

of graduate offerings. Theoretically, the size of the professional staff will be determined by the type of organization within the library, the college enrollment, the size and character of the collection, the teaching methods in use, the number of hours the library is open, the arrangement of the building, and the range of services. Obviously, the amount of funds which are provided for the operation of the library will critically affect the quality and the extent of its services and resources. It is the responsibility of the chief librarian to make the most efficient use of the funds which are available and at the same time work for adequate financial support for his developing program.

TRENDS, NEEDS, PROBLEMS

In the mid-1960s, strong emphasis in higher education on research methods, inquiry, and discovery learning and a growing belief that learning is "student-resource centered" rather than "faculty-classroom centered" have led to the further individualizing of instruction. The role of the library as a teaching instrument has been expanded and developed,[7] and as a result, new concepts of service and new instructional relationships have emerged and new types of library organization have been introduced. Several recent developments in higher education and in accompanying library practices are noteworthy:

1. The concept of residence halls as an "integral part of the learning environment," with classrooms, laboratories, libraries, and other academic facilities. In such living-learning centers, the library provides space for study, a basic reference collection, and materials related to freshman and sophomore classes.[8]

2. The emphasis on the multimedia approach to learning. In

[7] See Patricia B. Knapp, *The Monteith College Library Experiment* (New York: Scarecrow Press, Inc., 1966), a report of an experiment at Monteith College, Wayne State University, in coordination between the library and the teaching staff to change student use of the library.

[8] Stephens College is an example.

some colleges, the library is the center for varied collections of teaching and learning resources, such as programmed materials, tape and disc recordings, self-instruction carrels with facilities for recordings, audio-visual collections, electronic equipment, and computer-based instructional devices.

3. The learning resources center concept. This type of organization makes the library a department of a larger learning resources division, which has, in addition, a language laboratory, large-group and small-group facilities, classrooms, and television studios.

4. Extending independent study to all students rather than limiting it to the advanced and talented. Out of this effort has come the "library college" concept, in which the library becomes the center of the student's learning activities and efforts.[9] Mastery of library resources is fundamental to independent study, and new approaches to library instruction—including instruction in the use of all media—are necessary.

Other significant developments in college librarianship are:

1. Interinstitutional cooperation.[10] College libraries are participating in interinstitutional cooperative systems to strengthen and improve library resources and services by dividing responsibility for the acquisition of materials; sharing resources; maintaining location records of important materials or titles; preparing union lists of periodicals, reference works, or special collections; and exchanging cataloging and other bibliographical information.

2. The mechanization of certain library operations.[11] The use of mechanization in technical processes, circulation routines,

[9] See Louis Shores, "The Library College Idea," *Library Journal*, XCI (September 1, 1966), 3871–75.

[10] Examples of interinstitutional library cooperation among colleges within a state are (1) the cooperative library system developed by seven liberal arts colleges which comprise the Arkansas Foundation of Associated Colleges, (2) the Area College Library Cooperative Program formed by nine colleges in Pennsylvania; and (3) *Libras*, an organization formed by the libraries of eight Chicago-area private colleges for the purpose of interlibrary sharing.

[11] See also Chap. 23.

and acquisition procedures has resulted in improved library services for the college community and in more efficient use of time on the part of the professional staff.

Problems and needs[12]

Although the nature and direction of the college library program should be determined by the purposes and the teaching-learning activities of the college, it is too often determined by the amount of funds which the governing body and the administration allocate for its operation. Prolonged lack of the necessary funds has resulted in many substandard collections, in inadequate facilities and equipment, and in staffs insufficient in size and quality. The *National Inventory of Library Needs* estimated that more than 47 million volumes are needed to meet the minimum requirements of the American Library Association's standards in this area and more than 2,753 professional librarians are needed to meet ALA standards for professional staff.[13]

In short, if college libraries are to approach effectiveness in meeting the demands of increasing enrollments, in providing expanding programs of service required by the broadening and strengthening of instructional activities, and in becoming truly the central intellectual resources of their academic communities, they must have financial aid—in most cases a sizable amount beyond that now available to them. This aid is needed to bring their collections of both general and specialized materials up to at least a minimum standard of adequacy, to offer higher salaries to attract better qualified personnel and to increase the size of the professional staff, to provide more nonprofessional personnel to handle clerical and routine tasks, and to provide more efficient equipment and facilities.[14]

[12] See also pp. 273–74.
[13] *National Inventory of Library Needs, op. cit.,* p. 61.
[14] See p. 270 for a discussion of recent Federal legislative measures which provide some financial assistance in these areas of need.

CHAPTER 20
THE
UNIVERSITY
LIBRARY

A university is an institution of higher education which has a liberal arts college; offers a program of graduate study; has, usually, two or more professional schools or faculties; and is empowered to confer degrees in various fields of study.[1]

Before the Revolution all institutions of higher learning in America were called colleges. Following the Revolution, new state institutions called universities were organized and some of the private colleges were reorganized in order to assume the broadened university functions. The state university made its appearance in the late eighteenth century,[2] but the early state universities received little financial support from the state and the instruction which they gave was hardly advanced enough to qualify under modern standards as university teaching. The University of Virginia, established by Thomas Jefferson in 1825, has been called America's first real state university.[3] Deliberately planned as a public enterprise and completely undenominational, it offered a broader selection of subjects and more advanced work than existing colleges and predecessor universities.[4] In the course of westward expansion, universities were established under the leadership of educators from the Eastern states, and by the time of the Civil War twenty-one state universities and several municipal universities had been founded. Most of the

[1] Carter V. Good (ed.), *Dictionary of Education* (2d ed.; New York: Mc-Graw-Hill Book Company, 1959), p. 590.
[2] See pp. 83–84.
[3] Brubacher, *op. cit.*, p. 144.
[4] Thomas Jefferson laid down strict rules for the library of the University of Virginia, specifying that only books of "great reputation and too expensive for purchase by private means, and authoritative expositions of science and translations of superior elegance" should be acquired. (Brubacher, *op. cit.*, p. 94.)

municipal universities, however, appeared following the war with the development of large urban centers and were planned to provide publicly supported free higher education for the people who lived in the cities.

One of the major influences on American higher education in the nineteenth century was the German university. American students went in great number to study in Germany, attracted first by the advanced level of teaching and later by the German idea of scholarly research. The first American university to be founded in the true German tradition was Johns Hopkins University in 1876. "Non-sectarian and dedicated to the unfettered search for truth," it did not attempt to duplicate existing colleges, but aimed to supply the needs of the United States in certain special learned fields.[5] Following the example of Johns Hopkins, certain of the firmly established private colleges like Harvard, Yale, Columbia, and Princeton were reorganized and expanded into universities along the lines of the German tradition.

The German-educated scholars of the latter half of the nineteenth century brought back such new instructional techniques as the seminar, the laboratory method, and the lecture. The use of these new methods influenced not only the development of university organization and program but also the development and use of great university libraries. With reference to the prevailing intellectual mood and practice of the era in which he was writing, William Rainey Harper of the University of Chicago said that "in every subject . . . the laboratory method and the library method now hold full sway."[6]

Professor Brubacher has aptly summarized the early development of American universities:

The growth of universities in America was brought about by many factors—the rationalism and empiricism of the Enlightenment, the impact of the American and French Revolutions, the influence of the resurgent German universities of the nineteenth century,

---

[5] Brubacher, *op. cit.*, p. 176.
[6] William Rainey Harper, *The Trend in Higher Education* (Chicago: The University of Chicago Press, 1905), pp. 126, 134.

the utilitarian need for incorporating new fields of knowledge such as science and modern languages into the curriculum to serve the requirements of an expanding society.[7]

In the twentieth century the university has added many new and different fields of graduate education—journalism, pharmacy, nursing, agriculture, business, public administration, and library science—as well as research programs for the benefit of the university; of local, state, or Federal government; and of business and industry.

THE UNIVERSITY LIBRARY PROGRAM[8]

Purposes and functions

The purpose of the university library program is to support the university's total program. Since the range of the total program extends from the freshman to the doctoral candidate engaged in scholarly research, the university library must try to offer resources and services of comparable range.

For the undergraduate students, the library program provides materials and services specifically designed to meet their requirements. For the students pursuing advanced study, the faculty members involved in that level of study, and the resident or visiting research specialists, it provides resources and services to support each of the graduate programs and materials of sufficient quantity and diversity to support research of whatever kind in every subject field. It also provides resources for the university's program of continuing education, participates in the publishing program of the university as an active contributor and as the depository of the university's publications, and serves both as a repository and a generating source of knowledge and ideas.

[7] Brubacher, *op. cit.*, p. 139.
[8] See also pp. 271–73 and Chap. 21.
    The standard text in this area (now somewhat out of date) is Louis Round Wilson and Maurice F. Tauber, *The University Library, The Organization, Administration and Functions of Academic Libraries* (2d ed.; New York: Columbia University Press, 1956.)

The collection

The collection of the university library, which includes materials to meet the needs of the undergraduate student as well as resources of sufficient breadth and depth to support serious scholarship in all areas in which instruction is given, to encourage research, and to stimulate and support continuing study and specialization, embraces all subjects and provides:[9]

1. A general collection of materials of common interest to several fields and including the most recent editions as well as those which have historical value
2. General and specialized reference, curricular and research materials in both English and foreign languages
3. Rare materials, such as incunabula, first editions, manuscripts, papers, letters, museum objects, broadsides, and historical maps
4. Newspapers and periodicals in English and foreign languages
5. Publications of Federal, state, local, and foreign governments as well as those of the United Nations
6. Special materials, such as monographic studies, results of research, theses, dissertations, archives, clippings, visual and audio-visual materials, and microforms
7. Diverse forms of materials and equipment, such as disc and tape recordings, films, sound tracks, language laboratories, video tapes, listening and viewing apparatus, photocopiers, and—increasingly—computers and auxiliary machines

In listing the factors which affect the quality of graduate work, the Middle States Association states that:

> Graduate study in any field, even more than undergraduate, is dependent upon the library. It requires resources out of proportion to the additional number of courses and students concerned. Not only must the advanced courses be supported with a greater number and more specialized kinds of books, monographs, source materials, periodicals, and reference works in the fields of instruction and

[9] See also pp. 283, 301.

related areas, but the background material for many special investigations will be demanded, too. Lack of superior library resources or failure to use them well condemns the program to mediocrity at the start.[10]

Organization

The university library program is organized to support and serve effectively the total university program. Until about the middle of this century, the university library usually was a central library in which the collections crossed all lines of intellectual endeavor and served undergraduates, graduates, and faculty members, with departmental collections to provide specialized materials and services to each of the several schools or colleges of the university.

Today, a number of organizational patterns are in use in addition to the one described above. Some universities provide a library for undergraduates in a separate building, with all the materials, facilities, and services necessary to meet their basic needs. In these instances, the central library gives its attention to providing materials and services to graduate students, research staff, and faculty members; but both the central library and the undergraduate library are open to all students. In some universities, the undergraduate library is not housed in a separate building but occupies one or more floors of the central library. In other instances, the central library contains all collections, but special provisions are made for undergraduates, such as reading rooms with special reserve and reference collections. The library may include only traditional forms of library materials (chiefly printed) with audio-visual and other materials being administered by a separate division; it may be a total facility, offering all services and materials, both print and nonprint, which are required for study and research; or it may be a department of a larger division of learning resources, which also includes language laboratories, other learning laboratories, television and radio studios, and an audio-visual department.

[10] Middle States Association of Colleges and Secondary Schools, Commission on Institutions of Higher Education, *Graduate Work* (Document No. 4.72; New York: Middle States Association of Colleges and Secondary Schools, 1959), p. 3.

Services and staff

The university library serves the academic community by:

1. Introducing the student to the attitudes, techniques, and possibilities of investigation and giving him the opportunity and resources to pursue it
2. Acquainting students with bibliographies in their subject fields and giving instruction in their use
3. Giving assistance in bibliographical method
4. Assisting faculty members in developing their own bibliographical knowledge and in keeping up with current publications in their fields
5. Providing ready access to materials, facilities for uninterrupted individual study, and such aids as translation assistance, typing facilities, and photocopying devices

In an effort to provide more efficient service to the academic community and to the world of scholarship, the university library participates in cooperative undertakings in bibliographical service, such as:

1. Interlibrary lending[11]
2. Cooperative and centralized cataloging
3. Compilation of bibliographies and union lists
4. Development of the National Union Catalog at the Library of Congress and of regional and local union catalogs and bibliographical centers
5. Specialization in collecting materials[12]
6. Centralized storage centers for little-used materials[13]
7. Cooperative photographic projects[14]

The director of the university library must have the training, ability, and skill to develop and administer this highly complex part of the institution's intellectual life; to interpret his program to society in general, to those who use it, and to the staff; and

[11] The purpose of interlibrary loans is to make available unusual and out-of-print materials to graduate students, faculty, and other qualified researchers. "General Interlibrary Loan Code 1952," *College and Research Libraries*, XIII (October, 1952), 350–58. (Repr. in *American Library Directory*, 25th ed., 1967, pp. 1279–87.)
[12] See the Farmington Plan, p. 302.
[13] See Center for Research Libraries, pp. 302–03.
[14] See Library of Congress Microfilm Project, p. 157.

to secure support for it—financial and other. "His thinking and planning must be that of a teacher and scholar, not a curator or technician. . . He must know what scholarship is and what teaching entails."[15] He must understand the purposes, objectives, and policies of the university in order to relate the library effectively to the various curricula and to the total university program. The members of the staff should be professional librarians who have a broad general education and the specializations which are required in each area of service offered by the library, such as specialists in the subject fields, in languages, in materials of instruction and special types and forms of materials, in reader guidance, in research, and in technology. They must be competent both as librarians and as educators.

Problems and needs[16]

Some of the problems of the university library grow out of developments within the university: increased total enrollment; the growing number of graduate students and programs; new comprehensive areas of study, such as non-Western countries and civilizations, which require resources that are expensive, scarce, and difficult to acquire; the trend toward providing more opportunities for independent study; and an expanding extension program, which enrolled—in all universities—more than 2 million adults in 1962.[17] All these problems contribute to the need for additional facilities, staff, and resources, which in turn produce the urgent need for an appreciable increase in funds allocated on a reliable and continuing basis.

Two special and major problems derive from the increased scholarly undertakings of the university and the great expansion of potential library materials in every field of knowledge. The enormous increase in research in every subject field in a growing number of universities, requiring exceedingly extensive and highly accessible

[15] Middle States Association of Colleges and Secondary Schools, Commission on Institutions of Higher Education, *Evaluating the Library* . . . , p. 1.
[16] See also pp. 273–74, 306–07.
[17] "Statement by Francis Keppel . . . ," p. 6.

collections of books, journals, and reports as well as other kinds of materials in a diversity of forms and languages, has brought a recognition that "the concerns of Western scholarship and contemporary society cannot be parochial but must be based upon access to an understanding of all other societies and cultures in the world regardless of geographic location, language, or form of materials."[18] Since one university can acquire only a small percent of these materials and since some materials, although soon obsolete, must be kept by some institution, the university library is faced with the urgent problems of what to acquire, what to keep, and how to make materials immediately accessible. Pressing needs are for (1) more space for the library's active collection and for storage of little-used materials; (2) larger and better-trained staffs with more subject competencies to explain resources, prepare bibliographies, and locate materials in other libraries; and (3) participation in more cooperative activities in the acquisition and dissemination of materials.

Possible solutions of some of these problems, especially the problems of storage and access, are being sought in a program of information-transfer experiments being conducted at the Massachusetts Institute of Technology.

In the university of the future, as it is visualized at M.I.T., the library will be the central resource of an information transfer network that will extend throughout the academic community. Students and scholars will use this system not only to locate books and documents in the library, but also to gain access to the university's total information resources, through Touch-Tone telephones, tele-typewriter keyboards, television-like displays, and quickly made copies. The users of the network will communicate with each other as well as with the library; data just obtained in the laboratory and comments made by observers will be as easily available as the text of books in the library or documents in the departmental files. The information traffic will be controlled by means of the university's time-shared computer utility in much the same

[18] *Intrex, Report of a Planning Conference on Information Transfer Experiments*, September 3, 1965, ed. Carl F. J. Overhage and R. Joyce Harman (Cambridge, Mass.: The M.I.T. Press, 1965), p. 7, 8, *passim.*

way in which today's verbal communications are handled by the campus telephone exchange. Long-distance service will connect the university's information transfer network with sources and users elsewhere.[19]

The research aspects of the university library are discussed further in the next chapter, "Research Libraries."

[19] *Ibid.*, p. 1.

CHAPTER 21
RESEARCH
LIBRARIES

Every man is a valuable member of society who, by his observations, researches, and experiments, procures knowledge for men . . . it is in his knowledge that man has found his greatness and his happiness, the high superiority which he holds over the other animals who inhabit the earth with him, and consequently no ignorance is probably without loss to him, no error without evil.[1]

Emphasis on research, not only in the sciences of nature but also in the behavioral and social sciences and the fields of humanistic study, has been increasing steadily for generations in technologically and industrially advanced countries. This emphasis has been accelerated radically since World War II, largely as the result of a stronger and more widespread judgment that information and knowledge issuing from research—and particularly technical and scientific information—constitute the basic ingredient in economic growth and prosperity and the chief line of defense of a country's power, national position, and survival in an aggressively competitive and nationalistic world. The natural result of this judgment has been a very great expansion of research facilities and resources in universities, with a marked shift of research responsibilities from specifically skilled and motivated individual scholars to faculty members at large; a growth of research resources in government agencies and in large public library systems; an increased development of independent private research libraries and centers; and a very expansive development of library resources and services to support the research activities of private industrial and commercial companies.

The president of the Council on Library Resources has stated

---

[1] James Smithson, founder of the Smithsonian Institution, quoted in the exterior inscriptions, Museum of History and Technology, Smithsonian Institution, Washington, D.C.

that "the essential function of the research library . . . is to provide access in bibliographic and in physical terms to the records of human communication."[2] In terms of this function, research libraries cut across standardized group classifications, such as school, academic, public, and special. Consequently, not only is there not a precise category into which research libraries can be placed,[3] but also there are not, nor can there be, any published precise quantitative standards by which to evaluate all research libraries. The forms and the subject content of the collection of research materials will vary with the particular mission of a specific library; and the quantity of the materials will vary with a particular library's decision regarding the extent to which it will attempt to be locally self-sufficient, that is, the extent to which it will try to provide in its own collection all, or at least the most significant part of, the materials and resources which its users need as against depending on effective access to resources other than its own.

For example, the collection of an independent research library which specializes in science—such as the John Crerar Library in Chicago or the Linda Hall Library in Kansas City, Missouri—will differ from the research materials of a university in that the collection will be predominantly scientific, whereas the university will provide materials of research in the humanities and social sciences as well as in the pure and applied sciences. Also, the collections of the university's research library will be built upon the resources of the university's central library. The same type of difference applies in comparing the research collections of a university with the research materials of the Henry F. Huntington Library in San Marino, California, and the Newberry Library in Chicago—both of which are privately endowed libraries which emphasize literature and history.

Although quantitative comparisons of research collections are not feasible, quality and service standards for academic research libraries are promoted actively by two national professional orga-

---

[2] Verner W. Clapp, *The Future of the Research Library* (Urbana, Ill.: The University of Illinois Press, 1964), pp. 49–50.
[3] It is possible and appropriate to classify research libraries as "specialized" or "general" with reference to the field or fields of knowledge which are covered by the materials and services provided.

nizations, the Association of College and Research Libraries[4] and the Association of Research Libraries. In addition to the research libraries of universities, the Association of Research Libraries also includes in its concern large public libraries, independent research libraries, and national Federal libraries. The association was formed in 1932 with forty-four member libraries for the purpose of studying the common problems of scholarly libraries and improving cooperation among the group as a whole. In 1967, it had eighty members; and although most of them were university libraries, two large municipal libraries, three national Federal libraries, and four privately endowed research libraries were included. Membership in the association is by invitation and is limited to the largest research libraries in the country with collections of materials that are broadly based and nationally significant. These libraries constitute a network of cooperation in the sharing of resources with the Library of Congress at the center. In this network is concentrated a great mass of valuable materials for advanced study and research. The Librarian of Congress has noted that these libraries "control bibliographical materials of a magnitude and richness unparalleled in history."[5]

It is not meant to suggest that the member libraries of the Association of Research Libraries are the only ones in this country which fully merit being called "research libraries"; it is believed, however, that a general understanding of the basic purposes, functions, and cooperative activities of the association's members will be adequately indicative of all research libraries. In this chapter, therefore, the discussion will be limited to the *types* of research libraries represented in the association's membership. The numerous libraries and library services in business, industry, and government, which are maintained in support of technical and scientific inquiry, experimentation, and research, will be discussed in the next chapter, "Special Libraries."

Availability

The resources of a university research library are available to the students, faculty, university research staff, and visiting schol-

[4] See pp. 265–66.
[5] "68th Meeting of the Association of Research Libraries." *ACRL News*, No. 7 (October, 1966), 129.

ars. The materials and services of a research library in a public
library system are open to the public under the regulations and
conditions established by the particular library. Use of some independent research libraries is restricted to advanced scholars and
is permitted only by special arrangement; others are open to the
public under regulations limiting the locale in which the materials
can be used. The research resources and services of the three national libraries—the Library of Congress, the National Library of
Medicine, and the National Agricultural Library—are available to
scholars; to students; to the research staffs of government agencies,
businesses and industries; and to the general public under regulations
relating to the form and nature of the materials, the time and place
of their use, and the nature and importance of the particular project
on which the user is working.

Functions

The common basic function of all research libraries is to provide
the resources and services to meet the research requirements of
their users in the form in which they are needed and at the time
when they are required. In light of this purpose, the research library
has a special responsibility to keep its clientele up to date and intellectually stimulated by providing pertinent literature, not only in
areas of immediate concern, but also in areas of emerging and developing importance within the scope of a particular library's mission.
Two specific types of functions, set forth in *The Federal Library
Mission*, are applicable to all research libraries.[6]

> Providing factual information responsive to specific inquiries, in-
> cluding when appropriate, the selection and synthesis of informa-
> tion from various sources and directing the inquirers' attention
> to related information beyond the immediate scope of the query
> . . .
> Providing professional guidance to readers in the use of library
> collections and bibliographic resources, and acquainting them with
> other information sources such as individual subject specialists, in-
> formation centers, and research organizations

[6] The Federal Library Committee, *op. cit.*, p. 8.

The collection

The collection is of a highly specialized nature, selected and fashioned to serve the specific area or areas of interest to which a particular research library is committed; thus, only the kinds of materials needed and in the amounts required to serve the library's purpose and commitments are acquired. Cooperative arrangements are maintained with other research libraries and with general and special libraries so that users will have access to the supplementary and supporting resources they require.[7]

The forms of the materials will vary with the fields of research interest included in the library's purpose. For example, a collection in the areas of science and technology will include reports of original research, monographs, abstracts, handbooks, tables of formulas, microforms, conference proceedings and reports, and certain types of laboratory material, as well as journals and materials in traditional book form. The production of information and knowledge materials in scientific and technical fields is currently so massive that most of the materials in the holdings of the science research library may be of very recent date. Collections of research libraries devoted to the humanities and social sciences will have many of the forms of materials which a science collection includes. In these fields, materials will not be as new as they are in science and technology, nor will they become out of date as rapidly. In all fields of research interest there will be materials in several languages.

Services

By the very nature of its purpose for being, the research library offers many types of specialized services such as:

1. Acquiring, organizing, and preparing for use needed and pertinent materials without delay
2. Preparing and circulating lists of new acquisitions
3. Examining new materials and providing to appropriate users information about them in the form of reviews, abstracts, tables of contents, and photocopies of excerpts

[7] See Neal Harlow, "Levels of Need for Library Service in Academic Institutions," *College and Research Libraries*, XXIV (September, 1963), 362.

4. Maintaining highly specialized reference files and indexes
5. Conducting literature searches
6. Providing accurate, relevant information to inquirers
7. Preparing bibliographies
8. Translating publications wholly or in part
9. Providing cheap and rapid means of photocopying
10. Providing quick reference and referral service, person to person and by telephone
11. Operating a delivery service, on occasion
12. Extending the limits of its own resources by interlibrary loan and through such methods of bibliographical cooperation as union lists and catalogs and the exchanging of catalogs and bibliographies

Examples of cooperative activities[8]

Among the most notable examples of the cooperative undertakings of research libraries are the Farmington Plan and the Center for Research Libraries. The Farmington Plan, administered by the Association of Research Libraries, was initiated in 1947 "to make sure that at least one copy of each new foreign book and pamphlet that might reasonably be expected to interest a research worker in the United States will be acquired by an American library, promptly listed in the Union Catalogue at the Library of Congress, and made available by interlibrary loan or photographic reproduction."[9] Some sixty research libraries participate in the plan and each one has accepted responsibility for collecting the literature of a given subject area from a particular country or region, using assigned book dealers in the country or region both for selection and distribution. Beginning with Western Europe, the plan now extends to Africa, Australia, Latin America, the Far East, South and Southeast Asia, and the Middle East. All fields of knowledge are covered.

The Midwest Inter-Library Center, incorporated in 1949 by

---

[8] See also pp. 185–86. Current issues of professional journals offer numerous recent examples of cooperation.
[9] Edwin E. Williams, *Farmington Plan Handbook* (Cambridge, Mass.: Association of Research Libraries, 1953), p. 3.

ten universities, became the Center for Research Libraries in 1965.[10] It now has twenty-one members. Its primary purpose is to increase the library research resources available to cooperating institutions in the Midwest, and its activities include:

1. Housing for common use the infrequently used materials held by each participating institution

2. Cooperative purchase and centralized cataloging and housing of infrequently used research materials not already available to the participants, such as doctoral dissertations from foreign universities, new foreign scholarly journals and other scholarly periodicals which are not sufficiently available to members, other kinds of journals, academy and society publications, and foreign government documents

3. Centralized acquisition and cataloging of materials acquired by the participants for their own collections

4. Coordination of acquisitions to avoid unnecessary duplication

Membership in the center is limited to institutions with broad programs of advanced research and with large research libraries. The center has a collection of more than 2 million volumes and makes loans to libraries other than its own members. It has become a national rather than a regional research institution.

Federal legislation

In preceding chapters, Federal programs, legislation, and services of potential benefit—financial and other—to practically all types of libraries have been pointed out. Provisions of current and continuing legislative programs of value to research libraries include:[11]

1. The State Technical Services Act of 1965, administered by the Department of Commerce, provides for a three-year

---

[10] See Gordon Williams, "The Center for Research Libraries: Its New Organization and Programs," *Library Journal*, XC (July, 1965), 2947–51.

[11] All the references to Federal legislation in this section will be found in the special issue of the *ALA Bulletin* (February, 1966), entitled "Federal Library Legislation, Programs, and Services," which has been cited previously. See also *ALA Bulletin* (October, 1967), entitled "Federal Library Legislation, Programs, and Services: II."

program of matching grants to the states to stimulate the establishment and maintenance of programs and activities designed to enable businesses and industrial establishments to acquire and use scientific and engineering information more effectively through such means as reference services to identify sources of engineering and other scientific knowledge and skills; preparing and disseminating technical reports, abstracts, reviews, microfilm, computer tapes, and similar forms of scientific and engineering information; and the establishment of state and interstate technical information centers. These activities are in line with the types of services noted above as typical of those offered by independent research libraries which specialize in science and technology and by the research libraries of universities and public library systems which maintain collections of specialized materials in the natural sciences. Those research libraries which participate in the programs established in the states under this act should benefit in a number of important ways.

2. The National Foundation on the Arts and the Humanities Act of 1965 provided for a National Foundation on the Arts and Humanities and for the establishment of two national endowments as components of the foundation. One of these, the National Endowment for the Humanities, was authorized to provide nonmatching grants and loans for research, fellowships, training, the publication of scholarly works, and exchanges of information in the humanities. Federal assistance under this act can be extended to research libraries which give special attention to the humanities and to university and public library systems in the building and enriching of their collections and services in the broad fields of the humanities and arts.

3. The Higher Education Act of 1965 provided for varied kinds of aid to academic libraries. Of special interest to academic research libraries are those provisions of a five-year program to assist in the acquiring of materials needed for their expanded responsibilities in research, the enlargement of training for service in libraries, and the promotion

of investigation and demonstration projects designed to make library and information services more efficient. In this act, as in the two acts mentioned above, matching funds from the participating institutions were not made a requirement.

4. Title II, Part C, of the Higher Education Act of 1965 included a provision to make funds available to the Library of Congress to acquire—to the extent possible—all library materials currently published throughout the world of value to scholarship and to provide catalog information on these acquisitions promptly. This program, called the National Program for Acquisitions and Cataloging, became operational in mid-1966. Prompt cataloging is made possible through the cooperation of foreign national libraries, who make available to Library of Congress catalogers the entries for their national bibliographies. The Library of Congress accepts the cataloging used in these entries as the basis for its own cataloging of these materials. More than ninety libraries in the United States are now participating in this shared cataloging program.[12]

5. The Agricultural Trade Development and Assistance Act of 1954 (Public Law 480) was amended in 1958 to authorize the Librarian of Congress to use United States-owned foreign currencies, within the limits of such appropriations as might be made by Congress, for the purchase of foreign publications; for cataloging, indexing, abstracting and related activities in connection with the purchased materials; and for the deposit of the materials in libraries and research centers of the United States. Beginning in 1961 with pilot programs in only three countries, the United Arab Republic, Pakistan, and India, it was expanded in 1963 to include Indonesia and Israel. In 1967 Nepal, Ceylon, and Yugoslavia were added, and negotiations were underway to include Poland.[13] By June, 1966 more than 5½ million

[12] See pp. 160–61.
[13] "Overseas Acquisitions and Cataloging Programs of the Library of Congress," *Federal Library Committee Newsletter*, No. 10 (April, 1967), 3–6, *passim*.

publications had been acquired and distributed to more than three hundred libraries in the United States.[14]

Staff

The qualifications of the professional staff of a particular research library are implicit in the specific purpose and functions of that library. Obviously, the subject specialists will vary with the areas emphasized and served. The size of the staff, both professional and nonprofessional, will vary with the volume of work involved in serving a particular library's clientele; with the methods, techniques, and organizational system employed in serving the library's users; with the funds available for personnel; and with the availability of qualified personnel.

Certain qualifications should be common to the professional staff of all research libraries, including thorough specialization in the areas of knowledge emphasized and in some areas, especially in the pure and applied sciences, specialization in the subdisciplines; facility in the appropriate languages; sufficient training in scholarly investigation and in the most effective bibliographical methods to be adept in literature searching and, thus, capable of giving clear, accurate, and adequate information on demand; proficiency in selecting and evaluating materials; ability to work effectively with subject specialists and research teams; and an understanding of the interrelationships of the subject fields.

Problems

Among the problems which face the research library in the last third of the century are:[15]

1. How to provide bibliographical access to the vast and ever-increasing quantities of recorded materials in all areas of thought, knowledge, and experience in order to enable the inquirer to become aware of, to identify, and to locate the particular publication or other form of material or the specific item of information he needs

[14] *Annual Report of the Librarian of Congress for the Fiscal Year Ending June 30, 1966, op. cit.,* p. 36.
[15] See also pp. 294–96 and Chap. 24.

2. How to shorten the period of time between the publication of research materials, their acquisition by the library, and the cataloging of these materials[16]
3. How to improve techniques for the description, organization, and maintenance of the research collection, including the storage of little-used materials
4. How to increase and make more effective cooperative activities in the sharing of library resources
5. How to preserve deteriorating materials[17]

[16] See pp. 159–60 for a discussion of the Library of Congress' machine-readable cataloging pilot project, MARC.

[17] It is estimated that most of the books published in the first half of this century will not be usable by the end of the century, and according to studies made in 1961–1962, there are in American libraries materials totaling some 3 billion pages which require preservative measures. *Ninth Annual Report for the Year Ending June 30, 1965* (Washington, D.C.: Council on Library Resources, Inc., 1965), pp. 23, 30.

Under a grant from the Council on Library Resources, the W. J. Barrow Research Laboratory was established in August, 1961 in Richmond, Virginia, to conduct research and development for the council in the preservation of library materials by developing techniques and materials for treating bound volumes to prevent deterioration of the paper in them and by developing materials and methods to improve the permanence and durability of records. In addition, the Barrow Laboratory is undertaking for the Library Technology Project of the ALA the task of developing standards and specifications for library bookbinding. The Library Technology Project, established in 1959 by the ALA with the financial assistance of the Council on Library Resources, includes among its activities: tests and evaluations of equipment, supplies, and materials of various kinds; development of performance standards for material; systems studies; and dissemination of purchasing information.

CHAPTER 22
SPECIAL
LIBRARIES

The term "special" as applied to libraries currently has various meanings. At times it is used as an omnibus term to apply to all libraries that are not school, academic, public, or research; at other times it is used more inclusively to cover certain privately endowed specialized collections such as the John Crerar Library.[1] It is often applied to "subject branches or departments of public or university library complexes, such as the business branch of a public library or the industrial relations library of a university library system";[2] and it is used to designate certain types of agencies called "information centers."[3]

It does not appear to be significantly important at this point to try to search out a completely clear and fully agreed-upon meaning for the term "special"; it is important, however, that the student of librarianship begin to develop a basic understanding of the differentiating characteristics of that growing number of libraries which are called "special."

Dr. Shera has suggested that the libraries of the early historical societies[4] and the libraries serving state bar associations, law firms, and schools of law were perhaps the first of the special libraries.[5] At the turn of the century, public libraries began to extend special service to business and industry, and in 1909 a group of twenty-six librarians under the leadership of John Cotton Dana, a distinguished pioneer of library service to business, founded the Special Libraries Association, which had as its object "to promote the interests of

[1] See p. 292.
[2] Edward G. Strable (ed.), *Special Libraries: A Guide for Management* (New York: Special Libraries Association, 1966), p. 1.
[3] See the discussion of information centers, pp. 315–19.
[4] See pp. 75–76.
[5] Jesse H. Shera "Library," *American Educator Encyclopedia*, IX (1965), p. 141.

the commercial, industrial, technical, civic, municipal and legislative libraries, the special departments of public libraries, universities, welfare organizations and business organizations."[6]

Since that time thousands of libraries which call themselves special, or are given that label by others in referring to them, have come into being in the United States and Canada with the principal growth taking place since World War II, stimulated by the tremendous increase in the number of scientific, technical, business, and industrial research and development organizations; the flood of technological and scientific materials being produced; and the accelerating widespread interest in the transfer of information and knowledge which have an immediate utilitarian value.

Growth of special libraries

It was noted in the preceding chapter that since World War II there has developed a deeply grounded judgment that the information and knowledge issuing from research—and particularly technical and scientific information—constitute the key ingredient in the economic growth and prosperity and the chief line of defense of this nation's power. Technical innovation has become recognized in recent decades as a necessity, not an option, because every new advance in mechanization adds to the ability of inventors, engineers, and scientists to design and develop newer and more efficient machines, which in turn speed up the design and development of still further advances in mechanization. Industrial corporations, therefore, have become more and more conscious of technological innovation as their central and most crucial policy and activity.

Long ago specialization proved its effectiveness as a method for producing new and usable information; thus with each generation research and learning have become more specialized and fragmented, not only in the fields of science and technology, where the nation is currently placing its greatest emphasis, but in all major fields of human experience. Such parent sciences as chemistry, biology, and physics have been divided and subdivided, and within subdivi-

[6] Bill M. Woods, "The Impolite Librarians," *Special Libraries*, LV (July–August, 1964), 347.

sions there emerge specialized "specialties," such as microelectronics as a subspecialty of miniature electronics. In other areas of knowledge and professional practice, there are also multiplying specialties and subspecialties. For example, physicians specialize in physical diseases, psychiatrists and psychologists in mental and emotional disorders, and social workers in social adjustment. These specialists then subspecialize in particular diseases, in adult and child disorders, in probation, child placement, and so on almost endlessly.

Out of the research in these fragmented areas of knowledge, and particularly in science and technology, have come in ever-increasing numbers in recent years reports and monographs, as well as articles in journals and other periodicals, on highly precise topics and problems. One communications expert has estimated that as many science papers have been published since 1950 as were published in all the centuries before. He has remarked, in specific detail, that today "a new communication concerning chemistry is published somewhere in the world every minute; a report on physics every three minutes; and a report on medicine, biology and electronics every five minutes."[7] Not only has the production of materials on very specific topics and problems accelerated to a dizzy pace, but the time between the production of these materials and their practical application has so markedly decreased that those who have need for the information contained in these materials want to know about their existence much earlier and want access to them much faster than at any time in the past.

It is not surprising that in such a situation there should be a rapid and large growth of those types of libraries and information services agencies which are dedicated to the single purpose of identifying, collecting, and providing to specialized users the specific and accurate information and knowledge which they require in carrying forward their interests, objectives, and work.[8] Only a few

[7] David Sarnoff, *Education and the Challenge of the Future, Address Made at the Fall Convocation, Hendrix College, October 12, 1965* (Conway, Ark.: Hendrix College, 1965), p. 11.
[8] One of the best summations of the factors and forces leading to the development of new techniques and agencies to serve the specialized information needs of special clienteles will be found in S. C. Bradford, *Documentation*,

counts and estimates of the number of special libraries have been made. It has been estimated that by the end of the 1920s the number was perhaps around 1,000; by the middle 1950s, the number was at least 5,000; and by 1965, there were more than 10,000. The Special Libraries Association has expressed the belief "that 15,000 special libraries can be expected by 1970."[9]

In keeping with its purpose "to promote high professional standards," the Special Libraries association began in 1959 to provide a means of measuring the character and performance of special libraries and information centers.[10] Standards adopted by the association in 1964,[11] covering objectives, staff, collection, services, physical facilities, and budget serve also—along with its later publication, which has been referred to previously[12]—as guidelines in the establishment of special libraries and provide helpful information to persons interested in the special library profession.

Kinds of special libraries and distinguishing characteristics
Among the thousands of special libraries are those which serve:

Historical and similar societies

Schools of law, law firms, and state bar associations

Officials and agencies of Federal, state, county, or municipal governments

Medical schools, hospitals, and medical societies

Divinity schools, churches, and religious organizations

Large museums

Military installations and prisons

---

with Introduction by Jesse H. Shera and Margaret E. Egan (2d ed.: London: Crosby, Lockwood & Son, Ltd., 1953). See the entire Introduction, particularly p. 24ff.
[9] Strable, *op. cit.* p. 3.
[10] See pp. 315–19 for discussion of information centers.
[11] Special Libraries Association, "Objectives and Standards for Special Libraries," *Special Libraries*, LV (December, 1964), 672–80.
[12] Strable (ed.), *op. cit.* See p. 308.

Learned societies

Music organizations

Banks, insurance companies, advertising agencies, publishers, and other businesses

Associations and societies devoted to trades or professions

Engineering and management firms

Industries, large and small, and particularly large corporations in such areas of production as drugs, chemicals, petroleum, and electronics

One of the most apparent and easily distinguishable characteristics of this sampling of special libraries is that each is a unit of an agency, organization, institution, business or industry—private or governmental—with the sole purpose of providing the information and knowledge resources which are vital to the parent organization's clientele in the achievement of that organization's specific objective, product, or service.

Since the clientele is a limited one in terms of interest and work and since the objectives of the library are specific rather than general, the collection of books, periodicals, and other materials—of whatever sort and form—is relatively narrow in scope, being limited to a single specific subject area or to a group of related subjects which meet the requirements of the supporting organization.

In addition to the fact that the kinds of people who use and are served by special libraries usually are specialized in their interests and skills, some special libraries are most easily distinguishable from other types of libraries by the highly specialized form of the materials assembled and made available for use, as in the case of map libraries and picture libraries.

Special libraries are of various forms and sizes, and although some special libraries have collections numbering into many thousands of items, the majority of them tend to be small, employing only a few persons. The Special Libraries Association observes that "the 'typical' special library might . . . be visualized as small in staff size and, usually, small in space occupied and in size of collection."[13]

The emphasis of the publications of the Special Libraries Association is on the *purpose and function* of the special library rather than on its size, form, or other features, and special librarianship is strongly presented as a "point of view."[14] This emphasis and point of view can be summarized as follows: Other kinds of libraries may cover in their objectives education, scholarly research, aesthetic appreciation, and recreation; but the distinctive purpose of special libraries is to provide information for immediate utilitarian application and to bring together users and the information they require— in whatever form it may be available, in the most effective way possible, at the time when and in the place where they need it, if possible. The emphasis, then, is on *information services*, on providing the specialized user with *information* rather than with material; and, according to the Special Libraries Association, it was this "single-endedness of special librarianship that first drew the group of twenty-six librarians together in 1909. It is the reason that 'Putting Knowledge to Work' was chosen and is used as the guiding slogan of special librarianship; it is the characteristic that best defines 'special' in special library."[15]

The special library collection

As the major source of information in the organization it serves, the special library acquires, organizes, and maintains informational materials in fields pertinent to the work of the organization, for use by or on behalf of its clientele. The collection includes all basic, frequently used, and potentially useful materials to meet both the current and anticipated needs of its users. Depending upon the nature of the supporting organization, the library collection may contain a variety of forms—books, pamphlets, translations, dissertations, periodicals, newspapers, press releases, transactions, reports, archival materials, yearbooks, directories, research and laboratory

[13] Strable, *op. cit.*, p. 2.
[14] Anthony T. Kruzas (ed.), *Directory of Special Libraries and Information Centers* (Detroit: Gale Research Company, 1963), pp. 7, 8.
[15] Strable, *op. cit.*, p. 3.

notebooks, patents, trademark specifications and standards, audio-visual materials, sheet music, recordings, manuscripts, clippings, abstracts, maps, blueprints, punched cards, magnetic tapes, tables, photocopies, and microforms. The size of the collection is determined by the purposes of the library and the availability of materials in its special area; it may contain works of permanent or historical value, or it may contain literature which is only currently useful.

The determining factor in the organization of the collection is the necessity for quick and efficient access. Traditional systems of cataloging and classification can sometimes be used, but modifications and adaptations of these systems are often considered necessary, and efforts may be made to devise an entirely new system of bibliographic access including a new classification scheme, printed checklists, indexes, computer print-out catalogs, and electronic data-processing equipment.[16]

Services and staff

The "special" librarian serves his clientele of specialists by examining all new literature which comes into the library, evaluating it, and making certain that it reaches the right persons; providing quick reference service, using photocopies as needed; making literature searches and providing bibliographies, abstracts, summaries, and translations if necessary; using interlibrary loan to provide additional needed materials; helping specialists keep up with the literature in their fields; maintaining company archives; encouraging the use of the library through displays, lists of new materials, and liberal loan policies; and developing programs to retrieve information through the use of computers.

The special librarian must know the structure and policy of the organization or agency which he serves in order to be able to see the place of the library in the achievement of the organization's goals and objectives; he must be well grounded in the subject specialty of his library and efficient in the techniques of reference and information service; he must know both the literature he collects and the particular interests and needs of his clientele and be able

---

[16] See Chap. 23 for further discussion of these matters.

to match literature and client; he must be able to perform such special services as indexing, editing, abstracting, and translating, or know where these services can be procured quickly; he must understand the basic principles of classification in order to adapt or devise systems to meet the needs of the diverse materials and forms of materials; he must familiarize himself with outside sources which can be of assistance in locating authoritative information in the developing new areas of knowledge; he must have the tenacity to see a problem to its successful conclusion as well as be able to move quickly from one problem to another; he must be able to change established procedures for more efficient methods, to experiment, and to innovate; and he must be able to work under pressure; "the ideal librarian will also have received his professional education from an American Library Association accredited graduate school of librarianship and may have related library experience."[17]

The staff of the typical special library is small, often consisting of one professional librarian together with clerical assistants. However, some special libraries have a number of specialists on the staff, such as a translator, an abstractor, an indexer, or an information systems specialist.

A growing problem of special librarianship, as it is in all areas of librarianship, is the shortage of personnel. It is conservatively estimated that during the next decade an additional fifteen thousand professional librarians will be needed to staff new special libraries and reinforce the staffs of existing libraries.[18]

INFORMATION SERVICES AND FACILITIES

The increasing importance, value, and use of information as a commodity is shown in the rapid development of facilities for the purpose of identifying, collecting, analyzing, evaluating, and disseminating it and in the new methods which are being used

Strable, *op. cit.*, p. 30.
[18] *Special Librarianship: Information at Work* (New York: Special Libraries Association, 1965), p. 12. See also pp. 306–07 and Chap. 24.

in an effort to speed up these processes. During the past twenty-five years the library profession has seen more and more specialization of information service. This development had its start in government and industry, where the need first presented itself to organize more specifically, effectively, and speedily the recorded information of a narrowly defined subject field in support of intensive scientific research and technological development methods. Special libraries have pioneered in the development of mechanized systems for the improvement of library service, especially in the field of information retrieval and other information service, using electronic computers and auxiliary mechanized equipment.[19] Mechanized equipment has been used with varying degrees of success in a sizable number of special libraries to perform routine tasks connected with the acquisition of materials, maintenance of borrowers files, sending of overdue notices, and the checking in and out of serial publications. Electronic computers are being used effectively in printing bibliographies of useful references, producing catalogs, predicting what materials may be of use to an individual user and giving the source of such materials; they are being used experimentally in retrieving both documents and information.

The importance of new specialization in librarianship is underscored by the trend in library schools to include courses in the curriculum to prepare students for these areas of work. Recent additions to the curriculum include courses in the literature and methods of research in the humanities, the sciences, and the social sciences and in indexing, abstracting, documentation, information systems, and data processing in libraries. In addition to these kinds of courses, there are workshops, seminars, institutes, and conferences to keep the library profession and the special librarian up to date on new developments, trends, and needs. It is obvious that special libraries vary from high to low in their scope and ability in acquiring, organizing, and disseminating information and materials. In its *Special Libraries: A Guide for Management* the Special Libraries Association notes carefully that "special libraries are not interchangeable" and sets forth an outline of functions which realistically

[19] See Chap. 23.

takes into account "levels" of service.[20] Correspondingly, information centers, which are also of various sizes, are not interchangeable; they, too, provide levels of service. Usually, when the subject of information centers is being discussed, it is the specialized information center, and often the highly specialized one dealing only with technical and scientific information and staffed largely by technical personnel, which is under consideration.

In his volume on specialized information centers, Kent[21] indicates that such centers can be organized in terms of subject matter—such as chemistry, metallurgy, biology, pharmacology; by source material—such as reports and records, engineering drawings and technical manuals which are generated internally and journals, books, periodicals, and trade literature generated externally; by the numbers and varieties of people served; or by the types of service provided. Under types of service, the entire gamut of forms of service is run, from the traditional organization of materials so that individual users can conduct their own searches, through the provision of a bibliographic reference, an original document or copy of it, an abstract or extract of the source materials, to direct answers to questions. These are the types of service previously noted as characterizing special libraries, and in the *Directory of Special Libraries and Information Centers*, information centers which perform these kinds of services are included and are referred to as "this new library-like species."[22]

Simpson has offered a definition of a specialized information center which has received considerable acceptance:

> A scientific information center exists for the primary purpose of preparing authoritative, timely and specialized reports of the evaluative, analytical, monographic, or state-of-the art type. It is an organization staffed in part with scientists and engineers, and to provide a basis for its primary function, it conducts a selective data and information acquisition and processing program.[23]

[20] Strable, *op. cit.*
[21] Allen Kent, *Specialized Information Centers* (Washington, D.C.: Spartan Books, 1965), pp. 23ff.
[22] Kruzas, *op. cit.*, p. 9.
[23] G. S. Simpson, "Scientific Information Centers in the United States," *American Documentation*, XIII (January, 1962), 43.

Here, again, is a type-of-purpose and -service characteristic of certain self-designated special libraries.

Another point of view is offered by Weinberg in a paper presented at a meeting of the American Library Association and the Association of College and Research Libraries in St. Louis, Missouri, June 30, 1964. Among other things, Mr. Weinberg said,

> The specialized information center in our view is . . . not a technical library; it is more nearly a technical institute. . . . But the specialized center obviously must depend on the librarian in the most central way if it is to operate successfully. First are the obvious and traditional library functions, particularly retrieval, storing, and cataloging. Every information center must have on its staff librarians who are expert in these fields. But the demands of the information center are rather special and go somewhat beyond the traditional demands made on librarians. The information center is expected to achieve about 99.5 percent retrieval of the literature in the special field in which it operates.[24]

In connection with this concept of the specialized information center as a technical institute, Mr. Weinberg has argued that such a center must be run by recognized scientific leaders in their fields of science. He has noted further, however, that "as the information center grows, so will the library that supports the center."

It is proper that different points of view, sometimes bluntly conflicting, should be offered for study and evaluation, for at the heart of this exchange of views regarding information centers and libraries is a recognition in varying degrees of the high importance of recorded information and knowledge in this technologically advanced industrial society and of the need for quick, accurate, economical, and convenient access to those portions of recorded materials which will serve the requirements of users at a particular time. Although there is substantial common agreement as to this basic need, there remain differences of opinion as to the most effective ways and means of providing information services and as to the proper role of librarians, special librarians, information specialists,

[24] Alvin Weinberg, "Second Thoughts on Scientific Information," *College and Research Libraries*, XXV (November, 1964), 476.

scientists, and technicians in the total task of acquiring, describing, indexing, retrieving, and transmitting significant information in its most usable forms at the proper time.

The question of whether the function and scope of the specialized information centers are "the natural birthright and responsibility of the library profession"[25] is yet to be determined; so, also, is the question of whether a special library is an information center or whether a specialized information center is a special library. However important these and similar questions may be, it should be pointed out that the strictly informational facility is only one kind of special library—or "library-like" facility—and that even though it is receiving much of the attention that is now being given to special libraries, it is neither the most numerous nor the most widespread. Other types of libraries which are greatly concerned with the information and knowledge problem—such as medical, theological, law, military, church, museum, music, and hospital, as well as subject departments in public and university libraries and research libraries in the social sciences and in the humanities— continue to increase in number, in prestige, and in the contributions which they are making to educational, cultural, and economic progress.

[25] Alan M. Rees, "Librarians and Information Centers," *College and Research Libraries*, XXV (May, 1964), 203.

CHAPTER 23
AUTOMATION
IN
LIBRARIES

If there is any significant dissent from the proposition that the electronic digital computer is the most versatile and helpful of all the machines, instruments, and devices which have been produced to assist in carrying out many of man's important purposes, it is not noticeable. Indeed, the current multiple demonstrated capacities of the computer and its assumed potentials are so highly regarded that the "age of automation"—or the "age of advanced mechanization"—is usually thought of as dating from the time when the first of these electronic devices was switched on in 1946 at the Army Proving Grounds in Aberdeen, Maryland, for the purpose of providing high-speed computational assistance in the national defense program.

Discovery of new uses for the computer and auxiliary machines has continued steadily since that time, and today few if any areas of life have been left untouched—directly or indirectly—by the many constructive things which are being done by these machines. Along with the development of new uses, there has been steady improvement in the performance and capabilities of computers with regard to a large number of tasks to which they have been applied, especially in their calculating speed, their storage capacity or "memory," their compactness and flexibility, and the relative economy of their operation. One of the leading spokesmen of this age of automation has noted that the national computing power "will soon be sufficient to make the computer a genuinely universal tool" and has offered the prediction that science and technology will advance more in the decades immediately ahead "than in all of the millennia since man's creation," adding the judgment that "the threshold of the computer age has barely been crossed."[1] Whatever the ultimate pace of total technological advance may turn out to be, this forecast appears to be comfortably within the mood of the scientific and technological optimism which currently exists in the more advanced industrial countries, particularly with regard to the field of electronics and especially with regard to the field of electrical communications.

Applicability of automation to library activities

In the light of this optimism and of the need for more and better library services, it is understandable that for a good many years those who have had responsibilities for library and specialized information services have been turning to mechanical and electrical ingenuity for aid in solving some of their most persistent problems. In preceding chapters some of the specific conditions, needs, and pressures leading to this turn toward advanced mechanization have been noted.[2]

Although a number of electrical machines, including computers, are being used in the performance of certain library and information activities and although a considerable amount of experimental work has been and is being carried on in connection with other and more complicated activities, the fact remains that *the question of the extent to which library operations and services can be automated effectively and economically is still a very open and unsettled one.* In the ongoing debate and study of this multifaceted question, many points of view are being expressed and new and significant experimental projects are either planned or in prospect. Also, the literature bearing on this unsettled question is increasing both in volume and in diversity: books of theory and books dealing with practice; articles in a variety of journals covering specific aspects of the question; reports of progress on experimental projects, reports of conferences and institutes, and reports of national and agency advisory commit-

[1] David Sarnoff, "By the End of the Twentieth Century," *Fortune*, LXIX (May, 1964), 113. See also David Sarnoff, "No Life Untouched," *Saturday Review*, XLIX (July 23, 1966), 22.
[2] See Chaps. 20–22.

tees and councils; master's theses and doctoral dissertations; and outlines and courses of formal study.[3]

Keeping up to date on library automation

The more information a highly organized scientifically advanced society produces, the more that society becomes dependent upon ready and efficient access to it. Dean Shera has observed that the major problem that confronts the librarian today is not so much one of accumulation as of access to that which is accumulated."[4] Since it is the librarian's business to provide that necessary access, it is essential that he find and use the most effective means possible by which to do it. In the face of this essentiality, it seems clear that any student or practitioner of librarianship who fails to try to keep up to date regarding those machines which can perform library activities more effectively than they are now being performed will be seriously remiss in the preparation for, and the execution of, his responsibilities.

Trying to keep up to date, however, is not an easy task: Such a large part of the growing body of literature concerning the actual and potential uses of electronic equipment in library and special information services is so highly technical that many students and librarians often find it incomprehensible; the number and variety of experiments in progress or being planned are complicated and difficult to follow; and—perhaps most important—the computer family of machines has been promoted for so many different purposes and as the solution to so many problems that it is often "difficult to distinguish fact from fiction."[5] Following a tour of several weeks through the United States and Canada on which he visited thirty-eight selected libraries, the librarian of the University of Sydney, Australia, set forth some of his observations on American library automation. One of his findings was that some projects which had

---

[3] Regarding the general nature of these courses, see p. 131.

[4] Jesse H. Shera, "What Is Past Is Prologue: Beyond 1984," *ALA Bulletin,* LXI (January, 1967), 37.

[5] Joseph Becker and Robert M. Hayes, *Information Storage and Retrieval— Tools, Elements, Theories* (New York: John Wiley & Sons, Inc., 1963), p. 41.

been reported as being fully operational were, when carefully examined, found to be still in the project-development stage and that some systems which had been reported "in the full flush of initial optimism" were found "abandoned or modified out of recognition."[6]

In spite of the difficulty involved, the serious student of librarianship will make the strongest possible effort to keep adequately informed regarding the applicability of advanced machines to library activities. And in this context it is suggested that he cannot afford to accept unexamined assumptions and unyielding opinions— regardless of whether those opinions and assumptions are characterized by zeal for new machines as cure-alls or by fear of them as possible usurpers of some of the librarian's historic and cherished duties and functions. Susan Artandi has put the matter simply in saying that what are needed are "open minds that are willing to become informed, willing to weigh, willing to criticize and then accept or reject on the basis of objective facts."[7]

GENERAL POINTS OF VIEW

Many people have a significant stake in the discovery and development of more effective aids in collecting, organizing, storing, retrieving, and disseminating the great volume and the varied forms of information and knowledge materials now being produced. When, soon after its advent, the computer began to be used to perform many complicated and essential functions in government, business, and industry, the hope and belief developed in a number of quarters that electronic machines could provide a revolutionary "new dimension" in the handling and transmitting of information and knowledge. During the past decade, this general belief in the potentials of the computer family of machines in relation to the management of information and knowledge in libraries and special information centers has become comparatively deep set. Some examples are the strong affirmation that the general purpose digital computer "has opened up a wealth of possibilities, for it provides capa-

[6] Harrison Bryan, "American Automation in Action," *Library Journal*, XCII (January 15, 1967), 189.
[7] Susan A. Artandi, "Keeping Up with Mechanization," *Library Journal*, XC (November 1, 1965), 4716.

bilities enormously more powerful than those of any previous mechanical device for the handling of information";[8] the prophecy that although computers "have not yet solved the problem of our libraries, about to be swamped by the deluge of printed matter . . . some day they will";[9] and the admonition that "there would seem to be no limit to the potentialities that automation can bring to the transmission, storage, and retrieval of information, and if librarians do not take this technological revolution into account they will find themselves in a sorry plight."[10]

Other voices are being heard, of course. There are those who do not question the efficiency of electrical machines in the performance of certain important traditional library tasks but who offer cautionary opinions regarding the applicability of mechanization to some of the more complicated nonroutine library processes and services. For example, reporting on the use of electronic equipment in the Library of Congress, Samuel Snyder has noted that the operations which are required to produce an adequate bibliographical representation of a work and to recover the work upon request "are not easily automated."[11] On this same matter of using machines effectively in securing needed access to information and knowledge materials, Professor Hammer has observed that in a library "in which collections cross all lines of human intellectual endeavor, the contribution of present-day data processing systems to reference service is of somewhat limited value" and has offered the judgment that "the use of machines to accomplish the work of the university library will be limited to clerical tasks."[12] A professional information scientist identified with the administration of communication research has witnessed that long debate "has neither proved nor dis-

[8] Becker and Hayes, *op. cit.*, p. 112.

[9] Vannevar Bush, "Science Pauses," *Fortune*, LXXI (May, 1965), 119. Copyright © 1965 by Vannevar Bush.

[10] Jesse H. Shera, "The Propaedeutic of the New Librarianship," *Information Retrieval Today*, ed. Wesley Simonton (Minneapolis: University of Minnesota Center for Continuation Study, 1963), p. 16. This article is also found in Jesse H. Shera, *Documentation and the Organization of Knowledge*, ed. D. J. Foskett (Hamden, Conn.: Archon Books, 1966), pp. 54–71.

[11] Samuel S. Snyder, "Automation at L.C.: Philosophy, Plans, Progress," *Library Journal*, XC (November 1, 1965), 4710.

[12] Donald P. Hammer, "Automated Operations in a University Library—A Summary," *College and Research Libraries*, XXVI (January, 1965), 19, 27.

proved the alleged superiority in terms of effectiveness and efficiency of computerized over manual retrieval systems."[13]

It should be clear that these few statements of experience and opinion are not designed to cover more than a small part of a complex subject nor to represent more than a token of the ongoing debate and study in connection with the question of the applicability of advanced mechanization in library operations. Other points of view will emerge in the paragraphs which follow.

Practices in the use of mechanization in libraries

In any field of thought and endeavor in which both theory and practice are in a state of change, generalizing can be a hazardous business, but generalizations can be helpful as take-off points for more detailed and arduous study. Therefore, on the subject under consideration, it can be said that, in general, it is the more repetitive and routine library tasks which have to date yielded most readily to the capacities of advanced machines and that the use of computers and auxiliary machines—in school, academic, and public libraries in particular—has been limited very largely to assisting in such traditional operations as the acquisition of materials; the performance of sundry kinds of bookkeeping, payroll, and accounting work; maintaining inventories of supplies and equipment; developing and updating patron registration files; preparing catalogs; keeping up with circulation; and expediting serials work.[14]

In the performance of these basic functions, several unit-record machines are being used, both with and without a computer, including the card-punch, or key-punch machine, with a keyboard like a typewriter which punches holes representing coded information in special kinds of cards; the sorter, which arranges cards in numerical or alphabetical order depending upon the kinds of holes punched in them; the collator, which interfiles cards; the tabulator (or accounting machine, or printer), which can read the punched cards

[13] Alan M. Rees, "Librarians and Information Centers," *op. cit.*, pp. 200–201.
[14] See Bryan, *op. cit.* See also Donald V. Black and Earl A. Farley, "Library Automation," *Annual Review of Information Science and Technology*, ed. Carlos A. Cuadra (New York: Interscience Publishers, 1966), I, 273–303; and Lois C. McCune and Stephen R. Salmon, "Bibliography of Automation," *ALA Bulletin*, LXI (June, 1967), 674–694.

and print in readable form what it reads; and the reproducer, which reproduces cards. The computer can perform all the functions of the unit-record machines, but it has additional capacities in the handling and storing of certain kinds of information in that it has a magnetic memory[15] and can operate also under the control of a list of detailed instructions called a program, which tells it what to do.

By way of restatement, thus far where unit-record machines, computers, and other electronic devices have been introduced into the operation of school, academic, and public libraries, they have been used mainly as recording, tabulating, and printing devices—recording basic information so that catalogs of materials and lists of such items as accessions, overdue materials, serials purchases and holdings, materials at the bindery, faculty reading and research interests, payroll information, and circulation records can be readily prepared and distributed to those who may need the information.[16] In short, the dominant emphasis to date in school, academic, and public libraries is on the mechanizing of existing routine and repetitive functions and processes.

In most instances the installation of these mechanization activities has been taken in step-by-step order[17] rather than in all-at-once fashion and only after efforts have been made to define carefully the several individual operations under way in the specific library under scrutiny; to analyze the number, nature, and needs of the

---

[15] This memory can consist of magnetic tape similar to that used in tape recorders, which carries information in the form of small magnetic spots, or the spots can be put on cards, cylinders, or discs. To date, the computer has been developed largely as an arithmetic machine handling numbers or characters. In handling problems dealing with words, the computer must first convert the words into numbers or characters. Difficulties at this point will be noted later under the subtopic dealing with information retrieval, pp. 328–33.

[16] In the spring of 1967, public announcement was made of the availability of a duplicating device, designed for use with computers and other electronic equipment, which automatically copies and reproduces the page size directly from printer output. The machine takes the 15- by 11-inch continuous fanfold forms, which come from the printing devices, and within a short time turns them into collated sets of regular 11- by 8½-inch pages for binding and distribution, thus combining in one machine the several steps heretofore required for the printing and distribution of computer reports.

[17] See Ivan F. Jackson, "An Approach to Library Automation Problems," *College and Research Libraries*, XXVIII (March, 1967), 133–37.

library's users; and to evaluate the nature and adequacy of both the library's overall and specific goals. Other factors which are given important consideration are the size of the library, the competency of the staff, the equipment available at the time mechanization is being considered, and the adequacy of financial support.

As was noted previously, some practitioners are of the opinion that electronic machines likely will continue to be confined to assistance in the performance of such operations as those described above. There are those, however, who believe that such limited usage constitutes a dissipation of the most valuable use-possibilities of automation, which are considered to be in the storage and retrieval of information.[18] These persons may be willing to grant that in the use of computers and auxiliary machines to perform traditional operations, librarians are freed from time-consuming and often onerous routines and can give needed attention to more complex intellectual and managerial activities; but they hasten to contend that mechanization for such purposes does not go far enough and actually may be undesirable except as it is a planned step in the ultimate development of a comprehensive automated system for describing and organizing, for storing and retrieving, and for disseminating information. It will be recognized that those who take this position are assuming that any problems which now exist in connection with the use of machines to deal effectively with non-numerical matters can and will be worked out in due time. To exactly what extent this is a valid assumption has yet to be determined, and in connection with the proving or disproving of it many persistent and intensive efforts are being put forth—efforts which should command the attention of students and practitioners alike. Another assumption which is definitely implied in this position is that the library's chief business is that of transmitting usable information, in short, that the library is dominantly an information agency. This assumption requires broader and more careful examination than it has yet received by many of those who have concern for the library as a social, cultural, and educational institution.[19]

[18] Leonard H. Freiser, "Technology in the Library," *Wilson Library Bulletin,* XLI (September, 1966), 69–71.
[19] See Chap. 8.

Mechanization in information retrieval

The term "information retrieval" has been used a number of times in preceding discussions. The activity of information retrieval is not anything new. It has always been one major function of librarianship to organize whatever types and forms of materials have been available at the time; to recover—or find, or retrieve—information and knowledge from these materials; and to transmit them in some usable form to those who have needed or requested them. Indeed, the core of librarianship has been bibliography and reference service—a service in which the user and his requirements are given first place. For sundry reasons, many librarians have been and continue to be concerned about other things; even so, the function of providing effective access to library materials persists as a central concern and activity of librarianship and, historically, has covered any and all methods of locating information, knowledge, and materials.[20]

Although as an activity information retrieval is not new, as a specific term it is relatively recent. It came into wide use and received urgent attention following World War II when technical reports of all kinds grew in number and importance, when research-and-development was given new impetus by governmental support, and when there developed accelerated demands for specific bits and pieces of utilitarian information. Even though the term is now more widely used and discussed than ever before, it has not yet acquired a specific and exclusive meaning, still serving as an omnibus expression to cover a variety of recovery-of-information activities, such as:[21]

1. Reference retrieval, typified by the library card catalog or other indexes, in which a complete reference to a document (a full bibliographic citation) is produced, with or without the use of a computer
2. Document retrieval, in which the user is provided with

---

[20] See Joseph L. Wheeler, "Bettering Reference Service," *RQ*, VI (Spring, 1967), 99–113.
[21] See Charles P. Bourne, *Methods of Information Handling* (New York: John Wiley & Sons, Inc., 1963), pp. 2ff. See also B. C. Vickery, *On Retrieval System Theory* (2d. ed.; London: Butterworth & Co. (Publishers), Ltd., 1965), pp. 177ff.

full document texts (a copy of a book, journal, report, or manuscript) instead of with only a citation or reference

3. Data or fact retrieval, in which specific information, such as the gross citrus production of Florida or California in a particular year, is provided in answer to a specific request[22]

In summary, the basic effort in these varied activities is that of locating information and getting it to the people who need it—both before and when they need or request it—in the forms in which it is presumed to be most usable at the time. This effort is common to both librarianship and information retrieval, which is also called information storage and retrieval, information science, or documentation. Though the objectives of librarianship and information retrieval in its broadest sense are the same,[23] there are some noticeable differences of emphasis, such as in the top priority given by information scientists to the needs of specialists (scientific and technical specialists, in particular) and to nonbook information sources; and there are emphasis differences in the techniques employed, especially in the attempt of information retrieval to harness the assumed potentialities of computers.[24]

It is not surprising that the great majority of the mechanized information-storage and -retrieval experiments are found in special libraries and in specialized information centers in government and industry, for in carrying out their specific missions[25] the problem of retrieving quickly and accurately the materials and particularized information needed by their specialized users is considered by them

[22] This particular kind of retrieval is, in fact, a special form of document retrieval—sometimes called subdocument or microdocument retrieval—in which the documents are presented as a line or lines of figures or tabular lists or as concise independent sentences.

[23] Jesse H. Shera, "Librarians Against Machines," *Science*, CLVI (May 12, 1967), 346–50. See also Alan M. Rees, "New Bottles for Old Wine: Retrieval and Librarianship," *Wilson Library Bulletin*, XXXIX (May, 1964), 773–79, *passim.*

[24] More emphasis has been placed thus far on information engineering, that is, on the techniques and hardware for processing technical-scientific information, than on information science, that is, on the securing of maximum accessibility and usability.

[25] See pp. 313, 316.

to be appreciably more difficult than the problem of recovering and disseminating requested information and materials in general library collections.

ORGANIZING MATERIALS FOR INFORMATION RETRIEVAL

The methods by which the materials are described and organized are crucial in the performance of any recovery-of-information activity. Consequently, just as the index or classification or catalog scheme is at the heart of library reference service, so at the center of the "more difficult" problem of handling efficiently the specialized literature of science and technology are the indexing and classification techniques that are being used.[26]

In their recovery of needed information and knowledge materials, librarians have always been makers of bibliographies and catalogs and users of indexes; traditionally, however, they have normally cataloged a document as a whole (a unit), not its parts and subparts. Many of the handlers of the great volume of largely nonbook specialized technical and scientific literature have been insisting for years that this depth of cataloging is no longer adequate for their specialized needs. They have been saying that because the basic requirements of many of their users are for specific bits and items of information, cataloging must be in much greater detail than has been usual in general libraries; that it must provide an exhaustive analysis of the subject content of materials and cover every aspect of a subject, including its relationship to other subjects. In other words, it is necessary to catalog to the level of the *specific item* in a document.

Cataloging (also called indexing) to this depth has proved to be very difficult. For one thing, if a card catalog system is used, cataloging to the item of information which it is thought may be needed produces so many card entries that the file itself may become virtually unmanageable. If a printed book-form catalog is used, there develops the serious problem—in terms of time and cost—of main-

[26] See Grieg Aspnes, "The Current Situation in Documentation," *The Bowker Annual of Library and Book Trade Information* (New York: R. R. Bowker Company, 1965), p. 230.

taining and updating a volume of such size. For another thing, such detailed cataloging of highly specialized material, much of which is unusually technical in language and meaning, places upon the general cataloger the tremendous task of analyzing this material as if he were a subject expert. Faced with this task, the librarian may find himself having to try to decide whether he will catalog a few selected books and documents to the depth of the item of information or a larger selection of materials in less thorough detail.[27] In coming to this decision, he may have to make a judgment as to whether the smaller and more exhaustively analyzed or the larger and less thoroughly analyzed body of materials will meet the needs of his patrons more adequately. This means that he must carefully take into account the nature and number of the library's users, the kind and number of their requests, and the amount of time which he may be allowed in responding to their requests and needs.

Many persons who handle materials relating to scientific and technical activities in situations where the volume of daily requests for information retrieval is high and whose clients often want answers to their queries in a very short time believe that it is only through the use of electronic machines, in which a magnetic memory can be substituted for a card catalog, that their problems can be solved. Their difficulties in implementing this belief derive from the fact that most information is not in a form that can be received by the computer; consequently, the main difficulty is that of converting the large body of printed information into the digital form (a restricted set of characters) required for computer handling. Once information is cast in machine-readable form, the computer can receive it in amazingly large amounts, but there are many yet unanswered questions, such as:

1. What kinds of machine-readable identifying labels will be placed on the documents, specialized reports, and items and bits of information which are to be added to the memory bank of computers?
2. What kinds of symbols, marks, codes, indexing terms, or

[27] *Ibid.,* p. 231.

identification tags will cover most clearly and comprehensively the meanings embodied in the information content of their materials?

3. How can the important and usable material be so coded and indexed that in a machine retrieval system it is separated from the unimportant and extraneous?

4. How can the machine-readable identification tags used in indexing to the depth of an item of information be made to cover both the specificity and the broad range of the many questions which it is hoped the retrieved information will answer?

Writing on the situation which obtained in 1966 with regard to machine-based information storage and retrieval systems, Philip Leslie observed that "perfect correspondence between the information retrieved and the information needed involves more luck than many people would like to admit."[28] The superlative handling of data (facts and figures) by computers has long been a commonplace activity, but the heart of the problem now for the promoters and operators of electronic information-storage and -retrieval systems is that of programming computers for the effective handling of nonnumerical information. In wrestling with this problem, "the logic of language, the meaning of words, the philosophy of synonymy and the adequacy of subject terms have all taken on new significance."[29]

A crucial part of the problem has been stated by Arthur L. Kenney as follows:

The distance between the machine and the human brain is great and before we can get needed information fast and in a usable form, responsible public and scientific officials will have to grapple with the problem of "How do we codify information for adequate computer manipulation, so that we can be certain of accurate retrieval? And more importantly, how do we get people to agree upon such codes and use them once they have been devised and

[28] Philip Leslie, "The Current Situation in Documentation," *The Bowker Annual of Library and Book Trade Information* (New York: R. R. Bowker Company, 1966), p. 241.
[29] *Ibid.*, p. 242.

disseminated?" People who stress the hardware capabilities, without directing their efforts to software problems, such as codification, are giving time to what has become only a part of the information problem.[30]

As was previously observed, much research at this point has been going on for years and is still in process. Although current efforts to represent both the depth and quality of the contents of documents by a few words and symbols are noticeably awkward and inadequate in a good many instances, there is no apparent reason for believing that aggressive experimentation will be abandoned or even lessened. Undoubtedly experimental efforts will be pursued forcefully, but very likely on a considerably more coodinated basis than in the past and with fewer before-the-fact conclusions. The point under consideration here is a vital one. Much is at stake both for libraries and for specialized information centers in the continuing efforts to develop effective machine-readable cataloging (indexing) vocabularies.[31] Assuming that more coordinated efforts will in time result in the development of efficient computer-based systems for the storage and speedy and accurate retrieval of usable scientific and technical information, there is still the question of the applicability of these systems to other types of materials. The possibility that in the concept of automated information retrieval the link between theory and practice may be forged in some areas of information and knowledge does not automatically mean that the link will be forged in all areas. The Committee on Scientific and Technical Information of the Federal Council for Science and Technology has recognized that one type of system may be required for the adequate handling of scientific and technical literature, and other systems may be required in the effective handling of the literature of the arts, the humanities, and other literature which constitute the major portion of the general library's collection.[32]

[30] Arthur L. Kenney, "Instrumentation and Information," *Guide to Scientific Instruments: Science*, CLIVA (November, 22, 1966), 7. Copyright 1966 by the American Association for the Advancement of Science.
[31] One alternate solution which appears to hold some promise is the development of optical scanning devices that can read most types of print.
[32] Gordon N. Ray, "The Future of the Book," *ALA Bulletin*, LX (September, 1966), 788.

Suggestions regarding further study

At the beginning of this chapter it was noted that few if any areas of thought and endeavor have been left untouched—directly or indirectly—by the computer and auxiliary electronic machines. Advanced machines have already touched librarianship in a number of important ways, not only in the handling and expediting of library housekeeping functions and basic routine processes, but more significantly in bringing to librarians an awareness of new and powerful forces that are acting upon the profession—forces which demand understanding and continuous evaluation. Several years ago Dean Shera remarked that "a new understanding of librarianship may eventually prove to be the greatest single gift of automation to the library world, and whether there is in the future a push-button library may now be regarded as almost irrelevant."[33] More recently he has stated that "the mechanization of the library, and the emerging information science that it rests upon, are not transitory enthusiasms. Librarians are confronted by a movement that has been steadily developing over the past thirty years[34] and which, though it is very far from being immune from error, already has some impressive achievements to its credit. Librarianship is not going to be untouched by the machine."[35]

Clearly then—as has been urged a number of times—it is necessary that the student or practitioner of librarianship do his utmost to keep up to date on the portentous matters briefly discussed in this chapter. In this effort, it is neither possible nor necessary to try to follow closely all the many tryout operations now under way or which will emerge in connection with library mechanization and automated information storage and retrieval. Also, it is neither possible nor productive to try to read all the articles and books of theory and practice in these expansive fields. The librarian should, however, make a serious effort to do as many of the following things as are within his time and capacity:

---

[33] Jesse H. Shera, "Automation and the Reference Librarian," *RQ*, III (July, 1964), 7.

[34] Thirty years ago Dr. Ralph Parker published one of the first proposals to introduce the punched-card technique into librarianship. See Ralph H. Parker, "Mechanical Aids in College and University Libraries," *ALA Bulletin*, XXXII (October 15, 1938), 818.

[35] Shera, "What Is Past Is Prologue: Beyond 1984," p. 41.

1. Read regularly the announcements and articles on library automation; information storage, retrieval, and dissemination; documentation; specialized information centers; information networks; and so on[36] in such journals as *ALA Bulletin, Library Journal, Wilson Library Bulletin, American Documentation, Documentation Abstracts, College and Research Libraries, Journal of Education for Librarianship, Special Libraries, Science,* and *Library Science Abstracts.* It is equally important to read also the discussions in these publications on the aims and objectives of libraries and on the establishment of library networks.

2. Study the publications of the Office of Science Information, National Science Foundation, giving particular attention to the publication *Annual Review of Information Science and Technology.*

3. Examine the reports of projects set forth in the *Annual Reports* of the Council on Library Resources, Inc.

4. Keep up with the clinics, seminars, and institutes which are being conducted increasingly by the larger universities on various phases of the subject of the applicability of mechanization and automation to library operations and services and to specialized information services, and study as many of their reports as may be accessible. Announcements regarding these activities and the availability of reports which issue from them will be found in most of the publications noted above.

5. Follow as closely as possible the reports of progress and the outcomes of the growingly expansive experiment known as INTREX (Information Transfer Experiments) at the Massachusetts Institute of Technology. This is the most ambitious undertaking thus far established to probe the technical, administrative, and economic feasibilities of de-

---

[36] The subjects of pertinent articles are many and varied. "Automation," for example, is a word used in many different contexts; so, also is the subject "information retrieval." Since titles and meanings in these unsettled fields of theory and endeavor are not standardized, the student may find it difficult—at least in the beginning of his orientation—to separate the relevant from the extraneous.

veloping a systematic mechanized-automated program for dealing with the flood of information and knowledge materials now being funneled into university, research, and public libraries and specialized information centers. The project covers multiple types of experiments directed toward the ultimate design of integrated library services that might become available at M.I.T. and elsewhere in the decade beginning 1970. To date the costs of this wide-ranging project are being underwritten by grants from the Carnegie Corporation, the Council on Library Resources, Inc., the National Science Foundation, and the Advanced Research Projects Agency.[37]

6. Keep up with the activities of the Information Science and Automation Division of ALA through its *Journal of Information Science and Library Automation.*

7. Keep informed regarding the activities of the Library of Congress in the areas of automation and library cooperation as they are reported in the *Annual Report of the Librarian of Congress.*

[37] Many of the ideas and influences behind the INTREX idea are found in J. C. R. Licklider, *Libraries of the Future* (Cambridge, Mass.: The M.I.T. Press, 1965). A full report of the five-week planning conference which formulated the basic objectives and procedures of the project is set forth in *IN-TREX: The Report of a Planning Conference on Information Transfer Experiments,* ed. Carl F. J. Overhage and R. Joyce Harman (Cambridge, Mass.: The M.I.T. Press, 1965).

CHAPTER 24
WHAT
OF THE
FUTURE?

An institution is the embodiment of an ideal. In order to survive, an institution must fulfill two conditions: it must be sufficiently stable to sustain the ideal which gave it birth and sufficiently responsive to remain relevant to the society which supports it.[1]

Those institutions that move with change and maintain a position of relevance to contemporary problems will fulfill themselves. . . . Libraries are a facility of increasingly central importance in a society whose knowledge base provides the vital key to future progress and survival as a civilization. How well libraries adapt their various institutional forms to the conditions and requirements of the next few decades very largely depends on the capacity of library leaders to identify and interpret relevant trends.[2]

To what kind of society will it be necessary for the library to remain relevant? What are the conditions and demands of the future with which libraries must move? These are the kinds of questions with which each student and practitioner of librarianship will have to concern himself, while trying to maintain a balanced perspective on what constitutes increasingly better library service in the present and what may constitute adequacy and efficiency in the future.

It is obvious that no one can predict with any certainty the precise patterns and details of thought and activity in the future. There are at hand, however, certain signs and portents, many persistent problems and questions, and certain trends, which should be taken into due account. In the following pages a few basic fea-

---

[1] Eric Ashby, *Universities: British, Indian, African* (Cambridge, Mass.: Harvard University Press, 1966), p. 3.
[2] Ralph W. Conant, "Sociological and Institutional Changes in American Life," *ALA Bulletin*, LXI (May, 1967), 528, 529, 534.

tures of the future and a number of problems, questions, and trends are set forth briefly, representing, of course, only a small fraction of the matters which are pertinent to effective librarianship. It is assumed that the serious student has long since started the process of raising for himself many more questions than he will ever be able to find completely satisfying answers to—a process of critical significance to himself, his librarianship, and his society; for if ever he is able to find what he considers to be full answers to the problems and issues inherent in effective librarianship in a growingly complicated world, then either he will have ceased to think and to grow or librarianship will have become so routinized and functionally delimited that it will play only an inconsequential part in the important affairs of life. Neither alternative is a tolerable one.

BASIC FEATURES OF THE FUTURE

Change in a free society

Scientists, philosophers, and others speak of change as increasing "exponentially" today in all areas of human knowledge and existence. What is meant is simply that the amount of change which takes place is proportional to the amount that has already taken place; therefore, as more change occurs, the rate increases further. On this basis, even more and faster change than characterizes the present is inevitable in the decades ahead. The starting point, therefore, in both personal and institutional planning and functioning is the clear realization that *rapid change as a basic condition of tomorrow's life*—with all phases of life being deeply affected—must be dealt with in some fashion, willingly or reluctantly, efficiently or inefficiently.

Consider, for example, a national society which is committed to the maintenance of personal freedom and the efficient operation of the democratic process. It is the nature of this kind of society to face radical change head on and to strive—through its citizens and its institutions—to introduce increasing amounts of intelligence into its management. National societies committed to values other than those cherished by a free country can use such approaches in dealing with change as will fit the arbitrarily chosen objectives of their policy makers, but a democratic society must (1) trust that if its citizens become and stay as intelligently informed as the capacities of each will permit, they will make the right and necessary decisions about the problems and affairs of their society as well as about their own personal affairs; and (2) rely on its free institutions to find and use the required ways and means by which that trust can be realized. This has always been democracy's gamble of faith and effort. Today the stakes are higher and the task much larger and more difficult than heretofore because of the speed, volume, and far-reaching nature of current and impending change; the growing complexity of society's structure and problems; and the increasing amount and variety of knowledge which the individual needs to acquire in order to think and act intelligently and with social competency.

This trust and this reliance—in such times as are ahead—place upon citizens and their institutions many necessities, both immediate and long range, and place upon librarians the responsibilities of becoming and remaining knowledgeable about those necessities and of participating with growing aggressiveness and effectiveness in meeting them. For example, a vital necessity in the approach of a democratic society to pervasive change is that more and more members of that society develop and sustain the motivation to learn and acquire and maintain the skills of continuous learning. One immediate conclusion seems to be clear: unless the librarian—regardless of the particular professional or occupational role he may play in librarianship—is a constant illustration of how to become and remain a lifelong student, he will relegate himself to the role of an ineffectual spectator in the efforts going on around him. How can the school, or academic, or public librarian, for example, "arm the student with a spirit of inquiry for life"[3] unless he is fully imbued with that spirit himself and exhibits it in his actions and expressed thoughts? How can a reference librarian assist students

[3] Marguerite Murray, "Luaus in the Library," *Library Journal*, XCII (April 15, 1967), 1709.

as he should in learning how to carry on their own education unless the degree and quality of his reference work gives unmistakable evidence that he has mastered the skills required in continuous learning?

Another vital necessity is that more and more members of a free society develop the disposition and acquire the habits and skills of recognizing social problems, of analyzing them, and of knowing how to seek and find and use the knowledge needed in a reasoned attack upon them. No group in society has had as much experience as librarians in collecting, describing, storing, and making available for use the information and knowledge materials needed by citizens in making intelligent decisions and in initiating thought-through actions; and no group has been more concerned about the effective handling of the materials issuing from research in the physical and social sciences. How can librarians expect to bear their full load of responsibility as agents of a democratic society in producing problem-facing, problem-solving citizens unless they themselves are constantly seeking through coordinated study and research to define their own objectives, to understand their problems and needs, and to prove out through innovative experimentation the most effective ways by which to perform their functions and services?[4]

The last question implies a tremendous never-ending effort, and it is just that; but can anything less be expected of librarians? A free society expects that its members will learn how to recognize the important, to separate the trivial and the shoddy from the meaningful and the valuable, and to establish scales of significance and urgency and pursue them in the order of first things first. The price of mere busyness and aimless frenetic activity is too high either for an individual or an institution to pay. Librarians should be expected by society to set about with reasoned purpose to evaluate their many activities and problems, to separate the important from the peripheral and the trivial, and then to apply themselves with determination and cooperative design to learning through continuing research what the metes and bounds and expansive dimen-

---

[4] See "A Kaleidoscopic View of Library Research," *Wilson Library Bulletin,* XLI (May, 1967), *passim.,* 896–949.

sions of their job are in the society which supports and relies on them and how that never-static job can best be performed.

The extent to which librarians develop and maintain their own seek-search-find enterprise, well ordered in its priorities and drawing on all pertinent disciplines for the fullest possible help, may well determine the degree to which they will be classed as indispensables in the intellectual, cultural, social, and economic life of the future, for the consequences of whether librarians know what their job is and do it poorly or excellently have never been quite so decisive. In short, librarians can choose to be "Very Important Persons," the first step in the achievement and maintenance of that status being unqualified recognition that both the librarian and the library must be willing to be judged by what they are becoming and what they are determined to be—not by what they may have been and may have done in the past.

Increasing volume of information and knowledge materials

As long as the scientific community remains free to operate on the premise that the physical universe does not hold any inherent secrets and thus that all parts of it—including the human mind itself—are open to investigation and research, the production of scientific materials will increase. The same conclusion applies with regard to the production of technical materials. The chairman of the board of one of the world's leading publishing companies has aptly pointed out to librarians the current "endless loop of generating, stating, publishing, vending and using of technical information."[5] In the future the elements of this loop undoubtedly will vary in process and form, but that technical information will increase in quantity is assured. It must not be overlooked, however, that information and knowledge materials are accumulating in vast quantities in many other areas of experience. For example, the accumulation of court decisions is increasing by many thousands each year with many of these decisions carrying highly significant impli-

[5] Curtis G. Benjamin, *Everything Is Not Coming Up Roses,* An Address to the Science-Technology Division of the Special Libraries Association Fifty-Sixth Annual Convention, Philadelphia, June 9, 1965 (New York: McGraw-Hill Book Company, 1965), p. 2.

cations not only for the legal profession but also for those who make plans; initiate actions and programs; and seek to solve problems in social, economic, educational, business, governmental and other affairs.

In sum, the volume of recorded materials in all the major areas of thought and experience can be expected to grow steadily year by year. This rising flood of information will continue to come in a multitude of forms, both book and nonbook. Whether books will become outmoded and eventually replaced by other ways of packaging and preserving the world's accumulation of information and knowledge does not appear to be the question of greatest practicality or import at this stage of history. As far ahead as anyone has tried to see, it is judged that books instead of disappearing will become even more common and more widely available than now, and the business of printing and publishing will continue to grow.[6] For example, book sales in the United States in 1963 were almost three times those of ten years earlier, and sales of the publishing industry in 1966 were 15 percent greater than those in 1965. Also without question, nonbook forms will multiply greatly.

A much more pressing and practical matter than that of which knowledge form will replace or outnumber some other form is that of knowing what information and knowledge are produced, who produced them, who needs them, and how to provide timely and effective access to them regardless of the form in which they are recorded and where and how they are stored. This is not just one critical and practical matter: it is many matters and raises a multitude of questions:

1. Who shall attempt to keep up with the many sources of information and knowledge production?
2. To whom shall these sources be made known, by whom, and how? How is a determination made of who needs what portions of these materials—specialized and nonspecialized?
3. Shall there be a conscious planned division of labor between and among agencies in order to avoid wasteful competition and duplication?

[6] See Gilbert Burck, "Knowledge: The Greatest Growth Industry of Them All," *Fortune*, LXX (November, 1964), 267. See also John Tebbel "Book-Publishers' Salvation," *Saturday Review*, XLIX (July 23, 1966), 32, 33.

4. Shall there be a network of agencies, and what is the place of the various forms of libraries in such a network?

5. By what agencies and in what manner shall the attempt be made to evaluate the transitory or the enduring worth of the materials produced?

6. Who shall collect what portions and forms of the flood of materials? How shall they be described and stored? Who shall retrieve them?

7. To what extent will the form of recorded information and knowledge affect timely and effective access to it?

8. To what extent is access affected by the knowledgeability of the user in pursuing his own education or by the changing nature of his needs?

And so on.

It has been observed previously that the problem of becoming and of staying competently informed in any area of thought and action is a staggering one. The more anyone learns and knows—student, professional, nonprofessional, specialist, or generalist—the greater is his awareness of how much more there is to learn and to know. It would be an outcome beyond reasoned belief if the potential of a modern dark age were allowed to develop in the future because of too much information and knowledge instead of too little—as in times past—and because ways and means are not found by which the needed information and knowledge can be made available and used effectively in dealing with the world's problems and afflictions. One librarian has articulated the judgment of many social analysts in saying that "to keep society from being swamped by ignorance will require the utmost in ingenuity and leadership from librarians as well as from educators, sociologists, and politicians."[7]

Complexity and interrelatedness of problems

That modern society is highly complicated and its problems complex and interrelated is not a new fact, but discovery of the proportions and some of the meanings of that fact is relatively re-

[7] Ervin J. Gaines, "Intellectual Freedom," *ALA Bulletin,* LX (February, 1966) 119.

cent. In the midst of this country's greatest economic depression, the President's Research Committee on Social Trends set forth in the opening of its formal report the following theme statements:

> The outstanding problem might be stated as that of bringing about a realization of the interdependence of the factors of our compli- cated social structure. . . . It is the express purpose of this review of findings to unite such problems as those of economics, govern- ment, religion, education . . . to direct attention to the importance of balance among the factors of change. A nation advances not only by dynamic power, but by and through the maintenance of some degree of equilibrium among the moving forces.[8]

It was not until relatively recent years—a quarter of a century after the publication of this report—that there began to be an out- spoken recognition that "ours" is a truly "complicated social struc- ture" and that social, cultural, economic, educational, political and other categorized problems are extremely complex, arising out of multiple causes and requiring persistent joint efforts in their solution. As cities, rural areas, states, and regions in this country have worked at defining their major problems and projecting solutions for them,[9] there has begun to develop another belated but growing recognition, to wit: it is the nonspecialists, the generalists, the synthesizers— those whose purpose, training, and effort are directed toward trying to see and to understand total situations and problems as a whole rather than in their fragmented parts—who are so badly needed. Coincident with this recognition has come the jolting discovery that persons of such capacity are in short supply.

The paradox is that at the very time when there is growing out- side the academic and professional communities a need and demand for those who can integrate and synthesize knowledge, the emphasis on specialization inside the academic community not only continues to exist but in most instances to become stronger; and inside the professional community technical vocabularies and restricted per-

[8] President's Research Committee on Social Trends, *Recent Social Trends in the United States* (New York: McGraw-Hill Book Company, 1933), I, xii, xiii.
[9] See Ralph W. Conant (ed.), *The Public Library and the City* (Cambridge, Mass.: The M.I.T. Press, 1965).

spectives deter the achievement of mutual understanding and the effective coordination of purposes and efforts.

Dorothy Broderick, reporting on her participation in the Mid-Decade White House Conference on Children and Youth in Washington, D.C., which included psychiatrists, medical doctors, housing experts, social workers, teachers, and librarians, stated: "Most of the participants were so bogged down in their own special jargon, in their own narrow view of the problems facing youth, that they could not communicate with each other. We, the librarians, served as interpreters and, on occasion, mediators."[10] Later in her report, in setting forth her conception of the responsibility of the library in relationship to the integration of knowledge, she stated that her "basic bias was reaffirmed at that meeting: namely that the scholars of all disciplines (and the practitioners, since they are trained by the scholars) have shattered the Humpty-Dumpty known as knowledge and that it falls to us, the librarians, to do what all the king's horses and all the king's men couldn't do—put him back together again." Then she added that no group of librarians—public, academic, school, or special—is exempted from the "responsibility to serve as liaison agent among disciplines."[11]

The necessity of trying to understand total situations or whole problems and to deal with them in terms of cooperative efforts is not limited to such massive matters as economic growth and development, hunger, and disease. For example, increasingly in recent years—and with or without outside help—librarians have been engaging in the effort to define, analyze, and evaluate the current objectives of a particular library as well as its organizational parts; its specific operations and functions; its types and ranges of services; and the kinds of facilities, equipment, and methods it now possesses and uses. Those who have applied themselves to this critical enterprise have found that the effort to analyze a particular library as an organized program of aims which are "relevant to the society which supports it," and of activites which are relevant to those aims, is a highly complicated one.

[10] Dorothy M. Broderick, "The Librarian in Today's Society," *Library Journal*, XCII (April, 1, 1967), 1413.
[11] *Ibid.*, 1414.

What are the purposes of such an analytical effort: to arrive at an intelligent determination of whether or not the library's objectives, resources, services, and methods are adequate? If so, what is the measuring stick by which adequacy or inadequacy is judged? Suppose that at the end of the analysis the library staff and its governing body are able to say that today they are performing all activities faster and better than they did yesterday: what does this announcement actually mean? Was the analysis made and was the conclusion reached in light of all the needs and requirements of the library's users and potential users or only on the basis of what were considered the most essential needs and requirements of the current users? On what bases were essential and nonessential decided? What consideration was given to the nature and extent of the responsibility of other libraries to share in serving these users; to the practicality of having this library become a part of a larger system of similar or dissimilar libraries in order to provide more materials, facilities, and services relevant to its needs and purposes; or to cooperative efforts with agencies and institutions other than libraries in extending the range and impact of its services?

What is the most effective relationship between public, school, and academic libraries and specialized information centers? Between public libraries and information centers? Between research libraries and information centers? What is the proper and effective place of commercial information-transmission networks and systems in producing increasingly knowledgeable citizens?

The effort to see, to analyze, and to understand problems and situations in their full range and then to project feasible plans and actions is the most difficult task an individual, a group, an agency, or an institution can engage in, for the factors and forces do not stand still; they are moving. Problems, situations, and relationships change in their structure and meaning at the very time that efforts are being made to analyze them, understand them, and put them together into a viable pattern. If ever there were ages of placidity in librarianship—and by comparison with today and tomorrow there have been—there is no rationale by which they can be expected again. The chief question then is whether librarians now have, or can achieve, the necessary temperament, attitude, and capacity to accept the facts of life and to deal patiently, persistently, and intelligently with fluidity of existence and the growing interrelatedness of problems as basic conditions of future life in full realization that the quality of what they think and plan and do is of vital importance in the affairs of a complex democratic society.

MORE PROBLEMS AND TRENDS

It is logical that in a free society which relies on the knowledgeable judgments and decisions of its citizens for the proper management of their own and society's affairs, the process of informing and educating citizens should constitute a larger and larger portion of the total work load of that society.

Formal education

It is natural that such a society should look increasingly to its system of formal education to produce the kind of citizens it needs, for society's progress and destiny—which encompass the welfare and destiny of the individual—cannot be left to the chance outcomes of informal efforts. It is not surprising, therefore, that the dimensions of America's system of formal education are expanding yearly.

The amount of schooling considered necessary has been increasing steadily for decades, with the result that during the twenty years immediately following World War II, outlays for formal education increased three and one-half times and the baccalaureate degree became the accepted educational norm of society.[12] In mid-1966 the U.S. Commissioner of Education announced that Americans were spending "close to $50 billion annually on their schools and colleges" and suggested that "as more and more people begin their education earlier, continue it longer, and decide to invest more in

---

[12] See Harry D. Gideonse, "The Purpose of Higher Education: A Reexamination," *The College and the Student,* ed. Lawrence E. Dennis and Joseph F. Kauffman (Washington, D.C.: American Council on Education, 1966), pp. 23–46.

their children's schooling or have their government do so," growing amounts will be spent on education.[13] Thus, formal education has become—in the vocabulary of business—a leading "growth industry," absorbing a larger share of this country's gross national product (GNP)[14] than any other single category of activity except national defense and involving the great majority of library services—school, academic, public, and research.[15]

This expanding system of formal education has always had multiple aims and will continue to set for itself plural purposes, but one particular goal of education is claiming the increasing attention of educational and social philosophers, administrators, and government leaders. This objective is logically derived from an analysis of such basic features of the future as were pointed out in preceding pages and is aptly summarized in the following succinct statements:

> Most of all we need an education which will create the educated mind. This is a mind—not simply a repository of information and skills. . . .[16]

> The goal of education, if we are to survive, is the facilitation of change and learning. . . . The only man who is educated is the man who has learned how to adapt and change; the man who has realized that no knowledge is secure, that only the process of seeking knowledge gives a basis for security. . . . A reliance on process rather than upon static knowledge, is the only thing that makes any sense as a goal of education in the modern world.[17]

The immediately obvious implication of this vital objective is that the entire formal educational system—preelementary through graduate school and the continuing education of adults—should be

---

[13] Harold Howe II, "Realities of the Learning Market," *Library Journal*, XCII (January 15, 1967), 298.

[14] GNP: the dollar value of all goods and services produced in the economy.

[15] Dan Lacy, "The Impact of Universal Education," *Library Journal*, XCI (September 1, 1966), 3866.

[16] From an address by President Lyndon B. Johnson to the White House Conference on Education in 1965.

[17] From a speech by Carl R. Rogers at the annual meeting of the Association for Supervision and Curriculum Development held March 12-16, 1967, reported in "Facilitation of Change Seen as New Goal of Education for Man in Modern World," *NEA Reporter*, VI (April 21, 1967), 2.

organized around the purpose of helping students of whatever age to progressively develop and maintain the desire and the necessary skills to seek and to acquire knowledge, both old and new, and as a consequence carry on their own informal education throughout their lives. In this concept the school, at all levels, becomes an organized selective learning enterprise, characterized by inquiry, probing, search, discovery, critical analysis, creativity, and the synthesis of knowledge in which "every form of learning instrument, hard or soft, will be integrated into an effective teaching and learning package."[18]

In this concept, librarians and libraries become invaluable parts of the entire selective learning enterprise. Librarians, teachers, and educational administrators work toward the same fundamental purpose and thus are partners in planning and executing an integrated instructional program using all available media and facilities. This means that librarians must be accquainted with and make available all kinds of learning materials and keep up with whatever develops.

Educating all students progressively in learning how to learn makes it necessary that the library become the center of an increasingly important part of the student's learning activity. In this central relationship and function, the librarian is an educator—a teacher, a curriculum maker, and an integrator of learning resources; and every librarian becomes, in a very practical sense, a reference librarian, for "the more a student knows, the more he needs help in a progressively sophisticated manner."[19] The help he needs is considerably more than that of simply finding materials or of having them put in his hand. Materials finding or delivery is not automatically materials usage. The librarian and teachers, therefore, have the job of assisting students in the evaluation and use of learning materials.

This, in brief sketch, is a part of the theory of the education which is required by the kind of future ahead and of the place

[18] Edward E. Booher, "Frontiers of Knowledge in a Changing World," *Imprint: The McGraw-Hill Book Company Story* (New York: McGraw-Hill Book Company, 1967), p. 2.
[19] Bernard E. Richardson, "Last One in Bed's a Librarian," *Library Journal*, XCI (October 15, 1966), 4906.

of librarians and libraries in it. This is far from being a completely new concept. It was pointed out in Chapter 16 that as early as 1956 the American Association of School Librarians set forth the philosophy of the school library as an instructional materials center. More than a decade later the task of tracing out the multiplied implications of this concept for libraries—school, academic, public, and research, in particular—and for schools continues to be a major undertaking, one which not only merits but demands the priority attention of both librarians and educators.[20]

The blunt fact is that there is a vast gap between concept and practice; between the theory of what should be and what actually is. However true the affirmation that "the library is the fastest growing element in the modern school" may be by comparison with the past, the yet unsolved problems, the things yet to be done, and the people yet to be convinced are multitudinous when the great gulf between the actuality of the present and the needs of the present is recognized, to say nothing of the greater requirements and demands of the future.

One thing is clear: America's system of formal education faces large and multiple responsibilities, the most central of which is that of doing whatever is necessary to see to it that all students—from the lowest level to the highest—learn how to carry on and forward their own education, and unless these responsibilities are fully shared by the librarians of the country they will not be executed in the manner and to the extent required by a complex free society in a fast-moving world. In sum, no single concern of this country is more important or requires more concerted effort than that of developing unified goals for formal education and librarianship and of mobilizing the professional, political, and public support necessary to the realization of those goals.

Information retrieval and dissemination

For a number of years technological innovators have been envisioning the establishment of a new public utility—an information

[20] See Mary V. Gaver, "The School Library: An Intellectual Force?" *Library Journal,* XCII (May 15, 1967), 1989–91.

utility that will make utilitarian information and factual knowledge available at established rates to subscribers throughout the world in much the same manner that people now pay for heat, light, power, and water.[21] Technological advance toward an information utility has been appreciable. A new generation of computers, with much larger-scale memories than heretofore, is being developed.[22] It was noted in Chapter 23 that most information is not in a form that can be understood by the computer, and thus that one of the chief difficulties is getting the information into the computers. Even so, the optimism of the technologists regarding the translation of information into machine-readable form is such that engineers, the producers of electronic equipment, and business management consultants are prophesying that information retrieval and dissemination will be a multibillion dollar business by the early 1970s and that business information retrieval systems will represent a major portion of commercial computer activity during that period and thereafter.

The man who is generally credited with coining the term "automation" has observed that as computer capabilities are increasing, costs are decreasing, and within a few years there will be such a reduction in the cost of "completing a data-processing job" that we "will be able to do more with information technology than we now can ever imagine."[23] In anticipation of a growing and profitable "inquiry" industry, a number of major American businesses have established mergers, joint ventures, and expansions in recent years. The editorial staff of *Forbes* magazine has noted that "the boundaries between the different forms of mass communication are breaking down. . . . As things now stand, television set makers publish books, magazine publishers own TV stations, and educational research organizations and book publishers own schools."[24] Some observers are of the judgment that such mergers and joint ventures will increase.

[21] John Pfeiffer, "Machines That Man Can Talk With," *Fortune*, LXIX (May, 1964), 196, 198.
[22] See John Diebold, "The New World Coming," *Saturday Review*, XLIX (July 23, 1966), 17, 18. See also Sarnoff, "No Life Untouched," p. 21.
[23] Diebold, *op. cit.*, 18.
[24] "Nineteenth Annual Report on American Industry, Communications," *Forbes*, C (January 1, 1967), 118.

The establishment of special information centers is spreading. The *Directory of Special Libraries and Information Centers* for 1966 lists more than ten thousand information centers, special libraries, and documentation centers in the United States and Canada.[25] Although not all are specialized information centers, an appreciable percentage is, and undoubtedly the number will materially increase. The formation of major information retrieval centers is also well under way. For example, the Committee on Scientific and Technical Information of the Federal Council for Science and Technology (COSATI) has been doing preliminary work on the establishment of a network of computerized information centers and special libraries to provide retrieval service in the major scientific disciplines. Further, in March, 1966, the Committee on Scientific and Technical Communication (SATCOM) was formed with the objective of providing a "focus for participation by scientists and engineers—through their professional organizations—in planning national networks of information systems."[26]

The Interuniversity Communications Council (EDUCOM), established in mid-1965 with a grant from the Kellogg Foundation and involving eight institutions of higher education, had grown to a membership of forty-two in 1966. Membership is open to all accredited universities and colleges in the United States, Canada, and Mexico. The group's basic goal is "to optimize the use of the emerging communication sciences."[27] In 1966, seven library associations in this country banded together in a Joint Committee on National Library and Information Systems (CONLIS). The purpose of this committee is to draft a program designed to improve the access and availability of information through networks of information centers and libraries.[28]

These are examples of the vigorous and multiplying efforts

[25] Anthony T. Kruzas (ed.), *Directory of Special Libraries and Information Centers* (Detroit: Gale Research Company, 1966).
[26] See "Route '66," *Library Journal*, XCII (January 1, 1967), 61.
[27] *ACRL News*, No. 7 (October, 1966), 125.
[28] "Route '66," *loc. cit.* The associations are: American Library Association, American Association of Law Libraries, American Documentation Institute, Association of Research Libraries, Council of National Library Associations, Medical Library Association, and Special Libraries Association.

to establish systems by which the growing volume of specialized information can be handled and disseminated more effectively and widely. For private enterprise these efforts constitute a potentially broad and profitable growth industry, suggesting that there will be a growing role for commercial interests in maintaining special systems for both wholesale transmission and selective dissemination of specialized information.

Libraries are also developing varied types of system arrangements, not only those like EDUCOM and CONLIS, but those involving cooperation among states, cooperative statewide services, and regional, county, and metropolitan-area federations. Examples of these arrangements were given in Chapter 14. Interlocking and cooperative library service—characterized by many forms of structural organization and varied purposes—without question will continue to grow and expand both in geography and in range of functions.

As a pragmatic frontier people, Americans have tended to think of education largely as a means of transmitting information; as the nation has become more advanced industrially and technologically, they have continued to think of education in terms of information; and in recent decades—as science has joined with industry and technology—the drive has been to program individual talents in the direction of technical utility. And now increasing numbers of people are drawing word-pictures of "their" libraries as parts of a vast network of immediately useful information, which begins with the nearest library and comes full circle only when the information is in the user's hand. It has been noted that steps in that direction have been taken and others will be taken. It must not be overlooked, however, that not all the information and knowledge materials being produced are designed for immediate consumption and application. Science is only a part of life, technology is only a part of life, and specialization—although inevitable and essential— is also only a part of life. The very complexities of a scientific and technological age—the direct derivatives of specialization— make it unwise for the individual to remain solely a specialist and for the library to commit itself wholly to the chore of recovering and transmitting specialized information. Significantly, some scientists are expressing concern that academic programs "are not geared to produce multidisciplinary scientists," noting that "it is unusual for a young scientist to be able to work effectively in more than his one chosen discipline."[29]

Competition for status and control in the field of communicating and transferring information is heavy and will become heavier; and fact finding and data processing for utilitarian purposes is certain to become an increasingly large part of the work of the library, but the library has a deeper responsibility to a free society than to concentrate on providing factual and immediately useful information. The future will contain the specialist and massive quantities of his specialized materials; but it will also contain the synthesizer (even in science), the nonspecialist, the nonscientist, and the nontechnologist. Paul Buck has offered the proposition that "strong libraries are essential to the full exploitation of intellectual resources and to the maintenance of free access to ideas . . . the library must remain a humane institution; it must not become an information factory."[30]

Philosophy, in the broadest possible sense of the term, may well be the most practical subject in the curriculum of tomorrow's education. It is suggested that a pilosophy of value—from which objectives can emerge—is already the most practical and important, timely and defensible area of study to which both students and practitioners of librarianship can give their attention.

LIBRARIANS TOMORROW

What will be the basic and continuing tasks of tomorrow's librarians? Certainly these will be among them:

1. To read the signs of the decades ahead and determine—with the help of all disciplines which have any pertinent knowledge to contribute—what the conditions and aspirations of men and the problems and expectations of society will be

[29] S. F. Singer, "Planetary Engineering," *Saturday Review*, L (July 1, 1967), 42.
[30] Paul Buck, *Libraries and Universities, Addresses and Reports,* ed. Edwin E. Williams (Cambridge, Mass.: The Belknap Press, Harvard University Press, 1964), p. 160.

2. To determine the many kinds of needs men and society will have for information and knowledge: what kinds of information and knowledge, in what places, under what conditions

3. To establish aims and objectives for libraries in light of those needs and in view of the cooperation that can be established with other agencies and institutions which are performing effective functions in meeting any portion of those needs

4. To continuingly appraise what machines can and cannot do and to use them when and where they are applicable, as a deliberate way by which to implement the objectives of responsive librarianship

5. To remain students all their lives, always intellectually alert and socially sensitive and always probing and searching for the better answer and the more effective service

What will those who choose to work at the incomparably important job of meeting the needs of the members of a democratic society for multiplied kinds of information and knowledge be called in the future? By numerous names, perhaps, for there will be many kinds of specialties—some narrow, some broad; many technical functions to be performed, and many obligations to be met by generalists and synthesizers, managers and policy-makers. It is far too early to decide, as some appear to have already done, that all names and titles will or should be subsumed under "information science" or any similar vocational or professional category or that they will or should be subsumed under "library science." The principal issue of librarianship does not relate to names and titles but to objectives fitted to the social milieu, to the policies and procedures and the organizations and technologies essential to the most effective fulfillment of those objectives, and—most importantly—to the caliber and quality of the men and women who devote themselves to these matters. No job description, no position name or title, no administrative fiat, no legal statute can confer upon the librarian a status of respect, prestige, and honor. It is the quality of his motivation, his thought, and his action which will contribute most to such a desired status.

APPENDIX 1
GUIDES FOR PROFESSIONAL PERFORMANCE

THE PROFESSION[1]

The time has at last come when a librarian may, without assumption, speak of his occupation as a profession. And, more, a
better time has come—perhaps we should say is coming, for it still
has many fields to conquer. The best librarians are no longer men
of merely negative virtues. They are positive, aggressive characters,
standing in the front rank of the educators of their communities,
side by side with the preachers and the teachers. The people are
more and more getting their incentives and ideas from the printed
page. There are more readers and fewer listeners, and men who
move and lead the world are using the press more and the platform
less. It needs no argument to prove that reading matter can be
distributed better and more cheaply through lending libraries than
in any other way, and we shall assume, what few will presume
to dispute, that the largest influence over the people is the printed
page and that this influence may be wielded most surely and
strongly through our libraries.

From the first, libraries have commanded great respect, and
much has been written of their priceless worth; but the opinion
has been largely prevalent that a librarian was a keeper only, and
had done his full duty if he preserved the books from loss, and
to a reasonable extent from the worms. There have been noble
exceptions to this rule, but still it is a modern idea that librarians
should do more than this. It is not now enough that the books
are cared for properly, are well arranged, are never lost. It is not
enough if the librarian can readily produce any book asked for.
It is not enough that he can, when asked, give advice as to the
best books in his collection on any given subject. All these things
are indispensable, but all these are not enough for our ideal. He
must see that his library contains, as far as possible, the best books

[1] Melvil Dewey, "The Profession," *The American Library Journal*, I, No.
1 (September 30, 1876), 5-6.

on the best subjects, regarding carefully the wants of his special community. Then, having the best books, he must create among his people, his pupils, a desire to read those books. He must put every facility in the way of readers, so that they shall be led on from good to better. He must teach them how, after studying their own wants, they may themselves select their reading wisely. Such a librarian will find enough who are ready to put themselves under his influence and direction, and, if competent and enthusiastic, he may soon largely shape the reading, and through it the thought, of his whole community.

The time is come when we are not astonished to find the ablest business talents engaged in the management of a public library. Not that we have less scholarship, but that we have more life. The passive has become active, and we look for a throng of people going in and out of library doors as in the markets and the stores. There was a time when libraries were opened only at intervals, and visitors came occasionally, as they come sometimes to a deserted castle or to a haunted house. Now many of our libraries are as accessible as our post offices, and the number of new libraries founded has been so great that in an ordinary town we no longer ask, "Have you a library?" but "Where is your library?" as we might ask where is your schoolhouse, or your post office, or your church?

And so our leading educators have come to recognize the library as sharing with the school the education of the people. The most that the schools can hope to do for the masses more than the schools are doing for them in many sections, is to teach them to read intelligently, to get ideas readily from the printed page. It may seem a strong statement, but many children leave the schools without this ability. They can repeat the words of the book, but this is simply pronunciation, as a beginner pronounces another language without getting any clear idea of the meaning. Could the schools really teach the masses to *read*, they would be doing a great work. The children of the lower classes have to commence work at a very early age, and it is impossible to keep them in the schools long enough to educate them to any degree. The school teaches them to read; the library must supply them with reading which shall serve to educate, and so it is that we are forced to divide popular education into two parts of almost equal importance and deserving equal attention: the free school and the free library.

It is in the interest of the modern library, and of those desiring to make its influence wider and greater, that this journal has been established. Its founders have an intense faith in the future of our libraries and believe that if the best methods can be applied by the best librarians, the public may soon be brought to recognize our claim that the free library ranks with the free school. We hold that there is no work reaching farther in its influence and deserving more honor than the work which a competent and earnest librarian can do for his community.

The time *was* when a library was very like a museum, and a librarian was a mouser in musty books, and visitors looked with curious eyes at ancient tomes and manuscripts. The time *is* when a library is a school, and the librarian is in the highest sense a teacher, and the visitor is a reader among the books as a workman among his tools. Will any man deny to the high calling of such a librarianship the title of profession?

CODE OF ETHICS FOR LIBRARIANS

PREAMBLE:

1. The library as an institution exists for the benefit of a given constituency, whether it be the citizens of a community, members of an educational institution, or some larger or more specialized group. Those who enter the library profession assume an obligation to maintain ethical standards of behavior in relation to the governing authority under which they work, to the library constituency, to the library as an institution and to fellow workers on the staff, to other members of the library profession, and to society in general.

2. The term librarian in this code applies to any person who is employed by a library to do work that is recognized to be professional in character according to standards established by the American Library Association.

3. This code sets forth principles of ethical behavior for the professional librarian. It is not a declaration of prerogatives nor a statement of recommended practices in specific situations.

I. RELATION OF THE LIBRARIAN TO THE GOVERNING AUTHORITY

4. The librarian should perform his duties with realization of the fact that final jurisdiction over the administration of the library rests in the officially constituted governing authority. This authority may be vested in a designated individual, or in a group such as a committee or board.

5. The chief librarian should keep the governing authority informed on professional standards and progressive action. Each librarian should be responsible for carrying out the

policies of the governing authorities and its appointed executives with a spirit of loyalty to the library.

6. The chief librarian should interpret decisions of the governing authority to the staff, and should act as liaison officer in maintaining friendly relations between staff members and those in authority.

7. Recommendations to the governing authority for the appointment of a staff member should be made by the chief librarian solely upon the basis of the candidate's professional and personal qualifications for the position. Continuance in service and promotion should depend upon the quality of performance, following a definite and known policy. Whenever the good of the service requires a change in personnel, timely warning should be given. If desirable adjustment cannot be made, unsatisfactory service should be terminated in accordance with the policy of the library and the rules of tenure.

8. Resolutions, petitions and requests of a staff organization or group should be submitted through a duly appointed representative to the chief librarian. If a mutually satisfactory solution cannot be reached, the chief librarian, on request of the staff, should transmit the matter to the governing authority. The staff may further request that they be allowed to send a representative to the governing authority, in order to present their opinions in person.

II. RELATION OF THE LIBRARIAN TO HIS CONSTITUENCY

9. The chief librarian, aided by staff members in touch with the constituency, should study the present and future needs of the library, and should acquire materials on the basis of those needs. Provision should be made for as wide a range of publications and as varied a representation of viewpoints as is consistent with the policies of the library and with the funds available.

10 It is the librarian's responsibility to make the resources

and services of the library known to its potential users. Impartial service should be rendered to all who are entitled to use the library.

11. It is the librarian's obligation to treat as confidential any private information obtained through contact with library patrons.

12. The librarian should try to protect library property and to inculcate in users a sense of their responsibility for its preservation.

III. RELATIONS OF THE LIBRARIAN WITHIN HIS LIBRARY

13. The chief librarian should delegate authority, encourage a sense of responsibility and initiative on the part of staff members, provide for their professional development and appreciate good work. Staff members should be informed of the duties of their positions and the policies and problems of the library.

14. Loyalty to fellow workers and a spirit of courteous cooperation, whether between individuals or between departments, are essential to effective library service.

15. Criticism of library policies, service and personnel should be offered only to the proper authority for the sole purpose of improvement of the library.

16. Acceptance of a position in a library incurs an obligation to remain long enough to repay the library for the expense incident to adjustment. A contract signed or agreement made should be adhered to faithfully until it expires or is dissolved by mutual consent.

17. Resignations should be made long enough before they are to take effect to allow adequate time for the work to be put in shape and a successor appointed.

18. A librarian should never enter into a business dealing on behalf of the library which will result in personal profit.

19. A librarian should never turn the library's resources to personal use, to the detriment of services which the library renders to its patrons.

IV. RELATION OF THE LIBRARIAN
TO HIS PROFESSION

20. Librarians should recognize librarianship as an educational profession and realize that the growing effectiveness of their service is dependent upon their own development.

21. In view of the importance of ability and personality traits in library work a librarian should encourage only those persons with suitable aptitudes to enter the library profession and should discourage the continuance in service of the unfit.

22. Recommendations should be confidential and should be fair to the candidate and the prospective employer by presenting an unbiased statement of strong and weak points.

23. Librarians should have a sincere belief and a critical interest in the library profession. They should endeavor to achieve and maintain adequate salaries and proper working conditions.

24. Formal appraisal of the policies or practices of another library should be given only upon the invitation of that library's governing authority or chief librarian.

25. Librarians, in recognizing the essential unity of their profession, should have membership in library organizations and should be ready to attend and participate in library meetings and conferences.

V. RELATIONS OF THE LIBRARIAN TO SOCIETY

26. Librarians should encourage a general realization of the value of library service and be informed concerning movements, organizations and institutions whose aims are compatible with those of the library.

27. Librarians should participate in public and community affairs and so represent the library that it will take its place among educational, social and cultural agencies.

28. A librarian's conduct should be such as to maintain public esteem for the library and library work.

Adopted ALA Council Meeting, December 29, 1938.

AMERICAN LIBRARY ASSOCIATION
STATEMENT ON LABELING

In view of our own convictions and those of other practicing librarians whose counsel we sought, the Committee on Intellectual Freedom recommends to the ALA Council the following policy with respect to labeling library materials:

Librarians should not use the technique of labeling as a means of predisposing readers against library materials for the following reasons:

1. Although totalitarian states find it easy and even proper, according to their ethics, to establish criteria for judging publications as "subversive," injustice and ignorance rather than justice and enlightenment result from such practices, and the American Library Association has a responsibility to take a stand against the establishment of such criteria in a democratic state.

2. Libraries do not advocate the ideas found in their collections. The presence of a magazine or book in a library does not indicate an endorsement of its contents by the library.

3. No one person should take the responsibility of labeling publications. No sizable group of persons would be likely to agree either on the types of material which should be labeled or the sources of information which should be regarded with suspicion. As a practical consideration, a librarian who labeled a book or magazine pro-communist might be sued for libel.

4. Labeling is an attempt to prejudice the reader, and as such, it is the censor's tool.

5. Labeling violates the spirit of the Library Bill of Rights.

6. Although we are all agreed that communism is a threat to the free world, if materials are labeled to pacify one group, there is no excuse for refusing to label any item

in the library's collection. Because communism, fascism, or other authoritarianisms tend to suppress ideas and attempt to coerce individuals to conform to a specific ideology, American librarians must be opposed to such "isms." We are, then, anticommunist, but we are also opposed to any other group which aims at closing any path to knowledge.

ALA Bulletin, XLV (July-August, 1951), 242.

FREEDOM TO READ

A statement prepared by the Westchester Conference of the American Library Association and the American Book Publishers Council, May 2 and 3, 1953.

The freedom to read is essential to our democracy. It is under attack. Private groups and public authorities in various parts of the country are working to remove books from sale, to censor textbooks, to label "controversial" books, to distribute lists of "objectionable" books or authors, and to purge libraries. These actions apparently rise from a view that our national tradition of free expression is no longer valid; that censorship and suppression are needed to avoid the subversion of politics and the corruption of morals. We, as citizens devoted to the use of books and as librarians and publishers responsible for disseminating them, wish to assert the public interest in the preservation of the freedom to read.

We are deeply concerned about these attempts at suppression. Most such attempts rest on a denial of the fundamental premise of democracy: that the ordinary citizen, by exercising his critical judgment, will accept the good and reject the bad. The censors, public and private, assume that they should determine what is good and what is bad for their fellow-citizens.

We trust Americans to recognize propaganda, and to reject obscenity. We do not believe they need the help of censors to assist them in this task. We do not believe they are prepared to sacrifice their heritage of a free press in order to be "protected" against what others think may be bad for them. We believe they still favor free enterprise in ideas and expression.

We are aware, of course, that books are not alone in being subjected to efforts at suppression. We are aware that these efforts are related to a larger pattern of pressures being brought against education, the press, films, radio and television. The problem is not only one of actual censorship. The shadow of fear cast by these pressures leads, we suspect, to an even larger voluntary curtailment of expression by those who seek to avoid controversy.

Such pressure toward conformity is perhaps natural to a time of uneasy change and pervading fear. Especially when so many of our apprehensions are directed against an ideology, the expression of a dissident idea becomes a thing feared in itself, and we tend to move against it as against a hostile deed, with suppression.

And yet suppression is never more dangerous than in such a time of social tension. Freedom has given the United States the elasticity to endure strain. Freedom keeps open the path of novel and creative solutions, and enables change to come by choice. Every silencing of a heresy, every enforcement of an orthodoxy, diminishes the toughness and resilience of our society and leaves it the less able to deal with stress.

Now as always in our history, books are among our greatest instruments of freedom. They are almost the only means for making generally available ideas or manners of expression that can initially command only a small audience. They are the natural medium for the new idea and the untried voice from which come the original contributions to social growth. They are essential to the extended discussion which serious thought requires, and to the accumulation of knowledge and ideas into organized collections.

We believe that free communication is essential to the preservation of a free society and a creative culture. We believe that these pressures toward conformity present the danger of limiting the range and variety of inquiry and expression on which our democracy and our culture depend. We believe that every American community must jealously guard the freedom to publish and to circulate, in order to preserve its own freedom to read. We believe that publishers and librarians have a profound responsibility to give validity to that freedom to read by making it possible for the reader to choose freely from a variety of offerings.

The freedom to read is guaranteed by the Constitution. Those with faith in free men will stand firm on these constitutional guarantees of essential rights and will exercise the responsibilities that accompany these rights.

We therefore affirm these propositions:

1. It is in the public interest for publishers and librarians to make available the widest diversity of views and expres-

sions, including those which are unorthodox or unpopular with the majority.

Creative thought is by definition new, and what is new is different. The bearer of every new thought is a rebel until his idea is refined and tested. Totalitarian systems attempt to maintain themselves in power by the ruthless suppression of any concept which challenges the established orthodoxy. The power of a democratic system to adapt to change is vastly strengthened by the freedom of its citizens to choose widely from among conflicting opinions offered freely to them. To stifle every nonconformist idea at birth would mark the end of the democratic process. Furthermore, only through the constant activity of weighing and selecting can the democratic mind attain the strength demanded by times like these. We need to know not only what we believe but why we believe it.

2. Publishers and librarians do not need to endorse every idea or presentation contained in the books they make available. It would conflict with the public interest for them to establish their own political, moral or aesthetic views as the sole standard for determining what books should be published or circulated.

Publishers and librarians serve the educational process by helping to make available knowledge and ideas required for the growth of the mind and the increase of learning. They do not foster education by imposing as mentors the patterns of their own thought. The people should have the freedom to read and consider a broader range of ideas than those that may be held by any single librarian or publisher or government or church. It is wrong that what one man can read should be confined to what another thinks proper.

3. It is contrary to the public interest for publishers or librarians to determine the acceptability of a book solely on the basis of the personal history or political affiliations of the author.

A book should be judged as a book. No art or literature can flourish if it is to be measured by the political views or private lives of its creators. No society of free men can flourish which draws up lists of writers to whom it will not listen, whatever they may have to say.

4. The present laws dealing with obscenity should be vigorously enforced. Beyond that, there is no place in our society for extra-legal efforts to coerce the taste of others, to confine adults to the reading matter deemed suitable for adolescents, or to inhibit the efforts of writers to achieve artistic expression.

To some, much of modern literature is shocking. But is not much of life itself shocking? We cut off literature at the source if we prevent serious artists from dealing with the stuff of life. Parents and teachers have a responsibility to prepare the young to meet the diversity of experiences in life to which they will be exposed as they have a responsibility to help them learn to think critically for themselves. These are affirmative responsibilities, not to be discharged simply by preventing them from reading works for which they are not yet prepared. In these matters taste differs, and taste cannot be legislated; nor can machinery be devised which will suit the demands of one group without limiting the freedom of others. We deplore the catering to the immature, the retarded or the maladjusted taste. But those concerned with freedom have the responsibility of seeing to it that each individual book or publication, whatever its contents, price or method of distribution, is dealt with in accordance with due process of law.

5. It is not in the public interest to force a reader to accept with any book the prejudgment of a label characterizing the book or author as subversive or dangerous.

The idea of labeling presupposes the existence of individuals or groups with wisdom to determine by authority what is good or bad for the citizen. It presupposes that each individual must be directed in making up his mind about the ideas he examines. But Americans do not need others to do their thinking for them.

6. It is the responsibility of publishers and librarians, as guardians of the people's freedom to read, to contest encroachments upon that freedom by individuals or groups seeking to impose their own standards or tastes upon the community at large.

It is inevitable in the give and take of the democratic process that the political, the moral, or the aesthetic concepts of an individual or group will occasionally collide with those of another individual or group. In a free society each individual is free to determine for himself what he wishes to read, and each group is free to determine what it will recommend to its freely associated members. But no group has the right to take the law into its own hands, and to impose its own concept of politics or morality upon other members of a democratic society. Freedom is no freedom if it is accorded only to the accepted and inoffensive.

7. It is the responsibility of publishers and librarians to give full meaning to the freedom to read by providing books that enrich the quality of thought and expression. By the exercise of this affirmative responsibility bookmen can demonstrate that the answer to a bad book is a good one, the answer to a bad idea is a good one.

The freedom to read is of little consequence when expended on the trivial; it is frustrated when the reader cannot obtain matter fit for his purpose. What is needed is not only the absence of restraint, but the positive provision of opportunity for the people to read the best that has been thought and said. Books are the major channel by which the intellectual inheritance is handed down, and the principal means of its testing and growth. The defense of their freedom and integrity, and the enlargement of their service to society, requires of all bookmen the utmost of their faculties, and deserves of all citizens the fullest of their support.

We state these propositions neither lightly nor as easy generalizations. We here stake out a lofty claim for the value of books. We do so because we believe that they are good, possessed of enormous variety and usefulness, worthy of cherishing and keeping free. We realize that the application of these propositions may mean the dissemination of ideas and manners of expression that are repugnant to many persons. We do not state these propositions in the comfortable belief that what people read is unimportant. We believe rather that what people read is deeply important; that ideas can be dangerous; but that the suppppression of ideas is fatal to a democratic society. Freedom itself is a dangerous way of life, but it is ours.

Endorsed by: American Library Association Council, June 25, 1953; American Book Publishers Council, Board of Directors, June 18, 1953.

THE LIBRARY BILL OF RIGHTS

The Council of the American Library Association reaffirms its belief in the following basic policies which should govern the services of all libraries.

1. As a responsibility of library service, books and other library materials selected should be chosen for values of interest, information, and enlightenment of all the people of the community. In no case should library materials be excluded because of the race or nationality or the social, political, or religious views of the authors.

2. Libraries should provide books and other materials presenting all points of view concerning the problems and issues of our times; no library materials should be proscribed or removed from libraries because of partisan or doctrinal disapproval.

3. Censorship should be challenged by libraries in the maintenance of their responsibility to provide public information and enlightenment.

4. Libraries should cooperate with all persons and groups concerned with resisting abridgment of free expression and free access to ideas.

5. The rights of an individual to the use of a library should not be denied or abridged because of his age, race, religion, national origins or social or political views.

6. As an institution of education for democratic living, the library should welcome the use of its meeting rooms for socially useful and cultural activities and discussion of current public questions. Such meeting places should be available on equal terms to all groups in the community regardless of the beliefs and affiliations of their members, provided that the meetings be open to the public.

Adopted June 18, 1948, amended February 1, 1961 and June 27, 1967, by the ALA Council. By official action of the council on February 3, 1951, the Library Bill of Rights shall be interpreted to apply to all materials and media of communication used or collected by libraries.[1]

[1] See pp. 248–49 for the School Library Bill of Rights.

APPENDIX II
BIBLIOGRAPHY

BIBLIOGRAPHY[1]

GENERAL

American Library Laws. Edited by Alex Ladenson. 3d ed. Chicago: American Library Association, 1964.

————. *First Supplement, 1963–1964.* 1965.

————. *Second Supplement, 1965–1966.* 1967.

Anderson, Florence. *Carnegie Corporation Library Program, 1911–1961.* New York: Carnegie Corporation of New York, 1963.

The Bowker Annual of Library and Book Trade Information. New York: R. R. Bowker Company, 1956– .

Council on Library Resources. Annual Report, 1st– . Washington, D.C.: Council on Library Resources, 1956/57– .

"Federal Library Legislation, Programs, and Services," *ALA Bulletin,* LX (February, 1966), 139–68.

"Federal Library Legislation, Programs, and Services," *ALA Bulletin,* LXI (October, 1967), 1049–87.

National Inventory of Library Needs. Chicago: American Library Association, 1965.

Shaw, Ralph R. *The State of the Library Art.* 5 vols. New Brunswick, N.J.: Graduate School of Library Service, Rutgers University, 1960–1961.

Williams, Joel (ed.). *Library Statistics: A Handbook of Concepts, Definitions, and Terminology.* Chicago: American Library Association, 1966.

PART ONE

CHAPTERS 1–5.

Athenaeus. *The Deipnosophists.* With an English translation by Charles Burton Gulick. Rev. ed. (The Loeb Classical Library.) Cambridge, Mass.: Harvard University Press, 1951. 7 vols.

Barnes, Harry Elmer. *An Intellectual and Cultural History of the West-*

[1] Other titles are given in the text in footnotes. In this bibliography, titles are arranged by chapters, but many titles are useful for more than one chapter.

ern World. 3d rev. ed. New York: Dover Publications, Inc., 1965. 3 vols.

Bieler, Ludwig. *Ireland, Harbinger of the Middle Ages.* London: Oxford University Press, 1963.

La Bibliothèque Nationale. *Aide-Mémoire Pour le Personnel Chargé des Visites.* Paris: La Bibliothéque Nationale, 1962.

La *Bibliothèque Nationale.* (La Documentation Française Illustrée, No. 50.) Paris: La Direction de la Documentation, 1951.

The Belles Heures of Jean, Duke of Berry, Prince of France. With an introduction by James J. Rorimer. New York: At the Cloisters, The Metropolitan Museum of Art, 1958.

Boyd, Clarence Eugene. *Public Libraries and Literary Culture in Ancient Rome.* (A Thesis Submitted for the Degree of Doctor of Philosophy, University of Wisconsin, 1904.) Chicago: n.p., 1916.

Bury, Richard de [Aungerville, Richard] *The Philobiblon.* Berkeley, Calif.: University of California Press, 1948.

Dahl, Svend. *History of the Book.* New York: Scarecrow Press, Inc., 1958.

Downs, Norton (ed.). *Basic Documents in Medieval History.* Princeton, N.J.: Anvil Books, D. Van Nostrand Company, Inc., 1959.

Durie, John. *The Reformed Librarie-Keeper.* Privately printed, 1947.

Einhard. *The Life of Charlemagne.* With a foreword by Sidney Painter. Ann Arbor, Mich.: Ann Arbor Paperbacks, University of Michigan Press, 1960.

Esdaile, Arundell J. *National Libraries of the World.* London: Grafton and Company, 1934.

Evans, Joan (ed.). *The Flowering of the Middle Ages.* New York: McGraw-Hill Book Company, 1966.

Godfrey, John. *The Chruch in Anglo-Saxon England.* New York: Cambridge University Press, 1962.

Grant, Michael (ed.). *The Birth of Western Civilization: Greece and Rome.* New York: McGraw-Hill Book Company, 1964.

Hall, Frederick William. *A Companion to Classical Texts.* Oxford: Clarendon Press, 1913.

Harrison, Frederic. *Byzantine History in the Early Middle Ages.* (The Rede Lecture Delivered in the Senate House, Cambridge, June 12, 1900.) London: Macmillan and Co., Ltd., 1900.

Haskins, Charles Homer. *The Renaissance of the Twelfth Century.* Cambridge, Mass.: Havard University Press, 1927.

Hastings, Rashdall. *The Universities of Europe in the Middle Ages.*

New ed. Edited by F. M. Powicke and A. B. Emden. London: Oxford University Press, 1936. 3 vols.

Hessel, Alfred. *History of Libraries*. Translated by Reuben Peiss. 2d ed. New York: Scarecrow Press, 1955.

Hitti, Philip K. *The Near East in History: A 5,000 Year Story*. New York: D. Van Nostrand Company, Inc., 1961.

Irwin, Raymond. *The Origins of the English Library*. London: George Allen & Unwin, Ltd., 1958.

Johnson, Elmer D. *A History of Libraries in the Western World*. New York: Scarecrow Press, Inc., 1965.

Kenyon, Sir Frederic George. *Books and Readers in Ancient Greece and Rome*. 2d ed. New York: Oxford University Press, 1951.

Kramer, Samuel Noah. *History Begins at Sumer*. Indian Hills, Colo.: Falcon Wing's Press, 1956.

————. *Sumerian Mythology: A Study of Spiritual and Literary Achievement in the Third Millennium B.C.* Rev. ed. New York: Harper Torchbooks, Harper & Row, Publishers, Incorporated, 1961.

————. *The Sumerians: Their History, Culture, and Character*. Chicago: The University of Chicago Press, 1963.

Laistner, M. L. W. *Thought and Letters in Western Europe, A.D. 500 to 900*. Rev. ed. Ithaca, N.Y.: Cornell Paperbacks, Cornell University Press, 1957.

McMurtrie, Douglas C. *The Book: The Story of Printing and Bookmaking*. New York: Oxford University Press, 1943.

Montgomery, John W. (tr.). *A Seventeenth Century View of European Libraries: Lomeier's de Bibliothecis, Chapter X*. Berkeley, Calif.: University of California Press, 1962.

Muller, Herbert J. *The Uses of the Past*. New York: Oxford University Press, 1952.

Naudé, Gabriel. *Advice on Establishing a Library*. With an introduction by Archer Taylor. Berkeley, Calif.: University of California Press, 1950.

Nichols, C. L. *The Library of Rameses the Great*. Cambridge: Cambridge University Press, 1909.

Ostrogorski, George. *History of the Byzantine State*. Oxford: Basil Blackwell & Mott, Ltd., 1956.

Parsons, Edward A. *The Alexandrian Library: Glory of the Hellenic World, Its Rise, Antiquities, and Destructions*. Amsterdam: Elsevier Publishing Company, 1952.

Piggott, Stuart (ed.). *The Dawn of Civilization*. New York: McGraw-Hill Book Company, 1961.

Plutarch's Lives of Illustrious Men. Corrected from the Greek and revised by A. H. Clough. Boston: Little, Brown & Company, 1930.

Rice, David Talbot (ed.). *Dawn of European Civilization*. New York: McGraw-Hill Book Company, 1966.

Sandys, Sir John Edwin. *A History of Classical Scholarship: Vol. I: From the Sixth Century B.C. to the End of the Middle Ages*. 3d. ed. Cambridge: Cambridge University Press, 1921.

——. *A History of Classical Scholarship: Vol. II: From the End of the Revival of Learning to the End of the Eighteenth Century*. Cambridge: Cambridge University Press, 1908.

Seneca. *Moral Essays*. With an English translation by John W. Basore. (The Loeb Classical Library.): Cambridge, Mass.: Harvard University Press, 1958.

Steinberg, S. H. *Five Hundred Years of Printing*. 2d ed. Baltimore: Penguin Books, Inc., 1961.

Strabo. *The Geography of Strabo*. With an English translation by Horace Leonard Jones. (The Loeb Classical Library.) Cambridge, Mass.: Harvard University Press, 1960.

Symonds, John Addington. *Renaissance in Italy: The Age of the Despots*. New York: Henry Holt and Company, 1888.

Taylor, Henry Osborn. *The Mediaeval Mind: A History of the Development of Thought and Emotion in the Middle Ages*. 4th ed. Cambridge, Mass.: Harvard University Press, 1925. 2 vols.

Thompson, James Westfall. *Ancient Libraries*. Berkeley, Calif.: University of California Press, 1940.

——. *The Medieval Library*. New York: Hafner Publishing Company, Inc., 1957.

Thornton, John L. *Chronology of Librarianship: An Introduction to the History of Libraries*. London: Grafton & Company, 1941.

Wace, Alan J. B., and Stubbins, Frank H. (eds.). *A Companion to Homer*. London: Macmillan and Company, Ltd., 1963.

West, Andrew Fleming. *Alcuin and the Rise of Christian Schools*. (The Great Educators.) New York: Charles Scribner's Sons, 1892.

Woolley, Sir Leonard. *History of Mankind, Cultural and Scientific Development: Vol. I, Part 2: The Beginnings of Civilization*. New York: Mentor Books, New American Library of World Literature, Inc., 1965.

CHAPTERS 6 AND 7.

Ditzion, Sidney. "Mechanics' and Mercantile Libraries," *Library Quarterly*, X (April, 1940), 192–216.

Duché, Jacob. *Observations on a Variety of Subjects, Literary, Moral and Religious.* . . . Philadelphia: Printed by John Dunlap, 1764. (Microfilm.)

Franklin, Benjamin. *The Autobiography of Benjamin Franklin.* Edited by W. Labaree and Others. New Haven, Conn.: Yale University Press, 1964.

Garceau, Oliver. *The Public Library in the Political Process.* New York: Columbia University Press, 1949.

"Libraries and Historical and Scientific Societies," *History of Philadelphia, 1609–1884*, II (1884), 1173–1229.

Norton's Literary and Educational Register for 1854. New York: Charles B. Norton, 1854.

Pennington, Edgar L. *The Reverend Thomas Bray.* (Publication No. VII.) Philadelphia: The Church Historical Society, 1934.

Shera, Jesse H. *Foundations of the Public Library: Origins of the Public Library Movement in New England from 1629–1855.* Chicago: The University of Chicago Press, 1949.

Steiner, Bernard C. "Rev. Thomas Bray and His American Libraries," *American Historical Review*, II (1896), 59–75.

Titcomb, Mary Lemist. *Story of the Washington County Free Library.* Hagerstown, Md.: n.d.

U.S. Bureau of Education. *Public Libraries in the United States of America: Their History, Condition and Management.* Special Report: Part I. Washington, D.C.: U.S. Government Printing Office, 1876. (Reprinted by the University of Illinois Graduate School of Library Science, 1966; available from Illini Union Book Store, Champaign, Ill.)

U.S. Office of Education. *Commissioner's Report, 1920.* Washington, D.C.: U.S. Government Printing Office, 1920.

Utley, George B. *The Librarians' Conference of 1853: A Chapter in American Library History.* Edited by G. H. Doane. Chicago: American Library Association, 1951.

Ver Steeg, Clarence L. *The Formative Years: 1607–1763.* (The Making of America Series.) New York: Hill and Wang, Inc., 1964.

Wheeler, Joseph Towne. "Booksellers and Circulating Libraries in Colonial Maryland," *Maryland Historical Magazine*, XXXIV (June, 1939), 111–37.

———. "Thomas Bray and the Maryland Parochial Libraries," *Maryland Historical Magazine*, XXXIV (September, 1939), 246–65.

Whitehill, Walter Muir. *Boston Public Library, A Centennial History*. Cambridge, Mass.: Harvard University Press, 1956.

Wright, Louis Booker. *The Cultural Life of the American Colonies, 1607–1763*. (The New American Nation Series.) New York: Harper & Row, Publishers, Incorporated, 1957.

———. *Culture on the Moving Frontier*. Bloomington, Ind.: University of Indiana Press, 1955.

CHAPTER 8.

Butler Pierce. *An Introduction to Library Science*. Chicago: The University of Chicago Press, 1944.

Carnovsky, Leon, and Martin, Lowell (eds.). *The Library in the Community*. Papers Presented Before the Library Institute at the University of Chicago August 23–28, 1943. (The University of Chicago Studies in Library Science.) Chicago: The University of Chicago Press, 1944.

Heckscher, August. "Libraries and the Nation's Cultural Life," *ALA Bulletin*, LVI (September, 1963), 716–20.

Landheer, Bartholomeus. *Social Functions of Libraries*. New York: Scarecrow Press, Inc., 1957.

Martineau, Harriet. *Society in America*. New York: Saunders and Otley, 1837. 2 vols.

Ranganathan, Shijali Ramamrita. *The Five Laws of Library Science*. Bombay: Asia Publishing House, 1963.

White, Carl M. (ed.). *Bases of Modern Librarianship*. New York: The Macmillan Company, 1964.

PART TWO

CHAPTERS 9–11.

American Library Association. Board of Education for Librarianship. "Standards for Accreditation," *ALA Bulletin*, XL (February, 1952), 48–49.

———. Committee on Accreditation. "Standards and Guide for Undergraduate Library Science Programs," *ALA Bulletin*, LII (October, 1958), 696–700.

The American Library Journal, I (September 30, 1876).

Becker, Howard S. "The Nature of a Profession," National Society for the Study of Education. *Sixty-First Yearbook:* Part II: *Educa-*

tion for the Professions. Chicago: National Society for the Study of Education, 1962. Pp. 27–46.

Berninghausen, David K. "The History of the ALA Intellectual Freedom Committee," *Wilson Library Bulletin,* XXVII (June, 1953), 813–17.

Bevis, Dorothy. "Windows—Not Mirrows," *ALA Bulletin,* LVII (January, 1963), 47–52.

Carr-Saunders, A. M., and Wilson, P. A. "Professions," *Encyclopaedia of the Social Sciences,* XI–XII (1933), 476–80.

———. *The Professions.* London: Oxford University Press, 1933. (Second impression published by Frank Cass & Company, Ltd., 1964.)

Danton, Emily (ed.). *American Library Pioneers.* Chicago: American Library Association, 1951.

———. *Pioneering Leaders in Librarianship.* Chicago: American Library Association, 1953.

Ennis, Philip H., and Winger, Howard D. (eds.). *Seven Questions About the Profession of Librarianship.* 26th Annual Conference of the Graduate Library School, June 21–23, 1961. Chicago: The University of Chicago Press, 1962.

Freedom of Inquiry: Supporting the Library Bill of Rights. Proceedings of the Conference on Intellectual Freedom January 23–24, 1965, Washington, D.C. Chicago: American Library Association, 1965.

Gitler, Robert L. "Librarianship," *American Universities and Colleges.* 9th ed. Washington, D.C.: American Council on Education, 1964. Pp. 106–09.

Greenwood, Ernest. "Attributes of a Profession," *Social Work,* II (July, 1957), 44–55.

Harlow, Neal. "Misused Librarians," *Library Journal,* XC (April 1, 1965), 1597–99.

Hostetter, Anita M. "Librarianship," *American Universities and Colleges.* 7th ed. Washington, D.C.: American Council on Education, 1956. Pp. 137–40.

"How Libraries and Schools Can Resist Censorship, A Statement by the Intellectual Freedom Committee," *ALA Bulletin,* LVI (March, 1962), 228–29.

Issues of Freedom in American Libraries. Reprinted from the *ALA Bulletin,* Vols. 54–57, June 1960-June 1963. Edited Everett T. Moore. Chicago: American Library Association, 1964.

Jewett, C. C. "Second Annual Report of the Assistant Secretary of the Smithsonian Institution Relative to the Library—Presented January 2, 1850," *Fourth Annual Report to the Board of Regents of the Smithsonian Institution.* . . . Washington, D.C.: Printed by the Printers to the Senate, 1850. Pp. 32–43.

Leigh, Robert D. (ed.). *Major Problems in the Education of Librarians.* New York: Columbia University Press, 1954.

"Library Hall of Fame for the 75th Anniversary," *Library Journal,* LXXV (March, 15, 1951), 466–72.

Library Technicians: A New Kind of Needed Library Worker. A Report of a Conference on Library Technology Sponsored by Catonsville Community College, Held in Chicago, Illinois, May 26–27, 1967. Washington, D.C.: Communication Service Corporation, 1967.

Martinson, John L. *Vocational Training for Library Technicians: A Survey of Experience to Date.* Washington, D.C.: Communication Service Corporation, 1965.

Monroe, Margaret E. "Standards—Criteria for Service or Goals for the Future?" *ALA Bulletin,* LVI (October, 1962), 818–20.

Munn, Ralph. "The New ALA Headquarters, A Symbol of Accomplishment," *ALA Bulletin,* LVII (September, 1963), 729–33.

Norton's Literary and Educational Register for 1854. New York: Charles B. Norton, 1854.

Norton's Literary Register and Book Buyer's Almanac for 1853. New York: Charles B. Norton, 1853.

"Proposals for Accrediting Professional Programs, A Statement of Policy by the ALA Board of Education for Librarianship," *ALA Bulletin,* XLV (January, 1951), 7–10.

Reece, Ernest J. *The Curriculum in Library Schools.* New York: Columbia University Press, 1936.

Reed, Sarah R. *Continuing Education for Librarians: Conferences, Workshops, and Short Courses, 1966–67.* Washington, D.C.: U.S. Department of Health, Education, and Welfare, 1966.

——— and Toye, Willie P. (eds.). *Continuing Education for Librarians: Conferences, Workshops and Short Courses, 1965–66.* Washington, D.C.: Bureau of Educational Research and Development, 1965.

——— and ——— (eds.). *Library Education Directory, 1964–65.* Washington, D.C.: Bureau of Educational Research and Development, 1965.

"A Report from the Commission on a National Plan for Library Education," *ALA Bulletin,* LXI (April, 1967), 419–22.

"The Second Annual Report of the Board of Education for Librarianship," *ALA Bulletin*, XX (1926), 405–73.

Utley, George Burwell. *The Librarians' Conference of 1953, A Chapter in American Library History*. Edited Gilbert H. Doane. Chicago: American Library Association, 1951.

Vann, Sarah K. *Training for Librarianship Before 1923, Education for Librarianship Prior to the Publication of Williamson's Report on Training for Library Service*. Chicago: American Library Association, 1961.

Vollmer, Howard M., and Mills, Donald L. (eds.). *Professionalization*. Englewood Cliffs, N.J.: Prentice-Hall, Inc., 1966.

Wheeler, J. L. *Progress and Problems in Education for Librarianship*. New York: Carnegie Corporation, 1946.

White, Carl M. *The Origins of the American Library School*. New York: The Scarecrow Press, 1961.

Williamson, Clarence C. *Training for Library Service*. New York: Carnegie Corporation, 1923.

Yenawine, Wayne S., and Boaz, Martha. "The Conferences That Were," *Journal of Education for Librarianship*, IV (Spring, 1964), 191–95.

PART THREE

CHAPTER 12.

ALA Board on Personnel Administration. *Personnel Organization and Procedure: A Manual for Public Libraries*. Chicago: American Library Association, 1952.

American Library Association. Board on Personnel Administration. *Position Classification and Salary Administration in Libraries*. Chicago: American Library Association, 1951.

Asheim, Lester, and Others. *The Humanities and the Library: Problems in the Interpretation, Evaluation and Use of Library Materials*. Chicago: American Library Association, 1957.

Brown, James W., and Norberg, Kenneth D. *Administering Educational Media*. New York: McGraw-Hill Book Company, 1965.

Butler, Pierce (ed.). *The Reference Function of the Library*. (The University of Chicago Studies in Library Science.) Chicago: The University of Chicago Press, 1934.

Carter, Mary Duncan, and Bonk, Wallace J. *Building Library Collections*. New York: Scarecrow Press, 1959.

Geer, Helen Thornton. *Charging Systems.* Chicago: American Library Association, 1955.

Haines, Helen. *Living With Books: The Art of Book Selection.* 2d ed. New York: Columbia University Press, 1950.

Hutchins, Margaret. *Introduction to Reference Work.* Chicago: American Library Association, 1944.

La Montagne, L. E. *American Library Classification with Special Reference to the Library of Congress.* Hamden, Conn.: The Shoe String Press, Inc., 1961.

Piercy, Esther J. *Commonsense Cataloging.* New York: The H. W. Wilson Company, 1965.

Rowland, Arthur Ray (ed.). *Reference Services.* (Contributions to Library Literature Number 5.) Hamden, Conn.: The Shoe String Press, Inc., 1964.

Wofford, Azile. *Book Selection for School Libraries.* New York: The H. W. Wilson Company, 1962.

——— *The School Library at Work: Acquisition, Organization, Use and Maintenance of Materials in the School Library.* New York: The H. W. Wilson Company, 1959.

CHAPTER 13.

"Address List of U.S. Information Service Libraries, January 1, 1966." Washington, D.C.: United States Information Agency, 1966. (Processed.)

Allen, George V. "Books and the American Image," *The Atlantic Monthly,* CCVII (May, 1961), 77–80.

Annual Report of the Librarian of Congress. Washington, D.C.: U.S. Government Printing Office, 1906– .

Austin, Charles J. "The Medlars System," *Datamation, the Magazine of Automatic Information Handling* (December, 1964), 28–31.

"Decentralization of MEDLARS." Washington, D.C.: National Library of Medicine, February, 1966. (Processed.)

Facts About the USIA. Washington: U.S. Government Printing Office, 1965.

The Federal Library Committee. *The Federal Library Mission: A Statement of Principles and Guidelines for Their Implementation.* Washington, D.C.: The Federal Library Committee, October, 1966.

Grigg, William. "Medical Library to Salute Index Originator," *The Evening Star* (Washington, D.C.), sec. C, p. 1, June 16, 1965.

Havens, Shirley, "A Day with the Army," *Library Journal*, XCI (February 15, 1966), 894–900.

Mearns, David C. "A Fog-laden Panorama of LC's Collections, Part I," *Library Journal*, XC (April 1, 1965), 1600–07.

The MEDLARS Story at the National Library of Medicine. Washington, D.C.: U.S. Department of Health, Education, and Welfare, 1963.

Mumford, L. Quincy. "International Breakthrough: An Account of the Operational Beginnings of the Shared Cataloging Program," *Library Journal*, XCII (January 1, 1967), 79–82.

The National Archives. (National Archives Publication No. 66–1.) Washington, D.C.: U.S. Government Printing Office, 1965.

Rowan, Carl T. "USIA Overseas Libraries—1964," *Wilson Library Bulletin*, XXXIX (September, 1964), 41–43.

"Testimony of L. Quincy Mumford, Librarian of Congress, Higher Education Act of 1965, Education Subcommittee, Senate Committee on Labor and Public Welfare, May 19, 1965." (Processed.)

CHAPTER 14.

American Association of State Libraries. Survey and Standards Committee. *Standards for Library Functions at the State Level* Chicago: American Library Association, 1963.

American Library Association. Public Library Association. *A Primer About Library Systems.* Chicago. American Library Association, n.d.

———. Standards Committee. *Minimum Standards for Public Library Systems*, 1966. Chicago: American Library Association, 1967.

Bowman, James R. (ed.). *Proceedings of the Second Assembly of State Librarians Held at the Library of Congress November 16–18, 1960.* Washington, D.C.: Library of Congress, 1961.

Carl, Herbert A. (ed.). *Statewide Long-range Planning for Libraries.* Report of Conference/September 19–22, 1965/Chicago, Illinois. (OE-15060.) Washington, D.C.: U.S. Government Printing Office, 1966.

Cohen, Nathan M. *State Library Extension Resources and Services, 1960–61.* (OE-15009-A, Circular No. 766.) Washington, D.C.: U.S. Government Printing Office, 1966

The Federal Government and Public Libraries: A Ten-year Partner-

ship, 1957–1966. Washington, D.C.: U.S. Department of Health, Education, and Welfare, 1966.

"Library Cooperation for Reference and Research," *ALA Bulletin,* LX (December, 1966), 1133–55.

Long, Marie Ann. "Action vs. Advice: Conflict in Consulting," *ALA Bulletin,* LX (April, 1966), 356–61.

———. *The State Library Consultant at Work.* (Research Series No. 6.) Springfield, Ill.: Illinois State Library, 1965.

McKenzie, Mary A. (ed.). *Proceedings of the Third Assembly on the Library Functions of the States Held November 13–15, 1963.* Washington, D.C.: Library of Congress, 1964.

Monypenny, Phillip. *The Library Functions of the States.* Chicago: American Library Association, 1966.

Morin, Wilfred L., and Cohen, Nathan M. *State Library Extension Services.* Washington, D.C.: U.S. Government Printing Office, 1960.

Posner, Ernest. *American State Archives.* Chicago: The University of Chicago Press, 1964.

Schenk, Gretchen K. *County and Regional Library Development.* Chicago: American Library Association, 1954.

U.S. Office of Education. Library Services Branch. *State Plans under the Library Services Act, Supplement 2.* Washington, D.C.: U.S. Government Printing Office, 1960.

———. *Supplement 3.* Washington, D.C.: U.S. Government Printing Office, 1963.

Vale, Michelle R. "The Interstate Library Compact," *Library Journal,* XCI (May 15, 1966), 2419–22.

CHAPTER 15.

Access to Public Libraries. Chicago: American Library Association, 1963.

American Library Association. Committee on Postwar Planning. *A National Plan for Library Service.* Chicago: American Library Association, 1948.

———. Committee of the Public Library Association. *Costs of Public Library Service, 1963.* Chicago: American Library Association, 1964.

———. Public Libraries Division. Coordinating Committee on Revision of Public Library Standards. *Public Library Service: A Guide to Evaluation with Minimum Standards.* Chicago: American Library Association, 1956.

———. Subcommittee of the Public Library Association. *Interim Stan-*

dards for Small Public Libraries. Chicago: American Library Association, 1962.

Asheim, Lester (ed.). *A Forum on the Public Library Inquiry.* New York: Columbia University Press, 1950.

Berelson, Bernard. *The Library's Public.* New York: Columbia University Press, 1949.

Boaz, Martha. "The Situation We Face," *ALA Bulletin,* LIX (June, 1965), 470, 476.

Bowler, Roberta (ed.). *Local Public Library Administration.* (Municipal Management Series.) Chicago: The International City Managers' Association, 1964.

Bryan, Alice. *The Public Librarian.* New York: Columbia University Press, 1952.

Carnovsky, Leon. "The Responsibilities and Obligations of the Librarian Concerning Censorship," *Library Quarterly,* XX (January, 1950).

———. "Role of the Public Library: Implications for Library Education," *Library Quarterly,* XXXIV (October, 1964), 315–25.

Conant, Ralph (ed.). *The Public Library and the City.* Cambridge, Mass.: The M. I. T. Press, Massachusetts Institute of Technology, 1965.

Ditzion, Sidney H. *Arsenals of a Democratic Culture.* Chicago: American Library Association, 1947.

Garceau, Oliver. *The Public Library in the Political Process.* New York: Columbia University Press, 1949.

Joeckel, Carleton Bruns. *The Government of the American Public Library.* (The University of Chicago Studies in Library Science.) Chicago: The University of Chicago Press, 1935.

———. *Library Service.* (Staff Study No. 11.) Washington, D.C.: U.S. Government Printing Office, 1938.

——— and Winslow, Amy. *A National Plan for Public Library Service.* (Planning for Libraries, No. 3.) Chicago: American Library Association, 1948.

Lee, Robert E. *Continuing Education for Adults in the American Public Library, 1833–1964.* Chicago: American Library Association, 1966.

Leigh, Robert D. *The Public Library in the United States.* New York: Columbia University Press, 1950.

McDiarmid, E. W., and McDiarmid, John. *Administration of the American Public Library.* Urbana, Ill.: American Library Association and University of Illinois Press, 1943.

Martin, Lowell A. *Students and the Pratt Library: Challenge and Opportunity.* Baltimore: Enoch Pratt Free Library, 1963.

"The Metropolitan Public Library." *Wilson Library Bulletin,* XL (June, 1966), 917–29.

"Metropolitan Public Library Problems Around the World." *Library Trends,* XIV (July, 1965).

Monroe, Margaret Ellen. *Library Adult Education: The Biography of an Idea.* New York: Scarecrow Press, Inc., 1963.

Rose, Ernestine. *The Public Library in American Life.* New York: Columbia University Press, 1954.

Sinclair, Dorothy. *The Administration of the Small Public Library.* Chicago: American Library Association, 1965.

The Small Public Library: A Series of Guides for the Community Librarian and Trustee. Chicago: American Library Association, 1962–1963.

Student Use of Libraries: An Inquiry Into the Needs of Students, Libraries, and the Educational Process. (Papers of the Conference Within a Conference.) Chicago: American Library Association, 1964.

Wheeler, Joseph, and Goldhor, Herbert. *Practical Administration of Public Libraries.* New York: Harper & Row, Publishers, Incorporated, 1962.

Young, Virginia G. (ed.). *The Library Trustee: A Practical Guidebook.* New York: R. R. Bowker Company, 1964.

CHAPTER 16.

American Association of School Librarians. *Standards for School Library Programs.* Chicago: American Library Association, 1960.

American Library Association. Committee on Post-war Planning. *School Libraries for Today and Tomorrow.* (Planning for Libraries, No. 5.) Chicago: American Library Association, 1945.

Berner, Elsa. *Integrating Library Instruction with Classroom Teaching at Plainview Junior High School.* Chicago: American Library Association, 1958.

Bossing, Nelson L., and Cramer, Roscoe V. *The Junior High School.* Boston: Houghton Mifflin Company, 1965.

Brimm, R. P. *The Junior High School.* (The Library of Education.) Washington, D.C.: The Center for Applied Research in Education, Inc., 1963.

Certain, C. C. "Report of the Joint Committee on Elementary School

Library Standards," National Education Association, Department of Elementary School Principals, *The Elementary School Principalship: A Study of Its Instructional and Administrative Aspects.* (Its Fourth Yearbook.) Washington, D.C.: National Education Association, 1925. Pp. 326–59.

Cooperative Study of Secondary School Standards. *Evaluative Criteria.* Washington, D.C.: Cooperative Study of Secondary School Standards, 1936.

Council of Chief State School Officers. *The State Department of Education: A Policy Statement of Guiding Principles for Its Legal Status, Its Functions and the Organization of Its Service Areas.* Revised ed. Washington, D.C.: Council of Chief State School Officers, 1963.

———. *Responsibilities of State Departments of Education for Approval and Accreditation of Public Schools.* Washington, D.C.: Council of Chief State School Officers, 1960.

———. *Responsibilities of State Departments of Education for Instruction: A Policy Statement.* Washington, D.C.: Council of Chief State School Officers, 1958.

———. *Responsibilities of State Departments of Education for School Library Services.* Washington, D.C.: Council of Chief State School Officers, 1961.

Darling, Richard L. (ed.). *Public School Library Statistics, 1962–63.* (OE-15020-63.) Washington, D.C.: U.S. Department of Health, Education, and Welfare, Office of Education, 1964.

———. *Survey of School Library Standards.* (OE Circular No. 740.) Washington, D.C.: U.S. Office of Education, 1964.

De Young, Chris A., and Wynn, Richard. *American Education.* 5th ed. (McGraw-Hill Series in Education.) New York: McGraw-Hill Book Company, 1964.

Ellsworth, Ralph E. *The School Library.* New York: The Center for Applied Research in Education, Inc., 1965.

——— and Wagener, Hobart D. *The School Library: Facilities for Independent Study in the Secondary School.* Edited by Ruth Weinstock. New York: Educational Facilities Laboratories, Inc., 1963.

Flanagan, J. C., and Others. *Studies of the American High School.* Technical Report to the U.S. Office of Education, Cooperative Research Project No. 226. Pittsburgh: Project Talent Office, University of Pittsburgh, 1962.

Gaver, Mary Virginia. *Every Child Needs a School Library.* 2d ed. Chicago: American Library Association, 1962.

——— *Effectiveness of Centralized Library Service in Elementary Schools.* New Brunswick, N.J.: Rutgers University Press, 1963.

Grieder, Calvin, and Romine, Stephen. *American Education: An Introduction to the Teaching Profession.* 3d ed. New York: The Ronald Press Co., 1965.

Henne, Frances, and Others. *A Planning Guide for the High School Library Program.* Chicago: American Library Association, 1951.

Kennon, Mary Frances, and Doyle, Leila. *Planning School Library Development: A Report of the School Library Development Project.* Chicago: American Library Association, 1962.

Lohrer, Alice. *The School Library Materials Center: Its Resources and Centralization.* Papers Presented at an Institute Conducted by the University of Illinois Graduate School of Library Science, November 3–6, 1963. Champaign, Ill.: Illini Bookstore, 1963.

McCarthy, Imogene J. "The Professional Library in the School: A Tool for Supervision," *The Elementary School Journal,* LXIII (December, 1962), 160–67.

McVey, William E. "Origin and Development of Criteria for the Accrediting of Secondary Schools in the North Central Territory," *The North Central Association Quarterly,* XVII (April, 1944), 283–92.

Mahar, Mary Helen (comp.). *Certification of School Librarians: A Compilation of State Requirements,* 1958. (Bulletin No. 12.) Washington, D.C.: U.S. Government Printing Office, 1958.

——— (ed.). *The School Library as a Materials Center: Educational Needs of Librarians in Its Administration and Use.* Washington: U.S. Government Printing Office, 1963.

———. *State Department of Education Responsibilities for School Libraries.* (OE-15006.) Washington, D.C.: U.S. Government Printing Office, 1960.

———, and Holladay, Doris C. (eds.). *Statistics of Public School Libraries, 1960–61;* Part I: *Basic Tables.* Washington D.C.: U.S. Government Printing Office, 1964.

National Association of Secondary-School Principals. *The Bulletin,* XLIII (November, 1959).

———. *The Bulletin,* L (January, 1966).

The National Council of Chief State School Officers. *Our System of Education: A Statement of Some Desirable Policies, Programs and Administrative Relationships in Education.* Washington, D.C.: The National Council of Chief State School Officers, 1951.

National Education Association. Department of Elementary School Principals. *Elementary-School Libraries Today.* Washington, D.C.: National Education Association, 1951.

———. Department of Rural Education. *School Library Programs in Rural Areas.* Washington, D.C.: National Education Association, 1966.

———. Joint Committee of the American Association of School Librarians and the National Commission on Teacher Education and Professional Standards of the National Education Association. *The Teachers' Library: How to Organize It and What to Include.* Washington, D.C.: National Education Association, 1966.

——— and American Library Association. Joint Committee. *Schools and Public Libraries Working Together in School Library Service.* Washington, D.C.: National Education Association, 1941.

———. Project on Instruction. *Schools for the Sixties.* New York: McGraw-Hill Book Company, 1963.

———. Research Division. *The Secondary School-teacher and Library Services.* (Research Monograph No. M-1.) Washington, D.C.: National Education Association, 1958.

National Study of Secondary School Evaluation. *Evaluative Criteria for Junior High Schools.* Washington, D.C.: National Study of Secondary School Evaluation, 1963.

National Study of Secondary School Evaluation. *Manual for Evaluative Criteria.* 1960 ed. Washington, D.C.: National Study of Secondary School Evaluation, 1960.

North Central Association of Colleges and Secondary Schools. *Policies and Criteria for the Approval of Secondary Schools.* Chicago: The North Central Association of Colleges and Secondary Schools, 1965.

———. *Proceedings of the First Annual Meeting of the North Central Association.* Chicago: The North Central Association of Colleges and Secondary Schools, 1896.

The Northwest Association of Secondary and Higher Schools. Commission on Secondary Schools. *Manual of Accrediting Secondary Schools.* Eugene, Ore.: The Northwest Association of Secondary and Higher Schools, 1962.

Southern Association of Colleges and Schools. Committee on Elementary Education. *Evaluating the Elementary School Library Program, Cooperative Program in Elementary Education.* Atlanta, Ga.: Southern Association of Colleges and Schools, 1964.

———. *Proceedings of the Sixty-ninth Annual Meeting of the Southern*

Association of Colleges and Schools, November 30–December 3, 1964. Atlanta, Ga.: Southern Association of Colleges and Schools, 1965.

Southern Association of Colleges and Secondary Schools. *The Junior High School Program*. Atlanta, Ga.: The Southern Association of Colleges and Secondary Schools, 1958.

Spain, Frances Lander. "The Application of School Library Standards," National Society for the Study of Education, *Forty-second Yearbook*: Part II: *The Library in General Education*. Chicago: The Department of Education, University of Chicago, 1943. Pp. 269–92.

"Standard Library Organization and Equipment for Secondary School Libraries of Different Sizes, Report of the Certain Committee on Library Organization and Equipment," National Education Association of the United States, *Addresses and Proceedings of the Fifty-sixth Annual Meeting*. Washington, D.C.: National Education Association, 1918. Pp. 691–719.

Taylor, James L., and Others. *Library Facilities for Elementary and Secondary Schools*. (OE-15050, Special Publication No. 10.) Washington, D.C.: U.S. Government Printing Office, 1966.

Willson, Ella Jean. *Evaluation of Urban Centralized Elementary School Libraries*. (Ed.D Dissertation.) Detroit: Wayne State University Press, 1965.

CHAPTERS 17–21.

American Association of Junior Colleges. *1966 Junior College Directory*. Washington, D.C.: American Association of Junior Colleges, 1966.

———. *1967 Junior College Directory*. Washington, D.C.: American Association of Junior Colleges, 1967.

The Association of College and Research Libraries. "ALA Standards for Junior College Libraries," *College and Research Libraries*, XXI (May, 1960), 200–06.

———. "Standards for College Libraries," *College and Research Libraries*, XX (July, 1959), 274–80.

"Association of Research Libraries Membership List, Revised January, 1965." (Typewritten.)

Baskin, Samuel (ed.). *Higher Education: Some Newer Developments*. New York: McGraw-Hill Book Company, 1965.

Blauch, Lloyd E. (ed.). *Accreditation in Higher Education*. Washington, D.C.: U.S. Government Printing Office, 1959.

Branscomb, Harvie. *Teaching With Books: A Study of College Libraries.* Chicago: Association of American Colleges and American Library Association, 1940.

Brubacher, John S., and Rudy, Willis. *Higher Education in Transition, An American History: 1936–1956.* New York: Harper & Row, Publishers, Incorporated, 1958.

Buck, Paul. *Libraries and Universities, Addresses and Reports.* Edited by Edwin E. Williams. Cambridge, Mass.: The Belknap Press, Harvard University Press, 1964.

Campion, Howard A. "Financing the Public Junior College," *NEA Journal,* LIII (October, 1964), 67–68.

Clapp, Verner W. *The Future of the Research Library.* Urbana, Ill.: The University of Illinois Press, 1964.

Gleazer, Edmund J. *A New Social Invention: The Community College—What It Is.* Washington, D.C.: American Association of Junior Colleges, n.d.

———. "The Stake of the Junior College in Its Library," *College and Research Libraries,* XXVII (July, 1966), 263–66, 317.

Harlow, Neal. "Levels of Need for Library Service in Academic Institutions," *College and Research Libraries,* XXIV (September, 1963), 359–64.

Jordan, Robert T. "Libraries of the Future for the Liberal Arts College," *Library Journal,* XCII (February 1, 1967), 537–39.

Knapp, Patricia B. *College Teaching and the College Library.* Chicago: American Library Association, 1959

———. *The Monteith College Library Experiment.* New York: Scarecrow Press, Inc., 1966.

Library Trends, XIV (October, 1965).

Lyle, Guy R. *The Administration of the College Library.* 3d ed. New York: The H. W. Wilson Company, 1961.

Mayor, John R., and Swartz, Willis G. *Accreditation in Teacher Education: Its Influence on Higher Education.* Washington, D.C.: National Commission on Accrediting, 1965.

Metcalf, Keyes D. *Planning Academic and Research Libraries.* New York: McGraw-Hill Book Company, 1965.

Middle States Association of Colleges and Secondary Schools. Commission on Institutions of Higher Education. *Characteristics of Excellence in Higher Education and Standards for Middle States Accreditation.* (Document No. 3.00.) New York: Middle States Association of Colleges and Secondary Schools, 1959.

————. *Evaluating the Library, Suggestions for the Use of Faculties and Evaluation Teams.* (Document No. 4.81.) New York: Middle States Association of Colleges and Secondary Schools, 1957.

————. *Graduate Work.* (Document No. 4.72.) New York: Middle States Association of Colleges and Secondary Schools, 1959

Nevins, John F. *A Study of the Organization and Operation of Voluntary Accrediting Agencies.* (The Catholic University of America Educational Research Monographs, Vol. XXII, No. 3.) Washington, D.C.: The Catholic University of America Press, 1959.

Randall, William M. *The College Library.* Chicago: The University of Chicago Press, 1932.

Rider, Fremont. *The Scholar and the Future of the Research Library.* New York: Hadham Press, 1944.

Samore, Theodore (ed.). *Library Statistics of Colleges and Universities, 1960–61;* Part 2: *Analytic Report.* Washington, D.C.: U.S. Government Printing Office, 1964.

Sheehan, Sister Helen Beebe. *The Small College Library.* Westminster, Md.: The Newman Press, 1963.

Shores, Louis. "The Library College Idea," *Library Journal,* XCI (September 1, 1966), 3871–75.

————. *Origins of the American College Library, 1638–1800.* Nashville, Tenn.: George Peabody College, 1934.

Smith, G. Kerry (ed.). *Current Issues in Higher Education.* Washington, D.C.: National Education Association, 1965.

"Statement by Francis Keppel, Commissioner of Education, Before the Subcommittee on Education of the Committee on Labor and Public Welfare, United States Senate, Tuesday, March 16, 1965." Pp. 13–24. (Processed.)

Tanis, Norman. "Implementing the Junior College Library Standards," *College and Research Libraries,* XXII (March, 1961), 130–33.

Tewksbury, Donald G. *The Founding of American Colleges and Universities Before the Civil War.* New York: Bureau of Publications, Teachers College, Columbia University, 1932.

Williams, Edwin E. *Farmington Plan Handbook.* Cambridge, Mass.: Association of Research Libraries, 1953.

————. *Farmington Plan Handbook.* Revised to 1961 and abridged. Cambridge, Mass.: Harvard University Printing Office, 1961. (Distributed by the Association of Research Libraries.)

Williams, Gordon. "Academic Librarianship: The State of the Art," *Library Journal,* XCI (May 15, 1966), 2413–18.

———. "The Center for Research Libraries: Its New Organization and Programs," *Library Journal*, XC (July, 1965), 2947–57.

Wilson, Louis Round, and Tauber, Maurice F. *The University Library, the Organization, Administration and Functions of Academic Libraries.* 2d ed. New York: Columbia University Press, 1956.

CHAPTER 22.

Bradford, S. C. *Documentation.* With Introduction by Jesse H. Shera and Margaret E. Egan. 2d ed. London: Crosby Lockwood & Son Ltd., 1953.

Carlson, Walter M. "The Research Librarian in a Challenging Age," *Special Libraries*, LV (January, 1964), 11–19.

Foskett, D. J. *Science, Humanism and Libraries.* New York : Hafner Publishing Company, Inc., 1964.

Kent, Allen. *Specialized Information Centers.* Washington, D.C.: Spartan Books, 1965.

Kruzas, Anthony T. *Business and Industrial Libraries in the United States, 1820–1840.* New York: Special Libraries Association, 1965.

———. (ed.). *Directory of Special Libraries and Information Centers.* Detroit: Gale Research Company, 1963.

Objectives and Standards for Special Libraries. New York: Special Libraries Association, 1964.

Sarnoff, David. *Education and the Challenge of the Future, Address Made at the Fall Convocation, Hendrix College, October 12, 1965.* Conway, Ark.: Hendrix College, 1965.

Simpson, C. S. "Scientific Information Centers in the United States," *American Documentation*, XIII (January, 1962), 43–57.

Slamecka, Vladimir, and Taube, Mortimer. "Theoretical Principles of Information Organization in Librarianship," *Library Quarterly*, XXXIV (October, 1964), 352–61.

Special Librarianship: Information at Work. New York: Special Libraries Association, 1965.

Strable, Edward G. (ed.). *Special Libraries: A Guide for Management.* New York: Special Libraries Association, 1966.

Swanson, Don R. "On Improving Communication Among Scientists," *Library Quarterly*, XXXVI (April, 1966), 79–87.

Weinberg, Alvin. "Second Thoughts on Scientific Information," *College and Research Libraries*, XXV (November, 1964), 463–71.

Woods, Bill M. "The Impolite Librarians," *Special Libraries*, LV (July, 1964), 345–50.

CHAPTER 23.

Andrews, Theodora, and Morelock, Molete (eds.). *Papers Presented at the Meeting on Automation in the Library: When, Where, and How, October 2–3, 1964.* Lafayette, Ind.: Purdue University, 1965.

Annual Review of Information Science and Technology. Edited by Carlos A. Cuadra. New York: Interscience Publishers, 1966–.

Artandi, Susan A. "Keeping Up With Mechanization," *Library Journal,* XC (November 1, 1965), 4715–17.

Becker, Joseph. "Systems Analysis—Prelude to Library Data Processing," *ALA Bulletin,* LIX (April, 1965), 293–96.

————. "Using Computers in a New University Library," *ALA Bulletin,* LIX (October, 1965), 823–26.

————, and Hayes, Robert M. *Information Storage and Retrieval: Tools, Elements, Theories.* New York: John Wiley & Sons, Inc., 1963.

Bryan, Harrison. "American Automation in Action," *Library Journal,* XCII (January 15, 1967), 189–96.

Bush, Vannevar, "Science Pauses," *Fortune,* LXXI (May, 1965), 116–19, 167–68, 172. Copyright © 1965 by Vannevar Bush.

Chapman, E. A. and St. Pierre, P. L. *Systems Analysis and Design as Related to Library Operations.* New York: John Wiley & Sons, Inc., 1967.

Covill, George W. "Automation in the Library: A Review of the State of the Art," *Special Libraries,* LVII (May–June, 1966), 332–35.

Flood, Merrill M. "The Systems Approach to Library Planning," *Library Quarterly,* XXXIV (October, 1964), 326–38.

Foskett, D. J. *Information Service in Libraries.* 2d ed. Hamden, Conn.: Archon Books and Clive Bingley, 1967.

Freiser, Leonard. "Technology in the Library," *Wilson Library Bulletin,* XLI (September, 1966), 69–71.

Goldhor, Herbert (ed.). *Proceedings of the 1963 Clinic on Library Applications of Data Processing Held at the Illini Union on the Urbana Campus of the University of Illinois, April 28–May 1, 1963.* Champaign, Ill.: Distributed by the Illini Union Bookstore, 1964.

Hammer, Donald P. "Automated Operations in a University Library: A Summary," *College and Research Libraries,* XXVI (January, 1965), 19–29, 44.

Intrex: The Report of a Planning Conference on Information Transfer

Experiments. Edited by Carl F. J. Overhage. Cambridge, Mass.: The M. I. T. Press, 1965.

Jackson, Eugene B. "The Use of Data Processing Equipment by Libraries and Information Centers," *Special Libraries*, LVIII (May–June, 1967), 317–27.

Jackson, Ivan F. "An Approach to Library Automation Problems," *College and Research Libraries*, XXVIII (March, 1967), 133–37.

Jehoda, Gerald, and Accola, Ferrol Ann. "Library Records Prepared with the Aid of Data Processing Equipment," *College and Research Libraries*, XXVI (March, 1965), 129–37.

Kenney, Arthur L. "Instrumentation and Information," *Guide to Scientific Instruments: Science*, CLIVA (November 22, 1966), 7.

Knox, William T. "The Changing Role of Libraries," *ALA Bulletin*, LIX (September, 1965), 720–725.

Leimkuhler, Ferdinand F. "Systems Analysis in University Libraries," *College and Research Libraries*, XXVII (January, 1966), 13–18.

"Library Automation. Tomorrow Becomes Today," *ALA Bulletin*, LXI (June, 1967), 635–94.

Licklider, J. C. R. *Libraries of the Future.* Cambridge, Mass.: The M. I. T. Press, Massachusetts Institute of Technology, 1965.

Mumford, L. Quincy. "Libraries and the Everlasting Now," *Library Journal*, XCI (February 15, 1966), 901–06.

Parker, Ralph. "Are Reference Librarians Obsolete?" *RQ*, III (July, 1964), 9–10.

———. "Mechanical Aids in College and University Libraries," *ALA Bulletin*, XXXII (October 15, 1938), 818–19.

Ray, Gordon N. "The Future of the Book," *ALA Bulletin*, LX (September, 1966), 783–93.

Rees, Alan M. "Librarians and Information Centers," *College and Research Libraries*, XXV (May, 1964), 200–04.

———. "New Bottles for Old Wine: Retrieval and Librarianship," *Wilson Library Bulletin* XXXIX (May, 1964), 773–79.

Sarnoff, David. "By the End of the Twentieth Century," *Fortune*, LXIX (May, 1964), 116–19.

———. "No Life Untouched," *Saturday Review*, XLIX (July 23, 1966), 21–22.

Schultheiss, Louis A., and Others. *Advanced Data Processing in the University Library.* New York The Scarecrow Press, 1962.

Shaw, Ralph R. "The Fo n and the Substance," *Library Journal*, XC (February 1, 1965), 567 71.

Shera, Jesse H. "Automation and the Reference Librarian," *RQ*, III (July, 1964), 3–7.

———. "Bibliographic Organization," *Wilson Library Bulletin*, XL (April, 1966), 703–05.

———. "Librarians Against Machines," *Science*, CLVI (May 12, 1967), 346–50.

———. "Librarians' Pugwash or Intrex on the Cape," *Wilson Library Bulletin*, XL (December, 1965), 359–62.

- ———. "What Is Past Is Prologue: Beyond 1984," *ALA Bulletin*, LXI (January, 1967), 35–47.

Simonton, Wesley (ed.). *Information Retrieval Today*. Minneapolis: University of Minnesota Center for Continuation Study, 1963.

Simpson, G. S. "Scientific Information Centers in the United States," *American Documentation*, XIII (January, 1962), 43–57.

Snyder, Samuel S. "Automation at LC: Philosophy, Plans, Progress," *Library Journal*, XC (November 1, 1965), 4709–14.

Wheeler, Joseph L. "Bettering Reference Service," *RQ*, VI (Spring, 1967), 99–113.

CHAPTER 24.

Ashby, Sir Eric. *Universities: British, Indian, and African*. Cambridge, Mass.: Harvard University Press, 1966.

Benjamin, Curtis G. *Everything Is Not Coming Up Roses*. An Address to the Science-Technology Division of the Special Libraries Association, Fifty-sixth Annual Convention, Philadelphia, January 9, 1965. New York: McGraw-Hill Book Company, 1965.

Broderick, Dorothy M. "The Librarian in Today's Society," *Library Journal*, XCII (April 1, 1967), 1413–16.

Burck, Gilbert. "Knowledge: The Biggest Growth Industry of Them All," *Fortune*, LXX (November, 1964), 128–31, 267–70.

Dennis, Lawrence E., and Kauffman, Joseph F. (eds.). *The College and the Student*. Washington, D.C.: American Council on Education, 1966.

Conant, Ralph W. "Sociological and Institutional Changes in American Life: Their Implications for the Library," *ALA Bulletin*, LXI (May, 1967), 528–36.

Diebold, John. "The New World Coming," *Saturday Review*, XLIX (July 23, 1966), 17–18.

Gaines, Ervin J. "Intellectual Freedom," *ALA Bulletin*, LX (February, 1966), 119.

Gaver, Mary Virginia. "The School Library: An Intellectual Force?" *Library Journal*, XCII (May 15, 1967), 1989–91.

Howe, Harold. "Realities of the Learning Market," *Library Journal*, XCII (January 15, 1967), 297–301.

Imprint: The McGraw-Hill Book Company Story. New York: Mc-Graw-Hill Book Company, 1967.

Jennings, Frank G. "Carpe Diem," *Library Journal*, XCII (February 1, 1967), 531–36.

"A Kaleidoscopic View of Library Research," *Wilson Library Bulletin*, XLI (May, 1967), 896–949.

Keppel, Francis. "Libraries: Future Unlimited," *ALA Bulletin*, LVIII (December, 1964), 991–94.

Lacy, Dan. "The Impact of Universal Education," *Library Journal*, XCI (September 1, 1966), 3866–70.

Murray, Marguerite, "Luaus in the Library," *Library Journal*, XCII (April, 15, 1967), 1708–10.

"Nineteenth Annual Report on American Industry: Communications," *Forbes*, C (January 1, 1967), 100.

Pfeiffer, John. "Machines That Man Can Talk With," *Fortune*, LXIX (May, 1964), 153–56, 194, 196–98.

President's Committee on Social Trends. *Recent Social Trends in the United States*. 2 vols. New York: McGraw-Hill Book Company, 1933.

Richardson, Bernard E. "Last One in Bed's a Librarian," *Library Journal*, XCI (October 15, 1966), 4904–07.

"Route '66," *Library Journal*, XCII (January 1, 1967), 51–63.

Tebbel, John. "Book-publishers' Salvation," *Saturday Review*, XLIX (July 23, 1966), 32–33.

INDEX